A Courageous Fool

A Courageous Fool

Marie Deans and Her Struggle against the Death Penalty

Todd C. Peppers with Margaret A. Anderson

Vanderbilt University Press
Nashville

© 2017 by Vanderbilt University Press
Nashville, Tennessee 37235
All rights reserved
First printing 2017

This book is printed on acid-free paper.
Manufactured in the United States of America

Cover design by Rich Hendel
Composition by Dariel Mayer

Library of Congress Cataloging-in-Publication Data on file
LC control number 2016042799
LC classification number KF9227.C2 P45 2017
Dewey classification number 364.66092 [B]—dc23
LC record available at *lccn.loc.gov/2016042799*

ISBN 978-0-8265-2160-6 (hardcover)
ISBN 978-0-8265-2161-3 (paperback)
ISBN 978-0-8265-2162-0 (ebook)

For Marie

Contents

Foreword

But for Marie McFadden Deans, my life would have ended in a dank prison basement on 22 February 1991, fried at the hands of the Commonwealth of Virginia. That is not to say that there were not many other human beings, all deserving of their own books, who jumped in to help stay the executioner's cold hands. There are many unsung heroes responsible for my being alive to write these words. The reality is that, but for Marie Deans, those other heroes would not have come together on my behalf. No matter how my story gets spun, no one can deny that Marie was the force and linchpin that kept my case, and ultimately me, alive. She was the force right up to the moment she drew her last breath, and she remains that force and linchpin even in death.

Marie was an uncompromising abolitionist. In her eyes, killing was wrong. State sanctioned killing was just that: wrong. As uncompromising as she was on the issue of capital punishment, there was one thing that Marie was not. She was not a namby-pamby bleeding heart who was soft on crime or criminals. I personally knew murderers, rapists, and robbers who dreaded encountering Marie. They knew, as I did, that she was not in the least tolerant of rationalizing, excuse making, whining, and "woe is me" crap. Marie demanded, without exception, that each one of us accept and take responsibility for our lives and our actions. Even the guards and some wardens grasped that Marie would brook no nonsense from "her guys," and they were not above telling various inmates, "[When] Ms. Deans visits again I'll fill her in on what you've been doing." More often than not, the individual in question would cool his heels, including me. I recall that shortly after I left the death house, while at Augusta Correctional Center, I was getting into some things I should not have been getting into. I was summoned to the building's breezeway and was confronted by Major Daniel Braxton. He said, "Knock it off. Do not make me place a call to Marie and Mike Farrell and let them know . . ." This attained the desired effect.

Marie insisted that we reflect on ourselves and that we work to educate ourselves; she expected that we ask her how we might be of help or service to others, instead of always expecting others to help us. She demanded that we make ourselves better human beings and better citizens, and she expected us to be that whether on or off death row, in or out of prison. And more, she demanded that we treat each and every individual we encountered—without exception—with respect and dignity. That included our executioners. For Marie, it wasn't us versus them; it was just us, all of us.

Colman McCarthy, a former syndicated columnist for the *Washington Post* and founder of the Center for Teaching Peace, once referred to Marie as being a saint. Marie, puffing on a cigarette, bristled and snapped, "I'm no goddamned saint." I agreed with Colman but defined what I meant by saint: "a sinner who pulls herself back up when she falls and keeps moving." I still got a withering look from her, but I didn't get hit with any nearby objects. Marie is gone now, so I feel safe referring to her as a saint, with one caveat. Ambrose Bierce defined a saint as "a dead sinner revised and edited." Marie, like us all, would require a great deal of editing. Marie could be damned difficult at times. She could, and did, push hard on her friends, and she could be unforgiving if you fell short of her sometimes unrealistic standards. She could have a very sharp tongue. Marie was driven. She would make personal sacrifices that others, even I, would not necessarily make. She hurt the feelings of more than a few of her friends, and even alienated some. I know Marie quite well, and I'm certain that she would be the first to say, "Don't revise or edit; I am no saint."

One bit I would not edit is this. Once, after Marie spent two hours on the witness stand during a civil trial to determine whether the state had a duty to provide lawyers to those it was planning to execute, the late Federal District Court Judge Robert Merhige stated, "The world could use a thousand more Maries." What the judge, and others, did not know when he made that statement was that, immediately after testifying, Marie had to admit herself to a hospital to have a large tumor removed. Her doctors had wanted to do the surgery a couple of weeks earlier, but Marie had kept that secret from everyone because she knew that her testimony was crucial to winning the case. As she put it to me, she wasn't going to let "a silly tumor screw that up." I don't know if that qualifies her for sainthood or not, but I believe that, of all the players involved in that case, including me, Marie is likely the only one who would have taken such a personal risk.

US Court of Appeals Judge Kenneth K. Hall once said of Marie, "The Commonwealth of Virginia has failed in its constitutional duty to provide those it has sentenced to death with adequate and meaningful access to the courts and has, instead, relied on Marie Deans, a private citizen, to carry out their constitutional responsibility." At the time Judge Hall was considered one of the most conservative judges sitting on the bench.

In a letter I sent to the Virginia Parole Board in 2004, I described Marie as being akin to both Socrates and Jesus in the role she played and the effect she had on my life. Marie did far more than work tirelessly to save my life and the lives of those others on death row with me. She pushed on us to learn, to question, to grow. She taught me about empathy, compassion, forgiveness, responsibility, and about what it means to be a good citizen and human being. She insisted that I seek out and discover my own answers to those large existential questions. At times she pushed with tears of reluctance and deep gentleness, at other times with careful analysis, still at other times with fierce fire and angry wisdom. Sometimes she would be quiet and not correct me to remind me of a point made by Søren Kierkegaard (just one of the great minds she introduced me to) that only by investing and speaking one's vision with passion, will the truth, one way or another, finally penetrate the complacency of the world. Marie, in that sense, took all of Kierkegaard's writings to heart, and the cost to her was heavy.

For all who knew her, Marie was a force to be reckoned with. Whether she was a saint or not makes no difference to me. For me, Marie will always be my friend and hero. I hope in the pages that follow you will be able to catch at least a small glimpse of the Marie Deans that I knew and loved.

—Joe Giarratano
Deerfield Correctional Center

Acknowledgments

Over the course of researching and writing this book, Maggie and I have benefited from the kindness and generosity of Marie's family, friends, and colleagues. First and foremost, we want to thank Robert Deans, Marie's youngest son and literary executor, who gave us access to Marie's personal papers as well as permission to tell her life story. Both Robert and his older brother, Joel McFadden, graciously spent time sharing their memories of their mother and her work. William Tremper, Marie's first husband, also talked with us and provided critical insights into Marie's family and upbringing.

The one person most responsible for helping us recreate Marie's work with the condemned men of death row is Joe Giarratano, a former death row inmate and one of the last living eyewitnesses from that terrible time period. Joe spent countless hours with us, both over the telephone and in person, helping us understand Marie the person and her tenacious commitment to the men of the row. At times it was tough for Joe to relive these horrifying memories, but he never wavered in his promise to help us. To him we owe a special debt of gratitude.

Former death row chaplain Russ Ford also went the extra mile. Not only did he share his memories of stepping into the "vortex of evil" with Marie, but he also allowed us to extensively quote from his unpublished manuscript about the years he spent ministering to the men of Virginia's death row. Without Russ's manuscript, we would not have discovered some of Marie's most powerful moments in the death house. Russ is another key witness to the inhumanity of the death penalty, and we hope that he will someday publish his manuscript.

We want to acknowledge the assistance of another death row chaplain, Joe Ingle. Still serving as a chaplain on Tennessee's death row after almost three decades, as well as being a celebrated author and social activist, Joe took time from his busy schedule to not only talk about Marie but to also write the afterword to this book. It is the good works of people like Marie, Russ Ford, and Joe Ingle which inspired us to write Marie's story.

We would also like to thank the friends and colleagues who shared their stories about Marie. They include James Aiken, Toni Bair, David Bruck, Larry Cox, Molly Cupp, Marshall Dayan, Mike Farrell, Eric Freedman, Nancy Gowen, Frank Green,

Father Jim Griffin, Henry Heller, United States Senator Tim Kaine, David Kendall, Jon Klein, Denise Lunsford, Walter McFarlene, Dottie Morefield, Marney Morrison, Steve Northup, Bill Pelke, Sister Helen Prejean, John Sasser, Reverend Thomas Smith, Lloyd Snook, Bart Stamper, Pamela Tucker, Sheryl Giarratana Ward, United States Senator Mark Warner, Earl Washington Jr., Barry Weinstein, Bob West, Deborah Wyatt, Charlotte Zander, and Gerald Zerkin. Former journalist turned author Margaret Edds went the extra mile, digging through her files and providing both audio tapes and written notes of interviews with Marie which were made when Margaret was doing research for her book *An Expendable Man: The Near Execution of Earl Washington, Jr.*

A number of different Roanoke College students lent their research skills to this project (including Wendy Moore-Schaeffer, who helped scan and electronically organize Marie's personal papers), and they were ably assisted by Roanoke College reference librarian Piper Cumbo. Finally, multiple versions of the book manuscript were carefully edited by my administrative assistant Judi Pinckney, who has been a constant companion and proofreader on all my writing projects. Whether it's editing a book manuscript, babysitting your children and/or your dogs, proctoring a final exam when you have a migraine, or planning a campus event for three hundred guests, Judi can do it all.

As we wrote the book, we were fortunate to have a number of people look over the unfinished manuscript and provide invaluable feedback. They include Roanoke College professor and poet Melanie Almeder, author Phyllis Theroux, and screenwriter Claudia Myers. In our search for photographs, we benefited from the expertise and help of archivist Sister Anne Francis Campbell of the Sisters of Charity of Our Lady of Mercy, photographer Randall Greenwell of the *Virginian-Pilot*, archivist Nicole Kappatos of the *Richmond Times-Dispatch*, Marc Oram of *United Press International*, local historian Seldon Richardson, Steve Tuttle of the South Carolina Department of Archives and History, and former South Carolina Law Enforcement Division forensic photographer and author Rita Y. Shuler (who we nicknamed "Saint Rita" for the lengths she went to help us find pictures).

This project would not have been possible without the course releases and research funds provided to me through the Henry H. & Trudye H. Fowler Chair in Public Affairs. I would like to thank Roanoke College President Michael Maxey and Dean of the College Richard Smith in awarding me this prestigious honor. Additional thanks goes to Dean Smith for always being willing to help find additional funds for the various costs associated with the book, including photograph licensing fees and the hiring of a professional indexer.

Moreover, this project would have not seen completion without the support of the editors and staff at Vanderbilt University Press. This includes, but is not limited to, Director Michael Ames, Managing Editor Joell Smith-Borne, Design and Production Manager Dariel Mayer, Sales and Marketing Manager Betsy Phillips, and Marketing and New Media Associate Jenna Phillips. A special thanks goes to Michael Ames, for taking a chance on our book proposal and having faith in our abilities to tell a compelling story about an unsung hero. Michael's careful reading of multiple versions of the manuscript, gentle criticism, and spot-on suggestions were instrumental in producing a polished and readable final product.

You may have discovered this book thanks to the efforts of American University professor Gemma Puglisi and the students in her Strategic Public Relations Portfolio practicum. Each year, Gemma and her students take on a client and plan out a comprehensive marketing strategy; in our case, it included designing a website, sending out marketing materials, and planning an on-campus promotional event. We are lucky to have such an enthusiastic group of students willing to help promote our story of a courageous fool named Marie.

I would also like to thank my family for putting up with another one of "Daddy's books." When my son Sam was five years old, he told me that he was going to ask Santa to "make Daddy stop writing books so he will play trains with me." Santa did not grant Sam's wish, but I hope that my sons Ben and Sam believe that I did a good job of carving out time to be both a dad and an author. And, of course, I could not be neither a good father nor a productive scholar without the love and support of my wife, Michele. I especially benefited from her unwavering faith in me when I questioned whether this book would ever be completed. While both of my parents read an early version of this book manuscript, my only regret is that my mother Fran did not get to see it published.

—Todd C. Peppers

I would like to thank my family and friends for providing their constant love and support during my first book-length project. My parents, Betty and William, have always taught me to pursue my dreams and follow my heart, and I am forever grateful for that. I have always wanted to write a book, and I am so happy that they have been able to go on this journey with me. I would also like to thank my sister Emma for her support, enthusiasm, and professional advice when we first discussed launching a website for our book. Additionally, Chris Carter has been my rock through this entire project—I am sure he questioned my sanity when I would read and re-read the same few sentences out loud to ensure they carried the right message. Thank you for putting up with me.

I would also like to thank Roanoke College. Without this institution's creative approach to learning and opportunities for students to get involved with faculty research, I doubt Todd would have been able to approach me about assisting him with this project. I owe a big thank you to Roanoke College and Todd for believing in me.

Last, but not least, I would like to thank my colleagues and friends at Senator Warner's office for being my cheering squad. As my first work family, it still amazes me that I could walk into an office every day and be surrounded by people who care so much about the work they are doing and the people they are doing it with. Thank you for always being there to provide advice and a high five.

—Maggie A. Anderson

Introduction

I don't believe in the [legal] system . . . I play because I know the
dice fall our way occasionally, if for no other reason than to keep
the game going. I think I also play to make the record in the hope
that one day that may make a difference to another generation.
—Marie Deans, 1986

This book is the story of one of the most remarkable and complex women I have
ever met. She was a fighter, a storyteller, and a civil rights activist named Marie
McFadden Deans. This book also represents a promise that I made in the fall of
2008, when I pledged to Marie that I would help her write her memoir. When that
promise was made, my original intent was to serve as Marie's co-author and research
assistant. Yet Marie's declining health and premature death from lung cancer in April
of 2011 made it impossible for us to complete the task. So I honored my promise to
Marie by picking up the baton and carrying on, aided by my former Roanoke College student Maggie Anderson.

Unfortunately, Maggie never had the opportunity to meet Marie. In the year after
Marie's death, however, Maggie and I spent hours in Marie's townhouse in Charlottesville, Virginia, crawling through her dusty attic looking for death penalty files
and sitting on the floor of her living room, slowly going through box after box of
Marie's writings, speeches, and photographs. In the months following those trips
to Charlottesville, Maggie spent endless hours reading and organizing the personal
papers that we found in Marie's home. And she helped me interview Marie's former
colleagues, family, and friends; watched videotapes of Marie's public appearances;
and journeyed to a maximum security prison to meet with one of Marie's closest and
oldest friends, former death row inmate Joe Giarratano. After spending hundreds
of hours on this project, Maggie has had the curious experience of coming to know
Marie in death more intimately than many who knew her in life.

The death penalty has created heroes and victims, and it has caused collateral
damage to families and communities throughout American history. Marie Deans
fits into all three of those categories. Marie was a South Carolina native who yearned
to be a fiction writer, but a combination of circumstances thrust Marie into a world

which proved to be much stranger than fiction, a world in which minorities and the poor are selected in a seemingly random (if not deliberate) manner to be sacrificed to what former Supreme Court Justice Harry Blackmun called the "machinery of death." In this world, Marie would find herself fighting to bring justice to the legal process, to bring humanity to death row, and to bring mercy to the death house. She would find herself struggling to survive the daily horrors to which she was exposed. As the "modern" death penalty (that is, the death penalty as it has been practiced since the Supreme Court allowed the resumption of state killing in 1977) slowly grinds down—abandoned less from moral outrage than the enormous costs associated with capital trials, appeals, and executions—it is time to account for the toll that the death penalty has taken on our country and on the men and women who were sucked into Justice Blackmun's machinery of death.

Marie's work on death row began in South Carolina in the early 1980s, and it continued in Virginia for the next twenty years. During this time period, Marie wore many different hats: she found attorneys for men who were facing executions without legal representation; she worked to improve prison conditions and inmates' access to lawyers and legal research materials; she acted as a surrogate mother and spiritual advisor to the men; she assisted lawyers in the drafting of appeals and motions; and she helped create the role of mitigation specialist in which she interviewed the inmates, their family members, and experts in an effort to convince the jury that the inmate's life was worth saving.

Starting in the mid-1990s, Marie attempted to write her story. It was an agonizing process, with Marie battling writer's block that was triggered by reliving the terror of seeing men that she cared about being killed by the state. The struggles, however, went deeper. "Mom's problem with writing, and Mom's problem with becoming a writer, was that . . . all the stories that she's trying to tell are in her heart. There was so much emotion, [and] [the emotions] were such crucial parts of her, that she was unable to express in writing," explained Marie's oldest son, Joel "Mac" McFadden. I myself witnessed the strain that unearthing these memories placed on Marie. Once, sitting outside of a local Charlottesville restaurant on a cool spring day, I watched as Marie's large brown eyes filled with tears, and her hands shook so hard that she had to put her sandwich down, as she tried to talk about the execution of Morris Mason. Despite these barriers to writing, Marie refused to give up.

Over the course of approximately fifteen years, Marie battled her demons and fought to memorialize her story. At the time of her death, she had produced roughly seventy-five pages of memories—including her tumultuous childhood, the murder of her mother-in-law, her early involvement with Amnesty International, her endless quest to find adequate representation for the condemned men, and her relationships with the men of the South Carolina and Virginia death rows. Sometimes Marie was able to capture these recollections in complete chapters, other times she scribbled fragments of her story onto pieces of notebook paper. Her memoir, however, was never completed. Even during the final weeks of her life, Marie mourned her inability to finish the project. During my last meeting with her, two weeks before her death, Marie could barely get out of bed but still asked me to bring a tape recorder so we could work on the book.

When Marie died in the spring of 2011, I felt a deep sense of grief—not only for the loss of a friend, but for what I believed was the loss of my friend's story. Marie was an unsung hero in the fight against the modern death penalty, and I felt that the contributions she made were forever lost with her death. After receiving permission from Marie's youngest son, Robert Deans, to continue the project, Maggie and I began reviewing her personal papers, and we started interviewing those who knew Marie. Then, my sadness gave way to a fragile hope that maybe Marie's remarkable story could still be told. Over the course of researching and writing this book, there have been at least a dozen occasions in which I have turned to Maggie and muttered, "if only I had the chance for one more interview with Marie." And there are, unfortunately, critical moments in Marie's work on death row, as well as her inner thoughts and opinions, that cannot be recreated through the memories of others or by reviewing reports in her personal papers.

Nevertheless, this book represents our best effort at not only telling Marie's story but also infusing the book with Marie's unique style and voice. We have preserved Marie's own words throughout the chapters and built upon this foundation with our own research, which includes interviews of her family and colleagues as well as newspaper articles, reports, speeches, and letters found in Marie's voluminous personal papers. The goal is to present Marie the human being with all her strengths and foibles. Marie despised being called the "Angel" or "Saint" of death row, and she was neither. Marie was an incredibly bright and strong-willed woman who knew her own mind and did not suffer fools gladly. Her commitment to the cause was total, but sacrifices such as hers come with consequences. The years of stress undoubtedly shortened her life, and her unyielding fight damaged relationships with some friends and family members. Marie was aware of the price that she paid, and the consequences of those choices bore heavily on her in the last few years.

Despite all of the available resources, Marie's story could not be told without the insights and memories of Joe Giarratano, a former death row inmate who wrote the foreword to this book. Marie first met Joe in 1982, during a fact-finding mission on Virginia's death row. Over the next twenty-nine years, Marie would become a teacher, a mentor, a spiritual guide, a therapist, a mother, a best friend, and a savior to Joe. Through Marie's guidance, Joe himself would become a formidable death penalty abolitionist and prison lawyer who joined Marie's fight for prison reform and basic civil rights for his fellow prisoners.

The work of Marie and a band of dedicated lawyers resulted in a conditional pardon for Joe, a second chance at life which removed Joe from death row but placed him in a maximum security prison and a legal twilight zone where neither prison administrators nor state officials seemingly cared about his substantial claims of factual innocence. Because of this conditional pardon, Joe is one of the few living witnesses to the hell that was Virginia's death row in the 1980s as well as the extraordinary work Marie performed on behalf of the condemned men. Of the thirty-four men Marie visited in the death house, he is one of only three inmates who were not ultimately executed. Through telephone calls, visits, and letters, Joe has committed hundreds of hours to this project. His experiences with Marie and his love for her are threads that run through Marie's story.

As Marie shopped her unfinished memoir to publishers, she drafted several different descriptions of the manuscript. In keeping with our commitment to let Marie speak for herself whenever possible, we have knitted together several of the descriptions. Collectively, they let Marie explain her vision of the incomplete memoir.

"Unimagined Voices" is a non-fiction, investigative memoir that describes my personal journey from a Southern wife, mother, and writer at the scene of my mother-in-law's murder to the death chambers of South Carolina and Virginia and the founding of a national organization for the families of murder victims. It explores the reactions to murder of a family and community that caused me to choose this path, the hardships and horrors I endured, the successes I achieved through determination and pure stubbornness and how the journey changed me.

When my mother-in-law, Penny Deans, was murdered in 1972, our family was stunned to learn that the police believed they could comfort us by telling us they would "catch the bastard and fry him." People expected murder victims' families to prove their love for their murdered family member by seeking revenge through the death penalty. My husband recoiled at the idea that his mother should be connected in any way to an electric chair. Raised as a Lutheran, I was taught and wholly believe that I cannot justify my sins by the sins of another, and so I could never justify executions by the acts of those who kill. We needed help in dealing with our anger, pain and fear, yet we were isolated by the assumptions of others. Breaking out of that isolation meant challenging those assumptions publicly. Doing so brought us unexpected attention, and one day I found myself being escorted onto death row by a nervous warden who was desperate to stop an execution but not at all sure he should be taking a member of a murder victim's family to meet one of his death row prisoners.

I not only became an advocate for, and friend of, the condemned, I also came to know and understand those involved—the families of the victims and the condemned, the prosecutors and defense lawyers, the juries, the corrections officers, the death squad members, the chaplains and the governors. I saw murders and executions in their totality. As a mitigation specialist and investigator, I worked on over 300 capital cases at the trial, appellate and clemency levels, and I helped to save over 250 of those defendants. Thirty-four condemned prisoners asked me to "stand their death watch with them" and be present at their executions. These were dreaded, emotionally draining, horrific experiences, but I stayed with the men because of what I learned from my dying father-in-law and because of a question Dietrich Bonhoeffer puts to Christians: Would you leave Jesus alone on the cross? It was not that I believed these men Christ-like but simply that I believed them human and would not leave them to die alone. The book relates a few of these cases and executions that demonstrate the starkest reality of the death penalty and how it affects the human beings involved.

I call my book "Unimagined Voices" because the public forgets or can't imagine the people that executions affect. Would they imagine the head of the execution squad standing in front of a cell taking communion with and holding the hand of the man he would soon strap into the electric chair? Would they imagine this man, garbed in his special black uniform, sitting in the corner of the death house trying to control his tears? Would they imagine the woman whose mother had been brutally raped and murdered by one of my clients thanking me for staying with him and telling me she had prayed all night that the execution would be stopped and then for God to be with both me and this man who brought her so much pain? Would they imagine a warden who corrections people called "the meanest somabitch in the business" crying when I asked him what executions did to him? Would they imagine the mother who had vivid dreams every night that she is forced to plug in the electric chair her child is sitting in, or the mother with Huntington's Chorea, which eats away the mind, who collapsed on the floor of the death house keening out the one reality she could grasp, that we were about to kill her boy?

The timing of my experience and where I worked also make "Unimagined Voices" different. My work spanned the time when those doing legal defense work had no money and no resources. We did our work independently from the corners of our bedrooms, lived under the poverty level, and were forced to cover dozens of cases at a time. After a few years in South Carolina, I worked for over twenty years in Virginia, where the procedural rules always trumped evidence (even evidence of innocence), where the indigent defense system was a disgrace, where appeals were difficult to pursue, where the polls showed a higher percentage of people supported the death penalty than any state except Texas, and where the government, press, and media were extremely conservative. That work was overwhelming. Against the endless resources of the Commonwealth of Virginia, I had a desk, a typewriter, a telephone, a budget of about $1,000 a month, including my salary, and enough stubbornness not to cry uncle. Looking back on those years is like watching a "Roadrunner" cartoon. I, of course, was the coyote. There was never a break. There always was another victim's family, another person being tried for capital murder, another person being sent to death row, another investigation to carry out, another clemency petition to pull together and represent before the governor, another execution, another personal or family crisis.

Like others involved in death penalty work, I paid a financial and personal price for these years. Only now that I have stepped back to write this book am I realizing the path I walked both limited and expanded my life. I have seen things few others have even glimpsed and learned valuable lessons about life, death, redemption, forgiveness, vengeance, political expediency, close-mindedness, and unrestrained ambition. I have learned that evil does exist—that it strives to be acknowledged and to grow, but, more often than not, it is overwhelmed by the incredibly tenacious will to affirm one's own humanity. Again and again, I watched human beings claw their way through evil and fight their way back into the light of hope. "Unimagined Voices" is not only an intimate and unnerving first-hand account of life on the front lines of the anti-death penalty struggle. The book also describes a personal journey in which I went from being a victim to becoming a survivor and came to believe that God is the intention to life—and that to give up on any human being is to give up on life and, therefore, on God.

I hope this book will not be categorized as just another death penalty book. To me, the book is a personal journey of survival, reconciliation, and redemption. It is about my search for answers to the questions that my mother-in-law's murder raised in me. I wanted to know why we were so good at violence and so poor at love, and that led me to death row. Working on death row and with victims' families, I wanted to know why some human spirits survive and some do not. To me, survival is not simply staying alive—it is the ground that gives you the chance to survive. True survival is about stretching out to fulfill your potential. It is about affirming life, hope, and all the things that take you away from the darkness and into the light. I hope the stories in my book demonstrate how people come out of the darkness and move into the light, even under extreme circumstances.

I am a mitigation specialist, one who documents people's lives through their stories. When I began my work, mitigation specialists worked exclusively on capital cases; so I was working with men, women, and children who had killed, and with their families. It surprised me that not everyone could learn those stories, that so many people considered it amazing that I could learn them. If that was true, I didn't want to analyze how I did so, as if there might be some magic I'd ignorantly stumbled into and could lose at any moment. In time, I realized what was happening. I wasn't gifted. I had no magic. It was simply that wounded people recognize one another. Our wounds open and speak to one another.

For years I resisted telling these stories. I wasn't with the men in the death house, their families, or their victims' families as a reporter. I was there simply to be with them, to believe in their humanity, to be present in their struggle to come through what they had done or what had been done to them. I thought these times too private, too intimate to tell. Even as I heard them, I knew that answers about the human spirit were in those stories. Looking back, I still hear every man who was executed telling me he hoped his execution would be the last, and I've come to realize there was a deeper hope and prayer in those statements. And I hear the victims' families asking me how they can make a difference, how they can help stop the cycle of violence. They taught me so much. But the book will not be preachy. Instead, I want readers to walk this journey with me, to hear and experience these stories for themselves.

When author Truman Capote wrote *In Cold Blood*, he crowed that he had invented a new form of literature, to wit, "the non-fiction novel" in which he drew upon "reportage" to accurately and objectively tell a compelling story. Capote steadfastly insisted that he did not fictionalize dialogue or occurrences in his book, referring to his work as "immaculately factual."[1] Others, however, have challenged that assertion.[2]

The end product of our efforts is even harder to categorize. This book is many things: an autobiography, a biography, and, to quote Marie, an "investigative memoir." As explained by Gore Vidal, there is a subtle but important difference between a memoir and an autobiography: "a memoir is how one remembers one's own life, while an autobiography is history, requiring research, dates, facts double-checked."[3] The materials left behind by Marie combine the genres of memoir and autobiography. While much of her writing is carefully grounded in fact, occasionally Marie focuses on a specific experience—the death of her mother-in-law, the first time she walked onto death row, the execution of Ricky Boggs—and pours out the emotions that filled her heart during these experiences. While her emotions are true and real, they cannot be fact-checked or footnoted; they are from Marie's heart and soul, not from a database or reference source. But they provide the emotional core of the book, as Marie pulls back the curtain and shows us the pain and horror inflicted by capital punishment. As for myself, I will assume the role of a tailor who stitches together the fabric of this book by introducing important actors and issues, placing Marie's work into the context of the death penalty in the 1980s and 1990s. Finally, in order to make the book more accessible to a general audience, we have tried to minimize citations; unless otherwise noted, Marie's words come from her unpublished manuscript (these extracts are italicized to distinguish them from other sources), her personal papers, and our interviews and conversations. The same citation rules have been used for Joe Giarratano, who is quoted extensively in the book. All information comes from our interviews with Joe unless there is a citation to additional sources, such as newspaper articles about him.

With apologies to Marie, we have chosen a different title for this book. Once during a visit with Marie, I asked her how she wanted to be remembered. She took a drag off her cigarette, paused for a moment, blew a cloud of smoke toward the ceiling, and responded "as a courageous fool." When I pushed her to explain, Marie gave a throaty laugh and replied that she often tilted at windmills, but she was too stubborn or foolish to abandon the fight despite her fears and doubts—especially when it came to the lives of the men on death row. What follows is a requiem for that courageous fool, a complex and brave woman whose story will hopefully inspire others to take up her fallen banner and continue the good fight against our country's shameful and bloody embrace of the death penalty.

—Todd C. Peppers
Salem, VA

1

The Murder of Penny Deans

Every time I am about to meet a man, woman, or child on death row for the first time, I am thrown back into Penny's murder . . . I identify so strongly with the victims and their families that I spend days calling on God to help me remember that the man or woman that I am about to meet is my brother or sister.
—Marie Deans, date unknown

When Marie gave a public speech about the death penalty, she would often tell the story of the murder of her mother-in-law, Evelyn "Penny" Deans. The story of Penny's brutal slaying represented why Marie got involved in death penalty work. It also highlighted why Marie thought that the death penalty was ineffective and morally offensive. "My mother-in-law's killing was the crucial element, the key that motivated me to get into this work . . . I don't want to see anyone ignored or thrown away by society, whether they're the victims or the murderers."[1]

When Marie sat down to outline her book, she decided to start it with Penny's murder because it was "the key" to her work. We want to honor Marie's wishes by presenting Penny's story early in this book, but it is necessary to place the story in context. By the time of Penny's death in 1972, Marie was living with her third husband, Bob Deans, in Charleston, South Carolina. Marie's first two marriages ended in divorce. Marie had a tense relationship with her parents, but she quickly bonded with her new in-laws, Joseph Robert "Jabo" Deans and Penny. Marie finally had parental figures that loved and supported her. Marie remained a constant presence by Jabo's side during his slow death from cancer in 1971.

I'd always adored Jabo, but we'd become even closer during his two years in the hospital. I'd visited him every day after my older son left for school, taking him the collard greens, cornbread, pork roast, fried chicken, and other Southern dishes he wanted. We talked about everything from the latest Charleston gossip, to my writing, to his days as a jazz drummer, to what it was like growing up—or, in my case, spending my summers—on a Carolina tobacco farm.

Marie's relationship with Penny grew even stronger when Marie announced she was pregnant. "I had a mother now and she would love me all her life," wrote Marie. "Her love had been a precious and desperately needed gift."

On the evening of August 20, 1972, Marie received a telephone call that changed the course of her life.

We were lying in bed watching the news when the phone rang. Our digital alarm clock had just clicked to 11:22 p.m. We let it ring several times before Bob leaned over and picked it up. His voice quickly changed from irritation to alarm. "It's Bill. Someone broke into Mama's house. She's been shot." If the police had called, Bob would have told them they'd made a mistake. Penny and her six-year-old daughter, Rachel [not her real name], weren't expected home for several days. But there was no mistake, and to this day, the phone ringing late at night is like a tripwire setting off an explosion of adrenalin in me.

We lived around the corner and got to Penny's house in minutes, but police officers, reporters, TV crews, and neighbors already formed a small crowd outside of the house. Bill ran to meet us. He looked like a little boy calling out to his parents in the middle of a nightmare. He grabbed me and held on tightly until Bob put his arm around him. Bill turned to Bob, and the brothers came together. I had never seen them so close and so tender with one another. Finally, Bob asked, "Where's Mama?" and Bill pointed to the house.

"Wait, don't go in there." The urgency in Bill's voice stopped us. "It's a crime scene. They won't let you in there."

Bob made a "so what" sound, and we kept moving until Bill grabbed my shoulder. "No, Marie! You cannot go in there." He looked directly at my protruding belly, then at Bob.

Bob put his arm around my shoulder and started walking away from the house. I pulled against his arm. "Wait, Bob, don't. She can't be left alone. We shouldn't be out here. They don't understand. She can't be left alone."

"She's not alone," Bill said. "The paramedics are with her."

Bob suddenly whirled around to face him. "Rachel! Where is Rachel?"

Bill put his hand out as if to stop Bob. "It's okay. She's okay." He told us that he had gotten Rachel out of the house and taken her to a neighbor's before the police came.

"So Penny knows she's all right?" I asked him. Bill walked away. "Bill?" He kept on walking.

I looked at Bob, and he shook his head. "He didn't hear you. He's just more hyper than usual."

Bill lived down the street from Penny in one of the smaller homes closer to the entrance of the subdivision. He told us that he and a friend had been driving by and saw lights on in the house and a strange car in the driveway. Knowing Penny and Rachel were supposed to be in North Carolina, they stopped to investigate.

As they came up the walk, they heard voices. Bill's first thought was that

Undated photograph of Penny
Deans, whose violent murder led
Marie to become a death penalty
abolitionist. Personal collection
of Marie Deans.

*Penny was back and with some friend or neighbor. As he turned to go back to the
car, he heard shots. He immediately went back to the door and started banging
and kicking on it, trying to get in. His friend ran around to the back of the house
and saw a man sprinting from the garage.*

*We stood just off the wide front lawn, leaning against a police car, watching
the front door. The blue lights on the police cars kept searching the neighborhood
in hypnotic silvery sweeps. It should have sounded like a helicopter in a Vietnam
War report. Whomp. Whomp. Whomp. Instead, there was only the squawking of
the police radio.*

*Each time the light illuminated the front of the house, I expected Penny to be
standing there, throwing open the door. "Come on in. Why are you standing out
there?" It was not real to be standing here. This had to be a play, a nightmare,
anything but the reality that this was Penny's house and she'd been shot. Why
would anyone hurt Penny? She'd been through enough watching her husband
Jabo slowly die of cancer just a year ago, feeling her life fall out from under her,
feeling so afraid, and then this baby. I caressed my belly. Everything had changed
for her. She was so excited about being a grandmother.*

*Bodies blurred past us, moving between us and the door. I craned my neck
to see around them. I didn't want to miss her. Bill was pacing off to the side, now
and then pacing over to us and stopping for a minute. Bob was still, quiet.*

*A young police officer, his uniform black in the night, came over and put his
hand gently on my shoulder. "Don't worry. We'll catch the bastard and fry him."*

"What?" I could see the concern in his eyes, feel the gentleness of his touch. I

must not have understood what he said. What I heard did not go with those eyes, that touch. Suddenly Bill was there, reaching out for the officer and practically dragging him away from us.

"What is he talking about?" Bob asked. "Come up and say something like that to you. What is wrong with him?"

He had said what I heard. Did he really think the idea of "frying" someone was supposed to make me feel better? Nothing made any sense. I want to scream until someone told me why anyone would hurt Penny. I felt my body would fly into pieces if someone didn't tell me that Penny knew Rachel was all right. Was Penny hurting? Was she scared? Were her questions being answered? But all these people were running back and forth in front of us.

We were there for over an hour before we realized Terry, Penny's older daughter, knew nothing of what was happening. Bill insisted he would stay at the house, and I should go with Bob to get Terry. Bob called Terry's fiancé, P. A., and we picked him up on the way to Terry's apartment. She lived on James Island. We had to cross the Cooper River Bridge, the peninsula of Charleston and the Ashley River Bridge. It was Sunday night/early Monday morning. The Cooper River flashed silver streaks, but the marsh was dark and still. The streets of the city empty, the houses dark and shuttered.

Groggy and rumpled, Terry suddenly came awake when she saw the three of us standing outside. "What is it? What's happened?" P. A. put his arms around her. We couldn't see her. We only could hear first her gasp and then her crying and asking questions none of us could answer.

Coming back there was a blockade at the foot of the Cooper River Bridge. The policeman came over, shined his flashlight into the car, and started explaining that they were stopping all cars because they were trying to catch a man who had. . . . "We know," Bob said, "We are Mrs. Deans's children. We went to get my sister." The policeman was so flustered, he couldn't stop talking or waving his flashlight around inside the car. We waited while he told us he was sorry, but we shouldn't worry, they would find the man.

And then an ambulance coming off the bridge into town passed us. No warning light. For a moment, we debated following the ambulance. Then someone said maybe it's not her, and we followed the policeman's hands pointing up the bridge.

When we got back to the house, Bob confronted the police. Had Penny been in the ambulance we passed? Yes, they told him. They had sent her body to the hospital for an autopsy. That's how we learned Penny was dead. Somehow we could not or would not take that in. Bob insisted to the police officer that his brother had not told him his mother was dead, as if that was the deciding factor between her being alive or dead. Bill came up and pulled us away. "How could you not know? How could you not understand? There was blood everywhere. I had to step over her body to get Rachel."

Strangely, that memory, which was not even ours, became my most enduring memory of that night, along with another—which we also never saw—the terror *on Penny's face when she realized what was about to happen to her and might happen to Rachel.*

I wasn't angry that night. The only feeling I had was an overwhelming sense of loss and sadness. Penny had been so lost after Jabo died. She and Jabo had married young, and she could not imagine—and was fearful of—life without him. The baby I carried had been a miracle for her. For the first time since Jabo died, Penny had begun looking forward. You could see life welling up in her. She was so excited about being a grandmother that she couldn't contain herself. She had to go to North Carolina and tell each member of Jabo's family in person.

Why was her life taken now? Why are we so good at passing on violence and so poor at passing on love? The question mourned in me, becoming a mantra that kept me from wailing or crumpling to the ground. Why? Why? God, how I needed an answer.

I don't know how long we stood outside the house before the neighbor directly across the street came and got us. At her house, we sat bunched up on the hall stairs staring out of her open front door, facing Penny's front door. Why did we stay there watching? Now we knew she was dead. We knew even her body was no longer there, knew she would never throw open that door and beckon us in. Yet we stayed, watching, waiting. We knew, but we still could not or would not take it in. Maybe we believed if we left, we would make it true, and Penny would really be dead. But if we stayed, kept the watch, somehow that night would go away, and we, too, would start the morning with a new beginning of our routine lives. Maybe our bodies simply had forgotten how to move.

As the sky began turning light grey, we watched the police seal the house, watched the yellow tape go up, watched them collect up their equipment and pair off into their cars, watched as one turned around and looked at us, watched him walk toward us. "Go home now. There's nothing more you can do here. Go home." We needed someone to tell us what to do, yet his was the command we didn't want. We couldn't change anything.

Terry pushed her head against mine. I put my arm around her and kissed her hair. Slowly she stood up and pulled me up. She, P. A., Bob, and I went to our house, and Bill went to the neighbors who were caring for Rachel.

Bob went straight to our bedroom and shut the door. Terry clung to P. A. on the sofa. I sat alone in a chair facing them, listening to Terry's questions. Why had this happened? Why was her mother dead? What had any of us done to deserve all we had been going through this past year? Terry's face, her fear and outrage, made me feel even more helpless. She was just a girl, and I wanted so badly to give her some answer, something to help her, but all I had were more questions.

Later in the afternoon Bob emerged from the bedroom to take Terry and P. A. home, telling me to get some sleep. As they left, Bob picked up the evening paper from the stoop and handed it to me. I watched them drive off before glancing down at the paper.

Penny's murder was on the front page. I stared at it, slowly beginning to realize we were in the middle of a "sensational murder case." I dropped the paper on the hall table and headed for the bedroom, but I couldn't sleep. I couldn't even stay in bed. My mind was like Bill's pacing.

I got the paper and spread it on the kitchen table. At first it just wasn't real. I'd begin to read it, then get up and stare out the window, start reading it again, then roam the house for a few minutes. Finally, I forced myself to read the entire article.

The story stirred the first feelings of complicity in me. It posed numerous questions, like why had Penny cut short her vacation? Where and under what circumstances had she met up with the killer? How had he gotten into the house? There were interviews with neighbors who expressed intense fear when they heard the killer was on the loose. Many had left their homes and gone into Charleston to stay with friends and relatives. To me, the story said Penny was somehow responsible for bringing this violence into her life and the lives of her neighbors.

The man who killed Penny had escaped from prison in Maine, killed another woman up there, taken her car, and headed South. It was her car in Penny's driveway. The assumption was that he had seen Penny on the road and followed her. The police, who had told us virtually nothing, had given many details to the reporters. Now I read about the fight Penny had put up, that her fingernails had been torn and broken, where the bullets had entered her head, exactly where and in what position she had been found.

I saw the expression on Penny's face when she realized what was about to happen. I could feel her terror as if the gun was pointed at me. No one should die alone like that, terrified like that. No mother should have to imagine, even for a second, such a death for her child. I wanted desperately to have been with her.

Who would do such a thing? Penny was friendly, outgoing. She always expected the best from people. Had the man seen Penny on the road in her big new station wagon and decided she must have money he could steal? Had she smiled at him at a gas station or in a restaurant, and had he decided she would provide a haven for him? Was he some sick monster who got a thrill from preying on vulnerable women? If he escaped from prison, how had he gotten a gun? Why target Penny? Of all the people who must have been driving South that night, all the people this man could have followed, in God's name, why Penny?

Soon our phone began ringing. Neighbors and friends from Mt. Pleasant and Charleston came with food and offers of help. We learned that one neighbor had made rounds of our house during those early morning hours to be sure we were safe. And much later we learned he may have had good reason, because the gun used to kill Penny was found in one of the yards abutting our back yard.

Within a day or two, the sheriff came to tell us the man who murdered Penny had been caught. Wayne Northup had run all the way to Fayetteville, North Carolina, with Penny's blood on him. He'd gone to his sister's, and she had turned him in. The sheriff said the man's sister had expressed her deepest sympathy for us, her sorrow at our loss and the loss of the family in Maine. The sheriff wouldn't give us her name, just as he wouldn't give her any information about us, but he told us she seemed devastated, and he believed she was sincere.

I had been like most people, not really thinking about the families of murderers, but the message from this man's sister haunted me. Before long I began trying to walk in her shoes, feeling what it must be like to have a brother or son or husband commit murder.

Since then, every time I go to or near Fayetteville I wonder if I am close to her, if I could find her, if she is all right. I wonder if she knows that, because of her, the organization of murder victims' families I founded several years after Penny's death includes the families of those the state executes.

In the next days and weeks, we tried to ignore the murder case and the sensational news coverage and to deal with our family and our grief. Terry had gotten into a spat with Penny before she left for North Carolina and felt incredible anger at the killer for cutting off any opportunity to mend that temporary rift. I tried to assure Terry that she and her mother were fine, but the only real relief for her came when an aunt told us that the reason Penny had come home early was because she missed us.

"All of us?"

"Absolutely."

"Was she upset with Terry?"

"No, why would she be?"

Bill kept saying if he hadn't started back to the car, he could have gotten into the house in time to save Penny. Bob and I tried to reason with him, telling him that, had he gotten into the house, he and Rachel probably would have been killed as well. He would shake his head and say he understood that, but the distant look in his eyes told me he was back at Penny's front door, trying to get in.

Their feelings were irrational, but I understood them. I felt guilty for not being with Penny. She always had come to see me when I needed her, yet I had not been there for her. I had let her die alone.

Still, our biggest concern was Rachel. One of Penny's friends, Dr. Pat, was a psychologist, and Bill took Rachel to her. Dr. Pat was a wise and caring woman, and we followed her advice to the letter. We were lucky that the advice was good. We were all in shock and probably would have followed the advice of anyone who showed up on our doorstep offering any answers. That shock, which even we were unaware of at the time, and being willing to follow the advice and demands of others would cause additional trauma for Rachel before the "case" was finished.

Somehow we managed a funeral. Bill wanted it to be as normal as possible and asked that the casket be left open. Bob wanted the casket closed, but he agreed that, if it was important to Bill, it should be left open.

Friends and neighbors came, but there also were people none of us could identify, and they began questioning us about the murder. They asked if Penny had been raped, if she knew her killer, if she had let him in the house. A couple of our friends heard some of the questioning and asked those people to leave. Then the funeral director caught two people pulling Penny's head up the see the bullet wounds and moving her hands to see her fingernails. He closed the casket immediately.

That evening I started hemorrhaging. Dr. Durst, our family doctor, ordered me to bed and talked to Bob about the need to protect me from any more trauma. The pain of grief can be so dark and heavy it smothers out life. I couldn't get away from it through sleep or any other means. When Bob was gone, I lay curled up in bed, begging my child to be safe, begging Penny to come back.

I tried to make myself get back to some routine, but nothing worked. My mind, everything in or about me, seemed consumed by the physical pain and mental darkness of grief. It was my only reality. In order to protect me—and therefore our child—Bob, Bill, and Terry were trying to act like our life was normal. Instead, I simply felt cut off. It would have helped my own grieving to give what support I could to the rest of the family and to talk about Penny.

While I was being kept in the dark to prevent a miscarriage, the prosecutor in Maine convinced Bill that Rachel needed to come to the trial and identify the killer. I knew nothing about the trial, nothing about Bill and Rachel going to Maine. Sometime after they got back, Bob and Bill told me what had happened. Rachel had gone up to the witness box, turned around, seen her mother's killer, and gone into hysterics. Bill had gotten to the witness box, grabbed Rachel, and run out of the courtroom with her in his arms. As he was trying to soothe her in the hall, the prosecutor came up, clapped his hand on Bill's shoulder and said: "That was exactly what we needed."

Hearing that, I became infuriated. Given the chance, I would have kicked Wayne Northup and his prosecutor clean out of the world. I was equally angry with myself. While I had lain in bed sniveling, Bill had been manipulated by the prosecutor, and Rachel had been subjected to yet another trauma. I had let her down. I had let Penny down, and God had let us all down.

Northup would be put on trial for Penny's murder as well, this time in our own community, with newspapers and television reporting the trial and the details of Penny's murder on a daily basis, and we would be expected to be there. Bob was determined that we would not be put through that. The prosecutor in South Carolina was a friend and lived behind us. Bob went over to the fence and told him, "no more. We've had it." In the Maine trial, he had been given a life sentence. Bob told the prosecutor to leave him in Maine. "This family cannot endure another trial." We were lucky the prosecutor agreed.

I took most of my anger out on God. Sometimes when Bob was at work, I would go into the yard and hiss obscenities at God. I demanded that he prove himself to me by saving my baby and this family.

Slowly my rational side ascended, mostly because of Dr. Durst. Gently, but firmly, he told me I was not helping my baby. My fury over Penny's murder was endangering my child and keeping me from helping Rachel. Through long talks with myself, I came to the conclusion that, if I continued to be this angry, I was going to help Penny's killer add the rest of us, including my baby, to his list of victims.

My church (the Church of Sweden) teaches that you cannot justify your sins by the sins of another. There were no excuses. I was responsible for my own behavior, my own actions, and my own heart. No matter what Wayne Northup had done, I was responsible for the way I reacted. Just as his actions would not justify my participating in taking his life, either as a citizen or a stone thrower, they did not justify my endangering my baby and not taking care of my family. Nor did the actions of the Maine prosecutor. My anger was eating up my heart, and I was being self-indulgent to let it continue. The church teaches forgiveness, too, but I wasn't ready for it. I had to take this one step at a time. Later I would forgive God, Wayne Northup, and maybe even myself. For now, I would deal with my anger.

I got busy. Besides the hemorrhaging, I was RH negative, had low thyroid, and, at thirty-two, was considered old for pregnancy at the time. I became one of the first patients in Charleston's new problem-pregnancy clinic, going once a week to have my blood tested and then trooping over to the doctor's office. I was given the new ultrasound, seeing through the smeary black and white image the miracle child whose heart was beating in me.

When I wasn't going to be prodded and tested, I got the nursery in order and worked in the garden. Now and then, all my busyness and best intentions fell away, and I would vacillate between almost overwhelming sadness and a need to lash out and hurt someone or something. I learned to go into the nursery at those times. There I could remind myself that I couldn't change what had happened. No matter what I did, I couldn't take us all back to the day before Penny was killed and stop her murder. No one could. Not even God could take away her murder. All I could do, all any of us could do, was move forward the best way possible.

I talked to Penny a lot, especially when the sadness or anger came. I told her about my visits to the clinic and the doctors, about the ultrasound. I asked her if she liked the nursery. I even asked her if she could feel the baby kicking. And I told her I was afraid, that I didn't know if I was up to being the mother of this family, that I needed a mother myself. I needed her.

In late September, I got a letter from the South Carolina Arts Commission that a short story I'd written was one of the winning entries in a creative writing contest and would be published in The South Carolina Review. *I decided to force myself to get back to the discipline I needed to write again, but it was a futile effort, and it would be several years before I would publish another short story. I came to understand my own writing process when I made some innocuous comment to Bob one day, and he looked startled. When I asked what was wrong, he told me I hadn't spoken in four days. "I guess you've been writing," he said. A character and situation or event would begin to form in my mind, and I would go silent. I was listening to the characters tell me their story.*

That listening was my way of solving any problem, but clearly more fundamental problems were keeping my mind occupied. Later I would realize that I wasn't simply grieving—I was still in shock.

I also was listening to something else. The questions I'd asked outside Penny's house were still with me. I still had a burning need to understand why there was so much violence, why we seemed so good at it, and why we seemed so poor at love. I'd been something of an activist since I was barely into my teens, and I knew that beyond the questions that kept running through my mind was a call to some kind of activism that would respond to those questions. Unless I found a way to do something about the violence, I knew I could never truly honor Penny's life.

Honoring Penny's life also meant keeping our family together. I could never take Penny's place with her children, but I wanted to pass on some of the love and warmth and safety she had given to me. Thanksgiving and Christmas would be held at our home, and I spent weeks getting the house and food ready before each holiday. The house looked warm and inviting. We all oohed and aahed over our presents on Christmas and made a concerted effort to be thankful and cheerful. The food was delicious, but looking around the table I thought we were awfully young to be a complete family. There wasn't a grey hair among us, and we'd all had both too little and too much experience in our short years.

After the holidays, we began making those last-minute purchases and plans for the baby. I was huge and had trouble getting around, even having to be literally pulled out of the car or any chair I sat in. Having been skinny all my life, my body was unused to the new bulk, and I tired easily, so everything I did seemed to take three times as long as it should have. The ultrasounds and other tests had shown that I would have a placenta previa birth, which explained the enormous protrusion I was hauling around. I went to three doctors who were in practice together. Dr. Rivers believed I should have a C-section, Dr. Wilson took a "wait and see" attitude, and Dr. Sosnowski felt a C-section would be a last resort.

On the morning of January 22, I woke to a drenched mattress. I called Bob and got in the shower. When I got out, I all but flooded the bathroom. I showered and dressed again, only to ruin those clothes and have to start again. Before I could, Bob got home and told me not to worry about it, Dr. Wilson was waiting for me. The fluid would not stop coming, and I was embarrassed by the orderly following me through the hospital with a mop. Throughout the labor, the nurse was replacing stacks of pads under me every few minutes.

My first pregnancy had been extremely difficult. I'd dilated to a certain degree and stopped, although the labor continued. It had taken me thirty-four hours to deliver my first son, and he had been a blue baby. This labor seemed easier to me, but I outlasted Dr. Wilson, and Dr. Sosnowski took over. I liked Dr. Wilson a lot, but I adored Dr. Sosnowski, and I knew he would do everything possible to avoid a C-section. When he came in to tell me I was doing the same thing with this delivery I'd done with my first, but now they had a shot they could give me so I would continue to dilate, I was ready for it.

"It will cause the labor to be harder," he said. "Do you want something to help you with the pain?"

I didn't. A few hours before my first child was born, they had knocked me out, and I was determined to watch this child be born. The nurse and Dr. Sosnowski

Marie and Robert Deans
at his christening. Personal
collection of Marie Deans.

*said the labor would take a long time, but it didn't seem long to me. About 5
o'clock that evening, they rolled me into the delivery room.*

*For seven months we have been calling this child Catherine Anne, but the
minute the head emerged, Dr. Sosnowski said: "Marie, I don't think this is
Catherine Anne. I hope you've thought about a name for a boy." Sure enough, a
chubby, red-faced big baby boy was put in my arms. He looked like Jabo, and, to
me, still does.*

*As I looked into his face that moment after he was born, I began to hear
music, the most beautiful music I'd ever heard. Then the delivery room simply
went away; my son and I were amidst millions of stars. They were shimmering,
weaving, undulating together in a kind of dance, and the music swelled. It was
the most glorious thing I'd ever seen or heard or felt. It was life, past, present, and
future celebrating creation. I knew Penny was there. I saw her smile. I felt her
all around us. We were all here. I knew that each of us was connected, part of a
whole. In one form or another, life is eternal. I was not separated from God, from
Penny and Jabo, from my parents, or my first son.*

*Life itself is such a miracle. This baby, so endangered, had been determined to
rise out of the darkness and heaviness of grief, so determined not to let it smother
his life. In his birth, I had seen life as I'd never seen it before. Holding this child, I
felt pure joy. I had not let Penny's murderer take that from me.*

Wayne Northup was returned to Maine, where he was tried for a murder committed
in that state, and he spent the rest of his life in prison. Marie and her family agreed

with the prosecutor's decision to not have Northup extradited to South Carolina to stand trial for Penny's murder. Of the family's opposition to trying Northup, Marie stated: "Most people see this as proof that we are either saints or emotional freaks. We are neither."[2] And she explained that her initial reaction to Penny's death was anger and a desire to hurt Northup. "I wanted to take the killer into a room and beat and kick him for what he had done to her and our family. It was savage."[3] In the end, however, Marie and her family opposed the death penalty on the ground that they "simply wanted to prevent violence from being added to violence."[4]

In later years, Marie spoke about the series of events she believed led to Penny's death. Pointing to the fact that Penny's killer had been convicted of multiple crimes of violence against women but had never received any treatment, Marie argued that her mother-in-law "had paid for our society's inability to face its problems and deal with them effectively. We are more interested in satisfying our emotional needs than we are in finding real solutions to our problems."[5]

Penny's death proved to be the catalyst for Marie's decision to become involved in issues involving crime, the death penalty, and reconciliation. Within six months, Marie had joined Amnesty International, initially focusing on the plight of political prisoners in other countries before shifting her attention to the death penalty; by 1976, Marie had created a new organization, which she hoped would give a voice to those family members of murder victims who opposed the death penalty. And shortly thereafter Marie would step onto a death row for the first time to visit South Carolina inmate J. C. Shaw.

Marie's work was motivated not only by concerns over civil rights and justice but also by a need to understand the roots of violence. "From the moment Penny was killed, I never understood it, why she was killed. I came to the conclusion that we would not find out why unless we talked to the people who had done these things and [found] out from them. Of course they can't tell you why. You have to dig a lot deeper than that. I learned the answers to my 'whys' through working with J. C. Shaw and others on death row."[6]

In the years to come, Penny Deans would remain a constant presence in Marie's life.

> I still dream about Penny. At first, the dreams were nightmares about her fear.
> I would see the gun and her face, filled with the horrific knowledge of her own
> death. Then the dreams would be mixed up with the executions. Penny would
> be standing in a long line of men I knew, chained to them, waiting to be dragged
> into the death chamber and strapped in the electric chair. Finally, I began to
> dream about her as the grandmother she would have been.

While Marie's dreams of Penny evolved, one fact remained constant—Penny's murder was the rallying cry for Marie's quixotic battle against state-sanctioned death.

2

The Birth of an Abolitionist

Some things you must always be unable to bear. Some things
you must never stop refusing to bear. Injustice and outrage and
dishonor and shame. No matter how young you are or how old
you have got. Not for kudos and not for cash, your picture in the
paper nor money in the bank, neither. Just refuse to bear them.
— quotation on Marie Deans's desk from William
Faulkner's *Intruder in the Dust*

Marie's personal papers contain little information about her childhood. At first
glance, this seems like an odd oversight given the highly detailed descriptions
of her professional life that Marie left behind. Given the abuse and trauma she experienced at the hands of her parents, it is not surprising that Marie avoided discussing
her early years. To most people, Marie only referred cryptically to a childhood filled
with abuse and fear.

Marie was born on June 8, 1940, in New Zion Township, South Carolina. Although Marie's parents were living in Charleston at the time of her birth, Marie explained that her mother travelled to New Zion Township to give birth in her paternal
grandfather's bed because all members of the McFadden family had been born in the
Township for the last two hundred years. "I had to be taken up there to be born because, if you were a McFadden, you could not be born outside of Clarendon County,"
Marie later explained. Family tradition was important to Marie, and seventy years
later, in keeping with her wishes, she would be buried in the very same county in the
McFadden family cemetery.

Her mother was Eva Alice "Hettie" Jackson McFadden, who was a direct descen-
dent of Jonathan Jackson, the father of General Thomas "Stonewall" Jackson. Hettie
had grown up in relative wealth on a large orange tree farm near Deland, Florida, but
her family's fortunes were irreversibly damaged when their trees—along with seventy percent of the orange trees in Florida—had to be destroyed during a Mediter-
ranean fruit fly epidemic in 1929. Hettie was sent to live with an uncle who served in
the military, exchanging a life of privilege for a spartan military barracks in Panama
City, Panama. "[Reversal of fortune] has been a thing within the Jackson side of the

family since they came here," observed Marie's oldest son, Joel McFadden. "[When my grandmother] married my grandfather, they spent their entire lives climbing back up the ladder until they owned a magnificent home in downtown Charleston." Hettie herself worked at The Citadel for over thirty years, eventually serving as the secretary in the commandant's office. She was a highly competent and respected staff member, and a modest scholarship at The Citadel still bears her name.

Marie believed that her mother suffered from schizophrenia. The mother-daughter relationship was turbulent and unpredictable due to Hettie's dramatic personality swings. In Joel's eyes, his grandmother "was not a little off her rocker. She was a lot off her rocker." While baffled by her mother's destructive behavior and her inability to love her daughter, Marie recognized that her mother was "the hand that always moved the pieces on our family board" and that she and her father were mere pawns in some incomprehensible game that, because of Hettie's mental illness, no one could ever win. "[Mother] seemed to always want more than any one human being could possibly give to her," Marie explained. Even in her twenties, Marie still craved her mother's approval and lamented the fact that Hettie "never seemed able to say to me that she loved me for what I was."

As an adult, Marie commented that she could "not imagine" manipulating and hurting her children like her mother did, and she tried to comprehend what forces shaped her mother's destructive personality. Marie recalled the tension and anger that existed between her mother and her mother's sisters. "I've never seen a family so full of hatred for one another . . . something must have hurt my mother terribly for her to be so bitter and revengeful," and Marie believed that her mother had the "ability to destroy anything or anyone she decided had crossed her." For Marie, she had put herself in Hettie's crosshairs by favoring her father over her mother when she was a young child. "I know I've brought a lot of pain to her, and when I was younger I know I preferred my father, and I must have let her see that."

Joel echoes his mother, painting a picture of his grandmother as a manipulative woman who used threats and emotional blackmail to try to control people. "You have to understand that [Marie] was raised by people whose idea of love was abuse and then love, affection and [then] abuse," stated Joel. "Mom never really knew what real love was." While Marie suffered physical abuse at the hands of both parents, her mother was also emotionally abusive. Joel recalls the following, "My grandmother was much more manipulative [than my grandfather]. [She would say] 'If you leave here, I won't love you—I won't give you things. I'll give you anything you want if you stay and put up with me, but the minute you leave you're cut off.'" And, as Marie would learn, this was not an idle threat.

Marie's father was Joel Ellis McFadden II, the son of a tobacco farmer whose ancestors had immigrated to the United States from Scotland in the 1700s. McFadden attended watchmaking school after WWII, and he eventually owned two jewelry stores in Charleston. Joel remembered his grandfather as a weak, passive-aggressive man who was dominated by his wife but would viciously lash out if pushed into a corner.

As a young child, Marie was closer to her father than her mother, and she often

Marie's mother, Eva Alice "Hettie" Jackson. Hettie is standing in front of a monument to General Stonewall Jackson, whom she proudly claimed as a family member. Personal collection of Marie Deans.

confided in him. Their relationship was shattered when Marie discovered that her father had betrayed her confidences to her mother. "My dad needed you so desperately that he couldn't help betraying me," Marie wrote to her mother years later. "He was always trying to get both you and I to love him, so he would agree with me when I came to him about my troubles with you and then tell you exactly what I said. As a child I couldn't understand that." Hettie would only grow angrier when she learned of the conversations between Marie and her father. As a child Marie "felt like it was the end of the world" when her mother was angry, and she found herself facing Hettie's rages without her father to protect her.

It was not only a betrayal of her confidences that soured Marie's relationship with her father. In her book manuscript, Marie described her father as a prejudiced man who was a "molester and a sadist" and "morally insane." Marie never spoke explicitly about the type of abuse that she suffered at home, but she clearly identified herself as an abuse victim[1] and spoke in vague terms to her friends about the sexual abuse she suffered as a child at the hands of an unidentified male relative. And Marie felt like she was the frequent target of her father's temper, commenting that he would make a public show of loving Marie while "always humiliat[ing] me in front of others."

The emotional and physical abuse led Marie to believe that she was neither loved nor wanted by her parents. Hettie lost a male child during pregnancy, and she remained haunted by her inability to have a son. "Hettie wanted a male child very badly and she couldn't [have one]," explained Joel. "I think when Mom was a child her parents always were disappointed in her, primarily because she was female." When Joel was born, Marie wanted to name him John Scott after his maternal grandfather. Her mother, however, completed the birth certificate and named him after Marie's own father.

Together, Joel and Hettie McFadden created a home in which anger appeared as quickly and unexpectedly as a summer afternoon thunderstorm. Young Marie coped by avoiding conflict. "It seems to me that most of my life has been spent trying to please you on the one hand (something that seems to all of us almost impossible to do) and get away from you on the other hand," Marie wrote her mother in a 1972 letter. "Trying to avoid her mother at all costs was a big thing for her," Joel added. "I think she [Marie] really wanted to love her Mom, but she wanted to do it from afar."

Joel believes that loving people from a distance would become a pattern in Marie's life. "She [found] it very difficult to love somebody who's standing in front of her," he explained. "She want[ed] to love somebody but entirely on her terms, and, in order for it for it to be on her terms, the best thing is for them to be away." While the physical distance between Marie and the men of death row was often a matter of feet, the shackles and bars that divided them, and the rules that governed their interactions, would provide Marie with the opportunity to relate to the men on her own terms.

Because of Marie's dysfunctional family, we believe that she found it literally impossible to write at any length about her childhood. It is as if the things that went unwritten and unsaid allow us to piece together how miserable Marie's childhood was. The same can be said when it comes to photographs of Marie. "My Mom has one happy photo of her," Joel stated. "She's on a tricycle with a red towel tied around her neck being Super Girl [and she's] riding her tricycle up and down 10th Street. And if you think about a childhood—if a person can only tell you one moment in her life when she was happy, that says a lot."

When Marie was six years old she overdosed, and a family doctor removed her from her parents' care. He placed her at St. Angela Academy in Aiken, South Carolina. Marie later wrote that she overdosed because she was despondent over her parents' separation. The school was run by the Sisters of Charity of Our Lady of Mercy, an order founded in Charleston in 1829 and dedicated to caring for the city's sick, destitute, and orphaned. Marie not only attended the Academy, but she lived with the nuns in the nearby convent. Her time at St. Angela Academy was pivotal in Marie's moral development, and Marie wrote a short chapter about attending the Academy and living with the nuns who sheltered and loved her. The chapter, and some snippets from a speech which Marie gave, are some of a few glimpses that Marie herself provides into her traumatic childhood and the forces that shaped her character.

Marie and her father, Joel Ellis McFadden II. Later in life, Marie would speak of childhood psychological and physical abuse from both parents. Personal collection of Marie Deans.

During World War II, Charleston, SC, was not the lush colorful grande dame she is today. There was no money for paint, no money for renovations, and vegetable patches were crowded into our renowned gardens. In the spring when the wisteria, azaleas, and bulbs bloomed, Charleston looked like a black-and-white photograph that someone had hand tinted with daubs of color. My father had left for the war, and my mother and I lived alone in a small single house on Pitt Street—which was across the street from the carriage house my parents had lived in when I was born.

Even in Charleston, we ate poorly except for the occasional bus trip to my [paternal] grandparents' farm [in Sardinia, SC]. The buses were packed, and I learned to sleep standing up, leaning against my mother's legs. Uncle Roland was in the war, too, but Aunt Adelaide was still at the farm. She was always laughing and playing, and she made me laugh, even though I had no idea what we were laughing about.

My granddaddy let me help him move the milk cow to pasture at dawn every day, telling me he couldn't get her to cross the road unless I pushed her from behind. It never occurred to me to wonder who pushed her when I wasn't there. I loved following him around all day. He was quiet, gentle, and so closely knit to his land that it was hard to imagine him in another place.

Once my grandfather took me to the slave quarters on the old McFadden property. There were several long rows of tiny brick houses. The family was going to tear them down, and he wanted me to see them first. I don't remember all the words, but he told me that I should remember that our family had been involved in buying human beings to work for us and how wrong it was, and he made it clear that we needed to give something back for that. I remember seeing how sad those little houses made him.

I knew my grandmother didn't like me, and I tried to stay out of her way. When it was time to leave, my grandparents would fill a large cardboard box with vegetables, fruit, smoked meats, and butter. My mother and I would eat like queens for days.

I was four when we went to Camp Story, VA, to live for a few months with my father. There was no real housing, and we lived with another couple in what had been a woodshed. The shed was divided by sheets into three rooms. There was no heat, no water, and no bathroom. The bucket of water the adults collected every night and put in the makeshift kitchen would be frozen over in the morning. I liked it though. The other couple was nice to me, and my mother didn't have any of her spells while we were there. There were lots of other kids at the camp, and we played together all day. We bashed garbage can lids and used them as sleds to slide down the hills covered in pine straw. We piled more straw next to a storage shed, climbed up and jumped off, maybe a hundred times a day. Christmas Day it snowed. All the kids and their parents came out bundled for bear and played until it was too dark to see. To a child from Charleston, that snow was wondrous stuff.

Back in Charleston that summer I got malaria. Those months are a blur of crawling on the bathroom floor trying to get cool, vomiting constantly, the Coke truck bringing cases of Coke—the only thing I could keep down—Dr. Reynolds sitting beside me, and the smell of my mother's freshly starched cotton blouses and skirts when she bent over my bed. It was too much for my mother to handle alone, so we moved to my great aunt Lollie's in Lakeland, FL.

Aunt Lollie made Ovaltine doctored with vitamins and the home remedies she swore by for me every night, and my mother forced liquid quinine down me twice a day. Most of the time I threw it up, infuriating my mother. I suppose that quinine was precious fluid, but it had the nastiest, bitterest taste you can imagine. To this day anything grey with black spots will make me gag. Aunt Lollie pulled a daybed onto the sun porch so I could see outside, and I watched the kids play, pretending I was part of their games.

The malaria lasted longer than my mother had planned, and the next year we moved into a garage apartment. There were good things there. After a few months, I got to go out now and then. Somebody bought me a scooter and a pair of skates. Most of the time outside, I was on one or the other. I loved the movement. I also loved climbing the avocado tree in the backyard and got really good at biting my way into the fruit. There were guava trees, too, and I would eat three or four guavas, putting my nose into the flesh between bites. I thought they must smell like the Garden of Eden.

Mostly, though, it wasn't good. There was no one to stand between me and my mother's anger. Once, when I threw up in my plate at supper, she made me eat everything on the plate. It took all night, eating and throwing up, while she stood over me pushing my head down to the plate. That's the first time I remember her calling me Edna. Aunt Lollie told me Edna was my grandmother, who died when I was nine months old.

I got into trouble for crossing the street to play with neighborhood children. If I didn't get back before my mother found out, she would tie me to a tree until it was dark. I hated being tied to the tree, but I wanted to play with the children badly enough that I kept taking the chance. I never knew why I wasn't supposed to cross the street. There were so few cars in those days you would be lucky to see one a week, and the only thing I'd ever confronted in the street was a big black snake that had come out of the yard next door.

I went to kindergarten in Florida, but we moved back to Charleston just before my sixth birthday. We lived downtown in a big bedroom/sitting room of a family my mother knew. I don't know whether it was the malaria or missing Aunt Lollie, but I couldn't keep food down. The family had a cook named Maggie who carried on about me being so skinny and green around the gills. Her solution was white bread with butter and sugar. I ate it slowly. I could usually keep down a couple of pieces a day. Mother was gone most of the time. She'd started working and would go out at night. During the day Maggie let me stay in the kitchen with her, but at night I stayed alone in our room. I would lie on the sofa and watch the mice come out of the chimney and play on the floor. Those days seem silent and gray, except for Maggie's pleas to get me to eat. Mother didn't yell or anything. I don't remember her talking to me at all. I started school, but that didn't help. A lot of the kids came from the orphanage, and their favorite activity was beating up the kids they didn't know. I was one of those kids who got beat up.

My mother had migraines, and she kept the medicine on her bedside table. She'd caught me playing with the bottle once and told me to leave it alone. "Don't touch those. They can kill you," she told me.

"What would happen if they killed me?" I asked her.

"You wouldn't be here. You would be gone."

"Gone where?"

"I don't know. Gone forever. You wouldn't be here. You'd be dead."

Dead meant nothing to me, but not being here meant a lot. Maybe I'd be with my granddaddy. So one night when she was gone, I took all the pills in the bottle.

I woke up to Dr. Reynolds peering at me, nurses bustling around, and my stomach hurting something awful. It wasn't my granddaddy's farm or the gone forever I'd been promised, but things always seemed better when Dr. Reynolds was there.

I didn't go back to school. I went home and got fussed over by Maggie for a few days. Next thing I remember is standing in the middle of the sitting area of our room looking up at a bunch of adults, including Dr. Reynolds and my mother. Dr. Reynolds was holding my hand and being very stern with the adults.

A young Marie, likely taken around the time her family doctor took her out of the family home and placed her in the care of the Sisters of Charity of Our Lady of Mercy. Personal collection of Marie Deans.

Then I went with Dr. Reynolds on a long ride. He told me I was going to live in a convent with a bunch of sisters, that they would like me a lot, and I would go to school there and be a happy child.

He was right. I was a happy child with the nuns. They scared me at first. They wore funny clothes, seemed to have no hands and looked grim. The convent was huge and cavernous and rustled with the echoes of the nuns' murmurs, but I soon got over my fear, except of Mother Superior and my teacher.

The nuns had more rules than they had grits, and boy did they have grits—every morning, grits and stewed prunes. I guess I broke all those rules at some time, because the punishment was standing facing the wall and thinking about the rules for fifteen minutes before bedtime. The parish priest came in every night, and to this day I can't remember his face, because he always said goodnight to my back.

On those few nights when I didn't have to stand against the wall, I'd go into the novices' room. They would brush my hair and show me how to keep my shoes polished and my things neat. They told me how pretty I was, told me I was a precious doll and told me that I was going to make boys ache. They giggled and romped around in their underwear, which looked way too big and serious for them.

On Sundays we went on a hike after mass. I was with the Sisters of Charity in Aiken, SC, and the leaves had turned there. The colors were glorious—red, yellow, orange, burgundy. We had to stay together, but I was forever getting left behind looking at and touching the tiny gems of wildflowers, moss, and lichen.

School was fine, except that I had a crush on the little boy who sat behind me. I would twist around and answer him every time he whispered my name. The sister's hand, ruler attached, would come out of her habit sleeve, and I would get a whack across my knuckles. "No talking in class!" I never learned to be discreet.

Every day at recess one of the sisters would give each child in the school a piece of candy. The war was still going on, and candy was precious. We lined up to get our piece, moved away from the little kiosk and savored it quietly, letting it last as long as possible.

One day, one of the older girls started picking on me. I knew the rule and didn't respond, but she upped the ante when she said I was an orphan. I lit into her with fists flying. The fight didn't get far before habits were flying as well, and we were pulled apart. Our punishment was no candy for a week.

Three days later, another nun took over the kiosk at recess. When the other children formed the line, I sat drawing in the dirt and trying not to see hands reaching for candy. After all the children got their treats, the sister came over and asked why I hadn't come for mine. I told her I was being punished for fighting.

"Was it wrong for you to fight?"

"Yes, sister."

"Did going without the candy make you think about that?"

"Yes, sister."

The Sisters of Charity of Our Lady of Mercy in 1947. Sister Berenice McGregor (standing, second from the left) ran the school candy shop. She is likely the teacher who taught Marie a profound lesson about justice. Photograph courtesty of the archives of the Sisters of Charity of Our Lady of Mercy.

"Well, then, you've learned from your punishment. Punishment isn't to be mean. It's to teach you a lesson. Since you've learned your lesson, and that's what punishment is for, yours is over. Come get a piece of candy." Nothing like that had ever happened to me before. Punishment had been something that came for some reason or no reason and lasted as long as the person doing the punishment wanted it to.

As we walked over to the kiosk, the sister put her hand on my shoulder. "You know, Marie, you could have lied to me. I didn't know you were being punished. I would have given you the candy." She squeezed my shoulder. "You are a very good girl."

That praise tasted sweeter than the candy.

Until my first child was born I was a heavy sleeper. One night I slept through a fire alarm at the convent. I only woke up when sparks were flying around me and there was zapping and cracking loud enough to wake the dead, or at least me. I reacted in my normal way to fear. I froze. It felt like I was there for the better part of an eternity, but it couldn't have been many minutes before two of the nuns came running into my room. They pulled me off the bed, and one of them grabbed me up like a baby, wrapped her habit around me and took off. I got out untouched. I was unwound from the habit and set gently on the ground where the other sister leaned over me, touching me and telling me I was safe. They were as scared as I was, though, and I knew what it meant that they had gone back into that convent for me. The sister who carried me was rubbing her arm. She'd been hurt. None of the sisters ever let me know how or how bad.

I was not allowed to see my parents without at least one of the nuns present. Maybe that's why they never came to visit me and why the other children thought I had no parents. I didn't miss them. In my mind I was home, and I would stay there.

It didn't work out that way though. The day came when my parents came for me. For a long time, I remained so homesick for the sisters I felt I could lie down and never get up again. But they had given me something even I couldn't take away. I remembered the candy punishment, the praise, the fire, the many things they had taught me, the gentleness in their faces when they looked at me, even when I messed up on the rules. I knew they believed that I was a worthwhile child and that there was strength in me. They had shown me unconditional love and given me the stuff of a survivor, and I would remember and draw on those resources all my life.

The mental and physical abuse resumed when Marie returned home after a year at the Academy, with Hettie again exerting ruthless control over her daughter. During one of our conversations over take-out Chinese food, Marie—with an odd tone of detachment—recalled an occasion when her mother, angered by some long-forgotten triviality, decided to punish Marie by locking her in a closet for several days. Marie was forced to relieve herself in the corner of the closet, and she only ate when her father snuck food to her. For someone who would eventually counsel death row inmates, the image of a young child trapped in a small closet is a powerful and suggestive one. As is the image of Marie tied to a tree.

Those who knew Marie believed that the wounds from her childhood never fully healed. And Marie herself recognized this fact. In a 1984 letter to the *Richmond Times-Dispatch*, Marie alluded to her own story as she discussed the tragedy of child abuse:

> The results of child abuse go far beyond the physical and immediate emotional scars. Unless an abused child has a role model outside the abusive home, there is no way for him to learn that acts have logical consequences, nor is there any way to learn a sense of justice. The abusive parent acts out of his or her own childhood trauma and-or current stress. A child can be very naughty with no abusive results one day and perfectly behaved with intensely abusive results the next. What the child does learn is that violence is a legitimate and acceptable release. He also learns to have a love-hate relationship with authority that grows deeper and more volatile as his sense of isolation becomes more acute. I was lucky.
>
> When I was six, my family doctor arranged for me to live in a convent. There I was taught that acts do have logical consequences and that some authority figures do practice justice, even loving justice. But few are as lucky as I was.[2]

Marie's youngest son, Robert Deans, believes that the nuns of St. Angela Academy also taught his mother important lessons about kindness and charity. "[They] helped her understand that the world didn't have to work the way it did at home. The brief time she was there, she was able to absorb a lot of lessons on how the world really could be a better place solely through how people treated each other."[3]

The lessons learned by Marie at St. Angela Academy remained with her for the rest of her life. And Marie's growing sense of justice was reinforced by the diverse ethnic and religious environment in which Marie was raised.

> I think that I turned out as I have because I lived in a neighborhood where there were a lot of Jews who had escaped from Eastern Europe, including Germany and Poland. Many of them had lost most of their family members in concentration camps. Some had actually gone through the camps themselves and survived, and they told me their stories . . . of the impersonal, dispassionate killings [they witnessed]. No one took responsibility for those murders; everyone simply did their job. These stories had shaped me, but they also left me with a special, informed dread that an entire society can and will participate, either by omission or commission, in the killing of scapegoats that the society deems expendable. That special informed dread left me unable to admit that Americans of my generation would simply do their jobs, not interfere, and dispassionately take the lives of their fellow citizens.

In contrast to Marie's growing social awareness about prejudice and hatred was her father, who she described as "prejudiced about everything. He was particularly prejudiced about Jews and Blacks . . . colored people, as he called them." Marie described herself as a "curious child. I was never content with other people's opinions. I wanted to examine everything until I understood it for myself." She added:

> I had grown up at home and on my Grandfather's farm, and we would play with black children. In the South, you play with black children, and in Charleston, you live with black children, and they didn't fit what my father was telling me. My friends didn't fit, and what he was saying about the Jews didn't fit. I learned a lot from that.

As Marie grew older, she found herself perplexed by Jim Crow laws. "They made no sense to me," she recalled. "I would not drink from a 'white's only' fountain while my friends drank from a 'colored fountain.' "[4]

Confusion about segregation turned to disgust and outrage when Marie became a teenager, and her commitment to basic civil rights continued to mature. When she was thirteen years old, Marie took part in what she later called "an accidental sit-in" at a local Charleston Walgreens. After Marie walked into the restaurant and sat at the lunch counter, she noticed that four black teenagers were also sitting at the counter and were being ignored by the waitress. Seeing an acceptable white customer, the waitress walked over to Marie and said, with a smile, "Hi, Miss Marie. What will you have today?" Marie, finally realizing what was happening, replied "I'll have what they're having." The flummoxed waitress simply walked away, and, when the police arrived to arrest the protestors, they told Marie to go home.

Marie's voracious reading further fueled her moral outrage. One work that had a profound effect on the young teenager was Albert Camus's "Reflections on the Guillotine," in which the author argues against the death penalty. "It was Albert Camus who first made the death penalty more than an abstract reality to me." Marie later explained:

> I was repulsed by the idea that a people would capture and cage a human being and tell him or her: "We're going to kill you and here is how. Now think about it, picture it, feel it, imagine yourself being killed every minute of every day until we come for you." At sixteen I could not imagine there was a people left in the world who would carry out such a deliberate and inhuman act. Shortly after I read Camus, Caryl Chessman [a death row inmate turned author] was killed in a highly publicized execution in California, and I learned to my undying horror that *we* were a people who would carry out such an act.

Talking about the essay decades later, Marie recalled that Camus's graphic discussion of how the guillotined body slowly died made her vomit for three days. She would later joke that "Jung would say I couldn't stomach the idea."

Marie's opposition to the death penalty was also grounded in her religious upbringing in the Church of Sweden. "My mother and her family consistently reinforced the teachings of the church," explained Marie. "One of those teachings is that we cannot justify our sins by the sins of another. That certainly eliminates any support for the death penalty." Marie was dismissive of those Christians who spoke out in favor of capital punishment. She asserted that their support was "the equivalent of 'leaving Christ alone on the cross.' "[5] In a letter to the editor, written in response to a pastor's commentary that the Bible supported capital punishment, Marie wrote:

> It is, of course, no surprise that he [the editorial writer] does not mention Jesus in his arguments. When Jesus was confronted with the issue of the death penalty, he did not point to the offender or the offender's sins. He pointed to her would-be executioners and their sins. He pointed out their self-delusion of innocence. "Let he who is without sin cast the first stone." Jesus's own execution was the ultimate symbol of what human beings are capable of in our mad quest to take unto ourselves a power that is not ours—the power of absolute innocence, the power to destroy God's creation. The cross itself refutes man's ability to wield such power in moral purity.[6]

What Marie lamented most were Christians who went to church and Sunday school to learn about biblical teachings but promptly forgot their lessons when they returned home and resumed their daily lives. "Until we believe in the grace of God, believe that we can go to death row and to the broken community and bring about reconciliation, the violence in this country is just going to go on and on."[7]

At the end of her life, Marie's views on religion had changed and she lamented man's relationship with God. "I think if there is a God with consciousness, he/she/it is too appalled [by humanity] to show him/her/itself," she wrote in a letter to a former death row inmate. "Meanwhile, I'll stick with believing in the wonders I see with apologies to whatever accident created us and reminders that we, too, shall go away. To me our dreams of an afterlife have come to be an admission of what rotten, useless citizens of the universe we are, and the fact that we don't have a clue what to do with 'free will' and fear it a great deal."[8]

Marie graduated from Rivers High School in Charleston, South Carolina, in 1958. I have not been able to uncover much about Marie's time as a student. She was involved in a host of activities, and, as a "Teen Time delegate," she reported news on the high school's radio station and modeled "the latest fashions" at a local department store. While by all other accounts she was a popular student, Marie described herself as "guilt ridden and insecure."

Because of her stormy relationship with her parents and her desire to escape that environment, eighteen-year-old Marie immediately married a young Citadel student named William F. Tremper. They were introduced through Marie's mother, who was then working in the admissions office of The Citadel. "Hettie was very charming to us as cadets," recalled Tremper. "That is why [we] loved her so much." Hettie invited cadets to her home for dinner, and Marie met Tremper during one of those evening meals. "I passed Hettie's test. She liked me," explained Tremper. "At this time, cadets were not allowed to go overnight unless they were invited guests of [an] adult couple or parents. Hettie started to invite me to spend Saturday nights with them." Not surprisingly, the controlling Hettie had picked out a husband for Marie. "Hettie picked me for the first husband, and she picked Peter Anderson [not his real name] for the second husband," wryly observed Tremper.[9]

At the time, Tremper was not aware of the tension that existed between Marie and her parents. "I liked Joel, Sr.—I liked him a lot," he said. "He fixed me my first Manhattan and bought me my first suit. He was nice, pleasant, and a quiet listener. Always smiling, always cordial. But he was a door mat." As for the "charming" Hettie, Tremper said: "Marie and Hettie acted like sisters. Later, I was convinced that Hettie was capable of anything."

When I asked Tremper to describe Marie during their courtship, he replied: "I loved Marie for everything that she represented: pretty, well spoken, mature, and very polished. Her mother had trained her in the duties of a lady." As for the timing of the marriage, Bill added: "Either Marie wanted to get away or Hettie wanted to get her out of the house. That's why she married so young. And when we got divorced, she got out of the house again by marrying quickly."

Marie and Bill were married on August 18, 1958, at the Summerall Chapel at The Citadel. A short honeymoon followed at the glamorous Cloisters Hotel. Bill and Marie then moved to Florida, and Bill reported to flight training. Marie soon resented the long hours that Bill was required to serve, and he accommodated her by leaving flight training and starting infantry officer training. Still depressed and homesick, Marie told Tremper that she thought a child would make her happier. Once pregnant, however, Marie wanted to return to Charleston for medical care. In the fall of 1959, Marie moved back into her childhood home. Tremper visited Marie when he could. When he drove to Charleston in December of 1959 for Christmas, Tremper was met on the porch by Marie's father and handed legal papers. Reading the documents, an astonished Tremper learned that Marie wanted a divorce. The marriage was over.

After the divorce, Marie earned an associate's degree at Rice Business College and took English classes at the College of Charleston as she pursued her dream of becoming a writer. "I couldn't graduate from the College of Charleston because I couldn't pass math," Marie recalled. "So I went on to graduate school [at] the University of South Carolina in English and Creative Writing."

In 1961, Marie married a second Citadel graduate—Peter Anderson (we have changed his name to protect his identity). Marie considered Anderson the "love of her life," but his alcoholism doomed the marriage. Prior to meeting Marie, Anderson served in the demilitarized zone separating North and South Korea. While stationed in a forward position, Anderson's men were slaughtered by North Korean soldiers during a midnight raid. Although Anderson was not to blame for the incursion, he held himself responsible for the death of his men. Marie believed that he never recovered from the incident, and Anderson drank heavily through the marriage.

During the marriage, Marie worked as an assistant manager at her father's jewelry

Marie at seventeen years old, likely before one of the many dances and parties she attended at the Citadel. Personal collection of Marie Deans.

store, took creative writing classes at the University of South Carolina, and started submitting short stories to literary magazines. Marie's second marriage ended in divorce in 1967. During the separation period, Marie and her son again lived with her parents. The next year, Marie married Robert Deans.

The anger, hurt, and ambivalence Marie felt toward her parents was never resolved, and it reached a boiling point in the spring of 1972, when her eleven-year-old son announced that he wanted to live with his maternal grandparents in their grand Charleston home. Joel maintains that the decision was voluntary and triggered both by a lack of parental attention at home as well as being forced to attend a school where he was bullied. Marie, however, saw the move and subsequent custody battle as a betrayal that was later compounded by Penny's murder. Marie felt that her parents had manipulated and "kidnapped" her son, and she was distraught. "It was not a kidnapping," Joel retorted. "That [description] made it very comfortable for her, but it was absolutely my choice. And my grandparents were very ecstatic about it." He acknowledged, however, that Hettie "spent a lot of her time trying to take me from my mom."

In an undated letter to an aunt, Marie described how her parents set their plan in motion.

> *Last March Mother and Daddy said they were going to . . . a wedding and could Mac [Joel] go with them. Of course, Bob and I said yes. They left Thursday. On*

Friday I got a letter from Mac saying he couldn't live with me any longer and that he was going to live with Mother and Daddy. Well, I've run away from home a couple of times, so I figured we could straighten whatever it was out. But Mac said he and Mother had left Daddy in town so I could phone and tell him I wouldn't bother Mac, that he could live with Mother and Daddy. That made me suspect the whole thing had been planned (it turned out that it had been planned for some time between Mother and Mac and I suppose Daddy). I didn't want to believe it. I couldn't believe any Mother or Father would do such a thing to their child. They were supposed to come back by train Sunday night. I didn't hear from them, but I told myself they would get in late and call Monday morning.

By Monday evening I was literally sick. Bob and I went to see my doctor. He knows Daddy, and he said he thought Mac was probably upset about something and that Mother and Daddy just didn't realize what they were doing or, or rather, how serious what they were doing was. He gave me some medicine to keep my heart under control and called Daddy and asked to speak to Mac. I talked to Mac. We said we wanted to see each other, so he said he'd ask Mother if he could come to see me right then. When he got back on the phone, he said he was too busy. We went through several "how about tomorrow," "let me ask," "no," sequences; then I broke down and Dr. Durst took the phone. Dr. Durst asked me not to do anything but write Mother and Daddy and tell them how I felt about what they had done.

Dr. Durst got nowhere with Mother and Daddy. He said Daddy seemed to realize that what they were doing was not right, but that Mother was just hostile, and that Mac was obviously very confused and didn't really know what he wanted or what he should do. . . . one of the things that Mac said in his letter to me was that our house was not as nice as Mother's. We couldn't afford anything like that, but we found this house, which is a very nice house, in good shape, rather large, in a good, quiet neighborhood, with a huge fenced in yard, and even a tree house.

Marie would subsequently confront her parents during a group meeting at a doctor's office, but Marie found her mother to be "hostile" and "continually trying to start a fight." "I finally broke down crying, and I'm ashamed to say I got almost hysterical and ended up back in bed." She still had not seen her son. Marie was five months pregnant with her second child, a pregnancy that she thought impossible because of a thyroid condition. She had come close to miscarriage, and her family doctor recommended that Marie, who was still mourning the death of Penny, cease the confrontation with her parents until the pregnancy was over. Marie agreed, in part—oddly enough—because she was afraid that a court fight would result in her mother being forced to have a psychiatric evaluation. "Dr. Durst says that I mustn't do anything until this baby is born, but even then I don't think I can bring myself to drag Mother through that sort of thing," Marie wrote. Despite all the abuse she suffered, Marie took mercy on her mother.

Marie would ultimately not fight her parents in court. In an undated letter to them, she struggled to articulate her feelings about her relationship with her parents before announcing that they could keep her son.

I believe the time has come for us to drop all pretenses. We have had, at best, a very shaky relationship for the better part of my life. I truly don't know what you have sought in our relationship. For my part, I have sought two ambiguous things: one, a deep, abiding love and closeness and, two, to get away from you. I was never able to get rid of the torment these two desires have brought me. At times I have felt a degree of love from one or the other of you, and these times were joyous to me. At other times I have found only a bizarre form of competition from you, Mother, and from you, Daddy, humiliation.

I have tried to understand. I realize that you, Mother, must have had an unhappy childhood. Your feelings that Juanita and Johnny [Hettie's siblings] were preferred over you have perhaps made it difficult for you not to compete. And, Daddy, I've seen how you lack self-confidence, and so you could not help knocking others down in order to build yourself up. I, too, am a parent, and I know how terribly human all parents are, how they drag their own fears, hurts, and inadequacies into their relations with their children, how they must be constantly on guard less they allow their own sufferings, their own pains, to be passed on to their children.

I don't suppose that, as a child, I answered many of your needs. But I know how great your expectations must have been. I remember how badly I wanted Mac, and how sure I was that he would change my life. I thought that he would always be there to be loved by me and to love me. I learned slowly that it was I who should answer his needs. I have seen so many shattered adults that I came to want one thing for Mac above all, that he should grow up to be a confident adult who would be able to gain satisfaction from his life.

I suppose that, as an adult, I was even a worse disappointment for you, for I have felt, in the last few years particularly, that you resented me and had a desire to gain some sort of vengeance on me. I hope you will believe me when I tell you that I do not understand why this is so. I remember Daddy's fury when he told me: 'You made a mess of your life and by God you will pay for it.' I have tried to put myself in your place, Daddy, and Mac in mine to try to understand how a person could feel this way about his child. I haven't succeeded.

My son now says that he wants to live not with me but with you. I think all the way back to the time I first conceived Mac. Yes, he has given me many heartaches, but he has brought such joy, too. There is no way to measure that, is there? He is part of me, yet he is a separate human being. I have legal rights, but he has human rights. I want Mac with me more than I could ever make you understand, and there is no possible way to express what this has done to me.

Once I asked Mac why he lied about me to you. He told me he only did it when he was mad at me and that he did it because he knew it was the way to get me in trouble. I'm truly sorry that you, Mother and Daddy, and I made such a botch of being a family that you could not support me as a parent and were unable to care for me as your child. I know that you purposely set out to woo my child away from me. You have always seemed to think that you should have him and I should not. I don't understand those feelings, but I do understand that, to you, the taking from me gives as much pleasure as the 'winning' of Mac. Perhaps it gives you more pleasure, for I have never felt that you had a true love for Mac. You are too concerned with how Mac feels about you. To want someone to be tied to you and be dependent on you is not the same thing as loving someone.

But that is really not the point. Here is a child who has been torn between two sets of people until he can no longer stand the strain. I've not fought as you have, and I never will, because I cannot stand to see my child fought over like a 'thing,' a gold star to be won for somebody's list of self-conceived virtues. He is a living, breathing human being, and he is a particularly sensitive human being who has endured enough strife. Do you know that even though I saw this coming, I stuck by my intention of not letting Mac be fought over, and I hoped, against all hope it seems, that you would finally come to feel as I did. I hoped because I did not truly believe anyone would do what you have done. Once again I was naïve.

I mentioned my legal rights. I want you to understand that I am letting Mac be a visitor in your home only in the hopes that this will alleviate your constant fighting over him. This, in turn will, I hope alleviate my child's torment in trying to decide where his loyalties lie and will give him some peace. I believe you have used Mac (I do not know whether you have done this consciously or unconsciously, but the results are the same either way) to 'get at' me, and you have succeeded. I love Mac with all my heart, so by hurting him or taking him away, could you have failed? In this respect, you knew me well. I will exercise my rights in these ways (and possibly others which I may have overlooked in this letter).

Marie laid out a list of strict conditions for this new custodial agreement. She demanded that he continue to see a therapist, that her parents allow her to communicate freely with her son, and that she be "closely and strictly informed" of any changes in her son's medical or physical condition. It is unclear if her parents abided by any of these rules. They did, however, publish a classified ad in the local paper that Marie had been disowned and cut out of their will.

To her son, Marie wrote and apologized for failing him—not because she did not love him, but because, she wrote, "the love I feel for you did not get through to you."

There are many kinds of love. I believe a love that weakens the loved one, that causes him to be dependent, a love that says "I love you because you are like me," is a false love. To me that is a possessive love. We possess things, not people. I believe that true love strengthens the loved one, helps him find his own way of being, doing, and thinking. True love says "I love you for what you are, what you are growing toward, what you will become. It says, "I recognize our differences and appreciate them. I respect you and your right to be different, to be yourself." This is the way I love you, Mac. I wanted to have a child with all my heart. I didn't want to own that child. I didn't want to gain immortality through that child. I wanted to love that child, to watch him grow into manhood. I knew that growing would be painful. Childhood is not an easy time, clichés and slick writing to the contrary. I wanted to ease that pain. I wanted to help my child reach an adulthood that would be worth that pain and, at the same time, to make him know the security that comes from knowing that he is loved. That is where I failed . . . It was my mistake, and I am paying for it, but I still believe my goal was the right one.

But I do feel that love. I felt it when I carried you. I felt it when you were born. I feel it now. There is no piece of paper, no legal document, that can begin or end that kind of love. It doesn't automatically come with mother, either, but it came with you and me. It came, it stayed, and it is eternal. You may not see me as your mother, but I will always see you as my son.

To me signing these [custody] papers is an act of pain and love. Pain because I want to see you every day, to watch you grow and mature, to hold you in my arms. Pain because I am afraid for you. I know the depths of your emotions better than you would ever suppose me to know. I know how you hide your feelings, even from yourself. I know your anger and how it eats at you. I know your pain and how it torments you. I am afraid that without the true understanding you need you will grow up bitter and afraid as I once was. I don't want that for you. I want only the best for you . . . I want you to have the security, confidence, and understanding to live your life to the best of your capabilities. I want you to be a complete man, loved and loving, understood and understanding, and through these characteristics, fulfilled, your own man, successful in your heart and soul. My pain is that I must entrust you, a precious, growing human being, to the care of others and hope and pray with all I have in me that they love you and will help you achieve these most valuable and intangible goals.

While Marie professed to take full responsibility for the estrangement between herself and her son, she also pointed an accusatory finger at her parents. "From the moment you were born you were placed in a squeeze play I never understood," she wrote to Joel. "It was a competition I lost years ago simply because I refused to compete. A child's life is not something to fight over." Marie concluded the letter by expressing the hope that "someday you and I can be together in some way. Maybe you will be able to come see me, to let me be your friend."

Sadly, Marie and her son would never have a strong mother-son relationship. Joel accused Marie of having him briefly "institutionalized" and forced to undergo a battery of psychological testing before she allowed her parents to take legal custody. Marie did not see Joel again until he was fifteen years old and his father insisted that he visit his mother; Joel did not return to live with Marie until he was nineteen years old and attending the College of Charleston. Ironically, it was his grandparents' efforts to control and manipulate him that drove Joel out of their home. The final straw came when Joel's grandfather hit him over the head with a vase and knocked him out during a verbal altercation.

A year earlier, Bill Tremper attended a party thrown by Hettie in honor of Joel's high school graduation. [At the party] "they announced that Hettie had adopted Joel, and Joel was now Joel McFadden," Tremper said. "That broke my heart. And they re-wrote the will and left everything to Joel. They cut Marie out of everything." Tremper concluded, "That's when I realized that Hettie was the crazy one."

Living under the same roof again was challenging for both Marie and Joel, and he left within the year. Over the subsequent decades, the tensions between mother and son waxed and waned but never disappeared. Talking to a reporter at the time of her death, Joel would remark: "It's hard to share your mother. She had this emotional energy for it [fighting the death penalty], and she didn't always have that for everyone else. But I admired the hell out of her for it."[10]

For those who knew Marie as the seemingly fearless, hard-charging death penalty activist who marched into the lion's den of death row, her behavior regarding her son and her parents is baffling. There is no doubt that Marie loved her oldest son. If an inmate's life is worth fighting over, isn't a child's life? Especially a child who is being pulled into a destructive environment? Joel was not kidnapped and taken to a remote and unknown location. He was living in his grandparents' home in Charleston, only blocks away from Marie's house. Marie could have walked to her parents' home, taken her son by the ear, and dragged him home. And any court battle over legal rights would have quickly been resolved in Marie's favor. Yet Marie's ambiguous feelings about her parents paralyzed her.

Marie never found peace with her mother. Hettie died in 1983, shortly after Marie opened the Virginia Coalition on Jails and Prisons. Her father died two years later. Joel recalled a poignant scene during the last days of Hettie's life, where Marie sat beside her comatose mother's hospital bed, held her hand, and poured out her grief, anger, love and confusion to Hettie. It was only when Hettie was no longer a threat that Marie could confront her mother.

At the end, a love of reading was the only positive bond that Marie shared with her mother. Joel explains,

> My grandmother had this massive library of hardbacks. Every night at 7 or 8 o'clock, she would go to the library and read until 11 o'clock at night and then go to bed. Every single night of her life. And it was the only time that my grandmother was completely at peace and calm. She read Churchill's History of World War II. Great, great books. And Faulkner, Hemingway. She didn't read paperbacks. She thought that paperbacks were trivial. She just read. If you wanted to be loved by Hettie, you had to sit in a library and be read to. It was the only time that you ever got peace, comfort, and it was the only time Hettie was ever sort of in control of herself . . . if you were reading a book and you wanted to talk to her about the book you were reading, she would take the time to talk to you. That's where my love of reading comes from and that's where Mom's came from.

Marie remained a voracious reader until her death. Once during a telephone call in 2008, Marie told me that she had been crying. When I asked why, Marie said,

"Because I've been looking around my bedroom at my bookcases and my books. I realized that I won't be able to read them all again before I die." I didn't know what to say in response.

One goal of this book is to understand the individual who emerged from a childhood and early adulthood marked by abuse, pain, grief, and loss. Because I only knew Marie during the last years of her life, I have reached out to her family members, colleagues, and friends. Many speak of the sheer force of her intelligence, her "wicked" sense of humor, her rare ability to see the humanity of the men on death row, and her fierce devotion to ending the death penalty. Recalls actor and death penalty activist Mike Farrell:

> She was a spark plug. She was a bright, smart, dedicated, charming southern woman. She was full of stories and full of this incredible optimism about the human spirit and why it was that this work needed to be done. And how awful the system was and how unfair and inappropriate the conditions were in the system. She talked nonstop. She was kind of a veritable fountain of information about whatever cases she was working on at the time and about the people and the individuals—the sense that there was this great human potential that was being wasted by the blindness of the system.[11]

Tim Kaine, a former death penalty attorney who later became governor of Virginia, also recalled Marie's humor. "One thing I would hope a book about Marie would capture is not only her great humanity, but her great sense of humor and sense of fun," stated Kaine. "She was dealing with an incredible amount of stress, but she was always quick with a joke or to laugh at other people's jokes or see the humor in situations . . . anytime I was with her [or] we were with somebody on death row . . . she was funny and tried to lift people's spirits in that setting."[12]

Lloyd Snook, who met Marie in 1983, echoed Kaine's comments. "She chained smoked. She was funny. She was profane. She was—the person that she reminded me most of was a Virginia version of [Texas humorist] Molly Ivins."[13]

Marie's utter commitment to "the cause" was one of her defining characteristics. Sister Helen Prejean recalls being at a death penalty conference in the early 1980s, when Marie and another colleague discussed the idea of volunteering to hold hands with the men in the electric chair—thus exposing themselves to death as well—to demonstrate their solidarity with the condemned. When asked if Marie was serious, Prejean replied:

> I think Marie, being who she was, if she could have done that, she would have done that. I don't think she would ever bring up an idea that she wasn't ready to do. She was not an empty talker. That was not Marie Deans. She lived such a life of integrity, and if she offered an idea she's going be the first one saying "I'll go first." I absolutely do believe that about her and it's what I love about Marie Deans. It's what I learned from Marie Deans.

Throughout her interview, Prejean repeatedly used the word "integrity" to describe Marie. "Whatever she thought, she really tried to live . . . You absolutely trust[ed] her heart and her integrity and her fidelity."[14]

Marie's integrity was founded in an abiding belief in the basic humanity of the men on death row, men who society had condemned as monsters. "From Marie, I learned to see the guys on death row as human beings," explained former death penalty attorney Steve Northup. "No matter what they had done, she was able to see them as human beings. When you came under her influence, you would see the men in the same way."[15]

This compassion that Marie felt for the men of the row carried over to the death house, according to attorney Barry Weinstein. "Marie just had the personality, the traits, the characteristics of the very loving mother that inmates can be very comfortable with knowing that they're going to die . . . she was a friend [and a] spiritual advisor to these inmates. What transpired between them—especially during the last hour or so—there was just a calming effect."[16]

Seeing the humanity of the residents of death row, however, did not mean that Marie was soft on the men and their crimes. "She was also talking straight shit to them," said former Coalition attorney Bart Stamper. "She was calling them to the carpet . . . Marie didn't let them get off the hook but yet she showed a tremendous love in a motherly way. I mean tough love."[17]

For the young death penalty activists who worked with Marie, one benefit of their association was an education that stretched beyond capital punishment. "She was so well read," recalled Pamela Tucker. "She would give me books to read that I still haven't read. I learned so much from the people that were around her, it was almost like 'salons.' " And Pamela recognized the effect that Marie's dominant personality had on others. "I think that she collected people—I don't know if they gravitated to her or if she sucked them in."[18]

A few associates use the word "damaged" when talking about Marie, painting a picture of a haunted and insecure woman who often needed praise to support her shattered self-confidence. Remarked a former colleague:

> We all loved her, but she was an all-encompassing ego that was horribly damaged. She was a tortured person and she did a world of good for those without a voice. However, she hurt a lot of people along the way with her ego and need for devotion and adulation. There was never room for anyone else [in her life] other than the guys on the row and who she could save and be lauded for. That's why it's hard for anyone who knew her to talk about it. Certainly for me, there was a part of me that loved and admired her and a part of me that feared her. All of her relationships were like that. Many of us did our best to embrace the good in her to get the work done. But, in the end, most of us had to walk away or we were shunned for not doing it her way.[19]

Another colleague recalled Marie holding court at death penalty conferences, seeking the attention of the assembled activists and ignoring those friends who had disappointed her. "Maybe Marie needed the adoration," she said, "and I wasn't giving it to her anymore."

Yet it is too simple to conclude that Marie sought attention for the sake of attention itself. In the opinion of her oldest son, the attention confirmed that she was needed and valuable.

> If someone would come by and visit [the men of the row] and reassure them—I think that was a little bit of a comfort for her to be the person [who] would—to be able to go to a prison and be the person . . . befriending this person [who] has nothing else. I think it made her feel like she was really doing something great. Mom's motivation was to be accepted and appreciated. Everybody needs that at some level. I guess that's the basis of love—to be accepted and appreciated by somebody else. Her family never did that for her. Her husbands never did that for her. So when she was able to walk into a cell and she [was] all they had—you know that made her feel like she was worth something. Nothing else in her life ever made her feel like she was worth something.[20]

Former Amnesty International colleague Larry Cox echoed Joel's words about Marie finding purpose, and some measure of validation, in death penalty work. "I don't know what her life was like before, but you had the sense that this gave her enormous meaning and purpose and a sense of what she could do," remarked Cox. "I literally in those [early] years saw her transforming herself and becoming a real force . . . [and] a very intense force. I think she could scare people because she was so committed." Cox added that this intensity made him "wary" of Marie. "There was some dark part of her that was unhappy that was being filled up with all this work."[21]

Marie herself recognized that her unwavering focus on her work intimidated some people. In a letter to inmate and confidante Joe Giarratano, she wrote:

> [My] brooking no nonsense and being cutting I know is true. And it's also true that people think I stay angry at them. Those who know me well know better. And yes, people do say I'm always so serious. Remember Earl [Clanton] saying I didn't have a sense of humor, I had a sense of irony? Again, people who know me well, think I'm funny—at least at times, but even they say I have an 'unconventional' or 'dark' sense of humor. And you're right, this [death penalty work] is damned serious. Maybe if I sold houses for a living, I'd be funnier or more willing to waste time with stuff that doesn't matter.[22]

Writing back to Marie, Joe conceded that "most people are scared silly of you, Deans, even though your bark is really worse than your bite." As for the source of this fear, Joe hypothesized that her colleagues and friends admired Marie and "are afraid of letting you down more than they are actually afraid of you, per se. And just a glance from you can make them very aware that they are missing the mark . . . you don't allow them to make excuses or rationalize." Of course, it was easy to

Marie in the early 1980s, when she began working on South Carolina's death row. Personal collection of Marie Deans.

disappoint someone like Marie, who set impossible standards for herself and others around her.

If Marie sought the limelight to validate her own self-worth, Joel believes it was a futile effort because, in the end, there was only one person whose praise she wanted. "Mom spent her entire life trying to do something good enough for her mother to say, 'Good job, dear. I love you.' It never ever happened," explained Joel. "So Mom spent her entire life trying to be recognized for being successful by someone who was never going to recognize her. I could come and say, 'You're wonderful. We love you.' [But] it was never going to make her feel loved, because she wanted—everybody wants their parents to love them." When asked what Hettie did say to Marie about her work, Joel simply replied: " 'Those people deserved to die. You shouldn't waste your time.' "

The shell of self-confidence that Marie cultivated to mask her insecurities often led her to butt heads with attorneys and death penalty activists. For long-time Virginia death penalty attorney Jerry Zerkin, Marie's hard-nosed approach had both positive and negative effects. "She could be really rough on people who worked for her, but on the positive side she was very hard to say no to. As a result of that, [she] got people to do things [that] in their saner moments [they] wouldn't have agreed to. So I include myself among those."[23] Marie often grew angry when she believed that her colleagues in the death penalty fight were not making the same sacrifices she was, without recognizing that her own sacrifices were unrealistic and came at too high a cost to herself and those around her.

Marie's personality would also be shaped by pressures from her work. Former assistant Molly Cupp recalls that Marie "walked around with this deep grief that just became part of her. Not just because of individual people's stories, but just the whole—the whole horror of the whole thing—and that being a part of our society. She hurt not just for the men and their families but for modern society who wants to do this."[24] Once, in a moment of candor with a friend, Marie acknowledged the toll that the stress of her work had taken on her psyche, admitting that she likely suffered from post-traumatic stress disorder. Without missing a beat, the friend replied: "It can't be *post*-traumatic stress disorder, Marie, if you keep putting yourself in these situations. How can you heal?"

For Marie, the answer was clear—there wasn't time to heal. "For those of us who have made a full-time commitment to the human beings who are the victims of this killing machine, there is not even the luxury of time to heal, for the machine continues to grind on inexorably," Marie wrote to a colleague. She made a similar argument in a letter to an inmate. "There still isn't anyone else trying to stop this killing. It hurts that I work so hard to stop the killings and am f__king exhausted and then my family and friends carp at me, because I'm not paying enough attention to them." Marie conceded that she was "obsessive about this death penalty business," but pointed to the fact that her obsession was saving lives. She also recognized that work isolated her. "Mine . . . is a suffering that does not love company."[25]

Marie's frenetic pace took a physical toll as well: frequent migraines, weight loss, sleepless nights, hand shakes, and vomiting. In the final hours of his life in the death house, inmate James "J. B." Briley half-joked about the physical impact of Marie's work. After telling Marie that he would see her in the next world, Briley added that he knew it would be sooner rather than later because of the exhausting pace maintained by Marie. His words were prophetic. "I'm a seriously damaged person," Marie conceded in an October 31, 2000, telephone interview with author Margaret Edds. "You end up with bad health, your body's broken, you're running on spirit and you can't keep doing that. You can't do it the way I did and not pay some toll."

So who was Marie Deans? She was a woman who never escaped an abusive childhood and who remained scarred by that abuse until death. She was one of the most well-read individuals I've ever known, and her fierce intelligence could be intimidating—especially when she fixed those large eyes on you and peered into your soul. Marie did not suffer fools gladly, nor did she tolerate excuses from attorneys, paralegals, prison officials, and volunteers who were not working as hard as she was. And she was brave. Despite her fears, Marie steeled herself and walked into the death house so that thirty-four men would not die alone. When it came to her convictions about right and wrong, she was unyielding. Her devotion to the cause, however, exacted a terrible price.

3

Marie and the Men of the South Carolina Death Row

I believe that God is life and love. Those things that move
toward life are good things and godly things and sacred things,
and those things that move toward unnatural death are evil.
—Marie Deans, 1989

As Marie recovered from the murder of Penny Deans and the loss of her oldest son, she struggled to find a way to get involved in the fight for social justice. Marie had joined a letter-writing campaign to free Ukrainian author Valentine Moroz from a Soviet prison. In 1973, Marie read an article stating that Amnesty International (AI) was involved in a similar campaign. She wrote Amnesty International for information about its activities, and the materials that she received opened her eyes to the worldwide practice of imprisoning political activists. "I began to become aware of the whole human rights movement," Marie explained to a reporter in 1980. She jumped into that movement with both feet. Marie founded a Charleston chapter of Amnesty International in 1979. Her days became filled with circulating petitions, organizing volunteers, and supervising letter-writing campaigns. "I am fanatical about human rights, particularly today," Marie remarked. "I feel we are going to have a global conflagration if we aren't [already]."

In speaking of Marie's death penalty work, her friends and colleagues often mentioned her total devotion to the cause. The same commitment can be found in Marie's early AI work. "My life has changed because of AI," said Marie. "Forming the Charleston group has made life frantic." Little did Marie know that writing letters for political prisoners in foreign lands was the first step on her journey to her home state's death row. "Having anything to do with people on death row was not in my plans," admitted Marie years later. "I would have thought anyone who suggested such a thing had taken leave of their senses."[1]

I joined Amnesty International six months after Penny had been murdered. The concept of speaking up for those who could no longer speak for themselves and working against the violence being done to them appealed to me. Maybe I could be there for them when I hadn't been for Penny. The "them" I thought I would be speaking for were prisoners of conscience—political prisoners—in places like the USSR and Uruguay.I wanted to do more than write letters as an individual member and began forming an AI group in my hometown, Charleston, SC. AI was just moving into active opposition to the death penalty in the US, and the internal debate was noisy and sometimes ugly, so the US section staff made it clear that the issue of the death penalty needed to be addressed by all AI groups in the country.

Even so, one of the arguments used by proponents of the death penalty was deterrence, and regardless of my belief that the death penalty was wrong, I wasn't ready to jump into the debate if the death penalty did save innocent lives. I spent several weekends in the library pouring over every book and study I could find on the death penalty. What I found was a century of studies showing that the death penalty was no better at deterring murder than long terms in prison.

Within a year I was being asked to speak on behalf of AI, and I would include our position on the death penalty. Inevitably the question "what about the victims?" came up, and I would talk a bit about my own story. Occasionally, someone would come up after the talk and tell me a member of their family had been murdered, and, when they had voiced opposition to the death penalty, they had been treated like pariahs or saints.

I told Ray McClain, a friend of the Charleston AI group whose grandfather had been murdered, about the families I'd met and what had happened when they spoke out against the death penalty. Ray agreed that it would help families such as ours if we had our own voice.

I wrote the fifteen or so families whose stories of taking a position against the death penalty I'd heard or found, asking if they were interested in forming a group and if they would consider inviting the families of the executed as well. All but one responded, and I was heartened by their welcoming both the idea for such an organization and including the families of the executed. Between the letters and word of mouth, we soon had twenty-five family members of victims. It would be another four or five years before our first family member of the executed participated. For the first ten years, we called ourselves Victims' Families for Alternatives to the Death Penalty. In 1986, we changed our name to Murder Victims' Families for Reconciliation (MVFR).

We visited, talked on the phone, wrote each other, worked in our own communities, and sometimes went with members in neighboring states who were testifying before their legislative bodies or giving their first talk. Being able to say we belonged to a national organization of murder victims' families made us less susceptible to being dismissed, and supporting each other made us more willing and able to speak out. Slowly, but steadily, we added new members. It's good for activist organizations to grow, but for us, the tragedy that made new members eligible was always personal and sobering.

I quickly learned that our family's experiences were not unusual. Our members recounted stories of being used or dismissed by prosecutors. One woman

*whose daughter had been murdered kept calling the prosecutor trying to learn
first about the investigation and then about the trial. The prosecutor's behavior
toward her went from impatience to angrily telling her she needed to remember
that she was not the victim in "his" case. Another family told me that when they
expressed reluctance to have the offender executed, the sheriff told them the
man had vowed to get out and kill every member of the family and would do so
if they didn't help him secure a death penalty. They later learned the murderer
had made no such vow and instead had shown what they believed to be true
remorse.*

*Working with AI and MVFR felt like a natural part of the direction my life
was taking. I had recently published a short story and knew I would get back to
writing. I would take care of my family and watch over Penny's kids.*

Marie would not get back to her budding writing career. In 1976, Marie founded
MVFR. "I knew there were people like me . . . who were opposed to the death penalty," Marie recalled. "We had no voice and that was my goal—to give those people a
voice where they could speak out on their own." Marie felt that the families of murder victims need a "safe place from which they could speak out" because of tension
she perceived among the families, abolitionists, and attorneys. Specifically, Marie
observed that abolitionists often assumed that anyone related to a murder victim
automatically supported the death penalty, while attorneys representing defendants
in capital murder cases often thought that trashing the reputation of the murdered
individual increased the chances that their client would not get the death penalty—a
tactic which enraged family members.

Marie remained involved with MVFR until shortly before her death. The departure of her youngest son as the head of the organization caused Marie to resign. Furious and hurt at what she perceived to be mistreatment of her son, Marie demanded
that any mention of her name or her involvement with MVFR be stripped from their
website.

In the late 1970s, Marie was asked by Amnesty International USA (AI USA) to
become a charter member of an AI USA death penalty committee charged with the
responsibility of mapping out guidelines for an attack against the death penalty.
Within a few years, Marie was asked to join the board of directors of AI USA and
to be responsible for overseeing death penalty issues. Marie's job duties quickly extended beyond writing position papers and sitting on boards. She also began to visit
death rows and report on the conditions of confinement. In April of 1981, Marie met
with William D. Leeke, Commissioner of the South Carolina Prisons System and
toured the South Carolina death row located at the Central Correctional Institution
(CCI) in Columbia. This was the first time that Marie had set foot in a maximum
security prison.

On the day that she visited South Carolina's death row, Marie and two fellow
AI USA volunteers, Rose Styron and Larry Cox, first met with what Marie called a
"wary" corrections staff. Marie wrote that the staff started relaxing once the AI members spoke sympathetically about the difficulty the prison officials faced.

It was quite an education. The corrections officers and the Commissioner, who joined us for the last hour and a half, [are] against the death penalty. They feel beleaguered by the people. They hate "storing" their prisoners. They do not want any mistreatment, and they fear what was coming. Each time they told us something that was being done for an inmate, especially a death row inmate, they practically made us take an oath not to repeat it. One death row inmate was out that day having a root canal—this is not to be used—and the warden asked if we had any idea what the people would say if they found out a man under sentence of death was given a root canal.

Years later, Larry Cox credits Marie with defusing the tension in the room. "I was struck by the fact that Marie—[despite] the fact that she could be very intense and very uncompromising—really got along well with the prison officials," Cox recalled. "I was sort of surprised, and I felt like this was something I should learn how to do."[2]

Regarding her visit to the South Carolina death row, Marie wrote "we weren't allowed to speak to the inmates, which means it was like the classic nightmare of being in a zoo where the animals in the cages are human." Soon after her tour, Marie wrote to CCI Warden Joseph Martin and discussed how she was impacted by her prison visit.

I was shaken by the prison, the row . . . most of all I was shaken by you. It would be a great deal easier to think of you following those execution procedures if you were an insensitive clod. We've made it too easy for people to demand the death penalty and tell you to take care of the dirty work. I am not overly sympathetic to the murderers. I told you of my mother-in-law's murder. I reserve my sympathy for those I see as true victims—the murdered and their families and loved ones, the families and loved ones of the murderer, our children, who will have to live with this history, and—most of all—for the people in your position. That does not mean I care nothing for the inmates on death row. I do. What it does mean is that I have no sympathy for a man like Governor Riley, who says he is against the death penalty but won't go against the will of the people. I find people like him more culpable than the morally ignorant. And, again, he leaves you with the dirty work.

What is most striking about Marie's letter is the comment "I am not overly sympathetic to the murderers." This lack of empathy would dramatically change once Marie came to know the men of death row.

In 1982, AI USA sent Marie Deans and Rose Styron to investigate conditions on death rows throughout the South. "One by one, we're going to take a look at the state, at their prisons, and at the death rows, to see whether we can improve the situation," Styron explained in a joint newspaper interview with Marie Deans. "We know we can help," added Marie. "You have to remember that we're concentrated on the forgotten prisoners. . . . [for] most of us, if one comes out, it's worth what we've done."

Marie ultimately visited death rows in Louisiana, North Carolina, Oklahoma,

Tennessee, and Texas. Most of her time was spent in Texas, where its death row was packed to the rafters with 165 prisoners (most of whom did not have lawyers), who endured squalid conditions of confinement. In an interview with a local paper, Marie did not pull any punches on what she thought about death row:

> Texas is the worst I've seen. . . . It's sterile, no minister or other volunteers can come in from the outside, [and] lawyers have to visit with no privacy, just like other guests. They're in their cell twenty-three hours a day, and there are no contact visits at all. Notice I didn't say conjugal visits, but contact visits, not so much as a handshake with someone. You can't even touch your own kids if they come to visit.[3]

The fact that the men on death row could only visit with their loved ones through a thick metal mesh barrier seemed especially cruel to Marie. "This is a maximum security prison and guards are everywhere," Marie observed. "So why is all this necessary? It's all so closed in, so tight, and the tension is just rising."

Marie made it clear in the newspaper interview that AI USA and its volunteers did not consider the guilt or innocence of the prisoners to be relevant. The focus was on the method of punishment. "What we are saying . . . is that there is no justification for taking a human life, none."

Marie returned to Texas in December of 1982, when she attended protests in opposition to the execution of Charles Brooks Jr. He would be the first individual in the United States to be executed by lethal injection. Of his execution, Marie would write:

> When Charlie Brooks was executed in Texas last December for a murder committed during a robbery, three hundred students stood outside the prison laughing, drinking beer, and holding up signs like "Kill Them in VEIN." As Brooks was pronounced dead, one young man yelled: "Hey, the party's over!" A whoop went up in the crowd.[4]

The behavior of the crowd outside the death house was evidence, in Marie's eyes, of how the death penalty was dehumanizing society.

Marie also fought a public battle over Oklahoma's death row, which she found to be filled with violence and sexual assault. Marie was outraged when she learned that a young juvenile offender on death row had been repeatedly raped, but prison officials were baffled by Marie's distress because the inmate was under a death sentence. Why worry about the safety of a condemned man living within the shadows of the electric chair? Prison conditions on Oklahoma's death row did not change until Marie convinced a local newspaper to print a story about death row that shamed the prison administration into putting minimal reforms into place.

Besides visiting death rows, Marie corresponded with death row inmates. In her letters, she offered the inmates support and asked the inmates to describe their lives. The letters she received back were sobering. A death row inmate in Tennessee sent Marie this reply:

I have been on death row since December 11, 1978, practically four years, and the only way I can describe my existence is "just hanging on" by instinct alone. Just barely living, if it can even be called that. I think constantly about my case, hoping that something will change where my conviction might be reversed or that the death penalty will be ruled unconstitutional. I have also, for practically every day of the past four years, thought about the details of my execution. Having my head shaved, being dragged to the death chamber, being strapped into the chair and having the electrodes hooked to my body. At that point, there is always a lull in my thought for a moment, and then I force myself into something else to snap out of it.

These four years of isolation and deprivation, having little human contact, touch or sexuality, have built so much pressure on me that I really don't know how I'm able to go from one day to the next. This added to the constant threat of being executed, with the death chamber less than thirty paces from my cell, makes my existence almost unbearable.

I think that all of us (men on the row) realize that and believe that we are here for one purpose: to be, at some point, executed. But I guess, like all human beings, we cling to some hope that our situation will change. Most of us still hold onto some of the same hopes and desires as people in the free world and I'm sure we all still love (and need love) and care (and need to be cared for) about our friends, our families, and our fellow man.

There are sometimes visitors to death row. School groups, ministers, the county grand jury, and other people come down the row, view the men in their cells, and look at the electric chair. At these times, we here on death row feel at our lowest because we regard it as no more than people viewing us as animals in a zoo. And many of the visitors seem to have that attitude, looking on us with apprehension, anxiety, and fear—not appearing to even consider that we are men, human beings behind these bars.

I guess the one thing that causes more mental pressure and distress is the aloneness of each person on death row. Because of the isolation process we're subjected to, we are literally our own company for nearly every minute of every day, there is no sense of relating . . . to even the man in the next cell.

I'm sitting here waiting to be finally killed, yet hoping I won't, I often wonder how much of me will be left to kill after years of this tortuous, degrading, and dehumanizing kind of existence. The state may burn, gas, or shoot my body, but it's possible that my mind will have long ago ascended.

Living on death row, Marie, is like not really living at all. You don't have a future, cannot realize the present, and the past only provides painful memories of better times.

This letter, and others, gave Marie a more personalized and intimate look at the daily horror of the slow death suffered by men on the row. But Marie was still not meeting face-to-face with the condemned inmates—until she received a fateful phone call.

Having anything to do with people on death row was not in my plans. I would have thought anyone who suggested such a thing had taken leave of their senses, but I hadn't counted on a phone call from John Brown. John was with the Alston Wilkes Society, a prisoner support organization in South Carolina, and one in which my father had once served as president of the board. Even with his slow Piedmont accent, John had crammed so much into the first few minutes of the call he had left me breathless when he paused. Joseph Carl "J. C." Shaw had schizophrenia. He and another man, Terry Roach, had killed two teenagers. But the South Carolina Department of Corrections was giving J. C. treatment for his mental illness. Now J. C. was so horribly aware of what he had done, he had dropped his appeals in the hope that his execution would help the victims' families heal. The victims' families didn't know how they felt about an execution, and the prison administration was driven to drink by the idea that they might have to carry out the execution. Would I come talk to J. C.? Would I at least come talk with Warden Martin?

I'd asked John to let me think about it, and I spent the afternoon with half my attention on what I was doing and half on the phone call. There were two reasons I was even considering picking up this gauntlet. Several years before, I had learned my mother had schizophrenia. Most of the time she was simply distant, cold and odd, but she could also be violent. My aunt's earliest memory of my mother was of her trying to kill her younger brother. My own memories of her violence would erupt unexpectedly and cause me to react as if those memories were my only reality.

When I learned what was wrong with my mother, I read everything I could get my hands on about schizophrenia. Trying to understand this complicated mental illness sent me on a journey that would last for many years. Early in that journey, I realized I was trying to forgive my mother and find some way to love her. Maybe going to talk to J. C. Shaw would give me more insight into what schizophrenia can do to people. Shaw also presented the possibility of helping me answer the questions about murder that had been plaguing me since Penny's death. Surely, if anyone could answer those questions, it was someone on death row. I called John and agreed to meet with Warden Martin.

In approximately 1980, South Carolina death row inmate J. C. Shaw decided to drop his appeals and "volunteer" for death. A former military policeman, Shaw had taken part in a series of brutal crimes that resulted in the murder of three individuals, including seventeen-year-old Thomas Scofield Taylor and fourteen-year-old Carlotta Hartness. Their deaths were especially gruesome, with Shaw repeatedly raping Carlotta before and after her death. Joining Shaw in the bloody rampage was seventeen-year-old James Terry Roach, a mentally handicapped minor who would also be convicted of capital murder and sentenced to death in the South Carolina electric chair. If executed, Shaw would be the first inmate killed by South Carolina since the re-establishment of the death penalty in 1977.

We do not know how much Marie knew about the history of South Carolina's use of capital punishment as she prepared to meet J. C. Shaw. Like most southern states, South Carolina had a long history of vigorously imposing the death penalty. During colonial times, South Carolina joined other slaveholding states in enacting draconian legal codes to control its slave populations. Historian Stuart Banner wrote that both free blacks and slaves could be executed for a host of offenses, including "burning or destroying any grain, commodities, or manufactured goods, . . . for enticing other slaves to run away; and . . . maiming or bruising whites."[5] South Carolina also created a separate judicial system to try capital murder cases against its black population.

During the time of the "pre-modern" death penalty (colonial times to 1972), South Carolina executed approximately 641 individuals. More complete records reveal that from 1912 to 1962, 241 people were killed in the state's electric chair. Over eighty percent of those executed during this later time period were black—including a fourteen-year-old boy named George Stinney, executed in 1944. A crude booster seat was created out of large books so that the small teenager would fit in the electric chair. Stinney's conviction was based on such weak circumstantial evidence that his conviction was reversed seventy years later.[6]

From 1962 to 1972, there were no executions in South Carolina. This reflected a trend across the country as more and more states questioned the constitutionality and utility of the death penalty. In 1972, the United States Supreme Court formally halted executions in the case of *Furman v. Georgia*. The opinion issued by the Supreme Court, with all nine justices writing opinions, was fragmented and confusing; but, at the very least, the Court held that the current practices and procedures involved in the death penalty—including mandatory death sentences for specific crimes as well as a lack of guidance for juries charged with imposing sentences in capital cases—were unconstitutional. The Court, however, provided directions to the states as to how they could fix these problems, and, in the case of *Gregg v. Georgia* in 1976, the Supreme Court gave states who had adopted these reforms the green light to resume executions. Like many southern states, South Carolina followed the Supreme Court's guidelines and returned to applying the death penalty with renewed enthusiasm in 1977. One of the first men charged, tried, and convicted under South Carolina's new death penalty regime was J. C. Shaw.

It would be on South Carolina's death row that Marie Deans would first meet Shaw. She came to the row with the daunting challenge of trying to talk the depressed and uncommunicative Shaw into continuing to fight his death sentence. Marie was reluctant to meet Shaw and only came at the behest of a prisoner rights organization. The visit, however, would change the course of her life.

The parking lot is deserted. The rusted fence and scraggily weeds growing through cracked concrete makes it look like something left over from a failed urban renewal project. Am I in the right place? I check the directions again and decide to have one last cigarette, an appropriate thing to do before going onto death row. My hands are shaking so hard I almost light my nose. Why the hell had I agreed to do this? This is totally insane. But I can still see CCI Warden Joe Martin looking like he would peel off his own skin to get away.

South Carolina's death row. What struck Marie was the eerie silence of the row compared
to the endless noise and shouting in the main CCI prison. Photograph courtesy of the
South Carolina Department of Archives and History.

*I walk over to the stairs that lead to the pedestrian overpass. A sign warns me
that going beyond this point means I can be strip searched and that I can't bring
in explosives, guns, knives or other weapons. Am I going to need one of those?*

*The traffic swishes beneath me. I should be in one of the those cars, going
downtown to have lunch with a friend before heading back to Charleston, but
that friend would not be John Brown [a South Carolina prisoner rights advo-
cate], who had gotten me into this in the first place. I come down on the other
side of the overpass, crunch over gravel and go into the front doors of the prison.
A guard behind a half wall looks up and cocks his head.*

"I'm Marie Deans. I'm supposed to see Warden Martin."

*"Wait here," he tells me. I wait, jumping every time I hear a sound and mak-
ing up excuses for leaving until Joe Martin finally appears.*

"Hi, thanks for coming."

*I nod and shake his hand. "I wasn't sure I would, right up to the minute you
opened that door, especially after reading the strip search sign."*

*"Not to worry. You won't be strip searched or searched period. We don't usu-
ally strip search people anyway. It's just there in case. You have any questions?"*

"A hundred or so. No. Yes. How long do I stay?"

"We'd need you to leave by four."

I check my watch. It's a little after one. "Right. I doubt that will be a problem."

"J. C. is waiting in the visiting room. You ready?"

I nod again and follow Joe out of the administration area and into the prison.

A tiny cell on South Carolina's death row at the Central Correctional Institution (CCI) in Columbia. Photograph courtesy of the South Carolina Department of Archives and History.

The last time I'd seen Joe Martin, he had taken me on a disorienting tour of the prison as part of a fact-finding visit organized by Amnesty International. I'd recoiled reading about conditions in Russia, Yugoslavia, and Latin America, and here I had seen conditions I would never have imagined in the US. The place reminded me of a social science documentary I'd seen on television. Rats had been introduced, first slowly and then in growing numbers, into a confined space. The rats had gone from getting along, to getting into each other's way, to violence, to apathy and finally giving up, lying down and dying.

Besides the obvious overcrowding, the walls were crumbling, damp, and moldy. The windows running across the top of the buildings were so dirty they were more like opaque finger paintings than windows. The smell kept making me gag. The dorms looked and sounded like Bedlam, and the cells in the segregated blocks were so dark I wasn't sure anyone was in them until I heard a noise coming from one. I got a couple of steps closer and peered in. A filthy, gaunt man was curled up on the floor against the toilet, moaning. His body odor was pungent enough to cause me to back away immediately. I asked Joe if he was sick or hurt. He told me the man was mentally ill, stayed in the that position most of the day, and at night he hollered and screamed so much everyone in the cellblock yelled at him to shut up. "Creates a hellacious racket," he said. When I asked what he was doing in prison instead of a mental hospital, Joe raised his eyebrows. "You'd need to ask the legislators about that."

Later, in his office, Joe had talked about the scheduled execution of J. C. Shaw. His distress over carrying out an execution was so raw I agreed to do whatever I could to get Shaw to pick up his appeals. But today there is no sign of Joe's feelings about the scheduled execution. Instead he is cool and in control. I will learn that it doesn't matter what side of the bars you are on, in prison you do not show emotion. Now, walking beside Joe toward the visitor's cage, the confidence he is projecting makes me hope it has nothing to do with me, because I am the walking definition of inadequacy.

During an interview with Marie, I asked her to recall what it was like to walk into the Central Correctional Institution. Even thirty years later, the memories were clear.

What sticks out in your mind is the atmosphere. You can feel how much tension is or is not in a prison. You can feel what relationships are between the guards and the men and the administration. I can't unfortunately—other than telling long, long stories—I can't explain it any better than that, but you do feel it. CCI was extremely overcrowded and there were just men everywhere. They took me down a corridor, but there were men . . . everywhere. They were looking like they were going to fall over themselves or walk over themselves or something. The prison was falling apart and it was dirty and smelled—like really old socks after a hike or something. It was loud. And then you walked onto the row and it was suddenly silent.

She wrote about it as well:

The visitors' room is really a cage set off in a large area by a metal fence. It holds four tables with two or three chairs around each. In some nod to familial decor, the fencing has been painted white. Air Wick would have been a better nod. J. C. sits toward the back of the cage, his hands folded on the table. He is a big man with light brown hair and a soft face.

He reminds me of the caged bear in the park by my house. When I was in grammar school, I took a detour every school morning to say hello to him. He was so lonely, that bear. At night, when the wind was blowing south, I could hear his low growling. It sounded like crying. Sometimes I would cry, too.

Joe unlocks the cage door. "Stop by my office on your way out," he tells me. J. C. stands up. He's very tall. "J. C., this is Ms. Deans." Joe leaves, locking the fence door behind him. J. C. continues standing until I sit down. I sat across from him at a table so small that we had to turn our legs in opposite directions to keep from bumping our knees or stepping on each other's feet.

He looks a question to me, but says nothing.

"It's Marie. My name is Marie." He nods.

"You knew you were going to have a visitor. Did you know it was going to be me?" He nods.

"Did they tell you why I was coming?" He shakes his head.

Joe Martin had told me J. C. had been basically mute since the crime.

"I'm here because you dropped your appeals, because there are people who don't want you executed. The people in the administration don't want to do this."

Official mug shot of Joseph Carl "J.C." Shaw, the first death row inmate with whom Marie worked. A former military policeman who suffered from schizophrenia, Shaw participated in the violent murders of three individuals. Photograph courtesy of the South Carolina Department of Corrections.

He examines his hands. I hear the clock on the wall ticking. "They told me you think your execution will atone for the murders, bring the families some peace. Is that true?" He nods, still looking at his hands.

"I can't speak for them, your victims' families, except I was told they haven't called for your execution. I can't speak for them, but I'm a member of a murder victim's family, and I know it wouldn't help us. My mother-in-law, Penny, was murdered. Executing her murderer wouldn't help us. I'm married to Penny's oldest son. It disgusts him to think of his mother connected in any way to an execution. There are other ways to atone."

I'm talking so fast I don't even know if he can hear and sort through what I'm saying. I need to slow down. I'm not going to help anything just blurting all this out.

I close my eyes trying to calm down, but I see the newspaper pictures of the girl and boy this man killed. The girl's smile is lovely, frozen now. The boy . . . of course, he reminds me of my own sons. Maybe there is forgiveness, but atonement? How do you atone for wiping out those precious young lives? How do you make amends for that?

I open my eyes and see J. C. looking at me, but he says nothing. I try to snap back to why I'm here, but I'm doing no good at all. I should leave. I shouldn't have come. Why did they ask me, of all people? I can't stop thinking about the girl, the boy, their families. I wonder what they would think of my being here. I shouldn't have gone through a third party to find out what they think. I should have called them.

But there is Joe Martin, who shouldn't have to kill, and what if they had said "don't go"? I don't believe in killing this man. It would be just as wrong. More wrong in a way, because we are not mentally ill. And they did ask me. And I'm *here. There must be something I should say to stop this, but I have no idea what it is.*

"I don't really know what to say. I don't want you to be killed."

"Why not?"

His speaking startles me. He's not baiting me. His voice is apologetic.

"I don't know. I believe life is sacred. All life. That means your life is sacred, too. So I don't want you to die. Well, we all die, but not like this. This is wrong."

He ducks his head. In that brief second before his head goes down, I see something in his eyes. I recognize a yearning to go back, to start over, to wipe out that day. I have a momentary urge to cover his hands with mine, to tell him I understand what he longs for, to explain that he can't do that, he can't bring them back.

"I know what you did is horribly wrong. I'd be the last, well, almost the last, person to say it wasn't. I'm not giving you a pass, you know. I'm not saying you don't deserve to be punished. But executing you doesn't make it right. Executing you doesn't do anything to make it right. It's just another wrong. It really is just another evil act. You shouldn't . . . you can't make it right, and you shouldn't be part of another evil act." His head comes up quickly and he stares into my eyes. I sit back and look at him until he drops his head again. I didn't expect his face to be soft, his eyes to be so full of pain. I expected hardness. I expected some sign, like Cain's mark maybe. I expected his eyes to be dull. How can you brutally murder two young people and look so human? How can you murder and want so badly to take it back? Does Wayne Northup, Penny's killer, want to take it back?

I really want to get out of this place. I do not want to think about Wayne Northup. I do not want to think about these questions. I cannot be here, cannot do this.

I've failed. What will I tell Joe Martin? "Sorry, I couldn't change his mind. My own mind got too tangled up with the past. You're going to have to kill him. Hope you'll be okay with that."

"J. C., I don't know what to say. This is wrong. It's wrong to make these people kill you. You know two wrongs don't make a right. This is . . ." I stop, because I am about to tell him this is cheap grace. "Will you think about this more?"

I stand up and a guard quickly appears at the cage door.

J. C. stands up and shyly puts out his hand. I take it. His hand is soft, too.

"Will you come back?"

I want to drop his hand and bolt. I want never to see him again. I want never to see or hear of death row again. But what I hear come out of my mouth is "Yes."

"Thank you." Now I nod.

Joe Martin greets me with expectancy, but when I tell him about the visit, his body is suddenly smaller. He falls into his chair and takes a deep breath. "Well, he talked a bit. That's a good sign. He doesn't talk, you know. Just, 'yes sir, no sir.'"

"He didn't say much more, Joe."

"But he asked you to come back."

"Yes."

Now I can hear Joe's clock ticking. He watches as I shift in my chair. I can't stand it. I have to get out of here. I get up. Joe comes around the desk within arm's reach of me. "Will you?" He asks so quietly, I almost have to read his lips.

"I told him I would." I take a deep breath. "Yes, I will." I turn away to avoid the hope in his eyes.

On the two-hour drive home, I berate myself. Why had I said yes? Why hadn't I said I would think about it, or I'd let him know? What good had I done? I hadn't changed anything. The execution was still scheduled, and why shouldn't it be? I hadn't thought of anything meaningful to say. I hadn't come up with one decent argument. I punch the steering wheel, gritting "why" so many times that I know my hand will be swollen and blue in the morning.

A week after what seemed to me a totally useless visit, I went back to see J. C. After asking me how I was, he ducked his head and asked me if I would tell him about her. "Her" was Penny. While I talked about Penny, J. C. watched me with his head tilted to one side.

"You loved her like a mother."

"Yes, I came to. I did and do."

"I'm sorry." There were tears in his eyes. I couldn't stop looking at them. It slowly dawned on me that I was a surrogate for his victims' families, a role I would find myself in often through the years.

For months I made regular visits to J. C. After each visit, I stopped by Joe's office to report that J. C. still had not agreed to pick up his appeals.

J. C. was Catholic, and I'd asked John [Brown] to find a Catholic priest to visit as well. On one visit, Joe Martin had stopped me before I went in to see J. C. the day before they'd brought J. C. out for a scheduled visit with the priest John had found. J. C. had patiently waited in the cage for over two hours, but the priest had not come. Joe feared J. C.'s conviction that he should die had been reinforced by the priest not showing up. He was right. J. C. believed he had been given some sign that even God could not forgive him. I had come to feel responsible for keeping him alive and assuring Joe Martin would not have to carry out an execution. I had counted on the help of the priest and grumbled about pusillanimous clergy hiding behind their robes.

The stress of carrying that responsibility had begun to show. I hadn't had acne even as a teenager, but now my face was blotchy and puffy, and I rotated between being so hyper that, if I bared my teeth, I'd serve as a buzz saw, to being too drained to figure out how to walk across the room. But when I tried to lie down or go to sleep, I couldn't shut out J. C., Joe Martin, or the guards who kept thanking me for coming and trying. Neither could I shut out the boy and girl and their families.

The next morning I called the local Catholic Bishop, who was his usual gruff, dear self. He assured me that what I was doing was right and promised to send one of his best priests, and he did. After almost two more months of regular visits from Father John Duffy and me, J. C. agreed to pick up his appeals. It was the first time in months that I had slept through the night and had no nightmares.

Marie and J.C. Shaw in an undated photograph. Shaw insisted
that Marie not witness his execution because he feared it would
traumatize her. Personal collection of Marie Deans.

*While the regular visits with J. C. had been going on, I also spent time with his
lawyer, who let me read the appeal he would file. Along with all the legal issues
was a story that caused me to cry and rant for hours. It was the kind of story I
would come to hear again and again in the coming years. J. C. had been mentally
ill since he was a young teenager. He did fine on medication, and he had joined the
Army and become an MP. At first he hid his schizophrenia from the Army, thinking he had outgrown it or, miraculously, had been cured. After he began experiencing symptoms again, he tried street drugs, which only made his hallucinations
worse. Realizing what was happening to him, he twice went to the Army mental
health facility to commit himself. Both times the staff turned him away. The second
time was just before the murders.*

*Two young people, who could have been going on with their lives, were dead.
J. C. and Terry Roach were on death row. Four families had been devastated. J. C.
and Terry were accountable for their crimes, but they could have been prevented.
In my quest to learn why murder happens, the last factor I would have assumed
would have been the staff of a mental health facility.*

*The prison administration had been watching the way I handled myself in the
prison. Within days of J. C. picking up his appeals, Joe Martin asked me to see another man who was so deep in depression he wouldn't come out of his cell or talk
to anyone. Shortly after I began visiting that man, Bill Leeke, the Commissioner*

The men of South Carolina's death row in the early 1980s. When Marie visited the row, she met alone with the men in the prison chapel. Personal collection of Marie Deans.

of Corrections, asked me to be the liaison between death row prisoners and the administration in a conditions suit being brought against the prison. Bill had invited the suit because the legislature would not do anything about conditions at the prison.

"Look," he told me, "I don't like the death penalty. Among other things, it's counterproductive to good corrections. I'd hoped to never carry out an execution. Still hope for that. But we have a death row again. I can't stop what might happen, can't stop an execution, but I can make sure these men are treated decently, and I can keep the tension down. I'd like your help with that. That doesn't mean if you come in here and tell me they want furloughs or steak every night, they'll get it, but we'll do what we can."

Once a month, I met privately with the prisoners on death row in the chapel. The first time they crowded into the tiny chapel and the guard left and shut the door, I had a panic attack and wondered if I'd truly lost my mind. One of the guards later told me that when he questioned the arrangement, Joe Martin told him I would be safer in the chapel with those men than on the street.

Joe was right. The men clearly followed pre-determined house rules for their "guest." They always left the chair next to me for J. C. and always left space for James Butler, the second man I had visited, to sit on the floor facing me. Wesley [another inmate] was in charge of bringing me a perfect cup of coffee. The men learned that it was okay to gripe, but that I also expected them to be reasonable, to work out problems themselves whenever possible, and that we could brain-storm together about how to do that.

After meeting with them, I would see Joe and Bill Leeke, and sometimes Assistant Warden Jim Aiken and others in the administration. These corrections officials taught me a great deal about the hidden world of prisons and corrections. I still consider them mentors and friends and hold them in high regard.

I was surprised that Marie spoke so highly of the South Carolina prison officials, and I asked her to expand upon the lessons that she learned from them. "How [prisons] are run and what can happen in a prison if you're not careful—careful from all points of view," Marie explained. "What prisoners are like. How you can get fooled by them." Marie added that she also received encouragement from the officials.

> [Warden] Joe Martin would always tell me—he was so supportive—he would say "you did well" or "that was not your fault." There was a fight one time on death row over me, and I was devastated. A newcomer came. He asked me for a book of stamps. And that night he was beaten up because the guys had decided that I was coming there legitimately to help them, that I meant it, that I wasn't a groupie, that I wasn't taking advantage of them, and I was not to be fucked with. To them, asking me for something of material value was fucking with me—he had no right to do that and a lesson was taught. I didn't even know what really had happened. I knew there was a fight over me, and I was devastated.
>
> So I went to Joe, and Joe found out what had happened, and said "That was not your fault. None of us could have known how quickly they embraced you that way—that they were that protective of you. I knew that you were safe with them, but I didn't know how far they would go to call out somebody who stepped over the line."

Marie, unfortunately, would have a very different experience when she later tried to work with Virginia prison officials and was met with paranoia, scorn, and intimidation.

Prison officials and attorneys were impressed with Marie's work with the men of the row. In a letter written after Marie left South Carolina, David Bruck—himself a death penalty attorney—marveled at Marie's relationship with the condemned men. "Marie was the one person who seemed to be trusted and respected by even the most 'difficult' and prison-hardened of the men on the row," Bruck wrote. "While tireless in working on their behalf, she was at the same time . . . always realistic and firm in dealing with attempts at manipulation . . . I was very sorry when she left South Carolina, since folks like Marie can't be replaced."[7]

During her time on the South Carolina death row, Marie started doing mitigation work, namely, collecting information on an inmate's background as evidence that the death penalty was not merited and that the failure of the trial attorneys to present such evidence constituted ineffective assistance of counsel. Her first mitigation report was prepared for James A. Butler, a South Carolina inmate who would later be resentenced to life in prison because of prosecutorial misconduct during his sentencing hearing. Marie's detailed research dovetailed perfectly with her storytelling skills, and the mitigation reports often presented compelling tales of the lives of broken and haunted men.

In her essay "Living in Babylon," Marie discussed her ongoing relationship with J. C. Shaw. "[When] I was trying to get J. C. to pick up his appeals, he said to me several times, 'Stop, you are torturing me,' so when he was sitting in the Death House I asked him about that, and he said, 'Oh, no, no these have been the best years of my life, the best years, because I changed, I came back to God. I really would not have wanted to die back then."[8] The bonds between Marie and Shaw, whom she described as "my first client," ran deep. "J. C. was real shy and he would come up when I was doing general visits and would just stand beside me."[9]

Marie acknowledged that her description of the shy and faithful Shaw starkly contrasted with the public's image of a drug-abusing killer.

> He was certainly in a psychotic state when he killed. His family could not believe the change in him. J. C. could not believe it either. He had been on lithium as a youngster, but, when he was in the Army, he stopped taking it. He had been diagnosed as a schizophrenic. He had gone to the military hospital two or three times pleading that he be committed. The last time they were having a hot dog party in the back yard and they told him to come back the next day. That was just an afternoon before the murders happened. He would tell me 'I have lived this crime' and he named a number that was over a thousand, I think. The warden said that was the exact number of days since the murders. He had relived the murders every night since he had committed the crimes.[10]

Marie's work soon expanded. "After a few months of [my] regularly visiting this inmate [Shaw], he asked if I would see another man whose family lived too far away to visit," said Marie. "Before long I was visiting a number of the men individually . . . I also met and talked with most of the families who visited." Because of the friendships that Marie developed with the men on death row, she was often asked to "stand death watch" with the men—sitting in the death house with them and provide emotional support during the waning hours of their lives. Marie would ultimately stand death watch with thirty-four men in South Carolina and Virginia, an experience that left physical and mental scars.

"[Shaw] asked me to be with him at the end, and I went." At the time of the execution, Marie had moved to Richmond, Virginia, and started the Virginia Coalition on Jails and Prisons. Marie, however, did not watch Shaw's actual execution. "The day before [the execution] he held me and patted my back while we cried together. 'It's not hard except for this, Marie, how it hurts the people I love who love me' [said Shaw]. J. C.'s compassion was fully developed then. He never shed a tear for himself, but his grief for those who loved him, for his victims and their families, and even for his executioners, was intense."[11] He also told Marie that he did not want her to

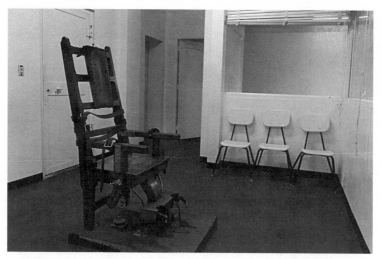

South Carolina's death chamber and electric chair. While Marie attended three executions at the South Carolina death house, she never watched the executions themselves. Photograph courtesy of the South Carolina Department of Archives and History.

witness his execution. "I don't want you here if you are afraid you may come to hate these people.' I don't think it would have happened, but I was afraid it might."[12]

Shaw's family met with South Carolina governor Richard Riley's staff shortly before the execution to beg for clemency. "J. C.'s stepfather, tears running down his face, asked: 'What harm would it do to let him live?' For him, for all of J. C.'s family, for us, he had asked a very real question," explained Marie. "For the governor, reality lay elsewhere. Governor Richard Riley's only answer was to order the execution [be] carried out."[1]

Shaw was executed in the South Carolina electric chair on January 11, 1985, in the early hours of the morning. He spent the prior afternoon visiting with his family, and his final meal was a simple pizza. After Shaw was placed in the electric chair, his attorney kissed him on the cheek, and then twenty-three hundred volts of electricity raced through his body.

In a final statement released to the press, Shaw implored opponents of the death penalty to "continue the fight against the hatred, violence, and revenge of this punitive form of punishment." Shaw also had a special message for South Carolina governor Richard Riley, who had denied Shaw's clemency petition. "Killing is wrong when I did it," Shaw stated. "It is wrong when you do it. I hope you have the courage and the moral strength to stop the killing."[14] As governor, Riley would not.

After the execution of Shaw, Marie took an early morning train back to Richmond, Virginia.

When I got home to Richmond, I fell across the bed and fell into a drugged-like sleep until the phone woke me up the next morning. It was my older son telling me that my father had just died of a massive heart attack. He had died exactly twenty-four hours after the death of J. C. My father and I had actually established a relationship by then (my mother had died two years before), and I'd had a wonderful conversation with my father by telephone the day before J. C. died. It took me a long time to get over that double whammy—I don't really believe in coincidences, I am too much low country Southern or something.

Marie had partially reconciled with her father after her mother's death in 1983. Of the reconciliation, she remembered her father's "constant crying and begging for my forgiveness, but we never talked about the abuse. I just told him it was over, and we could start from here." Two years later, both of Marie's parents were gone.

Almost exactly one year later, Marie would return to the death house at the Central Correctional Institution for the execution of Terry Roach. David Bruck, one of Terry's attorneys, described the young man as being "borderline" mentally handicapped. "What that meant, as a practical matter, was that in talking to him it seemed like you were talking to a twelve- or thirteen-year-old kid. He was very slow, he had a slack-jawed way of talking, he had a very limited understanding of why he was being executed."[15]

Peace activist and journalist Colman McCarthy visited with Terry on the day before his execution, and he offered a similar assessment of the young man:

> Roach, sitting behind a tiny coffee table, had an expressionless face except for his darting eyes. They showed bottomless fear. He had flaxen hair, wide shoulders, and skin with the kind of sallowness brought on by years of life without sun. Roach, mentally retarded with an IQ of between 75 and 80 and suffering from the early stages of Huntington's Chorea, an incurable brain disease, spoke in a thick-lipped rural Carolina accent that at times was indecipherable in its monotone. This was no eloquent Caryl Chessman or Jack Abbott offering quotable social criticism of the death penalty. Roach, with simple words that a child would use, was a terrified, cornered human being. He personified fear, not evil.[16]

Marie had stayed in touch with Terry after she moved to Virginia, and in January of 1986 she returned to her beloved home state to stand yet another death watch. The experience was brutal as Marie spent five days with the condemned man. On the day of the execution, Terry's family came to say goodbye. "I was with Terry and his family in the cell when they were told to leave," Marie wrote. "Terry's mother, who had full-blown Huntington's, collapsed, howling. The brothers began smashing their fists against the cell walls, and his father was threatening to kill everyone. His sisters and girlfriend were wailing."

Later that night, Marie Deans and attorney David Bruck arrived in the death house. "I had never thought that much about it, but when it was over, I discovered that it is the most natural thing in the world not to want to be alone when you die," said Bruck. "It is dying, and anyone should have support and reassurance when they die. Execution is such a degrading and humiliating death. The task was to block that out and make it as though it was just death, rather than a killing."

Official mugshot of James Terry Roach, a mentally handicapped minor who participated in Shaw's murders. Photograph courtesy of the South Carolina Department of Corrections.

Bruck recalls that Marie described their final hours with Terry as "like a campfire, and the conversation between the three of us was like throwing logs on the fire to keep away the darkness and the terror."[17] "At times the talk blazed brightly," said Bruck. "We read to Terry, and he listened, enthralled like a child at bedtime. His family minister came to visit and told Terry which prayers they would say: Terry asked him if those were the best ones to help him to heaven. Terry had little religious faith . . . but that night he needed to believe so much that he wasn't just at the edge of a void."[18] Despite their best efforts, however, Bruck conceded that "it was impossible to keep his attention diverted all night."

Marie and David stayed with Terry and continued to throw logs on the fire as the death squad prepared Terry for the electric chair. Bruck wrote:

> The guards arrived at about three thirty in the morning with a safety razor to shave his head. Shaving cream and everything. I had never realized that . . . I had just filed it away in the corner of my mind that they put conducting gel on his head. But what I didn't know was that they massage it in for over half an hour. It's a long process. This is after the barber ritual, the sheet around his shoulders, sitting in the cell like he was having [his] haircut. They cut his hair off with clippers, then shaved it with disposable safety razors and aerosol shaving cream, and then when they finished that and he had a smooth shiny head, they started caressing his head with conducting gel. They would work the gel in and then put more on and work that in and, when that was worked in, they would do it some more. This goes on and on, and all the time we were trying to make conversation.[19]

In a letter written after Terry's execution, Marie said that the guards themselves were fighting their own emotions. "The guards were distraught about this killing as well, and they were kind to Terry," Marie wrote. "He told them that he understood they didn't want to kill him, it was just their job, and he wanted them to know he had no hard feelings toward them."[20]

While Marie did not witness the execution, she walked with Roach to the death chamber. "They would not allow me to stay with Terry all the way through," Marie recalled. "He wanted my face to be the last thing he saw." As Marie and Roach stood in front of the electric chair, Roach asked Marie "who would you like me to say hello to?" Marie replied, "you tell the guys that we killed that I still remember them. They're still a part of my life and I love them all."[21] Earlier in the evening, Roach had promised to greet a friend of David Bruck's, a young woman named Susan who had died of cancer in the weeks before Roach's execution date.

Roach had practiced his final statement with Marie, and she wanted to remain in the death chamber until Roach read it. A government official, however, ordered Marie to leave, and a panicked Roach momentarily lost his nerve before he read his last statement from the electric chair.

> I leave you comfortable that I have been forgiven of my sins, just as I have forgiven those who have done this to me. . . . I pray that my fate will someday save another kid that ends up on the wrong side of the tracks. To the families of the victims, my heart is still with you in your sorrow. May you forgive me, just as I know that my Lord has done. To my family and friends, there is only three words to say: I love you.[22]

The angry protesters that Marie faced as she left the South Carolina death row on the evening of Terry Roach's execution. Photograph courtesy of Getty Images.

Having made his final statement, Terry turned to David, said the name "Susan," and gave a thumbs-up sign as prison officials covered his face with a black mask. Bruck then watched his client die as two charges of twenty-three hundred volts of electricity coursed through Roach's body and a cloud of smoke rose from the electrode attached to Roach's ankle. Upon learning of Roach's death, a group of two hundred death penalty supporters gathered outside the prison celebrated and waved signs stating "Let the Juice Flow," "Fry Him," "Plug Him In," and "Dim the Lights: The Party is Over!" A slight distance from the chanting mob was a small group of death penalty opponents, silently holding candles.

Recalling the execution years later, Bruck commented that he was struck by how quickly the death was carried out. "I suppose it would be better to say that the actual killing was incredibly disgusting, painful, gruesome, and gory to see . . . but to me, the truth is it was not as bad as that, and at the same time it was much worse. It was as easy as shutting a drawer or snapping one's fingers. It was fast." And the message that Bruck took away from the execution of Terry Roach was devastating. "To me, what it said was that they take a living person, who took twenty-five years to create . . . and within just seconds they converted him into a piece of junk to be wrestled out on a stretcher and carted away. To me, the message was that human beings are junk, and if you don't believe it—watch this."[23]

For Marie, the tragedy of Terry Roach had less to do with the young inmate and more with society. "My sorrow and my horror is not so much for Terry as for us," she stated. "That we could do that to him. It's very easy to kill somebody. Even if it takes fifteen minutes, you can do it. My question to my own people is, why? Is this macho America at work? That we can show how powerful we are by killing . . . a retarded boy with a terminal illness?"[24] To another reporter, Marie simply stated: "I can't understand what it is in us that makes us think we have to snuff out this life."[25]

One night shortly after the execution, Marie dreamed of the forgotten victims of the death penalty, namely, the families of the condemned men. "[The dream] began when I saw Mrs. Roach standing in a room all alone with tears streaming down her face," Marie recalled. "Her pain was so intense it was like waves pushing at me. Then the room began to fill with all the mothers, fathers, wives, children, siblings that I have held while their loved ones were killed and those whose loved ones are still alive, but waiting. The only way I can deal with that suffering is to go on fighting to stop it."[26]

On April 27, 1990, Marie made her final visit to the South Carolina death house as she returned for the execution of Raymond "Rusty" Woomer. A native of West Virginia, Woomer was sentenced to death for a bloody rampage across three South Carolina counties, which had left four people dead and a fifth maimed for life. In 1989 Marie had travelled to South Carolina to stand death watch with Woomer, only to see his death sentence stayed by the United States Supreme Court on the day of his scheduled execution. Shortly after the stay, Marie told reporters that Woomer was "in shock" over the stay and was "crying and thanking God and us."[27]

By 1990, Woomer's luck had run out, and no more legal options remained. Woomer became a born-again Christian during his last years on the row, and prison officials were startled at the serenity displayed by Woomer in his final hours. One of the prison officials most moved by the inmate's peaceful demeanor was Warden George Martin. Sitting on the bed with Woomer in his death house cell, Martin was stunned when Woomer pledged to go quietly to the chair and expressed the hope that his execution would not unduly burden the warden.

Woomer had the dubious distinction of being the first inmate scheduled to be executed at the new Broad River Correctional Institution. For almost eighty years, the electric chair had been housed at the CCI death house, and in that time 241 inmates had died in its fiery embrace. Now the antique chair had travelled to the "Capital Punishment Facility" (a much more politically correct name than "death house") at Broad River. And befitting a new home, a new execution protocol was followed during Woomer's early morning execution. For five seconds, 2,000 volts of electricity would be passed through Woomer's body, followed by eight seconds of 1,000 volts, and then two minutes of 250 volts. As the dead Woomer sat slumped in the electric chair, one of the witnesses muttered "that was too easy."[28] Outside yet another group of death penalty supporters cheered at the news of his execution.

Woomer's death ended Marie's ties with the South Carolina death row. Looking back on the time spent with the men of the row, Marie was able to move past the pain and remember the bond that she had formed, and the lessons that she had learned from the corrections officials, the inmates, and the inmates' families.

[The prisoners] showed their appreciation for my time and efforts in many ways. They "schooled" me in the way of prisoners, so I would never fall into the trap of being a "patsy." They made little handmade gifts for me. One Christmas when I had pneumonia, they pooled their commissary money and had the death row supervisor pick out and have delivered the biggest poinsettia tree I'd ever seen.

Some members of their families, whom I also met with as a group several times over the years, became friends. A few joined the local AI group and South Carolina Citizens Against the Death Penalty. Some baked cookies and cakes for me and my family, gave me cuttings for my garden or sent fresh vegetables from theirs.

The most important lesson I learned from the men on death row, their families, and the corrections people in South Carolina was that people on death row are not "the other." Maybe that's why a murder comes so early in the Bible and why God threatens sevenfold vengeance on any who would slay Cain. Death row may be the land of Nod, but it, too, is peopled by the Creator's own.

Convincing others that death row prisoners are not "the other"—but human beings —would prove to be one of the hardest tasks Marie would face.

4

Transitions

The car finally settled, listing to the left,
Cautiously I stood, then saw the water.
Grasping for belongings flung forward.

Watching the water rush against the car,
I thanked God my son was not with me.
And then I heard your voice.
"Take care of yourself, dear friend."

—Marie Deans, date unknown

The year 1982 was a turning point in Marie's personal life and professional career. It would see Marie suffer physical injuries that would leave her in pain for the rest of her life. And the year would end with Marie preparing to leave her beloved South Carolina to move to Virginia. The move would strain already tense familial bonds between Marie, her parents, and her oldest son, and it would signal the end of her marriage to her third husband.

For the first few months of the year, Marie juggled a dizzying combination of meetings, trips, and responsibilities. She travelled to Columbia to meet with the South Carolina Citizens Against the Death Penalty. She then went to New York and Atlanta to attend AI USA board meetings. She attended a reception at the South Carolina governor's mansion and remained involved in local community politics. She continued to spend time with the men of South Carolina's death row and prison officials. She spent a week in Texas on behalf of AI USA, investigating and reporting on prison conditions on death row, recruiting lawyers for the men of the row, and visiting local AI chapters in Austin, Dallas, and San Antonio.

On June 14, Marie concluded an AI meeting in Chicago, IL, and boarded an Amtrak train bound for Seattle, WA. Marie was scheduled to attend a national AI meeting in Seattle, and she decided to take the train rather than fly so she could see the Great Plains and the Rocky Mountains. When Marie purchased her train ticket, she had no idea how consequential her decision to eschew air travel would be. Below is a portion of a short chapter which Marie wrote about the tragedy that followed.

The tearing screech of metal writhing against itself in agony as my body is flung into a dead space, then a deep, heaving falump, falump, falump as something repeatedly smashes against my back and the dead space becomes a crevice to which my body is trying to adjust.

The noise and movement goes on, and I try to understand where I am, what has happened. First I think I am at home, awakened by an earthquake and I rolled off and under the bed, which then fell on me. Where are Bob and Robert? Slowly I remember I am on a train. Then the worst of the noise stops, and I hear screams and cursing. Then there is silence, and an occasional creaking sound. Now I hear water. I begin to push at the seat in front of me, then stretch out my arms and legs to find a way out between the seats.

As I'm looking for space, a male voice says, "You can crawl out this way." I feel a hand and grab at it. "You'll have to wiggle around. Can you? Are you all right?"

"Yes, I can. I just can't see anything."

He keeps talking to me as I wiggle through two pieces of metal, which must be seat braces. Once I get out and upright, he tells me there are seats toward the back that I can sit on, and he's going forward. My eyes are adjusting to the darkness, and I start looking for my pocketbook and brief case. It seems very important to me to find them for two reasons. My migraine medication is in my pocketbook, and a small keychain flashlight is in my briefcase along with the Amtrak ticket and route. It seems terribly important to me that I find out where we are. I do find them crunched under some seats toward the front of the car. I head back toward the rear, realizing that people are moving toward the seats, bunching up together. I find a space, dig into my pocketbook, and find the keychain. According to my watch it's three o'clock, and I start calculating where we must be. With all the water I hear, I think we must be in a river and decide it is the Missouri.

"Careful." A man's hand reaches up and touches my thigh. I look down. A body. An injured young woman.

"She had a baby with her," he says. "I think she was going to warm a bottle and got crushed between the doors. We need to find the baby."

He is about my size, a young voice. We both get up and step over the young woman and start looking. He tells others. A few are already looking, and in a few minutes the baby is found, peacefully asleep. Some people begin to move toward the doors, and a voice yells out: "This is the porter. Stay seated until the head conductor comes."

The other people in the car move back to their seats. I get up and look toward the voice.

"I think we're in a river, and I think we need to find out if we're safe in here or need to get out."

She starts to argue with me, and I turn toward the front of the car. The boy and I try to get the door open, but it won't budge. I tell him I think we're in a river.

"Yes, and those cars ahead of us are sleepers," he replies. "We can't get beyond these two connected cars, though, can't get through. I don't even know if we are still connected to the train."

We keep heaving at the door. I decide to go below to the luggage compartment and see if I can find an emergency hatchet or something to help us get the door open. I feel my way about halfway down before I realize my sneakers are squishing water. I come back up, and call to the boy.

"Water has risen halfway up the stairs. I can't see anything, but we've got to get out. Why don't these people help us?"

"Shock, I guess," he replies. "A few people forward are trying to get a window open and take care of the baby."

"I'm going back to try and talk to these people, get them ready to get out of here. Keep trying to get the door open. I'll be back." He nods and throws his body at the door again.

I start telling people they need to get up, to get out, that water is rising in the car. I beg them gently, quietly, but persistently, and slowly they begin to get up. "Stay together, form a line and make sure children are between two adults." I start back to the door when I hear another loud tearing of metal and freeze, looking for something to hold onto. I expect the car is going over sideways into the river.

Instead the boy yells, "Someone is out there. They are breaking through."

I get to the door just as it is torn open. There are two men in a boat.

"The baby," the boy says. "We need to get the baby to them." He turns toward the front.

I turn toward the rear of the car and yell out, "Some people are out here with a boat to help us, but we need to get a baby to them first. Get everybody up. Form a line."

The boy is back with someone who hands the baby out to the men in the boat. Another man is hanging off the train.

"You'll need to get out one by one," the man says. "You'll need to hang on the side of the car and make your way to the back, that way." He points to the rear of our car. "When the car ends, you'll be in water, but not as deep, but you'll have to stay in line with the car. That's track and land underneath the water. Stay single file so you don't fall off. There are people there to help you, get you on land. Someone there will tell you where to go."

Despite the protests of the porter, who continued to instruct the passengers to stay in their seats despite the slowly rising water and the car's ominous groans, Marie and the young, unnamed boy helped the passengers find their belongings and form a line. As the passengers organized themselves, Marie glanced out the window. "All around us was silver-lit water, the tops of blackened trees, and an empty, threatening sky," she recalled.

One-by-one, passengers walked down the steps of the double-decked passenger car, their shoes filled with flood water and their fragile nerves jumping as the car again groaned and shifted. "Those of us bringing up the rear tried to ignore the car's movement and kept urging the families to go ahead," Marie later wrote. "Until then I hadn't realized how many children were in our car. Once again, I felt relief that Robert was not with me."

Marie and her fellow passengers slowly moved through the flood waters, walking parallel with the train tracks and the remaining cars. At one point Marie slipped and fell into the rushing water, but she was quickly scooped up. All in all, the passengers walked almost a mile through the rain and darkness before reaching the bright lights of the rescue teams. Waiting for them was a group of school buses, which took them to a local town. The exhausted passengers were met by volunteers passing out blankets, hot coffee, and ham sandwiches. Marie wrote:

> While we slouched on the benches, drank coffee and smoked, volunteers came to sit with us and talk awhile. We learned they had been awake and heard the crash, because they had been rescuing their own people from rooftops. Their town was flooded. We heard stories of ruined farms, straying herds and endangered lives. These people had been rescuing first their neighbors and now strangers for 26 hours without sleep. Yet they hadn't hesitated to come to us, to share what they had, to be true neighbors to us. They not only rescued and fed us, they got a doctor for us, brought clothes and shoes, blankets and cots, arranged to bring in another telephone line, and stayed with us, serving and comforting us until the last of us left, leaving their school in a shambles. Weariness told in their faces, but they didn't seem to notice. They shrugged off our gratitude with smiles and jokes and offers of more coffee.
>
> We later learned over four hundred people, individually and in groups, had rushed to our aid. Without their help and demonstrated concern, I believe more of us would have died or received more lasting injuries. Without them, we might very well have given way to panic. As it was 150 passengers were injured and twenty-six were hospitalized. I don't think anyone who was on that train will ever forget Emerson, IA, nor the people who ignored their own fatigue and enormous problems to come to us. They are quiet, unselfish heroes of this story.

The wreck of the San Francisco Zephyr occurred near the small town of Emerson, where rapidly rising floodwaters had eroded the train bed and washed away the tracks. At the time of the accident, 3:15 a.m., over three hundred passengers were aboard. The Zephyr plowed into the floodwaters at seventy-six miles per hour, and twelve passenger cars were hurled into the dark waters before the locomotive came to rest under a small bridge. Teams of farmers and townspeople used boats to rescue the stranded and injured passengers. Over 150 passengers were injured, and 16 passengers were hospitalized, but nineteen-year-old Terri Thompson, the young mother from California who was in Marie's car, was the only fatality.[1]

Marie was ultimately diagnosed with a partially punctured lung, a fractured kneecap, and an injured back. She was treated in a hospital in Omaha, NE, but refused to be admitted. Instead she soldiered on to Seattle for the conference. Her son Joel believes that the back injuries suffered in the train accident changed his mother's life. "It carried her to the point where she couldn't go out and do anything without pain," he explained. "She was, all of a sudden, always in a physical state of pain, which was just another mental barrier for her . . . after that she hurt all the time."

Despite her injuries, Marie later wrote that the accident taught her a valuable lesson about humanity.

> We hear a lot about alienation in America, about those who pass by accidents and turn their faces away, those who won't even call the police when they see someone being mugged or stabbed. We hear about panic and self-centered pushing and clawing that causes needless loss of lives. Now and then, we hear about another spirit in America, the spirit of community that reminds us of the best in ourselves. Maybe it isn't as rare as we have come to believe. Nearly four hundred people in Emerson proved that we can still care about one another, work together, be true neighbors to one another. I will never understand why a young woman had to die in that train, but I do know why more didn't die, and I know I have been reminded of the best that is in people. It was a hard and tragic lesson, one that I hope I never forget.

In the spring of 1982, Marie started receiving telephone calls from friend and fellow abolitionist Joe Ingle, a Tennessee minister who cofounded the Southern Coalition on Jails and Prisons. Ingle had travelled to Virginia several times in the spring and summer of 1982, after death row inmate Joe Giarratano wrote him about a fellow inmate who had dropped his appeals and was scheduled to be executed. The inmate was Frank Coppola, a former policeman sentenced to death for the murder and robbery of Muriel Hatchell. Giarratano had sent over thirty letters to different individuals, law firms, and charitable organizations, seeking help for Coppola, but Ingle was the only person to respond. Ingle went to Virginia with the hope of convincing Coppola to pick up his appeals. If the death sentence was carried out, Coppola would the first person to be executed in Virginia in over twenty years.

During his visits to Virginia, Ingle found himself shocked at the lack of opposition to the death penalty in Virginia:

> I was stunned by the lack of organization, the barbarity of the treatment of the men and their conditions, and the utter contempt of the Virginia Department of Corrections and the Commonwealth of Virginia for those on death row. There were a few stalwart souls here and there. I was stunned with the conditions on death row . . . the men had virtually no rights. There were no lawyers for them. There was no outside organization really that amounted to anything to be against

Marie and the Reverend Joe Ingle, who requested that Marie move to Virginia and open the Virginia Coalition on Jails and Prisons. Personal collection of Marie Deans.

the death penalty. I mean you look across the board and everything you would like to have in a state Virginia had none of them . . . and Virginia was just about as backward a state as you could imagine on the death penalty, and I'd seen them all in the South at that point, so I knew what I was talking about.[2]

After his meetings with Coppola, Ingle would call Marie and report what he was learning about Virginia's death row. Despite her experience touring death rows in the South, Marie found Ingle's stories hard to believe.

[Ingle] did not go to death row then. He only went to the death house, visited Frank, and then went back to the hotel and called me. Just talk and talk and talk. He was telling me the things that Frank was telling him. Neither one of us was sure that those were real. Was Frank using hyperbole? Was he one of those prisoners that saw things from only his point of view? Or what was going on? Joe said 'Whatever happens, we've got to get somebody up here.'

The calls from Joe Ingle continued, and Marie decided to visit Virginia and investigate conditions on death row. Shortly before Marie traveled to Virginia, however, she and AI USA attorney Patricia Murray visited the men on South Carolina's death row in the little prison chapel. The date was August 10, 1982, the date of Frank Coppola's execution.

> The men who had been on the [South Carolina] row the longest were furious with Frank [Coppola]. They kept insisting that Frank's execution would open the floodgates. The men who had come on the row more recently were simply scared. I told them about the isolation and conditions in Virginia. A few of them quieted down, but one man blurted out: "I don't care how isolated he is, he's got to know there are over nine hundred more of us." Listening to the men, I realized that Frank had become a target for the anger and frustration they felt at being randomly picked out of so many murderers and put on death row, where they felt helpless to save themselves or others, and where they could do nothing to alleviate their loved ones' anguish and fear.
>
> When I told them that was what they were doing, they became quiet. Finally, they began to ask questions about Frank—how old was he, was he married, did he have children, were his parents alive, who was with him. Frank got a stay [of execution] after Pat and I left the row. We had supper, talked for a while, and then I started the hundred-mile trip back to Charleston. When I got home, I learned that Frank had been killed [executed], and I started throwing up. After a couple of hours of uncontrollable vomiting, I called my doctor, who drugged me enough so I could sleep.[3]

When Marie later learned of the last minute legal maneuvering by the Office of the Attorney General of Virginia to get Coppola's stay of execution lifted, she wrote, "my fury [over the execution] grew into hatred. I had to go off by myself to rid myself of the hatred, redirect the fury, and turn it into energy." The Southern Coalition on Jails and Prisons would offer Marie an opportunity to channel that energy.

Marie paid an initial visit to Virginia's death row in August of 1982. She was joined by AI USA volunteers Pat Murray and William Menza. At that time, death row was located at the new Mecklenburg Correctional Center in Boydton, Virginia, and the death house at the aging Virginia State Penitentiary in Richmond.

Unlike her first visit to South Carolina's death row, Marie did not have a lengthy meeting with the Virginia prison staff. "The administration tried to talk with me," Marie said. "They wanted to show me the files on all the men I was seeing." Marie recalled that she was "stunned" by the offer because, in her eyes, it was a transparent attempt to bias her against the men. Marie did ask the warden about the prison population at the Mecklenburg Correctional Center, wondering if it comprised only death row inmates or whether it included a general population. "He just laughed," recalled Marie. "He said 'we have the monsters.'" What he meant was that Mecklenburg had a general population composed of the most violent inmates in the Virginia corrections system.

Marie, Murray, and Menza were able to spend three hours speaking with death row inmates Earl Clanton, Buddy Earl Justus, Joe Giarratano, and Willie Lloyd

Turner, under a guard's supervision. The corrections officers were not happy to have visitors on the row, and tensions flared when Marie demanded that she and Murray meet privately with the men and that they be unshackled. "The men were just astonished. They had never seen one of their own lawyers stand up to the warden or even a guard in that prison," said Marie. "We became the talk of the row, and probably the whole prison. . . . [The inmates] all told me later that they'd just never seen anybody take on a guard. They just hoped that one of us would sure as hell come back."

During the three-hour meeting, the AI volunteers talked with the inmates about conditions of confinement, the violence on death row, the brutal punishment inflicted by the guards, and the lack of access to attorneys and a law library. What they heard were stories about mediocre food, limited recreational time, unfair grievance hearings, prisoner suicides, and guard-on-prisoner violence. The meeting convinced Marie that Coppola had not exaggerated. "I have to admit I was really stunned because there was no one here who could [even] tell me who was on death row," Marie stated. "The ACLU couldn't tell me. The Prison Project couldn't tell me. I went to the Virginia Supreme Court. They couldn't tell me . . . and seven of the men [on death row] had written the ACLU and said they were going to drop their appeals." To Marie, the lack of information was an indication of the indifference by Virginia prison officials toward the men of the row.

One of the inmates at the meeting was Joe Giarratano, with whom Marie would develop a life-long friendship. Years later, Marie still clearly recalled her first impressions of Joe.

> One of the things that I remember from that [visit] was that we were all impressed with Joe because he was so straight. If a prisoner had done something he shouldn't have done, Joe said that. If he broke a rule and got into trouble, he said that. I don't know how to explain this any better than most prisoners tell what's happening from their very narrow point of view. Joe would be almost like he could step back even when it involved him. He could step back and observe the whole thing and tell you from all points of view what was going on. I remember being really impressed by that. That is an unusual characteristic for a prisoner. That didn't tell us anything about his case but I remember us remarking about the fact that he seemed to have this ability to step back and relate with precision.

For Joe, what stood out from that first meeting was Marie's compassion and humanity—and her willingness to stand up to the guards.

> What struck me most was that she wasn't judging any of us. She wasn't judging me. She actually treated me like a human being. When she first came into the room and saw that we were handcuffed, she immediately told the guards to take the handcuffs off. And when the guards hesitated, she said, "Call the warden. I'm not going to meet with these men with handcuffs on." That was probably one of the first times that death row prisoners ever got un-handcuffed in the visiting

room in the administration building with people that weren't lawyers. It just wasn't allowed. And she just stood her ground. I got the sense that, "OK, this is a person who cares."[4]

Marie was less impressed with Earl "Goldie" Clanton, who announced during the meeting that he was dropping his appeals. In an effort to change Earl's mind, Marie left the large group and met privately with him. The meeting ended when Earl "got a little fresh" with Marie.

After meeting with the small group of inmates, Marie returned to South Carolina and told Joe Ingle that she would open up a Coalition office in Virginia. "My marriage was gone. I mean I could have stayed and worked for the South Carolina Department of Corrections, but they didn't really need me," Marie explained. "That was such a humane prison system anyway, and this [Virginia's death row] was so awful. The whole death penalty scene was so awful here . . . I'm not trying to sound like a martyr or a do-gooder, but the need was so great." It was time for a change.

Once Marie committed to opening up an office in Virginia, Ingle set to work raising money to support the new Coalition office. The new office's mandate was clear. "We're fighting the death penalty, and to abolish the death penalty you have to deal with it in all of its manifestations," explained Ingle. "That means reforming it so you can't execute the retarded, reforming it so you can't execute the juveniles, [and] getting lawyers for guys. [And] there's the whole prison conditions part, too, that you had to be aware of because usually the guys are confined in just barbaric conditions."[5]

In the months before Marie moved to Virginia, she started connecting with the men of Virginia's death row. In July of 1982, she received a handwritten letter scrawled on a piece of notebook paper from Edward "Fitz" Fitzgerald, a resident of Virginia's row. Several years earlier, Marie had founded a group called "Victims' Families for Alternatives to the Death Penalty" (later to be called "Murder Victims' Families for Reconciliation"), and Fitz sent his letter to that organization. He was seeking guidance on a fundamental question of life and death.

> I am a Death Row inmate in Virginia. The Virginia Supreme Court has just turned down my direct appeal. I have no attorney as of today and am considering not going forward with any other appeals. My main question I asked, is, if I were to be executed, would that hurt the other Death Row inmates in Virginia or elsewhere. I care not to live. But I do not wish to hurt the chances of the other inmates to stay alive as long as they can.

Marie wasted no time in answering back. "I admire your concern for your fellow inmates and suggest to you that a man who does not want to live and yet is more concerned about the safety of his fellow inmates than about his own feelings, is a man who has a contribution to make to this sad and tired old world." She urged Fitz to file his appeals, writing that he would be placing his friends in danger because "each execution that occurs in this country makes the carrying out of death sentences easier and more likely" and demoralizes other inmates. Marie concluded by urging Fitz to write her again. In her subsequent work with the men of Virginia death row, Marie would come to admire the "drunk monk" of death row, Edward Fitzgerald.

Marie found a young attorney named David Bruck to take over her responsibilities on the South Carolina death row, and, in January of 1983, she packed up her aging Chevy Nova and moved to a small apartment in Richmond, Virginia. Her ten-year-old son, Robert, remained in South Carolina with his father until spring to complete school. One question that I never was able to ask Marie is, "Would you have still gone if you knew the hell you would walk through in Virginia for the next decade?" Knowing Marie, the answer would have been an emphatic, "Yes."

5

The Virginia Coalition on Jails and Prisons

I am convinced that if Virginians truly understood what
happens from the trial on through the appeals in capital
cases, they would be outraged by its lack of fairness.
—Marie Deans, September 15, 1990

When Marie moved to Richmond, Virginia, in January of 1983, she did not fully realize the enormity of the task before her. "I spent the first few months trying to find out who was on death row, who their attorneys were (if they had attorneys), where their cases were in the courts, and trying to raise money." Moreover, Marie discovered that groups traditionally opposed to the death penalty were not willing to come to her aid. Some church organizations thought that Marie would interfere with their own fundraising operations, and the local ACLU and AI chapters feared that agitating about the death penalty would cost them public support and funding.

Lloyd Snook was one of the few attorneys in Virginia volunteering to take death penalty cases. A Charlottesville native who graduated from the University of Michigan School of Law, by the early 1980s the young attorney was struggling to manage the appeals of death row inmates Joe Giarratano, Morris Mason, Michael Marnell Smith, Willie Lloyd Turner, and Alton Waye. While attorneys representing death row inmates at trial in Virginia received, on average, the princely sum of $687 for their efforts,[1] Snook and other attorneys who handled death penalty appeals received no compensation and limited reimbursement.

Marie credited Snook with teaching her the relevant procedural and substantive laws involved with Virginia's capital murder regime, and, more importantly, for encouraging her during those initial difficult months. At first, Marie accompanied Snook on client visits. Marie was not working on the legal aspects of inmates' appeals, rather she went with Snook to death row to provide the men with emotional support. "For Marie to reach over [during these visits] and do something as simple as touching a guy on the hand could end up being a subtle but nonetheless important message of 'you're a human being to me,'" explained Snook. "I really thought that was part of what Marie was trying most to do—to make sure that the men remembered that they were human beings at a time when everybody else around them was trying to deny them their humanity."[2]

First and foremost, Marie came to Virginia to improve the conditions of confinement on death row, which was located at the Mecklenburg Correctional Center in Boydton. After its construction in 1977, it was hailed as a modern, state-of-the-art facility; by the time Marie arrived in Virginia, it had become a pressure cooker of unrest, violence, and corruption. "[Mecklenburg] was a very tense place," recalled Marie. "That was the thing that I always felt at Mecklenburg . . . [the] constant tension there. You could walk in and feel it. And it wasn't just me. I had a lot of experience going in and out of prisons, and I got to understand what I was feeling when I went. There is an atmosphere [to prisons]. And that is not to say that you don't always watch your back. You have to always watch your back. But there are some prisons [where] their administration feels it is their job to keep tension down. And there are other prisons in Virginia and Oklahoma, where they keep tension up."

In South Carolina, Marie worked in harmony with prison officials, but in Virginia she found open hostility from the very start.

> The prison administration [at Mecklenburg] constantly attempted to block the men's access to me and to their attorneys. Almost every time I went to prison, some incident occurred that I feel was designed to intimidate me. Although the prison is a super-maximum lock-down prison, twice I was threatened by "unescorted" prisoners. After an attorney would write a letter requesting an appointment, and follow with a phone call, I would drive two hours to the prison and be told that there was no paperwork for an appointment, so I would not be permitted to see the client or could see him only after a long delay. I have a collection of memos citing special rules that applied only to me. Once I was banned for talking about religion to my clients, and another time for "counseling" the men.
>
> My legal mail to the prisoners was opened by the officials, and no prisoner was allowed to talk with me on the phone. It was especially frustrating that they couldn't talk to me, because I was the only person recruiting attorneys and sometimes attorneys would literally disappear—just walk off the case. These were mostly appointed trial attorneys who were also appointed to do the direct appeal. They wouldn't tell anyone when the appeal was denied; they just wouldn't take the man's calls or answer his letters.

When Marie spent hours on the telephone trying to convince a death row inmate to resume his appeals, an assistant warden at Mecklenburg howled in protest. It was not the job of attorneys and paralegals, he argued, to provide "counseling services" to their clients. Another prison official was upset that Marie was talking to the men about God. A third complained that Marie called the inmates by their first names. Lloyd Snook fired off a letter in response to the Virginia attorney general's office. "I would respectfully suggest that [this argument] is utterly ridiculous. Counseling is a fundamental part of the practice of law, particularly in criminal and domestic relations cases," Snook wrote. "A relationship of trust and confidence does not burst forth, fully hatched, merely upon an attorney's uttering the magic words 'I am your lawyer, trust me.' " And Snook added that he relied on his paralegals, such as Marie, to help him build that trust.

For Snook, the newest effort to block Marie from talking on the telephone with inmates had little to do with institutional security or the appropriate role of a paralegal. It was a natural extension of the dim view that prison administrators took of the men they were warehousing.

> I have long suspected that the antipathy toward Marie, and, to a lesser extent, to me shown by some members of the DOC administration is due to the fact that Marie and I persist in our fanciful notion that our clients are human beings. An executioner does his job by denying the humanity of the person whom he kills. It is inevitable that the executioner will therefore be made uncomfortable by people who seek to remind him of the inmate's humanity. However, that discomfort cannot justify the interference with the investigation of psychiatric defenses, including cases of mitigation.

As for the timing of the Department of Corrections' newest outburst, Snook concluded his letter by offering an alternative explanation. "It seems as though every time Marie appears in the *Richmond Times-Dispatch*, the prisoner's right to call her is terminated," Snook mused. "This is, to say the least, curious."[3]

Throughout the summer of 1984, the harassment continued by Mecklenburg administrators. Legal mail was opened. Investigations were held to see if the attorneys and paralegals were friends with the inmates. Attorneys and paralegals were limited to ninety-minute meetings with their clients, and they were forced to keep the conference room doors open during those meetings. Only one attorney or paralegal was allowed to visit the prison at a time. Inmates were shackled when they met with their attorneys, despite requests that the restraints be removed. "For Mecklenburg, 1984 has become *1984*," Marie grimly noted in a letter.[4]

The Virginia Department of Corrections was forced to end their games in October of 1984, when a federal court found in favor of a group of death row inmates who sued prison administrators on the grounds that they were being denied their fundamental constitutional right to have access to legal services. In granting relief to the inmates, federal district court Judge Robert R. Merhige blasted the Department of Corrections' arguments that visits by attorneys and paralegals undermined institutional security at Virginia prisons as "public relations gimmickry" and ordered prison officials to stop their games.[5] "They stopped bugging me, for the most part," Marie later wrote. "They try to bug you a little bit, but you knew the game so you could go back to the warden's office and say, 'You are bugging me, why are you doing it? Let me see my client now or do I need to call Judge Merhige?' " Prison officials adopted an unspoken rule, which Marie delighted in repeating: "Thou shall not fuck with Marie Deans."

The fact that a federal judge backed Marie did not mean that the guards did not "bug" Marie from time-to-time. Prison Chaplain Russ Ford recalled,

> Guards messed with Marie once in the death house, locking her into a room when she was trying to leave after visiting with Ricky Boggs. They left her in there for about an hour. I was walking into the death house, and I discovered her. She came bursting out the door from the room where she had been locked in. Her face was red, her eyes narrowed, her fingernails in the face of the guard. "Just what the hell is going on? Do you know how long I was stuck in the foyer? Where the hell have you been," Marie said to the guard. "They called for you— are you deaf?" The Guard lied and said that he just heard the call to release her over the walkie-talkie. They were harassing her.

Russ concluded with a laugh, "Marie could be fiery."

While prison officials were stymied in their attempts to keep Marie from seeing the men, their efforts to smear and discredit Marie continued unabated. They seemed especially fixated on the long hours that Marie was spending with Joe Giarratano. An assistant warden called Giarratano's attorney to report that Marie was having an "amorous affair" with Joe, citing telephone calls and letters between Marie and Joe as evidence. Marie confronted the assistant warden and reminded him calls and letters could not be monitored, since Marie was working as a paralegal and their communications were protected by attorney-client privilege. He claimed that Joe's love letters to Marie had been floating around the prison. "I'm sorry to disappoint you," Marie wrote scathingly, "but if Joe writes love letters, I'm afraid they are not for me."[6] She added,

> Since I first began working with clients at Mecklenburg, I have been aware of the "us versus them" attitude. Along with many attorneys, ministers, and others who visit MMC, I am fully aware that this attitude encompasses not only the prisoners, but their attorneys, paralegals, ministers, friends, and family. This is an attitude that surprised me, and one I was not prepared for. One generally sees such an attitude only in institutions where there is something to hide from outsiders. It is also an attitude that only serves to make prisoners and those who work on their behalf . . . to become unnecessarily antagonistic toward the administration.

Tall tales of Marie's romantic entanglements with inmates continued to spread, much to Marie's fury. In January of 1988, a South Carolina death row inmate named Fred H. Kornahrens escaped while being transported to a court hearing. Marie had once met Kornahrens during a visit to the South Carolina row, and the FBI interviewed Marie to determine if Kornahrens had contacted her seeking help. Prior to interviewing Marie, FBI agents spoke to individuals in the Virginia Department of Corrections and the attorney general's office to assess "Deans's likelihood to harbor escaped death row inmates." Department of Corrections officials told the FBI that "Deans would willingly harbor captioned subject [Kornahrens] due to her extreme viewpoint on the dealth [*sic*] penalty and that Deans would be able to easily justify such action." The Virginia attorney general's office offered a slightly more charitable view of Marie. Although the AG's office called Marie a "semi-ideological zealot in her anti-death penalty viewpoint," it added that Marie "has never been known to behave unethically in her dealings with the death row inmates with whom she has almost daily contact."

As for Marie's relationship with the men of death row, the FBI report stated "Deans has been linked romantically by one of the Department of Corrections professionals to at least one current Virginia death row inmate." During their interview with Marie herself, the FBI agents asked her about this claim. Sarcastically, Marie responded, "What, only one? I'd have thought rumor mongers would have had it up to at least ten by now."[7] The agents dutifully took down Marie's words, but apparently missed the not-so-subtle humor. They subsequently wrote in their report that Marie "by her own admission has been linked romantically to at least ten or eleven death row inmates in Virginia and South Carolina." The agents concluded their report by noting that a "sincere" Marie firmly stated that she would not shelter a fugitive. "She venality [*sic*] denied that she would assist an inmate in escaping or provide us [*sic*] any type of assistance to him subsequent to an escape."[8]

When Marie obtained a copy of the FBI report through the Freedom of Information Act, she was stunned to see that the agents had painted her as a death row groupie. In a letter to the FBI, she wrote, "While I did acknowledge that some people make such comments about me or anyone else who works on the defense side of capital cases, I did not acknowledge having been romantically linked to any death row inmate. That is absurd."[9] The comments about Marie were absurd, but also sexist and predictable. Only a quivering heart and the starry-eyed fantasies of the weaker sex could explain why a woman would fight to save the lives of condemned killers. Looking back on the first two years of the Coalition, and her fights with the Virginia Department of Corrections, Marie was blunt. "The thing about these people that drove me crazy was their pettiness . . . and this fucking good ol' boy shit."

As for escaped convict Fred Kornahrens, he never made it out of South Carolina. Fifteen days after he shed his chains, overpowered two deputies, took their guns, and made his escape into the nearby woods, Kornahrens was captured by law enforcement officers and returned to his death row cell. On July 19, 1996, Kornahrens was put to death by a cocktail of drugs administered by South Carolina prison officials.[10]

From the start, Prison Chaplain Russ Ford was astounded by the fact that the Department of Corrections attacked Marie and kept her away from the men. "The Department of Corrections should have paid Marie," he said indignantly. "She had such a positive effect on the men. She wasn't coddling them. She could get the inmates to treat each other better. Marie tried to promote healthy relationships among the men. She humanized the men, taking them out of the clouds and making them responsible citizens." Russ added, however, that Marie was not a shrinking violet. "Marie had no problem telling a man that he was crazy, or a brute, or an animal. Marie could tame the dragon."[11]

The threats and insults leveled at Marie did not stop at the prison gate. "One morning in 1983, I found a convincingly stuffed body bag at my front door," Marie wrote. "About six months later, the outline of a body was painted in my parking space. I replaced six slashed tires in an eight month period, and I received countless threatening phone calls." Marie recalled a time when a group of people marched passed her apartment carrying a Confederate flag and yelling "Heil, Hitler." Marie told the protesters, "You have the wrong neighborhood. I'm the nigger lover. The Jew lives on the other side of town." (She was referring to a Jewish lawyer who worked with her on death penalty cases.)[12]

The insults were nothing new. In her short time as a death penalty activist, Marie had just about heard it all. "I have received more threatening remarks, letters, and telephone calls than I could begin to count," Marie wrote in a letter distributed to the men of Virginia's death row. "I've been told I'm a Communist, a traitor to victims, a tramp . . . and assorted other cute labels. I've been threatened with every known torture and told I should be put in your laps when you go to the chair."[13] But Marie pressed on, undeterred by intimidation and verbal abuse.

In terms of its history and traditions regarding capital punishment, Marie could not have picked a more blood-soaked state than Virginia. The first execution in the colonies took place in Virginia in 1607, and since that time Virginia has executed 1,187 men, women, and children. Until 1796, the penalty of death was imposed for all felonies in Virginia, and citizens were executed for such crimes as murder, rape, attempted rape, theft of farm animals, counterfeiting, and sodomy. Even after the criminal laws were reformed, and the number of death penalty offenses narrowed, free blacks and slaves in Virginia were executed in much higher numbers and for a wider number of offenses than whites. This disparity in executions between the races continued well into the twentieth century.

It was not Virginia's long embrace of the death penalty that offended Marie as much as the state's dismissive attitude toward basic due process rights for defendants charged with capital murder. Attorneys without experience in criminal matters could find themselves appointed to death penalty cases. Judges were quick to try death penalty cases, and the courts were slow to provide attorneys with the necessary resources to retain expert witnesses or conduct pre-trial investigations. And those who received the death penalty were not provided with attorneys for all of their appeals.

What most infuriated Marie about Virginia was its notorious "twenty-one day rule." In short, the rule held that defendants only had twenty-one days from the time that final judgment was entered in their trial to introduce additional evidence of factual innocence. The rationale behind the law was simple: if such a law didn't exist, then attorneys and their clients would not be motivated to present their best case at trial. This assumed, however, that attorneys had the time, skills, and resources to find all existing evidence of innocence before trial—an assumption that was not borne out in the truncated trials of many of the men on Virginia's death row.

Virginia's steadfast devotion to the twenty-one day rule meant that the attorney general's office would vehemently argue against the admissibility of exculpatory evidence, regardless of its evidentiary value, in death penalty appeals where claims of actual innocence were asserted. As Virginia attorney general Mary Sue Terry once famously stated in regards to such a claim, "evidence of innocence is irrelevant."[14] Of course, Marie had a powerful response. Of the inmates barred from introducing new evidence, Marie called them "the fatted calves being sacrificed on the altar of legal technicality."[15] This was the unbalanced battlefield upon which Marie would fight.

Soon after opening the doors of the Coalition, Marie learned that prison conditions had not improved since her initial visit in 1982. In several different letters to friends and colleagues, Marie lamented the deplorable conditions suffered by the men of the row in retaliation for an escape attempt.

Men on death row at Mecklenburg have been on total lock-down for three-and-a-half months, coming out of their cells (which have solid steel doors) for twenty-four minutes a week to take eight-minute showers. When shower day comes, the guards go outside the pod grill, pop one door, and tell the man to go directly to the shower. If he isn't back in his cell in eight minutes, the goon squad comes in after him. Three weeks ago they came in after five men, one at a time, of course. Eight men with plexiglass shields, helmets, and steel cored wooden sticks after one nude, soapy prisoner is not pretty. If the man speaks to another man as he passes his cell, he gets a delay and hindering charge, and they take away the only thing they have left—their radio.

The AG [Virginia attorney general] must have told them the lack of exercise cannot stand up in court, because they are now building twelve of what the prison itself calls "kennel-like runs"—a five-foot-by-twenty-five-foot [cage] of chain link fencing and razor wire for the men to "exercise" in individually. Dog runs! My God! The only other time they can come out is for legal visits.

Men are allowed only ten books and/or magazines and ten pieces of personal mail. Recently one prisoner's letters from his mother were destroyed because he tried to keep all of them. They receive three wool blankets, underwear, dungarees, and denim shirts, a denim jacket, a towel, toilet paper, legal paper, and envelopes from the prison. The prison will send out one free letter a week if the man can't afford postage. They must buy their own shampoo and other toilet articles.

There is a psychologist and a psychiatrist assigned to Mecklenburg. Frankly, I do not think much of their treatment. In the case of one man who has been on suicide watch several times, the psychologist told him to keep himself busy by putting together jigsaw puzzles. Another man, who had been "treated" by these doctors committed suicide after the Catholic priest who visited him and held services for the Catholic men was banned from prison. The usual "treatment" is massive doses of Thorazine and other psychotropic drugs. Such drugs might be treatment for some people. Here they are used [for] management more often than for treatment.

It is considered a security risk for anyone to take a picture of them. Pictures of death row inmates are not allowed, even when they face imminent execution. I could go on and on, but the simple truth is the men are treated more inhumanely than any prisoners I have ever seen or known.

Random beatings of the men, forcing the men to stand at attention for hours in the summer heat, continual shake-downs of their cells, and abrupt rotation of the prisoners from cell to cell also occurred. The men whom the prison guards labeled as the leaders of the escape were thrown into insolation and threatened.

One form of intimidation and abuse, which the inmates were embarrassed to discuss, was sexual assault. "This goon squad also abuses some of the men sexually," Marie recounted.

> I want to go to the press about it, but again, it is so embarrassing to the men
> that they don't want me to. Their method of doing this is to shackle and cuff the
> men so they can't help one another and then grab their private parts and make
> humiliating and suggestive remarks to them. They do this every now and then,
> and it is clearly a form of rape or sexual assault designed to show power and keep
> the men disoriented and feeling helpless . . . sometimes they strip the men. At
> other times they just stick their hands down their pants."[16]

Ironically, conditions became worse when Virginia opened its new death row at the Sussex I Correction Center in 1998. Admittedly, stories of abuse at the hands of corrections officers died away. There was no longer prisoner-on-prisoner violence or rape. Yet the men on the row had entered a new type of hell. No longer would inmates be allowed to congregate in a common pod area, where they could play cards, watch television, talk, and eat their meals. The condemned men were placed on twenty-four hour lock-down with no opportunity to interact with other death row inmates. Empty cells were maintained between the occupied ones, so the men could not communicate through their food slots. The inmates left their cells for three ten-minute showers each week as well as five hours of individual recreation time in a small area nicknamed the "dog cage." The recreation area had no weights or exercise equipment. None of the men were allowed to attend religious services or educational programming. They were entombed in a concrete mausoleum, awaiting death.[17] The practices by the Virginia Department of Corrections withstood constitutional challenge in federal court until October 2015.[18]

In the 1980s, Marie bemoaned the fact that the public was unaware of the inhumane conditions on Mecklenburg's death row, but she explained to the inmates that reaching out to television reporters and journalists was not necessarily the answer. "Think about TV," she wrote. "You watch enough of it. It is quick images. The quick image of MCC [Mecklenburg] is that of new buildings in good condition with flowers planted outside, cells with brightly colored doors and such luxuries as TVs, radios, typewriters and even tables and chairs." Viewers would not see the real story. "The viewers would see what they and the administration wanted them to see," she said. "They would not see beatings, gassings, macings, bad food, inadequate medical care, children banging on plexiglass to touch their fathers. They would not see the rotten conditions, tension, threats, and pettiness you deal with every day." Throughout her time as an activist, Marie was leery of the press and would only reach out to a handful of reporters who she believed were trustworthy.

In Marie's eyes, this type of chaos and fear was used to control and break down the condemned men. "I don't think of death row as a place so much as a process," wrote Marie in an unpublished interview. "And it's a process of dehumanization . . . Complete disorientation, constant disorientation. There is no routine, rules change every day, then they don't follow the rules. It is very hard to describe. They rotate the guards. They rotate the men."

Marie believed that the men were particularly susceptible to the banality and brutality of the row because of their mental state. "Perhaps death row represents what a state fears most, and I think that because mental health problems are so extensive that is their particular fear," explained Marie. "Most of the men on death row . . . were in and out of institutions before they killed someone . . . each death row is different, each state has a different set of crimes that are predominant, and ours [Virginia's] are the impulsive, mentally ill, mentally retarded, brain damaged." And Marie believed that the majority of the men on the row were the victims of sexual abuse. "Now that is something we don't talk about, except in confidence, because you can't live in prison if you have been sexually molested [and it's publicly known] but they talk to me because . . . sooner or later, they have to deal with it." These were the damaged human beings who populated Virginia's death row in the late 1980s.

Finally, Marie believed that that the prison administration was not only terrorizing the men of death row, but was actively working to speed up the execution process by asserting that the men were competent to be executed (an inmate cannot be executed if he does not understand what is happening to him and why). "The prison authorities here want the people on the row dead," Marie said. "They write affidavits [such as those regarding prisoner competency] to support their executions." Many of those writing affidavits, asserted Marie, were prison guards and counselors who were threatened with termination if they did not sign the documents.

Marie often remarked that it is easy to kill a monster but hard to kill a human being. Because the Department of Corrections worked mightily to shield both death row operations and the men of the row from public scrutiny, it was especially challenging for Marie to show the basic humanity of the men to the outside world.

When speaking against the death penalty to groups around the country, I often ask what they think death row might look like. Surprisingly the pictures they conjure up are pretty much the same: concrete walls, brick or stone walls, tiers, iron bars, guards with guns and circles of jangling keys, noise. A few embellish, adding TV sets bolted to walls, peeling paint, glaring lights. Some will even go so far as to envision men with crew cuts dressed in white T-shirts leaning against their cell doors. I suppose these similar imaginings can be attributed to Edward G. Robinson and late-night television.

But their men never have faces, and the question that always comes back to me is: "What are they like?" I know why they ask, what they are searching for, but I can't give them the answer, because it doesn't exist. There are only two factors the men and women on our death rows share. They are poor, and they

Marie striking a characteristically defiant pose outside of the offices of the Virginia Coalition on Jails and Prisons. Anonymous threats and acts of intimidation were aimed at Marie when she opened the Coalition, but she remained undeterred. Photograph courtesy of *Richmond Times-Dispatch*.

have been sentenced to death. They are disproportionately made up of minorities. All but a few were abused, neglected, or institutionalized as children or youths. Most of the younger men and women turned to drugs, the older ones to alcohol. Far more than half appear to be mentally ill to some degree. In many cases, they or their families sought help again and again. They all gave out clear signals that they were in trouble long before they killed. None received the help they needed. Why? Because they were our society's throwaways long before they murdered. One of the saddest facts about the people on death row is that once you know their true stories, the wonder becomes not that they murdered, but that they didn't murder sooner and more often.

As she planned out the structure of her book, Marie wanted to explore this common denominator of poverty with the story of Derick L. "Baydar" Peterson, a young black man sentenced to death for the shooting of a grocery store clerk. Below is a partial summary of Peterson's childhood and early adulthood written by Marie, based on her conversations with Peterson and his family.

On August 22, 1991, at 11:13 p.m., it was pronounced of Derick Lynn Peterson "this man has expired." My promise to Derick and myself less than an hour before, after he had been shaved, showered, and suited up for his execution and was carefully writing out his final statement, was to answer one question. Why?

Most people would say Derick was killed because he had killed a man during a robbery, but my work brings one in contact with hundreds of prisoners who have committed such crimes who are serving time and are eligible for parole. So why Derick in particular? For me, his life answers that question.

Derick was born into the southern, black underclass of Newport News, VA. His mother Eloise, one of nine children born in Georgia, was also raised in the projects of Newport News. Eloise was a strong woman with too much energy and too little ability to accept her "place." She married and bore her first child, Derick's older sister, at age sixteen. Cooking and cleaning for rich white people while being treated as if she weren't there solidified her hatred of whites and, therefore, of all authority. She began escaping through a bottle and trying to find her identity through the men who admired her good looks.

After her husband left, Eloise and her two children piled into her mother's already overrun apartment in the projects. Eloise worked as a cook in an all-white country club. When Derick was eight years old, Eloise got an apartment of her own in the projects. On weekends she held "selling parties" in the apartment for more money. "Selling parties" are gambling parties where illegal liquor and drugs are sold. They go on non-stop from Friday night through Monday morning. Derick and his sister helped out at the selling parties. Derick saw and heard it all. He watched men and women get drunk and bed together. He watched fights over cards. He watched people shoot up drugs. He heard the black hatred of the "man." It's a sorry environment for children—for anyone—but so are the projects, so is poverty, so is racism. If Eloise had gone on welfare, we'd have called her good-for-nothing, lazy, a leech. His mother was a queen there. He was a runt. He dreamed of being a bank robber.

Derick would drink the leavings in the glasses of liquor at these parties. He also began sniffing glue every day and shoplifting. Nobody questioned where he got the clothes and trinkets he gave his family and friends. The [only] attention he got was beatings from his mother. They didn't relate to his shoplifting. They didn't seem to relate to anything but Eloise's frustrations with the world. By the time he was ten years old, Derick went to school drunk every morning and was smoking a lot of marijuana.

Newport News and Hampton, VA, run together. In both cities poverty and wealth run together as well. Old, run-down projects that look like they were slapped down on the dirt with no foundations abut lushly landscaped middle- and upper-class neighborhoods. The demarcation lines are startling to the passerby. To those who live in the densely overcrowded projects, those demarcation lines look like barbed wire fences.

Derick was still a preteen when he began crossing those lines to bring back bits and pieces of that wealth. He was a tiny burglar who would soon move to armed robbery. A week before he was killed, a woman from his neighborhood told me they had thought of Derick as a modern Robin Hood.

At age 15, Derick was arrested for armed robbery and sent to Hanover School for Boys—a reform school just above Richmond. He loved Hanover. His

Undated photograph of Virginia death row inmate Derick Lynn "Baydar" Peterson. Like many men on the row, Peterson's childhood was filled with poverty, neglect, and violence. Personal collection of Marie Deans.

eyes would shine telling about the camping trips, the teachers, and the house fathers. "They really paid attention to you," he said. "It was wonderful." While at Hanover, his daughter, Keshane was born to his thirteen-year-old girlfriend. He and his girlfriend thought it was "neat" to have a baby girl.

We are not a people who want to see beyond individual responsibility. We keep looking for the "criminal gene." We want to believe in the bad seed. It exonerates us. The authorities did not look into Derick's environment or family life. They had given him his opportunity to straighten up at Hanover. The rest was up to him. After eight months, they released him back to his mother, back to the shot house.

Derick didn't go back to school. He became the bartender and one of the drug dealers for the shot house. He went back to drugs, shooting up downers, then speedballs (a combination of downers & uppers) while drinking and smoking marijuana. During the day, he became one of the robbers stalking Newport News and Hampton. He robbed only white establishments. And Derick and another girlfriend had a little boy, Peanut. Derick adored his children, but he was still a child himself and too much into drugs to take care of them.

On February 7, 1982, twenty-year-old Derick and a friend boosted their courage with wine in the parking lot of the Pantry Pride. They'd already shot up two speedballs, and they'd been smoking marijuana since they got up late that morning. Finally, after going in and out of the store three times, Derick decided to go get the money he'd seen the manager counting. His partner pulled out a gun for Derick to take with him. The prosecutor said that, after Derick had taken the money, he willfully shot Howard Kauffman, the white store manager, for no reason. Derick's memory was that Kauffman had blocked his exit and that he kept telling Kauffman to move. Derick shot Kauffman once in the stomach and ran.

The defense can offer evidence of mitigation about an offender's life, drug history, mental health, or anything that might help the jury understand what led a person to commit murder and whether he is redeemable. Derick had a wealth of mitigation. He not only was young, had been brought up in a horribly unfit environment, and had been abused and neglected, but Derick suffered from brain damage and neurological problems from birth. In addition, Derick's record at Hanover proved that he did extremely well in a structured environment. He was immediately redeemable. But Derick's lawyer did not present any of his evidence at the sentencing hearing.

In terms of guilt or innocence, the case against Derick Peterson was unambiguous. Three store employees witnessed the shooting, while three customers placed Derick at the scene of the crime. At the sentencing hearing, victims of two other robberies committed by Derick offered testimony to support the prosecution's claim that Derick posed a risk of future dangerousness. Only three witnesses testified on Derick's behalf at his sentence hearing—a probation officer who prepared a report on Derick's criminal history, a neighbor, and Derick's mother. No expert witness was retained to rebut testimony of future dangerousness, nor was evidence offered regarding brain damage.

With the story of Derick Peterson, Marie hoped to illustrate the undeniable fact that the men of death row came from childhoods filled with instability, violence, and despair. She wanted to show her readers that these men came into the world with two strikes against them. She wanted us to understand that the men were flawed and damaged human beings, not monsters. And she wanted to show their basic humanity.

To the outside world, Derick was a monster. To Marie, he was a loving and empathetic young man who called her "Mom" and who committed a terrible crime. Derick worried about Marie. In his death row letters he repeatedly thanked Marie for her help and cautioned her to slow down and take care of herself. "I hope that you are holding up all right under all the pressure," he wrote in a November 1990 letter, "I wanted you to know that I am here for you . . . remember that we all love you very much." And Marie loved him.

There is an ironic footnote to Derick's execution. Inside the death chamber, prison chaplain Russ Ford read the following prayer after Derick was strapped into the electric chair.

My Brother, we all pray that your death will somehow help cure the violence that so many years of painful poverty, oppression, and slavery have fashioned. And bring an end to our madness. May your execution yield abundant fruit for all the tragic victims—even those of us here who participate in this ritual, which so bruises and demeans our humanity. May your violent death here quicken our hearts to the empowering words of Jesus who ruled on an execution by drawing in the wisdom of the sands of time and proclaim that only those without sin can cast such violent stones. Continue your spiritual quest. And may God bless you, my brother Baydar.

Inmates Roger Coleman, Timothy Bunch, and Edward
Fitzgerald (left to right) celebrating Christmas on death row.
Marie would subsequently visit all three men in the death house
prior to their executions. Photograph courtesy of *Richmond
Times-Dispatch.*

After Baydar was killed, the head of the Virginia Department of Corrections angrily
confronted Russ and accused him of using the prayer to bring politics into the death
house.

Marie wanted people to understand the impact that death row had on the inmates. In a sense, Marie was drawing on Albert Camus's claim that the wait for gallows was more emotionally shattering than the fear experienced by the condemned
man's victim. "The devastating, degrading fear imposed on the condemned man for
months or even years is a punishment more terrible than death itself, and is one that
has not been imposed on his victim," wrote Camus. "A murdered man is generally
rushed to his death. . . . For the man condemned to death, on the other hand, the
horror of his situation is served up to him at every moment for months on end. Tor-

Virginia death row inmates Derick Peterson, Willie Leroy "Woo" Jones (top row, left to right), Charles Stamper and Johnny Watkins (bottom row, left to right). After a prison fight left him partially paralyzed, prison guards used a wheel chair to move Stamper into the death chamber. Personal collection of Marie Deans.

ture by hope alternates only with the pangs of animal despair."[19] For Marie, the years spent on death row were a form of torture the men struggled to escape.

> *Human beings naturally seek to understand their environment and what is happening to them. They naturally seek the ability to have some control over their lives, to make choices. But death row is an environment so alien to all that is human, so bizarre to any system of logic, and so devoid of choice that the mind goes through all kinds of twists and turns to deal with it. For those who are actually on death row, the only truly human way to deal with it is to leave it. Men, women, and children on death row leave in many ways. A few choose the concrete method of dropping their appeals and demanding speedy executions.*
>
> *Some leave by going into a stupor, signing up for the "yard pills" or "zenes" prison administrators hand out indiscriminately as management tools. Some choose the stupor of electronic pacifiers—blaring radios that overpower the sounds of steel doors clanging, keys rattling, disembodied commands screeched out over loud speakers, and men sobbing in their cells. Or they stare fixedly at the blurred images of a TV bolted to the wall outside of their tier.*
>
> *Some leave through simple denial. "I have a good case," or "I have the best lawyer in the state," or "they wouldn't kill an innocent man," or "they'll never*

get me in that damned chair." Some leave through religious fanaticism, pouring over their Bibles day after day looking for personal messages of forgiveness and hope.

Some leave through insanity. God alone knows where Alvin Ford is [a Florida death row inmate who went insane during his incarceration], but it has got to be better than death row. The paradox of Alvin's insanity may be that it is the only sane response to death row.

Some miraculously grow out of death row, developing spiritually, intellectually, and morally. They are the ones who are informed by their own appointed deaths and become truly transformed. If prison officials fear anyone on death row, it is these men and women, because in them prison officials are confronted with the unvarnished truth of the ritualized murder they call execution.

What Camus said about the contemplation of one's death being worse than the death itself is also true. Every person I've worked with on death row—and I've worked with hundreds—has told me about execution nightmares. I have listened as well to their imaginings about what their deaths by gassing, lethal injection, and the electric chair will be like. I have heard their fears of what their families will face when they recover their bodies. They do not experience their horrific deaths once, but daily and nightly for years.

Families and loved ones of those on death row live in what I call "death row's anteroom," a place just as illogical, bizarre, unnatural, and almost as isolated and devoid of choice as death row itself. Just like their loved ones, the only way they can deal with it is to leave. For them, the leaving is all too similar to that of their loved ones.'

Like the men who drop their appeals, some desert or torment their family members on death row, tearing the family apart. Other family members choose the stupor of drugs, alcohol, television, or the reverse stupor of frenetic lifestyles. Others become religious fanatics. A few change, grow, develop into stronger individuals. A few go insane. Most cling to denial.

They can't believe what is happening. Even after the methodical killing of one man while his nine-year-old son sobbed "I want my Daddy," even after seeing hundreds of their fellow citizens outside the prison carrying nooses and "Fry the Nigger" signs and cheering when the hearse goes by, even after every politician in the state runs on a pro death penalty ticket, families cling to their denial. Not my son. Not my father. Not my husband.

And yet they can't deny it. A mother has recurring nightmares of being forced to plug in the electric chair. A wife has execution flashes—she walked in front of a truck once while "seeing" the execution of her husband and was almost run over. A fourteen-year-old son becomes withdrawn, drops out of school, and attempts suicide. A fifteen-year-old girl who had been a cheerleader and class president begins to run wild. Both, and so many more children, try to hurry what they feel is their fate because their fathers are on death row. Only the strongest families and the strongest family members can survive the anteroom intact, and *even they are so changed by their stay there that few can remember what they and the world were like before they entered that room.*

While Marie felt tremendous empathy for the men, she did not coddle them. "I think it's demeaning for people to be treated like children," Marie stated. "I'm very demanding of them."[20]

> Even wardens tell me I'm harder on the inmates than they are. The guys on the row call me the "Slam Dunker," because I am hard on them. I will not take any——off them. And I don't want to hear them whine. I want them to take responsibility. I want them to know what they have done. They can't change until they take responsibility.[21]

Joe Giarratano is one of the only death row inmates remaining who can talk about his observations of Marie's interactions with the men of the row. In explaining these relationships, Joe echoes Marie's message of the basic humanity of the men, the need to confront the evil within, and tough love.

> Whether she was working with a death row prisoner, a judge, a member of the death squad, a lawyer, a police officer, a victim, a prosecutor, or a college student, her interaction was driven by her conviction that human beings should not be killing each other, and that we do great harm to ourselves when we do. Marie believed that when we kill we dehumanize ourselves. She understood that no human being could actually deprive another of their [*sic*] humanness, but that in the attempt to do so, one can, and does, dehumanize oneself. Marie understood the profound ramifications of that. She grasped that where there is an increase of dehumanization there is also an increase in evil; where human beings lose grip on their identities so, too, they lose grip of their souls.
>
> It was Marie's core understanding of that that guided all of her interactions with the men on the row, and all who were directly involved in that dehumanizing process. Marie was extremely good at what she did, e.g., recruiting attorneys to represent the men on the row, investigating cases, developing mitigation, spotting legal errors on novel legal issues, and fundraising. But she was [also] extremely good at connecting with those she interacted with and with finding ways to cultivate, stimulate, and/or rattle the humanity of the individual with whom she was interacting. Be it someone like Lem Tuggle, a condemned murderer, or with those who were paid to kill him by deliberately, with premeditation, strapping him into a heavy wooden chair, attaching electrodes to his head and leg, and then repeatedly zapping him with electricity until they fried the life out of him. Unlike Tuggle or the executioner, Marie refused to deny the basic humanity of the other and instead chose to respect it and honor it.
>
> Because of this, it would be a mistake to label Marie "a bleeding heart." Marie could be hard as nails, especially with those of us on the row. She did not tolerate the men making excuses for what they did, or otherwise not accepting responsi-

bility for their actions, or rationalizing things away. Most of the inmates got that, and most tried to show their love and appreciation in any little way they could; and not just by trying to help Marie, but by caring for each other, by treating the guards with respect and as human beings.

None of us were perfect. Sometimes there would be arguments and fights, some guys could be petty, but when Marie found out, she would lay into them; and grown men would stand there like little kids. You could always tell when Marie was getting on one of the guys over the phone for doing something stupid. You could see them fidgeting. If they had been arguing with someone, whoever happened to be on the phone would call the other party over and hand him the phone for his chewing out. Sometimes it was really funny.

Marie's attempt to help the guys re-humanize themselves was utmost in all of her interactions with them, and only intensified when they went into the death house with an execution date. There in the death house, life and death became extremely amplified and focused for all who were present. Because Marie was part of the legal team, she basically had twenty-four-hour access via visits and phone calls. I was not privy to the conversations that Marie had with the men at that point, though sometimes she would talk about those times with me afterward. At those times Marie was mother, father, sister, victim, priest, lawyer, psychologist, friend, sage, and comforter. She could be the devil's advocate, prosecutor, and angry citizen as well—whatever it took to get the individuals to rediscover empathy, compassion, and humanity. More often than not she succeeded. Many, though not all, of the men Marie sat with during those last hours had deep experiences of self-discovery and transformation; they were more alive and more human than those who extinguished their light with legal mechanics.[22]

When Marie moved to Virginia, she had not planned on working with inmates on their appeals; she believed that she would be finding lawyers to handle these appeals as well as working with prison officials to improve conditions of confinement on the row. That changed within the first twenty-four hours of the Coalition's existence, when Marie received a frantic telephone call from an attorney asking Marie to convince his client to pursue his appeals and not "volunteer" for the electric chair. The inmate was a brain-damaged man named Buddy Earl Justus, whose killing of three women in three different states had landed him on Virginia's death row. Within days of arriving in Virginia, Marie found herself in a courtroom—whispering to Justus to tell the judge that he would be filing an appeal.

We went to the hearing. I sat right behind Buddy. The sheriff let me sit right behind him. I remember when the judge asked him whether he was going to pick up his appeals or not—this was his last chance . . . to pick up his appeals or not—Buddy turned around and looked at me, and I went "yes, you are." He turned around and said, "yes, I am going to pick up my appeals." I wanted to hop, skip and jump all over the place. But I behaved myself.

Buddy would be the first in a long line of Virginia inmates who Marie would convince to pursue legal appeals and not walk meekly to the chair. In the winter of 1983, there were seven inmates who had decided to drop their appeals—and other inmates would follow suit in subsequent years.

A powerful example of how Marie struggled to get the men to pick up their appeals and fight is found in the case of Joseph John Savino III. Born and raised in Mt. Vernon, New York, Joseph claimed that, as a child, he was subjected to sexual abuse at the hands of priests who taught at his school. After serving time in a New York prison on a robbery conviction, Joseph moved to Virginia in 1988 and lived on a Bedford County farm with Thomas McWaters, a man with whom Joseph was sexually involved. The relationship came to an end on November 29, 1988, when Joseph, a heavy drug user, beat McWaters to death with a hammer while high on drugs. Subsequently, Joseph would allege that McWaters tried to control the younger man with the lure of drugs as well as threats of legal prosecution.

After his conviction of capital murder, Joseph decided not to pursue his appeals. In a document that he later gave Marie, entitled "Death Row Suicides," Joseph wrote that he wanted to "kill myself through legal suicide" because of the guilt he felt over the murder and the hopelessness that he felt.

> I did not want to spend the next eight or ten years on Death Row . . . I could not stand the isolation, being treated like an object instead of a human being, the absolute idleness, being chained like wild animals with every movement, every minute decision being made for me, watching the torture my loved ones were enduring . . . I felt like nobody was doing anything for us on death row . . . that we were the dregs of society and something less than human.

Joseph decided that suicide would not draw sufficient attention to what he viewed as the horror of the death house, and he also petitioned to have his execution publicly televised. "I would like to say that since my trial and everything else was public, that my execution be made public," Joseph stated. "I think it should be if it's to be a deterrence to anyone else."[23] His request was swiftly denied on the grounds that "it wouldn't be proper."[24]

Joseph was transferred to the death house in June of 1990. It is not clear whether Joseph knew Marie Deans prior to his transfer (most likely he did), but she came to the death house with the single purpose of getting him to pursue his appeals. In "Death Row Suicides," Joseph explained what happened next.

> I was sitting in my "Death Cell" counting the hours and the days to the day of my "release" from all of this hell, when a lady by the name of Marie Deans from the Virginia Coalition on Jails and Prisons came to visit me. She at first listened to all of my reasons for wanting to give up my appeals and die. I knew that she was there to "try" to change my mind . . . I was adamant that she wasn't going to change my mind, but we made a deal that I would listen to her and her reasons why I should change my mind. Marie ["I call her "Saint Marie"] promised me

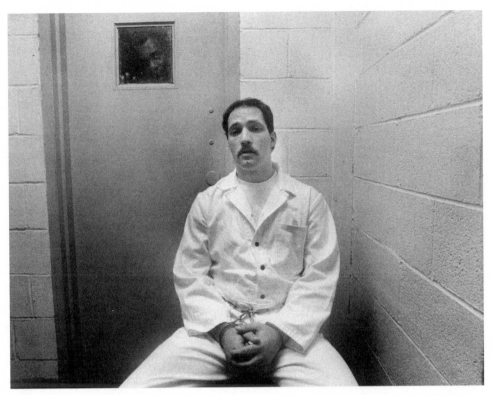

Undated photograph of Virginia death row inmate Joseph John Savino III. A close bond formed between Marie and Joseph after she convinced him to "pick up his appeals" and fight his death sentence, and Joseph referred to Marie as "Saint Marie." Photograph courtesy of *Richmond Times-Dispatch*.

she would not file a "Next Friend Petition," which would block my execution. She promised that she would help get my "message" out; that she would help my family through my execution, and that she would help me through the "Death House" experience. She held up to all her promises, except I found out later that she was going to file the "Next Friend Petition" on me, but that justs [*sic*] shows how committed she is to stopping state murders.

Without a doubt if it had not been for Marie I would have been executed. Marie showed me that all of the reasons I wanted to be executed were wrong and that I had conjured up the wrong conclusions based on misinformation. She showed me that there were many people working on getting the death penalty abolished, and that many people did care about me and the others on death row.

The whole time I was in the "Death House," Marie would faithfully show up every day and listen to me for hours. Everything I would say in support of my decision to kill myself by allowing my execution, she would turn it around and show me how empty and wrong my arguments were.

On the day I decided to pick up my appeals [five days before my execution], I had a very emotional visit with my family. They were all begging me to pick up my appeals. Right after they left, Marie came in and I talked for hours . . . she just listened. She got up and left, and in about ten minutes she returned with two lawyers . . . We all went into the "Cool Off Room," which is the room where they put the body of a man that has just been executed to cool off. Marie and the two lawyers bombarded me with ALL the reasons why I should pick up my appeals and go on fighting. They broke me down completely. I looked down the hall at a guard that was watching us, and then I looked at these three wonderful people who cared whether I lived or died, and who were willing to help me live.

It suddenly became very clear to me that if I got up and walked away with the guard and let the state kill me, that I would have been going with the enemy, and would have been letting everyone that loved me and cared about me, down! But if I picked up my appeals I would be with a great team . . . a "Life Team," and I would be able to [do] a lot for the "cause" by staying alive. Marie convinced me with her beautiful logic, that if I allowed myself to be killed, that everything I had done up to that point would be LOST! Marie made me realize that I can make a difference, and that my life still had meaning. I decided to pick up my appeals, and since then I have seen the truth to all that Marie and the others told me, and I am glad that I did not allow myself to be killed.

Joseph subsequently issued a press release regarding his intentions of pursuing his appeals, stating, "if all these people are willing to fight, I should and will do my part. Now, let's kick ass."

As Joseph was writing "Death Row Suicides," he was dealing with the death of Ricky Boggs—a fellow inmate who was executed on July 19, 1990. In a letter written six days after Boggs's death, Joseph shared his feelings about his dead friend with Marie. "While I was writing this paper about 'suicides' for you, I felt Rick—watching me—or helping me. I don't know, its [sic] hard to explain—but it felt great because since Thursday night, I've kinda [sic] felt like I let Rick down because I was supposed to be 'waiting for him' on the other side. But today I felt really good—or like I was doing something that pleased him. I don't know. What I do know is I miss him so much."

The experience in the death house created a tight bond between Marie and Joseph Savino. He filled Marie's mailbox with greeting cards and letters, constantly thanking Marie for her friendship and advocacy. In one card he wrote the following:

Well Saint, it's one year ago today the state almost had their way with me. Had it not been for you—I would've been gone, forever. You showed me that my life is not over, and that I can still make a difference. It's been a tough year—but I feel like I've done my best and I feel like I have made a small difference. I can never thank you enough Marie, for dragging me out of that death house.

In another card, Joseph told Marie that he had "learned so much from you, mostly how to forgive myself. I would've never been able to do that if I didn't get to know you." Marie had helped Joseph rediscover his humanity.

Although Joseph renewed his battle against his death sentence, he did not fully escape his other demons. In May of 1994, Joseph survived a near-fatal overdose of heroin. He initially claimed that corrections officers tried to kill him to cover up the murder of fellow death row inmate Wayne DeLong (DeLong committed suicide on death row in 1993),[25] but later admitted that he voluntarily took the drugs after purchasing them from a Mecklenburg corrections officer.[26] Maintaining his innocence to the end, Joseph was executed on July 17, 1996, by lethal injection. Death came as a relief to Joseph. "I don't really see this as a punishment for myself," he told a news reporter shortly before his execution. "To be very honest with you, I don't want to live anymore like this, anyway. So, I'm glad, to a certain degree, that this is over."[27] Marie did not stand death watch with Joseph. He worried about how his execution would affect Marie and insisted that she not be there.

Marie's acts of kindness extended to some of the forgotten inmates of death row, those men who died before their date with the executioner. One of those men was a Cuban national by the name of Manuel Quintana. In the passage below, Joe Giarratano tells the story of how Marie fought to secure adequate medical care for Quintana.

Manuel did not speak any English. When Marie began to review his case in 1982, she discovered that virtually nothing was known about him, and that his trial attorney had made no real effort to obtain information. All the information was based in Cuba.

When Marie could not get the information directly from Cuba, she went through friends who contacted other friends who had contacts at the Embassy and who then obtained copies of all the available records on Manuel in Cuba. Turns out that Manuel was some type of doctor in Cuba, had for a time served in the military there. That his father had been detained and killed by the military regime under Castro. Manuel spoke out and then fled the country. Marie also suspected that Manuel might not have committed the crime for which he was convicted.

While all that information was coming to light, Manuel had a major heart attack. Though he survived, doctors at MCV determined that he needed major open heart surgery or he would die in a short span of time. The Department of Corrections would not allow the surgery and returned him to Mecklenburg once he was able to move. There was some debate in the media about whether taxpayers should have to pay the cost of surgery for someone sentenced to death. This went on for a couple of months. Marie weighed in and made it clear that legal action was on the way, along with more publicity.

Manuel suffered another major heart attack on the row. The guard in the unit refused to call for medical help; he said that Manuel was faking. I picked up a chair and chased the guard out of the unit (I didn't hit him, just threatened him). He called a "10–33 Code Red" over the prison intercom system. [He] then went to Manuel to administer CPR. The medical team and more guards came. Manuel was rushed to the local hospital, stabilized, then taken to MCV, then transferred to the infirmary at the old State Pen. Marie went to visit him. The DOC caved and agreed to allow the surgery. Marie gave him the news, but Manuel said "no más." Through a translator, he essentially said that he was tired. Marie sat with him for a few days, trying to convince him to change his mind. She was there with him when he died.

At that time, there were a lot of ministers who visited the row. Marie asked all of them [if] they would help bury Manuel. None would, and that really angered Marie. I suggested that Marie contact Bishop Walter Sullivan of the Diocese of Richmond, and I gave her a letter to give to him as well. The Bishop did not hesitate. He made all the arrangements. He celebrated the Mass himself at the Cathedral, and the graveside service as well. Marie and Bishop Sullivan became good friends over the years, and the Richmond Diocese gave donations of money to the Virginia Coalition on Jails and Prisons for all the years it operated.[28]

In a newspaper interview after Manuel's death, Marie stated that his decision to refuse medical treatment was the result of the inmate being a victim of "the process of death row"—a process Marie described as "getting a human being dehumanized to the point where he can go to the chair or to the gas chamber without tearing the world apart. And I think if you look at past executions it's a successful process."[29] For Manuel, the row had broken him. Death was preferable to life.

As the years passed, the men grew more and more dependent on Marie. This allowed her to exert her authority over the men and bring down the level of violence on the row. There were several men that Marie leaned on as "pod leaders," including Joe Giarratano and Wayne "Buffalo" DeLong.

On death row for the shooting of a Richmond police officer, Buffalo subsequently assaulted a fellow death row inmate—Charles Stamper—and left him partially paralyzed. When Marie met with Buffalo after the death row assault, she let Buffalo know exactly how she felt. "I'm out here living on a pauper's wage and trying to raise my son and working like 120 hours a week here to prove that y'all are not a future danger, and you just go out and prove that you are" a furious Marie told the contrite Buffalo. "I'm trying to keep your ass out of the electric chair and you're trying to put everybody's in it." The message was received.

Marie came to trust Buffalo, and she relied on him to maintain order on the row. For example, when a seventeen-year-old inmate named Douglas Christopher "Chris" Thomas arrived on death row, it was Deans who ordered Buffalo to make sure that Thomas was not assaulted and raped. Marie did not always let the other inmates see her invisible hand at work; she never told Chris Thomas that she had ordered Buffalo to protect him. "Chris never knew I intervened [on his behalf]. The idea was to let Chris think of himself as being a man on the row. He was dealing with serious shit, and he didn't need to think that somebody was treating him like a child."

Buffalo himself came to care deeply for Marie. Shortly before his suicide on death row, he wrote the following note to her: "Your wonderful friendship and love have enriched my life . . . I only wish like hell I didn't have to attain it on death row." Buf-

Undated photograph of Virginia death row inmate Wayne "Buffalo" DeLong. On death row for the murder of a police officer, DeLong helped Marie maintain order on death row until his suicide in June 1993. Personal collection of Marie Deans.

falo continued to help Marie maintain order on death row until June 13, 1993, when he got drunk, took an injection of cocaine, and strangled himself with an electrical cord with the assistance of another inmate.[30] Buffalo had been scheduled to be executed on July 15, 1993. An inmate escaping a date with the executioner via overdose did not go unnoticed, and an embarrassed Department of Corrections tried unsuccessfully to find the source of the drugs and the syringe in the face of scathing publicity.[31]

In the early months of the Coalition, a panicked Marie raced to find attorneys for the condemned men. In basic terms, death row inmates get three appeals. The first appeal is called the direct appeal, which is an automatic appeal heard by the Virginia Supreme Court. Inmates are assigned attorneys during their direct appeal, and the Virginia Supreme Court looks to see if the trial court judge made any mistakes and if the death sentence was appropriately applied. A defendant who is unhappy with the Virginia Supreme Court's ruling can file an appeal with the United States Supreme Court.

The second and third appeals are called state and federal habeas corpus, respectively. These appeals raise broader claims about the defendant's trial and conviction, such as the claim that an inmate was denied his constitutional right to competent legal representation. In the 1980s, inmates did not have a right to have a lawyer represent them on the state and federal habeas corpus claims. When Marie created the Coalition, there were several death row inmates facing execution who did not have attorneys and had not filed these later types of claims. In short, these men were

We the undersigned are among the 73% of the people of Virginia who do not support the death penalty when given the alternative of 25 years imprisonment before parole eligibility and restitution to the victims' families. We therefore call upon the Virginia legislators to abolish the death penalty and enact the alternative.

NAME   Address

An anti-death penalty petition that circulated around death row and was subsequently given to Marie Deans. All but two of the men who signed the petition (Joseph Payne and Earl Washington) were subsequently executed. Personal collection of Marie Deans.

facing the electric chair without having exhausted all their legal appeals—and the Virginia attorney general's office and the Virginia Department of Corrections did not care. "The wonder of it is why half the men on the row weren't dead by the time I got here," Marie mused in a newspaper interview.

Marie spent hours on the telephone, begging attorneys to represent inmates on their appeals. In essence, Marie was asking these attorneys to take the cases pro bono and spend hundreds of hours on appeals that would likely make no difference. Her efforts on behalf of one inmate alone produced a five hundred dollar telephone bill, and Marie herself described the telephone calls as a combination of "arm-twisting, guilt tripping, and begging."

Marie and Robert Deans in the offices of the Virginia Coalition on Jails and Prisons. From a young age, Robert was involved in all aspects of Marie's death penalty work. Personal collection of Marie Deans.

During one of our conversations prior to her death, I asked Marie to explain all the different "hats that she wore" in running the Coalition. Marie listed so many responsibilities that I had to ask her to repeat the list several times—much to her irritation. "Why are you so interested in labels," she grumbled at me. Here is the list which I created as she talked. Marie was a prison reformer, trying to improve the miserable conditions of confinement at Mecklenburg's death row. She was a de facto prison administrator, using her influence with the men to bring order to the row. She was a paralegal and, for all intents and purposes, a skilled lawyer. She was a drafter of clemency petitions. She was an educator who taught continuing legal education seminars. She ran a pre-trial tracking service for new capital cases, providing informational packets on the basics of defending death penalty cases to the appointed defense attorneys. She recruited expert witnesses for capital murder trials. She was a spiritual advisor, a therapist, a drill sergeant, and a mother figure. She was an abolitionist, who continued to campaign to abolish the death penalty while she simultaneously tried to save the men already condemned to execution. She was an agitator and a social activist, who used the press to shine a light into the dark corners of the death house. She was a reluctant fundraiser for the Coalition. And she was a mitigation specialist.

There was one additional "hat" which Marie wore during her years with the Coalition, namely, single mother. When Marie moved to Richmond in January of 1983, her ten-year-old son Robert stayed in South Carolina with his father and completed the school year. When Marie picked her son up at the train station that summer, she did not recognize him—Robert's father had fed him a steady diet of fast food, and Robert had gained an enormous amount of weight.

From the start, Robert was involved with Marie's work with death row inmates. He came to Marie's office every afternoon after school, and there he would do homework and read comic books and science fiction novels. Occasionally Robert would relieve a weary Marie and talk on the telephone to the condemned men. Robert entertained the inmates with tales from his comic books and updates on his Lego projects as well as talking about sports or music.

Some of the men and women who worked with Marie questioned the wisdom of having a young boy talking to death row inmates. And they believed that Robert had to compete with the condemned men for Marie's attention. It is undeniable that Marie's work resonated with Robert. Marie herself revealed that a young Robert would pray at night for the "hurting soul" of J. C. Shaw. And Robert got emotionally involved in the men's pending appeals, talking at night with Marie about the specific cases and even attending execution vigils. The grief that Robert felt over executions is reflected on the cover of this book, where an anguished Marie holds her distraught son outside of the death house.

Russ Ford disagrees with the claims that Marie's work negatively impacted Robert. "I challenge the idea that it was damaging for Robert to talk to death row inmates," Russ said. "Marie saw his relationships with the men on the row as being positive and educational. Robert was part of her world. He was curious. He asked questions about her work. And Robert at age ten or eleven was more informed about the death penalty than most adult voters."

Once Robert arrived in Richmond, he became a co-equal partner in running the home. He and Marie shopped together, Robert did much of the cooking, and he made sure that his mother came home to a clean apartment. Money was always tight, so presents at holidays were limited and outings to their favorite cheap Italian and Greek restaurants were infrequent. At night they watched old movies together, laughing at the antics of the Marx Brothers and delighting in the suspense of Hitchcock. Marie introduced Robert to art, music, and literature, passing on her love of reading to her son. In short, there was a strong bond between mother and son.

Robert was very aware of the stress and anguish Marie was experiencing, and during especially rough times he worked to reduce the size of his "emotional footprint" at home. Marie, in turn, fretted about Robert. "Marie was concerned about how her choices impacted Robert," said Russ. "She did not shield him from the fight but did things to make his life as normal as possible." Marie worried about the fact that Robert's father was not playing an active role in his life, and the men around Marie and Robert—including Russ and Joe Giarratano—tried to fill that void.

Of all her professional hats, Marie was most proud of her role as a mitigation specialist, a position that Marie practically invented. She wrote:

> I am a mitigation specialist, one who documents people's lives through their stories. When I began my work, mitigation specialists worked exclusively on capital cases, so I was working with men, women and children who had killed, and with their families. It surprised me that not everyone could learn those stories, that so many people considered it amazing that I could learn them. If that was true, I didn't want to analyze how I did so, as if there might be some magic I'd ignorantly stumbled into and could lose at any moment. In time, I realized what was happening. I wasn't gifted. I had no magic. It was simply that wounded people recognize one another. Their wounds open and speak to one another.[32]

Under the laws of every state with the death penalty, an inmate charged with capital murder faces a "bifurcated" trial. First, a jury must decide if the defendant is guilty of the crime. If found guilty, a sentencing hearing is held and a jury must decide (or recommend to a judge) whether the defendant should be put to death or be given life without parole. In Virginia, during the sentencing hearing the prosecution must prove to the jury that the defendant poses a future risk of dangerousness to society or that the defendant's "conduct in committing the offense was outrageously or wantonly vile, horrible, or inhuman; in that it involved torture, depravity of mind, or aggravated battery to the victim."[33] If the prosecution carries this burden, then Virginia law allows a defendant to present mitigating evidence.

> Facts in mitigation may include, but shall not be limited to, the following: (i) the defendant has no significant history of prior criminal activity, (ii) the capital felony was committed while the defendant was under the influence of extreme mental or emotional disturbance, (iii) the victim was a participant in the defendant's conduct or consented to the act, (iv) at the time of the commission of the capital felony, the capacity of the defendant to appreciate the criminality of his conduct or to conform his conduct to the requirements of law was significantly impaired, (v) the age of the defendant at the time of the commission of the capital offense, or (vi) . . . the subaverage intellectual functioning of the defendant.[34]

Here is where the storyteller in Marie could make a difference by gathering information on the lives of the defendants and putting a human face on those who the prosecution claimed were monsters.

Marie talking with her staff at the Virginia Coalition on Jails and Prisons in September 1992. Shortly after this photograph was taken, Marie drove to the death house at the Greensville Correctional Center to spend time with condemned inmate Willie Leroy "Woo" Jones. Photograph courtesy of the *Virginian-Pilot*.

Marie worked as a mitigation specialist on both the capital murder trials of defendants as well as on their appeals. Over a twenty-year period, both as the director of the Coalition as well as the executive director of the Virginia Mitigation Project, Marie acted as a mitigation specialist on approximately 220 death penalty trials. Only three of the murder trials resulted in a sentence of death.

Marie's success with the Coalition led to increased doubts about her role on death row. As explained by Joe Giarratano, Marie questioned whether her work simply gave legitimacy to a system that she despised.

> It is important to remember that though she was heavily involved in the legal aspects of the cases she assisted on, and was damned good at it, her involvement there was born out of necessity. First and foremost, Marie was an abolitionist, and it pained her deeply that she could not devote all of her efforts to that cause. Her work as a mitigation specialist (even before that label become popular), as a paralegal, and as director of the Virginia Coalition pained her deeply. She never stopped questioning whether or not she should be doing that, i.e., whether she should be directly participating with the system that was doing the killing rather than standing against it. The state's killing system only works, and has the air of legitimacy, because of the people who participate in it.

Throughout Marie's time at the Coalition, financial crisis loomed in the horizon. Marie did not enjoy fundraising, but again and again her time was taken away from the men as she raised money to keep the Coalition operating. During its first year of existence, the Coalition was supported by a $14,000 grant from Charlottesville architect Leonard Dreyfuss, a long-time supporter of the Southern Coalition on Jails and Prisons. Marie received additional funds from the Southern Coalition as well as the Lutheran Church.

> *I was getting an $11,000 salary—and no health insurance—and most of the time I didn't even get the full $11,000 because I had expenses to pay. Gas was cheap thankfully. Phones and what have you. I was using somebody else's office space and then I moved into my bedroom. First my dining room and then my bedroom. There was no money to do much of anything. Work was really what was keeping me running. I remember working Christmas day after we opened presents at home. There was no vacation. There was no day off. You could see the history of it if you look at the execution schedules. First there were these seven men who were threatening to drop their appeals. I got them to pick up their appeals. Then Joe [Giarratano] drops his appeals and then the escape [from death row] happens. And we've got execution after execution after execution. And it just starts going like that. And I'm doing trials and I'm doing the only work that's being done on death row on conditions and access and legal work and recruiting lawyers and doing all that. We had no money. There was no time to say, "Okay, I'm going to stop everything and go write a grant." So I was really kind of like that gerbil on the wheel.*

Finding money, time, and resources to run the Coalition was a perpetual struggle, made all the more desperate by the well-funded foe Marie was fighting. In a letter that appeared in a prison newsletter published by prisoners in the Louisiana State Penitentiary, Marie described her struggle against Goliath.

> In my office you will find me, an old typewriter donated by the New York Public Defenders' Association, an old copier donated by a local doctor, and a bank balance constantly in the red. You will also find that we must put our legal pleadings on a bus and find some good hearted abolitionist to pick them up and deliver them to the court . . . in the attorney general's office you will find an array of attorneys, paralegals, secretaries, investigators, word processors, computers, collators, and other fancy equipment. Standing by are Lear jets and state police cars with state police for chauffeurs to carry the pleadings to the courts. The budget for our office is $35,000 to $40,000 a year, IF we can raise it. Most often we can't. The budget for the attorney general's death penalty appellate office has no ceiling. It runs up to several hundred thousand dollars a year. Unlike us, they don't have to raise it. They simply tax it out of you and me.[35]

In the mid-1980s, the Coalition faced a crisis as its funding dried up. "The death penalty again has become routine, and fighting it is no longer fashionable," wrote journalist Tony Germanotta. "The Lutheran Church, which used to supply Deans's

$14,000 annual salary, has pulled out. Although several individual congregations offer assistance, the major religious organizations . . . pay only lip service to the capital punishment issue. 'They've abandoned the men on the row,' Deans said. 'They'll hold their hands when they die, but they're not going to pay for legal work to help keep them alive.' "[36] By 1986, Marie decided not to draw a salary from the Coalition, channeled those funds into operations, and supported herself and her young son, Robert, with a monthly unemployment check of $536.

Rescue came not from the concerned citizens of Virginia but from Europe. Recounted Marie:

> In November of 1986, British ITV aired a documentary done on my work in Virginia. The documentary showed how few resources the Coalition had and the kind of work we did for those sentenced to death. They also showed footage on death row, including an interview with Joe Giarratano. I was amazed by the reactions in Europe. People there began to raise money for the Coalition, which always was in danger of folding due to lack of funds. Europeans almost single-handedly kept the Coalition going for two years, and we continued to receive donations from them until the day I closed the Coalition's doors for good in 1993. One of those donors who most touched me was a mason in Liverpool who sent five pounds a month "for your work with the laddies."

The Virginia Coalition on Jails and Prisons operated at a critical time in the history of capital punishment. Opened shortly after Virginia's first execution in the modern death penalty era, the Coalition kept defendants charged with capital murder off death row and fought tirelessly to keep those on death row from being executed. While Marie was at the center of the Coalition, she did not do the work alone. Lawyers and volunteers freely donated their time and expertise (often after being strong-armed by Marie) and citizens donated funds to keep the Coalition afloat. There was one person, however, who figured most prominently in Marie's work with the men of the row. His name was Russ Ford, and he would walk side-by-side with Marie during some of the most terrifying times of her life.

6

Marie and Russ

To do this work, I like to tell Russ, you must be a courageous fool.
—Marie Deans, undated

For most of her time working in the death house, Marie had Russ Ford at her side. A native of Richmond, Virginia, Russ was the son of a brick mason who was raised in the Baptist Church. He attended Averett College and then Southeastern Seminary in Wake Forest, North Carolina, before he began working at the Virginia State Penitentiary in 1984. Russ soon rose to the position of senior pastor, and his responsibilities included counseling the men of death row and the death house. "I didn't choose death row. I arrived there," Russ once explained to a newspaper reporter. "We thought we would rotate through. But the other chaplains weren't connecting with the men and weren't as effective, so I wound up being the lead. My gifts matched in that sense. It wasn't so much a choice as that I was chosen."[1]

It took Marie some time to bond with Russ, and, in the early years of her work in the Coalition, Marie had a tense relationship with the volunteer chaplains who counseled the men on death row and during their final hours in the death house. "The chaplaincy service would come in just before the execution, shake their [the inmates] hands, say hello, and go into the execution chamber," said Marie. "And I balked at that because I was the one who told Bishop [Walter] Sullivan, 'Don't go in there and watch an execution. Go there and be with the man. If you can't go there and be with the man, don't go there and be with the act. The men have got a sea of people in front of them, all wanting them to die, and they don't even know you. They need somebody they know in there, and it is a cheap break to go shake their hand and watch them.' Bishop Sullivan agreed, and he started coming in and actually visiting with them before."

Russ started visiting the men in the death house soon after Marie's initial confrontation with Bishop Sullivan, and, not surprisingly, Marie lashed out at him. With a smile and laugh, Russ recalled the first time that he met Marie.

I was going into the death house to see Morris Mason. Marie was coming out. We were on the steps leading down to the death house. She was coming out red

Chaplain Russ Ford on May 22, 1994. The senior pastor at the Virginia State Penitentiary, Ford was a close friend of Marie's and often stood "death watch" with Marie and the condemned inmate. Photograph courtesy of *Richmond Times-Dispatch*.

faced and steaming. And she said, "you damn preachers—you want to save their souls and not their lives." At the time, all a minister had to do to see an inmate waiting execution was to show up at the front gate and announce that they were a minister. Some soul-saver had upset Morris Mason. He told Morris that he was going to hell, and Morris was depressed about that. He had never thought about hell. Morris was limited—he never grasped his own mortality.[2]

Ford quickly took steps to shut down the practice of letting "bible notchers" walk in off the street to see the condemned men.

In the early months of their professional relationship, tensions continued as Marie felt that Russ was infringing on her space in the death house. Marie wrote:

He was mad at me at one point because [death row inmate] Michael Marnell Smith said, "I don't want you to take up my time here [in the death house]. I want to spend time with Marie." Russ had come down [to the death house] right before the last meal to shake his hand, and I don't think he intended to stay, but Michael said, "I am glad to meet you, but I don't really want you here because I am only allowed one person and I want that person to be Marie." Michael was a very, very religious person and his brother was a minister, so he said he wanted me there. He certainly didn't want a minister he didn't know there. So, Russ accosted me about this, [arguing] that I was taking up space in the death house. So, we had this sort of fight that broke down the battle between the chaplaincy service and the Coalition. I wasn't angry with Russ, I was just saying, "No. It's this way. I have known these men since they first came on death row, and that is why they are asking for me. And you don't know them and that is why they are not asking for you."

Russ went away, and thought about that, and then he called me and said, "You're right. Who am I to go down there and carry my little Bible, what is that?" And I said, "That's 'Bible notching' and I am glad you don't want to do it." And so, he asked me, "Can we go in together some time?" I said, "Sure, I go down the day they come and I go down every day." Well, it took him a while—at first he would come in [to the death house] for a little bit. After a while, he really saw what was going on, I think, and he really decided that what I was doing was right.[3]

For Russ, the tension eased and the partnership between him and Marie began after he started advocating with the prison administration on her behalf. "When I first met Marie, I was already supportive of her efforts," explained Russ. "I would say Marie eased up and understood my position better when I pushed the warden and Department of Corrections to give her more access to the men."

Like Marie, Russ also watched over the men of death row. While Marie concentrated on finding the men lawyers, litigating over prisoner's rights, and preparing mitigation reports, often speaking to the men from her Coalition office, Russ was a constant presence on the row. And what he offered the men was unconditional friendship. When I asked Joe Giarratano how Russ differed from other prison chaplains, he replied as follows:

Russ cared about us as individual human beings; he cared about how we were treated, and he had no qualms about taking the DOC to task when mistreatment occurred. Prisoners, generally, and the guys in the row, specifically, trusted Russ. He didn't spend his time trying to convert us; he didn't spend his time trying to save our souls; and he didn't refuse to help us if we weren't interested in religion. His caring was genuine and real. Russ had no agenda other than being there for the individual. His spirituality was truly authentic. He could hold his own with any preacher. If you wanted to talk about the Bible, religion, morality, baseball, poker, or whatever, that is what got talked about. If you had a problem, Russ was there if you called on him. He never violated a confidence. He would sit down and eat with us. If we needed to contact family members, you could count on him.

Russ was unlike those chaplains who couldn't remember our names from week to week, who had no problem with the state killing us, and who would say things like, "We can't concern ourselves with that. We are concerned about your soul. Have you been saved?" Russ, like Marie, wouldn't tolerate that nonsense.

An enraged Russ talking to the press after the August 23, 1991, execution of Derick Lynn Peterson. Russ was furious with prison officials for callously disrupting the minister's final prayer with Peterson. Photograph courtesy of *Richmond Times-Dispatch.*

Ask one of that bunch to send a letter to the governor, or to the director of the DOC, and you would be told, "Sorry, we aren't permitted to do that. That is not our purpose."

Russ not only loved Marie, like we did, but he also tried to always support her in every way that he could, and that alone gained him much respect from prisoners across the board. We loved Russ. Period.

Marie and Russ did not have a religious agenda when working with the men sitting in the death house. "We weren't there to save the men, unless they wanted to be saved," said Russ. Instead they used different approaches and tools to speak to "the different strands within the men to help them prepare to die." Sometimes they told the men stories. Sometimes they told jokes. Sometimes they held hands with the condemned man and sat in silence. Sometimes they sang hymns and prayed.

Preparing the men to be killed did not mean that Marie and Russ wanted the men to give up hope. Instead, they urged the men to be alive and present to the very end. "You tell the men, in advance, that the execution team is going to try to take your heart and put it in their pocket," said Russ. "So we told the men not to let the guards take their heart away. Marie and I used that expression to empower the men." Empowering the men was not what the Department of Corrections wanted. "Comfort was not part of the punishment," explained Russ. "Nor was having the men 'be alive' at the execution." It was especially galling to prison officials that one of the comforters, Marie, was also fighting tooth and nail to save the men from the electric chair. Prison officials started telling new guards that Russ and Marie "were the enemy."

While Marie and Russ provided comfort and support in the condemned men's final hours, they could only walk so far with the men on their final journey. This is best illustrated by the execution of Albert Clozza. The death row inmate was sentenced to death for the rape and murder of thirteen-year-old Patty Bolton, whom Bert had kidnapped as she walked home after visiting a book mobile. Bert resisted efforts by Marie and Russ to reach out to him while on death row, and it was not until his final days in the death house that he asked Russ for religious guidance. "Bert was convicted of one of the most ghastly crimes in Virginia, and on death row he had proven to be a self-absorbed whiner," wrote Marie. "Yet Bert's death watch was miraculous. I have never witnessed such a spiritual awakening."

In the waning minutes of the death watch, Marie, Bert, and the head of the execution squad joined hands as Russ administered the sacraments. Russ thought that Bert began to glow as he received communion. When asked if anyone wanted to say something, the squad leader said: "There are none righteous, oh Lord. No, not one." Bert's attorney, Steve Northup, later said that "it was one of the most profound religious experiences of my life."[4] Russ then accompanied Bert to the death chamber as Marie left the death house.

As Marie and Russ drove home after the execution, Ford was overcome with the memory of staring into Bert's eyes as he was strapped into the electric chair.

> "Russ was crying," Marie recalled. "He was just sobbing and I was holding him and rocking him." [She] told Ford he had been on the banks of the river Styx with Charon the boatman, making sure that Bert had a pence in his shoe to pay his toll across the river. "But I told him he hadn't stayed on the shore that he had crossed over the river with him." Ford knew he had tread into a sacred place. He determined to never again gaze into the eyes of a man as he is being executed.[5]

Of the experience itself, and the effect that it had on Ford, Marie had a simple explanation: "To do this work, I like to tell Russ, you must be a courageous fool."[6]

Years later, Russ still could not explain what he witnessed in Bert's last moments. "I haven't spent time trying to find words for what I saw. The best I can do is go back to *The Divine Comedy*. Virgil led Dante through hell and purgatory but he could only go so far. A guide can go only two-thirds of the way . . . there is a point at which death is a private act, something between you and your Maker."[7] As a testament to how much the experience affected the execution team, one of its members purchased the headstone for Bert's grave.

Russ and Marie did not always reach the inmates. One inmate that Russ said they "failed" was death row inmate Mickey Wayne Davidson, who killed his wife and two young stepdaughters with a crowbar after his wife announced that she was leaving him. Throughout his incarceration Mickey had remained ambivalent about his appeals, and he ultimately decided not to pursue them. Russ wrote:

Mickey Davidson was an alcoholic who bludgeoned to death three innocent family members. While on the row he used alcohol and drugs to self-medicate, but nothing wiped the memory of his victims and what he had done from his mind. Mickey was tormented by voices and claimed to speak with the devil. I spent many hours with Mickey talking through a crack in the steel door of his cell.

Mickey owned his mental condition and sought to silence the voices and be removed from the madness of his mind. Mickey spoke of demon possession and prayed for relief and found it only by having the state assist him in suicide. Mickey was housed in segregation for a long time and went totally insane.

Marie and I assisted Mickey in picking up his appeals several times, but then he would tell the attorney general and his own lawyers that he wanted to be executed. He knew that the courts and the attorney general's office stopped taking his request seriously because of how often he changed his mind. I believe they were looking for reasons to blame Mickey's indecision on me and Marie—like we were interfering with Mickey's death wish through some form of psychological and religious manipulation. The Department of Corrections and the attorney general knew we were working with a demented man, but they were fighting to kill him and saw him being led astray by "those do-gooders, Marie and Russ." To them we were the villains, and they were the good guys protecting Mickey's right to be executed. Marie and I knew he would be killed. We were attempting to help a very troubled man with a death wish. We failed to help him gain his sanity.

Marie and Russ travelled to the new death house at the Greensville Correctional Center in the days before Mickey's first execution date in August of 1992, trying to support the emotionally disturbed man. Their counseling sessions came to a halt when Russ determined that a guard was taping the conversations for the attorney general's office. The eavesdropping "shatter[ed] the trust and rapport" among Marie, Russ, and Mickey.[8] Russ demanded that further meetings take place in the private visiting room, but the frigid temperatures made conversation all but impossible. When Marie and Russ asked for blankets, their request was denied.

After hours of meetings with Marie and Russ, Mickey resumed his appeals and was returned to death row. Marie and Russ were able to delay his execution, but they were never able to pull Mickey back from the abyss of insanity. By the time of Mickey's last execution date in the fall of 1995, neither Marie nor Russ were actively working with the men of the row. Although Marie and Russ stayed in touch with Mickey, they refused to attend his execution because they thought that he was committing suicide with the help of prison officials.

Mickey was killed by lethal injection on October 19, 1995. After being strapped to the gurney, the condemned man declined the offer to make a final statement. "I'll say my last words to the Lord," he said. "I guess that's really all that needs to be said."[9] One could argue that Mickey had some earthly last words as well; he had purchased a burial plot next to his murdered wife and left instruction that he be buried there.

Each death watch touched Marie and Russ. Sometimes they were shaken by a condemned man who went to the chair consumed with denial and fear. Sometimes they were heartened by an inmate who found inner peace or salvation. And sometimes they were angered by the brutality of the death squad and the callous indifference of prison administrators.

The execution of Richard T. "Ricky" Boggs profoundly affected Marie and Russ, and they both wrote accounts about his death watch in their respective unpublished book manuscripts. We have taken their writings and supplemented them with facts contained in the unsuccessful clemency petition drafted by Ricky's lawyers. Our hope is that the following account will be greater than the sum of its parts and that it will provide a window into the most haunting death watch stood by Marie and Russ.

Ricky Boggs was born on September 13, 1962, in Portsmouth, Virginia. Ricky's mother drank during her pregnancy. It was not until his final days in the death house, however, that Ricky was diagnosed with fetal alcohol syndrome. By the sixth grade, Ricky was using alcohol, marijuana, and tobacco on a regular basis. His drug and alcohol abuse continued through high school, with Ricky both smoking and selling pot. Regarding his drug use, Ricky would later tell a psychiatrist, "in comparison to other people, I felt physically smaller and not like the rest of people. I wanted to be accepted by somebody and the drug users accepted me. I never had a girlfriend and I didn't feel worthy of women. Alcohol took the place of people." The psychiatrist concluded that Ricky is "an individual who has very low self-esteem and self-worth through his lifetime. He compensated for this by using drugs and alcohol to excess."[10]

Faced with the prospect of failing out of high school, Ricky dropped out during tenth grade and joined the Army after his eighteenth birthday. His drug and alcohol abuse continued, and Ricky attended three different rehabilitation programs in quick succession. Despite a documented history of significant drug and alcohol addiction, the Army gave Ricky an honorable discharge in the winter of 1983. Ricky promptly returned to live with his parents.

For the next year, Ricky worked at night as a bricklayer and at a company that manufactured swimming pool liners while he took day classes at Tidewater Community College. By all accounts, Ricky did well in his coursework despite spotty class attendance. While Ricky was not drinking as much, he continued to smoke pot regularly. He could not fully shake his addictions.

In the afternoon and early evening of January 25, 1984, Ricky consumed a variety of different drugs—several shots of bourbon, three joints, six beers, and an unknown quantity of speed—before leaving his parents' house. As he exited the residence, Ricky placed a four-inch wide chunk of metal in his pants pocket. At 7:00 p.m., Ricky walked two doors down to the residence of Treeby Shaw, an eighty-seven-year-old widow and a long-time neighbor of the Boggs family. Ricky's father had been close friends with Treeby Shaw's husband, and, after Mr. Shaw's death, the elder Boggs routinely checked on the older woman. Ricky himself had known Mrs. Shaw since childhood, and he had been an altar boy at the Episcopal Church that Mrs. Shaw attended.

Ricky entered the Shaw residence on the pretense that he wanted to borrow a book, but he really wanted to steal money to purchase drugs. Ricky visited with Mrs. Shaw for over an hour as the unsuspecting woman served him three cups of tea. At 8:30 p.m., Boggs suddenly rose and repeatedly hit Mrs. Shaw with the round piece of steel. She fell to the floor. Ricky started looking for valuables but stopped when he heard the ragged breathing of the unconscious and bleeding woman. He walked to the kitchen, grabbed a butcher knife, and stabbed her three times. One of the thrusts pierced Mrs. Shaw's heart, killing her instantly. Ricky's lawyers later claimed that "he heard her struggling to breathe and stabbed her in the side to put her out of misery." Ricky then robbed the dead woman, removing several diamond rings from her fingers and stealing her silver candlesticks and flatware.[11]

News of the murder spread through the tightly knit neighborhood. Ricky was not a prime suspect and was not questioned by the police. The Shaw and Boggs families were so close that Ricky's father was a pallbearer at Mrs. Shaw's funeral. It is unclear whether Ricky himself attended the funeral.

Ricky's drug and alcohol abuse continued in the days following the murder. On February 17, 1984, a drunk Ricky struck and killed a black pedestrian. Ricky fled the scene, only to be followed and arrested by the police. During a routine inventory search of Boggs's blue Volkswagen, police discovered the items stolen from Mrs. Shaw's home. Ricky subsequently confessed to police that he had murdered Mrs. Shaw. Still intoxicated, a weeping Ricky told the police that, "Man it was hard to kill her. The woman was so nice, so kind to me. . . . I really didn't want to kill her, but I needed money for drugs." He then made the following bizarre statement to his interrogators: "I want to kill the enemy on the other side, which is me, the white all over the world. I want to kill niggers."

Ricky's confession, as well as his racial slur, was read into evidence at his trial despite his attorney's objection. Listening to the statement was a jury composed of black and white citizens, who quickly convicted Ricky. For the killing of Mrs. Shaw, Ricky received the death penalty. He was later tried for first-degree murder for the hit-and-run and received a thirty-year sentence. Prior to the deaths of Mrs. Shaw and the pedestrian, Ricky had never been investigated, charged, or convicted for any violent crimes.

Marie first met Ricky in 1984, after he arrived on death row. In her notes, Marie recorded an initial conversation that she had with Ricky Boggs, who she called "Bird."

He was a tiny, bird-like creature. The first time I saw him, I'd brought two very pretty young women from one of the country's largest and most prestigious law firms to death row to interview a number of the inmates about a civil suit. I imagined the men would be completely taken up with ogling these young women.

Bird man was a complete surprise to me. I'd heard that he moved around death row "with his chest poked out like he was something special." Indeed, Bird carried himself like a knob: chest out, shoulders back, chin in. I half expected him to salute the guard when his handcuffs were removed, but he ignored him. After the obligatory handshakes, he also ignored the young women.

He sat down and turned his chair to face me. "I've been waiting to meet you. They told me upstairs that your Mama was murdered."

"My mother-in-law, yes."

"So you know what I did to her [Mrs. Shaw's] family?"

"Will you tell me?"

"Did I ruin their lives forever? Is there any peace for them? If I die, will that be peace for them?"

I searched his eyes for motive. Voyeurism? Did he get off on hurting this family? Did he want to know that he had that much power? What I saw was enormous pain.

"Please," he said. "Do you know what I did?"

And then he told me in detail how he had killed his elderly neighbor. He told me what a good, kind person she had been to everyone in the neighborhood. As he told me, one tear ran down his face. I stared at him. I'm told that my emotions are clearly reflected on my face, but Bird Man didn't flinch from my stare.

"Is that what I am? Is that all I am, a monster?"

"No, Bird. You did a monstrous thing, but the sum total of a human being is not the worst thing they ever did."

"But how can I make up for killing her?

"You can't. No one can."

"Then what should I do?"

"The only thing you can do is try to make the rest of your life meaningful, even here, even under these circumstances."

And that is what Ricky did—work to understand himself and make his life meaningful while he did his time. There were setbacks, and in his first years on the row Ricky succumbed to the escape offered by alcohol and drugs (both readily available on the row) and made one serious suicide attempt. After becoming violently ill from drinking some homemade wine, on December 25, 1986, Ricky vowed to stop using drugs and alcohol. Of his decision to go clean, Ricky wrote the following:

> I had to deal with this problem myself and start dealing with the reality that my drinking was literally killing me. Since I stopped drinking and taking medication, I have been able to face up to reality every day. I am trying my best to understand and cope with life on death row—a life with very little to look forward to. I am dealing with myself, or at least trying, in the best way I can without trying to hide behind a bottle of booze or a shield of drugs.[12]

In the same cathartic passage, Ricky acknowledged other painful truths. "I have to face the fact that I do not have a very good education, something that I am ashamed [of]." Ricky worked hard to overcome his educational deficits, and, in the fall of 1989, he earned a second GED (he had already earned a GED in North Carolina while in the Army). "I want to be among those that choose to do something positive with their lives in prison, even on DR," he explained to a friend.

Ricky's path to self-understanding accelerated once the fog of drugs and alcohol lifted. Russ taught him how to meditate, and Ricky threw himself into the study of hatha yoga. Meditation did not bring Ricky instant peace. "Meditation at first brings the demons forward, later it ushers them out," observes Russ.

Russ discovered that Ricky and a handful of other death row inmates craved a diverse diet of spiritual thinking, and Russ fed their minds.

> The group of men was drowning in their victims' blood. They came in damaged and crazy. The murder, the trial, and coming to death row had been a long whirlwind. They usually were spinning out of control when the murder occurred. Their murders were senseless acts. Something evil got ahold of them. Coming off of the madness took time. They hoped to escape through drugs, legal and illegal, but that only made them stupid. A yearning to understand and to be understood rose from within their nightmare and they reached out. We handed them a line of rope, which guided them out of the labyrinth.

Standing at the bars to the pod area, or talking through the food slots at the individual cells, Russ and the inmates debated a wide range of topics: Christianity, Taoism, Buddhism, Hinduism, Carl Jung, Jesus Christ, Indian shamans, New Age writers, mandalas, medicine wheels, the caves of Qumran, and the Dead Sea Scrolls. Often, the discussions were led by Edward "Fitz" Fitzgerald, a death row inmate whom Russ affectionately described as a "drunk monk." Despite the fact that Fitz enjoyed getting high, he mastered the basic tenets of eastern philosophy and helped the other men understand classic Taoist texts. Fitz was also known on the row for the elaborate soap sculptures that he fashioned of Chinese spiritual leaders, using only his long fingernails as carving tools.

For Russ, studying ancient texts with "wounded, cursed men birthed the peaceful warrior Ricky became, a warrior who directed his battles inward and sought understanding." The man who emerged from years of study, yoga, and meditation was very different from the man who murdered Treeby Shaw in cold blood. Ricky had not forgotten about his crime, and he worried about the effect that his execution would have on his family members. "I am concerned that my friends and relatives are going to suffer more because they in turn will be the victims of my crime," he wrote to his grandmother. And he explained to Marie that he wanted to protect his relatives from the shock of his execution by minimizing their emotional ties.

> I love my relatives, but I do not want to write to them a lot, or at all because I do not want to build up a relationship that will end one day with my death in the Chair. I feel that I will hurt less people if I have not built up years of writing back and forth to all of them. . . . I know that I am guilty, and my relatives do too. It would be great to get off of the ROW, but I honestly feel that it is not going to happen, so the less people that I write, the less people will be hurt by my Death.

Marie holding a soap sculpture created by Virginia death row inmate Edward "Fitz" Fitzgerald. A student of eastern philosophy, Fitzgerald studied classic Taoist texts with other inmates and carved elaborate soap sculptures with his fingernails. Photograph courtesy of Getty Images.

These are not the comments of a remorseless killer. Ricky had found his humanity.

The years passed, appeals were exhausted, and the date with the executioner's chair drew near. While there were small but fleeting legal victories—such as when a federal district court judge overturned Ricky's sentence because his racial comments were read to the jury, only to have the ruling overturned by an appellate court—Ricky, Russ, and Marie knew that time was running out.

Two weeks prior to his execution date, Ricky was transferred to the death house at the Virginia State Penitentiary. That is when a transformation began occurring, a metamorphosis which Marie and Russ did not anticipate. Russ's story begins several days before the execution, after Ricky has been moved from death row to the death house.

Even now, Ricky struggled with the senselessness of the crime, wondering what drove him to such an act. And though at this moment there was another legal battle raging about the cruelty of the electric chair, Ricky knew he was going to die. He was preparing himself to die. Besides constant exercise, he meditated and practiced a limited vegetarian diet of raw tomatoes, onions, carrots, honey, and peanut butter.

In his center cell in the small death house, Ricky was against the back wall standing on his hands and doing pushups. He wore white, state-issue boxer shorts and nothing else. I watched him for a moment without speaking, eating from the little paper cup of ice cream I'd taken from the death house refrigerator in the foyer. At the desk in the center of the aisle, two members of the death squad were into *General Hospital* on the television.

"Ricky," I said.

"Hey, Chaplain." There was not a trace of strain in his voice, although I knew he had probably been doing these pushups for an hour or more. I'd seen him do it. I'd had long sessions with him during which time I never saw him right-side up. He was a short man, not more than five feet four inches tall, and was as lean as someone who had been relentlessly preparing for an athletic event. He had shaved his hair off before he came to the pen. His face was unusual, though, flat with narrow eyes and a widely spaced nose. His head was small and his ears were oddly set.

Ricky moved up and down a few more times, then slowly brought himself back down and stood. Immediately, he began a self-styled Tai-Chi, his arms moving in a graceful and fluid motion, pushing the air around.

"I asked for the granola cereal you and Marie recommended," he said. "Check it out."

I glanced at the bowl on the food tray. "You didn't eat it."

"Look closer. It's alive."

I did. The cereal was full of lively, white larva. "That's right," I said. "You're not a meat-eater."

He smiled, still dancing. He worked his way over to the bars. "Marie was in here an hour ago."

"I know. I just passed her."

"She brought the results of my tests."

"And? What did they say?"

Richard T. "Ricky" Boggs, whose death-house transformation stunned Marie and forced her to decide whether or not to intervene to stop Boggs' execution on the grounds that he was mentally incompetent. Personal collection of Marie Deans.

"*Fetal Alcohol Syndrome. You know what that is?*"

"*Yeah. You seem relieved about this.*"

"*I guess this explains it,*" *Ricky said.* "*But it doesn't excuse it. You know, if I hadn't been caught, I could have hurt others.*"

"*Yeah,*" *I said.*

There was a pencil behind my ear; I pulled it out and passed it through the bars. Ricky took it and pressed it gently between his hands. During the psychological testing several days ago, he had become intrigued with the wood around a portable chalkboard. He had stopped in the middle of one test, closed his eyes, and felt the frame with his index and middle fingers, moving with the grain of wood. When asked by the psychologist why he had done this, Ricky said he'd not touched wood for a very long time. Now, whenever I visited him, I would bring little bits of wood to him.

From beyond the cell area, there was a loud clack and thump, then the distinct, high-pitched whine of electricity as it was fired through to check the voltage to the chair. I could see Ricky flinch. One of the guards at the desk scraped his plastic chair abruptly against the floor as though trying to drown out the hum.

"*Whoa, they been doing that for hours,*" *Ricky said.* "*Drove Marie up the wall. I'm not sure how I'm going to handle it.*"

"*No one is. They didn't write a user's guide.*"

Ricky laughed. Then he rubbed his hands down the length of his arms as if he had a chill.

"*If you fight the chair it will tear you apart. Somehow you have to just let yourself go with the flow.*"

"*Yeah?*" *Ricky spun away, his body swaying with the flow of the electric hum next door. Then he came back to the bars. He said,* "*Bill Jones talked with me about doing a communion service with my mom and dad on the last day. I'm not sure I want to do it. They'll just get upset. It would be the last time we're together. I know what I'm doing. I don't need something that might make it worse for them and harder for me.*"

"*Give it some thought,*" *I said.* "*Your mother is the one who suggested it. But it's your call.*"

Ricky agreed to think it over, then he went silent again, stepping away, his eyelids lowered, his mouth slack, his hands caressing the spaces before him.

Outside the death house, I paused on the steps, looked around to make sure no one was watching, then moved my own hands through the air, trying to grab for whatever it was Ricky had discovered.

In the second selection from Russ's manuscript, it is now approximately ninety minutes before the execution. Russ and Marie are with Ricky in the death house.

He had been prepped, his bald head shining with a fresh cut, and a patch of his right leg shaved. He was moving slowly around the perimeter of the holding cell, eyes still closed, wearing only boxer shorts, the jeans and Velcro-button shirt lying on the cot. His hands were on the wall, touching the surface in feather light strokes. He didn't appear to be aware of anyone's presence in the room and made no acknowledgement of Bill, Marie, and me as we came in and stood before his cell door. Guards Harper and Mullings gave me a look that said, "What the hell do we do now?"

We watched silently until the lawyer, who had been standing near the guard's desk, came over and said, "We could do a Ford on Ricky."

I shook my head. A Ford was a court order, declaring a man mentally incompetent to be executed. It might delay the execution, but they would only drug him up, bring him back in three months, and we'd be facing this night all over again. Besides, Ricky was not psychotic. "I don't think that's a good idea," I said. "He's not sick. These are not hallucinations."

"Ricky's worked too hard to put him through this again," said Marie.

"And there's something else going on here," I said. The lawyer shrugged and returned to stand by the guard's desk.

Ricky circled the cell twice more. His fingers probed the wall as if decoding some esoteric message. A bond had formed between Ricky and the ancient walls.

Marie bent to my ear. "When he came back from the service [baptism] and visited with his parents this afternoon, did you notice something strange about his appearance?"

My mouth went dry. I had, but I thought it was just me. "What do you mean?"

Marie took a long drag on her Virginia Slim. She looked at Bill then back at me. "He was so glad you did the service. He showed me where you anointed him on his forehead and I could have sworn he was glowing."

I answered, "I could have sworn it, too."

Bill nodded uncertainly.

Ricky came back around to the front of the cell and I said to Marie, "Why don't you reach in and touch him?"

Marie dropped her cigarette to the floor and pressed it out with the toe of her shoe, then walked over to the bars and reached in. As Ricky passed their hands touched. Instantly, Ricky was anchored. In the same gentle motions he'd used with the wall, he took Marie's hands and moved them across the top of his head and down along this shoulders. I came over beside Marie. Ricky reached out, never opening his eyes, and found my hands. He brought them in and they joined with Marie's and his.

In the minutes that followed, our hands merged, we were weaving a fabric of intimate energy with a life of its own. I could not distinguish between my hands and that of Marie's or Ricky's. Bill pulled a chair over and slid it under Marie. When she sat the rigid bars forced my arms over her, bringing my chest across her lap. Ricky moved down as we did, setting himself on his knees firmly against the concrete floor. His hands came in and joined ours.

Ricky spoke. "Do you see the colors?"

"What do they look like?" I asked.

"They're lavender and blue. I want you to see them." His voice was calm and clear. Although I didn't see them, I knew he did. I angled my face upward and looked at Ricky. Around his head and shoulders was a yellowish glow. Much like the glow I'd seen after the service, only more pronounced now. The four of us remained together, sharing in Ricky's last forty minutes.

Harper tapped my leg. "It's time to go," he whispered.

I could hear the squad coming in. Carefully, we disengaged. I had a hard time standing; the circulation had been cut off in my legs. The squad assembled near the cell, and Johnson banged on the bars, barking, "Put the clothes on! Now!"

Ricky stood but didn't put on the clothes.

"Put the clothes on! Now!"

Ricky's right eye came open and he looked at me.

I motioned my hand and said, "Just move with it, Ricky."

With the same easy movements we'd seen over the past fifteen days, Ricky dressed.

Marie's account of standing watch begins moments after Russ's story ends, as Ricky puts on his clothes and the death squad moves into position.

Metal rasping against metal and the steel door slams against the concrete wall. My body jerks. The adrenalin tastes sour. My heart beats to the execution squad's boots whomping the floor in unison. Quick step. Quick step. Their nametags and ranks are covered with duct tape against their black uniforms. Are we suddenly supposed to forget their names and ranks? Chosen in part for their size, they form a thick, impenetrable wall. Another black uniform blurs into my peripheral vision. An arm comes out and moves me aside. Oddly, it is gentle. I hear him murmur, but I don't hear the words. Is there a footnote for those words in the procedures manual?

The wall parts at the door of Cell One, leaving a path to Ricky. The warden appears in the doorway and walks up the path with a piece of paper in his hand. He clears his throat and begins to read the death warrant. I move closer to the bars of the cell next to Ricky's so he can see me. He turns his head, opens his eyes, and gives me a mournful smile. The warden stumbles over the words authorizing the Department of Corrections to "carry out the order of the court." Ricky closes his eyes. The warden asks that Ricky's soul be blessed, turns, and leaves the death house.

I hear the key slam into the cell door lock and see the top of the cell door swing from one side of the phalanx to the other. A shiver goes through Ricky's body, and his facial muscles tense. I call his name, and he nods. Hands reach out and pull him from the cell into the path. Then the path and Ricky disappear as the wall solidifies. Once again the whomping quick step, quick step. I listen for Ricky's normal footsteps, crane my head to see him within the wall, but there is only the wall and the triumphant quick step pounding the floor and my chest.

Suited DOC officials move away from the door in a ragged line as the black mass stomps lockstep into the death chamber.

From my left comes a woman in a navy blue suit, crouched over, a stopwatch in her hand. She is whispering into the watch. Another woman, Conga line like behind her, repeats the whispers into a walkie-talkie. The women walk past me and follow the wall into the death chamber. The male suits bunch up again in front of the door, but they make a little room as I come up beside them.

The phalanx is now before the chair. It is crude, heavy, dark, waiting. I remember the other men I've seen go to the electric chair. As if truly there, they appear one by one, their bodies arch, and then they disappear—zapped out of existence.

Ricky is regurgitated out of the black mass into the chair. The guards swarm around him. Right arm, left arm. Right ankle, left ankle. Chest. Each guard has his job. "I am right ankle." Done in concert. Mechanical. What covers over their souls like the tape over their nametags?

Ricky is so small trussed into the oak throne. His hands are delicate, pale against the coarse, dark grain of the wood. He lifts his fingers, as far as they will go, one by one they rise and fall back onto the wood, as if he is tapping out a message. Russ, the chaplain, is there, touching Ricky, saying something. What does Ricky hear, see, feel? I want him to see the lights he has been seeing all night—the beautiful green lights that made his face glow, that only he saw. The mask goes down over his head. I feel the rough leather as if it is against my face. I am gone even from his peripheral vision now, and I step back, feel the steel door against my heel, move further back, back, back, away from the door framing Ricky in the chair, to the steel bars of Cell One.

The suits are looking at me. I search their eyes, but there is nothing there. No regret, no sadness. Just dispassionate eyes. They are used to watching people be killed. It is, as they keep telling me, "simply part of the job." I can't look away from their eyes. What happens to human beings when horror becomes routine?

I cradle the envelope of Ricky's possessions hard against my chest so my heart won't explode. I expect the concrete floor to crack open, the creatures of the underworld to appear, dripping with Faustian slime. Surely they will come for all of us.

A scream! Was that me? No. Then a loud click, a mechanical huffing and the drone of the converter. It grows louder, overbearing, a sound that becomes pressure inside my skull and rib cage. It goes on and on. It fills the death chamber, moves into the death house, my head, my chest with building pressure. I don't know if I can contain it.

Sudden quiet outside of me. Did they kill him? Is he still alive? I want to go to him and take a step toward the door. No. "I will be there, Ricky. You'll know I'm there. As long as I can see your face, I'll be there. But I won't watch them kill you. When the mask goes on, I'll step away."

"I'll know," he had told me. "I'll know."

I caress the envelope. "I'm still here, Ricky."

No expression on the suits' faces. They simply stand there, waiting. One rocks back on his heels. My God. Let him be dead. There is no air moving, nothing moves but the eyes of the suits, back to me. Why do they keep looking at me? Have I become part of their ritual, or are they part of my nightmare? I close and open my eyes, but they are still there. My heart is pounding against my chest, some separate thing in me trying to get out. Do they hear it, see it?

The click, then the converter again. I'm shaking hard enough to lose my balance and fall against the cell bars. The drone moves outside my head again. Louder. It goes on, slowly eating the space around me and in me. This is an eternity. Penny. I clamp my teeth. NO! Don't go there. This is not Penny. This is Ricky. I can't breathe. The smell of Ricky's flesh is smothering me. I push against the bars for support.

"Marie! Marie!" I rush toward his voice. "I'm here, Russ. I'm here." The outside door is thrown open. Russ pulls me out. We jog up the steps. Into the night air, back into the administration building, still jogging, but in place, waiting for the steel doors to open and close behind us. Now another set of doors, and we're through. We reach the inside steps and collapse.

"They almost killed me," Russ says. "I still had my arms around him. They were in such a hurry they almost killed me!"

"Was that you who screamed?"

"No, that was Bair [the warden]. He saw me. He saw I was still holding Ricky. If he hadn't seen me . . ."

A woman from the prison staff leans over us. "Are you all right?"

I look up at her. "Are we supposed to be all right?" She backs away. Russ is still talking. I know he will hit anyone else who comes near us. "Can you stand up now?" I ask him.

"I think so."

"Let's try. I have to get out of here."

We stand up, checking ourselves as if our bones may have turned to ash or our joints won't remember how to work. Maybe both our hearts will burst when we try to get out. We hold on to each other, stumbling through the hallway and out the door.

The tower lights have turned the night sulfuric yellow. We gulp air, but it is too close to the prison to be clean. Further. We have to get further away. The blocked off street is deserted. We can hear muffled noises from the vigil on the side street, but we turn away from the noise and head for my car.

How long did we huddle in the car smoking cigarettes—Russ raving, me totally quiet, shaking—until we had braced ourselves enough to go to Ricky's parents?

They were in a motel somewhere. How did we find it, get into the room? I remember Ricky's mom grabbing me, hugging me, holding on to me. Like Ricky, she was so little. Her body quivered. Her hair looked like Penny's, the same color and length. I sat beside her on the bed. I can still feel her small hand gripping mine. She kept thanking me for staying with her son, saying they wouldn't let her *be there. How did she bear it? I wanted to cradle her. I wanted to give him back to her. I failed her so. I failed them all.*

Ricky's ashes were buried in his grandfather's grave. He always needed someone to take care of him.

Marie believed that Ricky was psychotic in his final hours of life, and she later questioned her decision not to try to halt the execution. "Marie's instincts were to stop executions," Russ explained, "and her decision cut against those instincts. But I thought that she acted courageously." There was no guarantee that a lawyer could have convinced a judge to intervene, and, even if the execution was halted, Ricky would have been returned to the death house once he was pumped full of psychotropic drugs. And Ricky did not want any further attempts to obtain a stay of execution. Whether psychotic or not, Ricky had found his peace.

The sights, sounds, and smells of Ricky's execution haunted Marie for years. Marie lived in an apartment that had an aging air conditioner that came to life with a mechanical groan and an audible "click." Whenever she heard these sounds, Marie had a momentary surge of adrenalin and dread—suddenly finding herself thrust back into the death chamber with Ricky Boggs.

7

Inside the Vortex of Evil

> [Russ] calls the death chambers the "vortex of evil"
> and you feel that when you are in the death house,
> because it is banal, it is incredibly banal.
> —Marie Deans, 1989

In our rambling conversations around Marie's wooden kitchen table, Marie and I talked in depth about a wide range of issues involving capital punishment. The death house, however, was not typically one of those topics. Whenever the conversation edged close to the death house, the normally talkative Marie fell silent as the shadows of what she called the "vortex of evil" drew near.

While Marie could speak in generalities about being in the death house (how many men she visited, how the death house was configured, the rodents, and the basic rules and procedures in the death house), the time that she spent standing "death watch" with the men was holy and difficult to discuss for Marie—a ritual that had been sanctified by blood, and death, and moments of grace. "The emotional impact of being moved to the death house is extreme," Marie explained in a letter to a colleague. "A human being is immediately and forcefully involved in the ritual of his own pre-determined death. Everything moves toward the state killing, and that movement looks like a freight train gathering speed and bearing down on you while you are tied down to the tracks."

There is a method to the madness surrounding the rituals and procedures of the death house. The men of Virginia's death row are transferred to the death house approximately two weeks prior to their execution, and there they are monitored as they prepare for their final walk to the death chamber. A special team of guards arrives with the prisoner. Handpicked by the warden for their large size, their express goal is to keep the prisoner alive and calm until the execution. Every telephone call the inmate makes—every visit to the toilet the inmate takes—is noted and logged. While it may sound bizarre, more than one Virginia inmate has been placed on suicide watch in the death house because corrections officers did not want the inmate to kill himself and "escape" punishment. "They keep you safe and make sure you don't hurt yourself so they can do it," commented death row inmate Derick "Baydar" Peterson. "Pretty sick. It's the system. They're like, 'No, let us do it.'"[1]

In the last hours of an inmate's life, a special set of rituals takes place. "Their belongings are boxed up. Their heads and right legs are shaved, and they are showered and given a special set of clothes to wear for their executions," stated Marie. "They are moved to a stripped down holding cell and given a final meal of their choice. Then conductor gel [is] applied to their heads and right legs." The final result of these rituals is that a human being is turned "into a conductor of electricity."

The rituals of the death house produce a compliant and broken man as his freedom and identity are completely stripped away. By the final evening of his life, his last meal is seldom eaten because, in the words of one death squad officer, "food is the last thing they got on their minds."[2] Packing up their belongings can bring even the most hardened con to tears, as their remaining worldly possessions are ripped away from them. And the shaving of the head is the last step. Although the removal of hair makes for a more effective transfer of electricity from electrode to human flesh, it also has the benefit of robbing the inmate of his very identity. A prison guard explains:

> When you get to the point of shaving a man's head, that usually will take just about all the strength a man has out of him. It's not long before he actually becomes a walking dead man. Because he knows that there is no more hope after that point . . . like when Delilah cut Samson's hair, that was it. It took all his strength. There was nothing left.[3]

The condemned man is weighed, photographed, and placed in the "death cell"— an empty cell closest to the death chamber. All that is left is for the warden to appear and read the death warrant. "They have devised a process so that when the time comes, the man walks up to the electric chair and allows them to strap him in it without a fight," Marie said. "The prisoners have the weight of a whole society bearing down on them."[4]

Most of the executions Marie attended were in the "old" death house located in the basement of A building at the Virginia State Penitentiary. The first execution in the death house occurred in 1908, when twenty-two-year-old Henry Smith had the misfortune of becoming the first inmate executed in the new electric chair. The Virginia Department of Corrections was pleased with their killing machine, and a Virginia Penitentiary doctor praised the electric chair as "a swift, sure, solemn, and awe-inspiring mode of punishment, and to my mind is infinitely more humane than hanging."[5] Of course, nobody could ask Henry Smith what he thought. Nor could they ask the other 245 men and one woman electrocuted between 1908 and 1962.

By the time Marie first went to the old death house in 1983, it was a decrepit and claustrophobic facility groaning under the weight of its own bloody history. Russ Ford once accompanied a group of prison reformers on a tour of the Virginia State Penitentiary. Russ's description of that tour, and the behavior of a member of the execution team that guided the group through the death house, is chilling.

It was no secret that the Virginia State Penitentiary in Richmond was considered the most dangerous and corrupt in the state. The Department of Corrections wasn't high on letting the public know, but the public knew. The place was ancient, some of the buildings one hundred years old and failing fast. Incidents of stabbings, beatings, and murders had been escalating; riots and lockdowns had become routine. The human slave trade boomed. Drugs and weapons were readily available. If the local media ever found themselves lacking for action-packed news, there was always something happening at the pen.

The Department of Corrections had talked for years about closing the place down, but there was always a reason they needed to keep the place running just a little bit longer. Men in Cell House B were double-bunked, crammed into cells just large enough for one man. Cell House A had been condemned but then, out of necessity, reopened. The old metal shop in the back of the complex had been converted to a dorm structure for additional prisoners. Beds stood side by side down long rows, and men rambled around with no programs and little super-vision. Few guards would put themselves at risk [by going into] the metal shop dorm.

This was the situation when a national task force from Presbyterians USA came to tour the prison. The trip through the administration building was quick, and then it was down to Cell House A's basement and the death house. We were greeted at the door by corrections officer James Johnson (not his real name). I knew the moment I saw him that he intended to thoroughly enjoy his chance to perform. He was carrying the wooden riot attack stick he used when confronting high school students in the prison's "Scared Straight" program. He made a point of letting the cluster of keys on his hip jangle as he walked. His white shirt with its gold badge was just a bit too tight on his arms and chest. In his free time, he pumped iron in the guards' lounge next door.

"Glad to show you folks around," he quipped. He smiled and led us into the cell area, all the while explaining the difficult job of keeping a man in line during his last fifteen days. The team listened intently, with only a few asking simple, clarifying questions.

The death house was a small portion of Cell House A's basement. It had nine steel cells, a shower and bathroom, the execution chamber, and a cool-down room. This part of the prison had been built around the turn of the century, so nothing was soundproof. When the chair was tested, everyone knew it. The hum came right through the chamber walls into the room with the cells so intense it would stand your arm hairs on end. Occasionally, rats ran through the cell aisle, escapees from the sewer beneath the prison. The cockroaches here were big enough to scare a pigeon.

At the far end of the cell aisle were two windows over which blue sheets would be draped on execution nights in case someone happening along Spring Street might decide to sneak over the stretch of grass, kneel down, and take a peek. The walls of the death house were painted in standard, institutional puke green.

Johnson led us into the execution chamber. The Presbyterians gazed at the dismal walls of the small room, the witness box, the metal-hooded lights and the chair. Johnson then strolled up to the electric chair, sat down, and draped his leg over the arm. He slouched back and wiggled his eyebrows.

"Let me tell you about electrocution. We bring our man in, struggling and fighting lots of times." The riot stick in his hand alternately poked at the air and smacked the wooden platform on which the chair sat. "We get him down, strap him in: ankles, chest, arms. Put on the helmet, which has a sea sponge on it that's been soaked for nearly a day in saline so it'll carry the charge good. Put on the mask so his eyes don't fall out to his lap." Johnson tipped his head back and laughed. The team was silent.

"That spot over there on the column is where the warden turns the key. The green light over it comes on, letting the executioner in the switch room know its time. He's peeking out that little hole in the back wall. He flicks the switch and the juice flows. Two thousand five hundred volts for 55 seconds. Then again. Two thousand five hundred for 55 seconds. The man's blood boils. His joints fuse together. Ain't that something?"

No one answered.

"We get 'em pretty regular now. Remember Morris Mason back in '85? He was fried here. Good riddance. He raped two girls and beat 'em up bad," said Johnson. He smacked his lips. "Mason then raped an old woman, put her in a chair and hit her with an axe. Then he set her house on fire and burned her up. Killed her. Some people tried to stop him from getting his. Tried to talk the governor into letting him live. But he was a real monster." Johnson paused, then brightened. He hopped from the chair, whirled his hand and said, "Come on, got more to show you."

The team was shown through the back door of the chamber to the cool-down room, where a stretcher and sandbags waited for the next man. The stretcher was to roll the man out to the ambulance; sandbags helped straighten fused joints so the body could fit more neatly into the body bag.

I was more than ready to leave the death house as we came out of the cool-down room, when Johnson said, "There's one more thing!" Across the hall from the cool-down room was the switch room. This private space from which the executioner would watch for the green light go-ahead reminded me of a walk-in closet, big enough to house one person, the equipment, and not a whole lot more. I had never known this room to be shown during a tour, so I was surprised when Johnson unlocked the door and turned on the light.

"Switch room," he said. I went inside behind him, along with another man. There was no room for anyone else. The rest of the team stood outside the door, peering in.

Johnson pointed out the tiny window the executioner used to see into the chamber. He pointed out the mechanisms, the switch. Then he pulled a wooden lock box from a shelf and with yet another key from the mass on his belt, he opened it.

"Look," he said, holding up the death mask so the old man could see. "See

The death chamber at the old Virginia State Penitentiary, including the electric chair and the witness room. Under Virginia law, up to six citizens can serve as witnesses at an execution. Some Virginians have signed up to watch multiple executions, including a business owner from Emporia, Virginia, who has attended a dozen executions. The electric chair was built in 1909 by prison inmates, and it has sent 265 men and one woman to their deaths. Photograph courtesy of *Richmond Times-Dispatch*.

here, where these bulges are in the leather? That's where the man's eyes try to pop out from the pressure!" He grinned and put the mask on the shelf, then pulled out the helmet. He turned it over in his hands and stared inside. He laughed suddenly and abruptly. "There's a piece of Alton Waye still in here!"

He tipped the helmet so we could see. There, clinging to the metal and sponge inside, was a charred piece of meat. A piece of burned scalp.

The man beside me recoiled. My stomach clenched in disgust and shock. Alton Waye had been executed just weeks earlier.

"Piece of Alton," Johnson repeated as if savoring the discovery. He put the mask and helmet back into the lock box.

I escorted the team out of the death house and back to the Yard.

In the coming years, Marie and Russ would be appalled by Johnson's petty and cruel behavior toward the men in the death house.

Marie stayed with the men until moments before they were led from the death cell to the death chamber. These final tension-filled hours left an indelible mark on Marie, both physically and spiritually. "I never went to the death house unless the men asked," Marie once explained to Russ Ford. "If the man wanted me there, he asked for me and I went. It just turned out that all the men did want me. J. B. [Briley] called [from the death house] and said, 'Where the hell are you?' I said, 'Well, you haven't said you wanted me.' He [replied], 'Why do I have to say I want you. You know I want you down here.'" Marie would honor the wishes of the men, but it came at a price. "I hate the death house. It's like a tomb. It's uncanny. It gives me the willies. . . . I always come out of there feeling filthy."[6] Often before entering the death house, she paused, steeled herself, and whispered a mantra: "Go through the fear."[7]

Marie never watched the moment of death. She was frankly relieved to be spared the shock of watching the men being cooked to death as over two thousand volts shot through their bodies.

> I'd be there with them in the cells. The team would come get him and take him into the chair, and I would walk over to the door [of the death chamber]. Usually there were a bunch of suits there from the administration. They would move a little bit so I could see. The leg irons—the leg restraints and arm restraints go on first. Then the mask was pulled down. They can't see through that mask. My preference was to be with him as long as I could be with him, [but] not to witness the execution itself. Not to give a stamp of approval or something to the execution. So, when he could no longer see me, I would back away back into the [death house] cell.

"Most of the guys have made me promise that I would never witness an execution," Marie explained. "They have a lot of strong feelings about that. They don't want people who don't want to kill them to see an execution . . . I've seen enough of them in my dreams," concluded Marie. "I don't need to see them."[8]

The images in Marie's dreams were informed by the stories she heard of botched executions. This included former policeman Frank Coppola, whose execution in 1982 was the first to be held in Virginia in twenty years. Although the electric chair had been re-wired and its rotting leather straps replaced, the execution did not proceed as planned.

> Coppola received two separate jolts of electrical current, each lasting about fifty-five seconds. The second jolt produced flames, smoke, and burning flesh when Coppola's leg became inflamed. During the second application of current, smoke began to flow from Mr. Coppola's head and leg. Soon, flames erupted from Coppola's leg near the site of the leg electrode. This flame and smoke continued until the current was turned off. [His attorney stated] "I observed smoke rising to the ceiling in sufficient amounts to fill the entire death chamber with a smoky haze. . . . Although I was in an isolated booth with other witnesses separated from the death chamber by glass and wall, I could smell an acrid odor that I assume was the smell of burning flesh. During the second application of current, a sizzling sound could be heard that sounded like cooking flesh . . . Shortly after Mr. Coppola's leg caught on fire, the Commonwealth turned the current off. Within minutes, a medical examiner pronounced Mr. Coppola dead.[9]

One of the prison officials who struggled to remove Coppola from the electric chair was a former military corpsman, and even he was affected by the sight of the burned

Former Virginia death row inmate Wilbert Evans. Chaplain Russ Ford believes that Evans' execution was botched and that Evans was tortured. Photograph courtesy of *Richmond Times-Dispatch*.

Coppola lying in the stretcher with his arms and legs "locked up" as if he was still in the chair. As the guards carried Coppola's body out of the death house, a prisoner's voice called out: "You all are killers."[10]

Virginia continued to have trouble with the electric chair in subsequent years, although the Department of Corrections staunchly maintained that there were never any botched executions in its death house. In 1990, the execution of Wilbert Evans at the old Virginia State Penitentiary proved especially gruesome. It is a memory burned into Russ's psyche. He wrote:

> There was the hum as the electricity was turned on. A woman screamed, "Oh, my God," I glanced to my side and saw a member of the death squad grimace and shake his head. Behind me, I heard a groan and then a burst of sound much like that of steam escaping a pressure cooker, loud and hissing as if a kettle was about to explode. I looked. Blood was streaming from beneath the death mask, running down Wilbert's chin and dripping to his chest. The shirt was drenched in scarlet. The cloth was saturated, adhering to his skin and revealing the shape of his twitching body. A puddle was forming on the floor beneath the chair. His mouth was pinched and twisted along the base of the death mask. Spittle shot upward from his lips, and the air forced from his burning body caused the terrible whistle.
>
> The second jolt was administered. Several of the witnesses covered their faces. One sobbed and ranted uncontrollably. When the current shut off, we all stood watching as the drips continued to splash. Five minutes later, Wilbert was pronounced dead and we were allowed to leave.

In the days after Wilbert's execution, prison officials offered a litany of excuses for what happened in the electric chair. A nosebleed triggered by Wilbert's head jerking when the first charge hit him. A death mask that was too small. High blood pressure caused by Wilbert's final meal of pigs' feet. One prison official actually conceded that Wilbert might have been in pain. "Well, that's possible. When you touch a circuit you're going to feel a little something."[11]

The Virginia Department of Corrections, however, steadfastly maintained that the electric chair worked perfectly. "We know it didn't [malfunction] because there was no need to administer any additional surge of electricity . . . the machines involved operated properly . . . different people react differently."[12] And, of course, different people have different definitions of what constitutes torture. Later, the Department of Corrections would release multiple documents related to the maintenance of the electric chair—including the startling fact that a local sales and service branch of General Electric performed routine maintenance of the chair.

Even when the electric chair performed perfectly, it inflicted terrible wounds on the men. Russ Ford recalled that J. B. Briley was "torn to pieces" when the electricity coursed through his body, and his contracting muscles pulled against the restraints. When former marine Timothy Bunch was executed, Marie recalled that the electricity left "ghastly red holes in his eyelids. Like a bullet had come out—an exit wound."

In 1991, the electric chair was moved to its new home at the Greensville Correctional Center. The old death house was scheduled for demolition, although Marie commented that Virginia "ought to leave it [standing], like Dachau."[13] Before being installed in the death chamber, the chair was re-wired and prison officials adopted a new practice of administering a single jolt of electricity to the condemned man. Derick Lynn Peterson was the second inmate executed in the refurbished chair. A short, slight young black man who had grown up in the projects, Derick ended up on death row for the shooting of a grocery store manager during a robbery. Derick was one of the six men who escaped from death row in 1984, but was arrested twenty-four hours later as he and fellow inmate Earl Clanton drank wine and ate cheese in front of a North Carolina laundromat. Derick became very close to Marie in the years after the escape, referring to her as his "second mother."

Even before Derick was taken into the death chamber, Russ was enraged because the loud laughing and gawking from prison officials had disrupted Russ's efforts to administer the sacraments to Derick. Perhaps buoyed by Russ's emotion, Derick defiantly read his last statement after being strapped into the electric chair.

> I wore a mask long before this one goes on.
>
> I've never picked cotton or lived in a little dirty hut, but I and all blacks young and old feel the pain and oppression that they suffered then still today.
>
> I hope that my death finds in some way to open our eyes to this legal murder, because we all know that this chair is made out of the same tree that we once were hanged from.
>
> The hovels of the plantation are no different than the hovels of the projects.

The strikes of the overseers were no different from the strikes of the electricity that you will send through my body.

If I thought that you can hurt me anymore, I would not be so calm, so strong, but that the people that are really being hurt are the ones left behind and they the blacks of this land need to speak out and stand for no more of this madness . . .

To the surprise of corrections officials, the first jolt of electricity did not kill Derick. Seven minutes passed as Derick's heart continued to beat. A second jolt was administered, and another five minutes elapsed before Derick's body sufficiently cooled for the doctor to determine that his heart had finally stopped. Again, the Department of Corrections challenged any claim of inhumane treatment. "He was brain dead, there was no question about that," Virginia Department of Corrections Director Edward W. Murray confidently declared. "We're dealing with brand new equipment. . . . I think you have to make adjustments as you use the equipment."[14] As for Marie, she was distraught when she learned of the botched execution.

While Marie did not see the actual executions, she explained that she could still feel and smell the electrocution while standing in the death house:

If you could imagine a rather big, older [machine]—like a big air conditioner—turning on and then sitting on a concrete slab. You're on the same slab. You can feel the vibrations. What you hear also sounds like an industrial air conditioner coming on. It's that kind of revving up and then this sort of loud grinding [sound]. Then, it's done twice [the electrocution] so I don't know how long it goes on. It feels like an hour. It feels like it's inside you. I don't know if it's the vibration plus the sound, but it feels like it's in your chest and it's pushing against the chest like your chest is going to burst. I don't know what causes that but maybe it's a combination of the sound and the vibration. It's like it's sucking all the air out. Then it's gone and then it comes back again.

[And] it does smell like burning. When I was a young girl, maybe twelve or so, there was a terrible fire in Charleston right down from my dad's store. Everybody left their stores and went down to the fire. As soon as we started walking toward it we knew that people had been burned in that fire. My dad turned around and brought me back. But I've never forgotten that smell. It smells—I don't know how to define it—but it smells like burning flesh.

The trauma did not end when Marie exited the death house. The Virginia Penitentiary was located in downtown Richmond, and executions often drew a crowd of death penalty supporters and opponents. The first execution Marie attended was the execution of Linwood Briley, a notorious death row inmate whose killing spree across Richmond, Virginia, had landed both himself and his brother, J. B., on death row. Linwood's celebrity increased after a death row prison break in the spring of 1984, when Linwood and J. B. managed to elude a dragnet for a month.

As Marie left the death house shortly before Linwood was electrocuted, she

Pro death penalty protesters outside of the Virginia State Penitentiary during the execution of Linwood Briley. Photographs courtesy of *Richmond Times-Dispatch*.

found herself in the middle of a surreal scene. Police had divided the crowd into two different camps, with the demonstrators on one side of Belvidere Street and the death penalty advocates on the other. Police officers stood between the two groups. As opponents of the death penalty held candles and sang, on the opposite side of the street supporters waved Confederate flags and held up signs reading "Fry the Coon," "Kill the Negro," and "Burn, Briley, Burn."[15]

Looking over the teeming mob, Marie spotted her ten-year-old son, Robert, yelling at a group of protestors. Wading into the crowd, Marie dragged her crying son back to safety and held him as death penalty supporters yelled, "Fry the son of a bitch." "I'm glad it's happening, honey," a bystander told a reporter. "As a taxpayer, I'm tired of paying for his room and board." Inside the death chamber, a prison doctor named Robert Fry pronounced Linwood dead after the electricity raced through Linwood's body and the scent of burning flesh permeated the death chamber. The announcement of Linwood's death was met with a thunderous cheer and the crackle of fire crackers, and a death penalty supporter yelled, "He's gone, brother . . . he's gone to hell and got burned."[16]

Standing death watch took a physical and mental toll on Marie. Sometimes she and Russ would return to the Coalition office to smoke, drink coffee, and cry. At other times, they would be unable to talk about the execution. And in the days after the execution, Marie would be stricken with crippling migraines, which drove her to a darkened bedroom until the pain subsided.

One fascinating aspect of Marie's work on death row, and in the death house, is that it extended not only to the inmates, but some of the corrections staff as well. Not surprisingly, prison insiders like Marie and Russ saw the toll that executions took on the executioners. What is surprising is that Marie reached out to the very men who were operating the machinery of death.

When Marie started becoming involved with specific death penalty cases in the early 1980s, she found herself struggling to understand how prison officials and corrections officers voluntarily took part in the killing of human beings. "I began wanting desperately to understand people who could work for and carry out executions," Marie wrote. "I thought there must be something we could say to them to make them see what they were doing. I thought if I could understand, maybe I wouldn't come to hate them."[17] Over time, Marie believed that she did understand the executioners.

> I did not come to hate these agents of state killing, these surreal priests of death. I came to understand them, and when I did, I let go of my informed dread. I let go, because I realized that what I had feared most of my life was already here. These people are no different than most. They are basically decent people, and basically decent people will follow orders. Just do their jobs and not interfere. They will tell themselves it is all right, because they are killing just murderers, and it is the law, and it is good for society, and it must be done. . . . Tomorrow they may kill the retarded and mentally ill who haven't murdered, and they will tell themselves that, too, is all right and for the good of society. Whoever they kill, the killings

never have and never will have anything to do with the good of society or any other rationalization they give. They have to do with our fear of death.[18]

Marie also acknowledged the pressures faced by the members of the execution team. "I feel very sorry for these men and women. . . . They've gotten trapped in our ugly doings, and it is hurting them in ways some of them don't even realize. What is surprising is how good some of these men and women are, how they have maintained their humanity, how long some stay because they don't want to turn the men over to brutal officers and administrators and instead stay to protect and offer what comfort they can." Marie added that a few of the execution team members found solace in religion. "One said he felt he was doing these guys a favor because he was helping them go to God. Some carry Bibles into the death house and sit there reading them."[19]

"Getting to know someone and then putting your hands on them and taking them into a place and setting them down and being a part of a machine that takes their life takes a physical and emotional toll," explained Russ. "Doesn't the average person think that if somebody went out and hooked up electricity to another person and then watched them cook—I mean smelled their body and then handled that body, you know, put it in a body bag, take and put it in a hearse and then drive it out of the facility—that somehow they'd be affected by doing that? The chemistry in your body is altered by what you've seen."[20]

Russ added that some of the execution team falsely claimed that they were not affected by the executions. "What you hear is a lot of people blocking that. . . . I think there was a lot of denial. Of course, some of these people didn't think they were affected at all. I remember one man who was on the team said he just went home, ate a sandwich, and drank a couple of beers. Two executions later, he didn't want to be there." Some execution team members self-medicated with prescription drugs, while others took the tension of the job home to their families.[21]

Marie was conflicted when it came to the members of the execution team. Discussing the arrival of the team at the death house in the days before an execution, Marie commented that "the guards leave one by one and come back wearing black uniforms with no name tags. You want to laugh. Do they really think you have forgotten who they are? They have removed themselves from what they are doing. They walk around like robots. They have become technicians of murder."[22] Despite her harsh words, Marie recognized the pain felt by some members of the execution team and—as with the inmates on death row—she reached out to them and tried to provide comfort. Joe Giarratano wrote:

There was a captain named Anthony Parker who oversaw the death house and death squad when executions were scheduled. Parker had a few personal experiences while overseeing that process—one during my last trip into the death house, one while Ricky Boggs was there, and another while Richard Whitley was there. Marie wouldn't go into the details, but she did tell me that Parker came to her for advice, I believe after Ricky was killed. Parker was going to quit his position in the death house, he was beginning to see it as conflicting with his Christian beliefs, but he was conflicted. He knew that there were some of the death squad who could be very brutal and he also knew that the person who would take his place was very brutal. He recognized that his presence in the death house held that in check. Marie, after long discussions, advised him to stay on and aim to be a humanizing influence. He struggled with it for a time but ultimately decided to stay for a while longer.[23]

Russ also urged Parker to stay. "[I told him] we needed him. And the men needed him. He acted like a human being. He didn't play mind games with the men like the execution team did. He didn't take their [the inmates'] hearts and put them in his pocket." When Parker later transferred, Marie and Russ were saddened because the men had one less ally in the death house.

"When we lost Parker, we lost someone who was fair," said Russ. "He knew that we weren't going to betray him, so he could help us. And he was compassionate with the men." The effects of Parker's departure were immediately obvious, as the death squad became much more hardnosed and rough.

Attorney Barry Weinstein also remembers how Marie related to the execution team, commenting that the execution team respected Marie. "The respect grew not only from the fact that Marie was a 'straight shooter' with the corrections officials about her beliefs, but that Marie reached out to the staff members. These guards . . . were going through something very traumatic. Many of them were first timers to this process, and I saw the interaction between Marie and the execution team," said Weinstein. "Marie wanted to be assured that the execution team was going to do what was necessary to protect the inmate . . . [Marie] counseled [and] assisted them in understanding what they were going through . . . so they would be able to do their work. She wasn't part of the execution per se though she was important in their relationship to the inmate. And it all plays on each other. It truly does."[24]

In one of our conversations around her kitchen table, Marie explained her own religious views and what she saw as her role in the death house.

> I believe that God is whatever force there is toward life. We don't have a real language for this stuff, but I see God more as a creator—whether it was a puff of gas or whatever the hell it was, something in this universe drives toward life. And there is something in this universe that drives toward death. Stars die, we die. But I see this drive toward life as being so important that we must honor it by trying to fulfill our potential. We were given this incredible potential and we must fulfill it. Or at least understand it, in some way.
>
> I don't impose this on the men, I never impose this on anyone. But very often the men [in the death house] would say to me, "I want you there because I need to deal with things and I don't know how to do it." [So] I would test out how far they wanted to go. And if they really wanted answers, [if] they really wanted to understand, I would go with them. I would spend . . . it didn't matter how many days or how many hours. I have fallen asleep in the death house from lack

of sleep. It didn't matter. But I didn't think I was there to say, "Accept Jesus and everything will be fine" because I don't believe that and they know I don't. They knew I didn't believe that, so that is not why they were asking me there. That is cheap grace[25] to me. And I can't imagine taking a human being, to be murdered by us, and giving him cheap grace. Nor can I imagine thinking this is my place [to give cheap grace].

To me, the people who had committed murder had survived intense abuse, brain damage, and/or mental illness that had factored into their becoming killers. They were, however, alive, and they could survive. So, I sat with them, called their names, talked to them, until we passed through words, and whispered to their spirits. I asked them to know themselves, even if the battle to so do seems agonizingly eternal and the reward momentary. I asked them not to die, even if they were killed; I asked them to do this to honor life, especially the life or lives they had taken as well as their own. They could have told me to go home and leave them alone. None did. They could have told me to talk about ordinary things. Some did. Most took the agonizing journey into the heart of their own souls, seeking their own truths, no matter how despicable those truths were. And when they did, there was a presence in the death house that was not there at any other time.

One of the things that I dealt with over and over again was [having to take] lawyers out of the death house and say, "I need you to understand that you will be here tomorrow to deal with your emotions and how much this is hurting you, but this man will not be here tomorrow and all of our focus needs to go to him and his needs and the way he wants to do this." I have seen people again and again and again who [place their focus] on themselves. That is what I came to love about Russ [Ford]. The focus was not on Russ. The focus was on that man.

In their final days and hours in the death house, Marie observed that the inmates tried to find a meaning or purpose in their deaths. "They try to keep that chair as much out of their minds as they can, but it's always there," explained Marie. "There are some things I've learned over time to understand, and one of them is that in every case of anybody I've been in the death house with, the person wants this to mean something. For almost all of them, their hope is that their execution will be the last. They cry about other men; I've seen a lot of that. They cry about other men coming behind them. They cry for their families. They cry for me."[26] And Marie cried with them.

8

Standing Watch in the Death House

> The world is drenched in mutual slaughter. . . . Held to
> be a crime when committed by individuals, homicide
> is called a virtue when committed by the state.
> —Saint Cyprian, quotation on Marie Deans's desk

M arie wrote sparingly about standing watch with thirty-four men in South Carolina and Virginia. Perhaps it was because she could not find the words. "There
is nothing to describe the horror, the sense of soul-filth, you feel when you come
out of there," Marie said. "There is nothing to describe the irony, the stupidity, the
bizarreness of being in the death house."[1] Moreover, Marie wrote that she did not
want her book "to be mired in [my] death watches," since "to write a litany of death
watches would make them banal." Marie did, however, want to focus on a few death
watches that were "particularly dramatic" and important.

Throughout her personal papers, Marie left behind some accounts of standing
death watch. I have combined these fragments with the writings of Russ Ford, attorney David Bruck, and anti-death penalty activist Joe Ingle. In stitching together
this quilt of memories and partial stories, I have tried to capture Marie's experiences
in the death house with inmates Morris Odell Mason, Willie Leroy Jones, Alton
Waye, Michael Smith, Greg Beaver, Richard Whitley, and Earl Clanton. The stories
are grim, raw, and tragic. They involve the final days and hours of men's lives, when
many crumbled under the pressure and became walking dead men. Collectively, the
stories paint a picture of death at its most senseless, terrifying, bureaucratic, and
absurd.

Morris Odell Mason (executed June 25, 1985)

Born in Philadelphia, Morris Odell Mason was raised by his mother in Northamp-
ton County, Virginia. He struggled academically and did not complete high school.
Morris's first psychiatric hospitalization occurred when he was seventeen years old,
triggered because he was setting fires. This hospitalization did not prevent Morris
from subsequently enlisting in the Army.

Mason served approximately one year in the Army, receiving a discharge for a back injury. Shortly after he left the Army, his claims of hearing voices resulted in a second hospitalization and formal diagnoses of mental retardation (with an IQ of sixty-six) and schizophrenia. Tragically, Mason did not receive any post-hospitalization treatment. Mason would, however, be incarcerated for the next two years for multiple acts of arson.

After his parole in the spring of 1978, Morris's criminal behavior increased. He briefly spent time in jail for fraud, and Morris repeatedly requested that his probation officer place him in a halfway house. The request went unanswered. On May 13, 1978, Morris raped a seventy-two-year-old woman, killed her with multiple blows from an axe, and set her house on fire. One day later, he assaulted two sisters—raping the twelve-year-old girl and shooting the thirteen-year-old girl—and tried burning down an empty home. Morris did not appear to understand the enormity of his monstrous acts, announcing at his bench trial (he waived his right to a jury), "I'm the killer of the Eastern shore. I made the Eastern shore popular."[2]

Once on death row, his mental incapacity became obvious to those around him. Marie remarked that Morris often did not comprehend what Marie was saying to him, but he understood the love behind her words. "Morris always said I loved him," Marie stated. "And he would tell other people "I think she's my momma." What Morris could talk about was sports, and he would rattle off statistics, scores, and names of players at the drop of a hat—especially when it came to his favorite team, the Miami Dolphins.

Marie believed that Morris developed an interest in sports so he could talk with the other inmates and not come across as mentally impaired. "None of this [sports] stuff had any meaning to him," observed Marie. Often his obsessive recitation of sports trivia had the opposite effect, irritating the other inmates and driving them away.

Like many of the men on the row, Morris received mail. He couldn't read the letters, however, without the assistance of his fellow inmates. "He had absolutely no reading comprehension and could barely spell his name," said Joe. "Morris would ask me, or one of the other men, to read his mail to him. He would ask us to write out responses to the letters he would receive. Then he would copy the words down in his own handwriting: large block print letters."

Morris's mail included what Marie called "freak letters"—letters from women who sought romantic encounters with death row inmates. Linwood Briley would read the letters to Morris and write responses for him, resulting in a cascade of new letters with lewd content and nude photographs. Marie was unaware of the "freak letters" until she visited Morris in the death house and he proudly showed them to her. She wrote:

So he had a whole stack of freak letters back from all these women [and their] pictures. Morris—if he loved you, he wanted to share everything in the world with you. And so Morris drags out his freak letters to show me. I start reading these letters and I'm like, "Oh, my God." The guards knew he had all these freak letters. At 6:00 p.m. [on the night of his execution] he had to pack up all his stuff. One of the guards said, "Morris, you don't want her to see those letters." I started blushing . . . they're very graphic, [and Morris] didn't know what they said. The guards starting carrying on. . . . They were all laughing at me. I was really embarrassed. I started looking at the pages and saying, "Wow, lots of people wrote you."

Linwood was quite aware of Morris's limitations. When Linwood heard that prison officials thought that Morris might have been involved in planning the 1984 prison escape, he was incredulous. "Linwood said that we could have given Morris the key [to the prison] and he would have gone and sat on the curb and waited until the warden came and got him," Marie said.

Writing to Joe Ingle, fellow death row inmate Joe Giarratano described Morris as child-like:

The only description that would aptly describe Morris Mason is that he was a child in mind who had no concept of reality. Morris was the same every day, and always seemed to live in his own little world. Living with him was like living with a hyper-active eight-year-old. He could never sit still, and was always talking. Morris had no concept of death, and didn't have the slightest idea of what being on Death Row meant. Morris just existed here from day to day talking about sports. He always had a perpetual grin on his face, and was docile as a lamb as long as I knew him.[3]

Astonishingly, a married social worker wrote to Morris and later claimed to be in love with him. "At first it [writing Morris] was a Christian thing, then she fell in love with him and she didn't know what to do," recalled Russ Ford. "She was a death house groupie. She was emotionally insecure and in love with Morris, who could not emotionally return her affections." The woman insisted on visiting Morris during his final day in the death house. "She wept and acted out the part of being his broken-hearted girlfriend,"[4] Russ recalled, and he later spent time on the telephone consoling the woman. Marie was incredulous. How could an adult woman with a child fall in love with a death row inmate operating on the level of an eight-year-old? "Death house groupies" were not an unusual phenomenon on death row,[5] and during his time as chaplain Russ Ford performed several marriages whose origins began with women writing the men of the row.

Given his profound mental limitations, it is not surprising that Morris did not understand that he was going to die. "Even after his execution date was set, and the guards came to take him to the death house, he told us that he'd see us in a couple of days," wrote Joe Giarratano.[6] Morris's inability to comprehend his own death carried over to the death house, where he spent his final days meeting with his lawyer, Lloyd Snook, Marie Deans, and the Reverend Joe Ingle.

In his book *Last Rights*, Ingle describes the final visit that he and Marie had with Morris.

On June 25, 1985, Marie Deans and I visited Morris Mason in the basement of the Virginia State Penitentiary. Morris was scheduled for electrocution at 11:00 p.m. Our afternoon visit was spent talking with Morris while he packed his meager possessions in a box. He showed us letters he'd received, proud to have been sent mail even though some letters urged his killing. All Morris understood was that people were writing to him, and usually that didn't happen. He was very tender with Marie and me. He gave Marie a bracelet when she started crying. Looking at her as a child would look at any unhappy mother, he sought to comfort her: "Don't cry. Don't cry. It's all right. It's for you. Promise me you won't give it away." Marie clutched the bracelet and promised.

Morris gave me a photograph of himself in his cell on Death Row. He showed us all the pictures he had. He was proud of the few things he could show off to us. As the afternoon progressed, I felt like a father to him. He so much wanted our approval and kept trying to take care of us.

The guards kept interjecting into the conversation, always trying to keep the mood light. Marie and I left for supper. We came back afterward, accompanied by Morris's lawyer. The lawyer and I shared sports enthusiasm with Morris. At one point, Morris looked up and asked: "What does it mean to die?" Marie responded: "It means you'll be with your grandmother." That seemed to satisfy Morris, and he chatted on about basketball. Suddenly, he stopped and told Marie: "You tell Roger [another Death Row prisoner] when I get back, I'm gonna show him I can play basketball as good as he can." The concept of death eluded Morris as it does any child.

For attorney Snook, it was not until a final conversation about the funeral that he realized that Morris did not have the mental capacity to understand his own death. In a subsequent interview with a local newspaper, Snook recounted the following exchange:

Mason . . . asked Deans and Snook what he should wear to his funeral. "Maybe you could talk to your mother about that," Deans suggested gently. "Maybe she could bring some clothes and they could dress you in them after the execution." Mason didn't get it. Why would someone else have to dress him? He could dress himself, he told Deans and Snook. "I remember being really astounded," Snook says. "It just sort of slowly dawned on us at the same time. He didn't know he would be dead after the execution. Marie and I kind of looked at each other . . . and then we talked about the fact that execution meant being dead. He understood what death was—he had, after all, killed people—but in talking to him about it, what it meant to him was that he would be with his grandmother in heaven."[7]

Morris's child-like demeanor was reflected in his choice of a final dinner. "He ordered four Big Macs, two large orders of fries, two ice cream sundaes and a couple of large grape sodas," noted *Washington Post* reporter Evans Hopkins, "and he shared

Virginia death row inmate Morris Mason. The profoundly mentally handicapped Mason did not understand that he would not survive the electric chair. Photograph courtesy of *Richmond Times-Dispatch*.

with two guards, perhaps the same ones who . . . [strapped] him into the old oaken chair."[8]

At approximately 8:30 p.m., Deans, Snook, and Ingle were asked to leave the death house while the members of the death squad prepared Mason for his execution. Ingle recalls the jarring sight of returning to the death house to find Mason with his head partially shaved.

When we returned we found Morris lying on his bunk, the back of his shaved head glistening from the light outside the cell. He turned to us and sighed: "Oh, Marie, look what they've done to me now." The clothes they had given him dwarfed his small frame. The blue denim shirt and blue jeans made Morris look clownish.

We sat outside the cell, the minutes slipping away. Marie held Morris's hand. He asked us about death again. Before we could answer, his expression brightened, and he said: "Does it mean I get to order anything I want for breakfast?" For Morris, selecting his own meal after years of being fed in his cell represented the ultimate idea of heaven.

It was 10:30, and we only had fifteen more minutes with Morris. Morris was absolutely determined to make Marie and me "proud" of him. He kept saying: "You tell the men [on Death Row] how strong I was. I'm gonna be strong. I'm gonna be brave. I'm gonna make you proud." It was like a litany. Morris was holding to this refrain, even as he trembled, to get through the next few minutes. "I'm gonna be strong, I'm gonna be brave. I'm gonna make you proud."

The overwhelming feeling of bidding good-bye to a child struck me. Marie and I were Morris's parents for his last minutes. We knew he would make us proud and that it was his gift to us. At 10:45 the death squad assembled outside Morris's cell. Morris said to us: "I love you. Don't be sad. Don't cry." We told Morris we loved him too.

Morris's arrested development was evidenced in his final words to Russ Ford. As Morris entered the death chamber with Russ, he turned and said " 'Russ, don't forget to tell the men back at the row that I was a big boy.' As Mason's knees began to buckle, Ford put his hand on the man's shoulder and said, 'You'll be OK.' 'Sure enough, Morris walked on in there like a big boy, sat down in the chair and was executed,' Ford said. 'I went in reading Psalm 23. Do you think he understood any of it?' "[9]

Of the execution itself, Russ would write:

> I wasn't prepared for what I was about to see. After telling Morris, "God bless you," and after the straps were secured and the mask tied on, I stepped back yet kept my eye on him. I would never forget the next few minutes; it would haunt me for years. The current was cut on with a grinding, deafening roar. Morris lunged, his head jerking, his hands raising off chair arms as if a demonic puppeteer was making him wave. Sparks flew from his right leg where the adapter was connected. His feet tapped up and down in a horrendous dance. His body began to smoke and his forehead began to swell, grow red, and blister over the top of the death mask. The smell, which later became part of my recurrent nightmares, was that of burned pork.[10]

Years later, what Russ would remember most vividly about the execution was the rise and fall of Morris's hands, which reminded Russ of the fluttering of dark-colored doves. It was the last execution that Russ ever watched.

In the cooling room, the guards used sandbags to break Morris's fused joints before placing him in a body bag. Earlier, Morris had seen the sandbags in the death house and asked Marie why the bags were there. Marie had "made up some story" and changed the subject. Outside over two hundred death penalty supporters roared in approval when prison officials announced his death.

Morris was buried at his family farm in an unmarked grave. "Someone opened the ground up, dropped him in, and covered [the coffin] over," said Russ. "My understanding was that there were few people in attendance and no service. I believe Morris's family felt anxious about the community's reaction to the whole affair and did not want to draw any more attention."

Alton Waye (executed August 30, 1989)

Alton Waye was sentenced to death for the October 1977 murder of LaVergne Marshall, a sixty-seven-year-old woman who made the mistake of letting a drunk Alton into her home to use the telephone. Alton subsequently raped, beat, and stabbed the woman approximately forty-two times before placing her body in her bathtub and dousing it with Clorox. Alton later called the police and confessed to the murder. In the weeks before his execution, anti-death-penalty groups argued that it was immoral and unjust to execute the "borderline retarded" Alton.[11] Their informal appeals for clemency went unanswered by the governor's office.

"Alton was a strange individual," recalls Joe. "He wasn't as mentally slow as Morris Mason, but he wasn't too far off. He would stand in his cell and yell out the door all hours of the night, preaching from the Old Testament. He also tried to play the part of a bully, and Alton got his nose twisted for it more than once." Most of the time, Alton avoided the other men of the row. "He was, for the lack of a better description, anti-social by the row's standards," Joe added. "He looked down on us sinners."

While many inmates closely followed the status of their appeals, Alton was disinterested. "Alton really didn't care about what was going on with his case. He never initiated contact with Marie," said Joe. "Marie visited him a few times and asked to speak with him on the phone more than a few times. Alton was polite but never very communicative. Marie always reached out to him, but never could get any kind of rapport going with him."[12]

In his unpublished book manuscript, Russ writes of Alton's execution. Although these are not Marie's words, Russ provides an insider's account of a death watch Marie attended. The night before, Russ baptized Alton in the small prison chapel at the Pen. The members of the execution team participated in the religious ceremony, including taking communion, singing "Amazing Grace," and reciting the Lord's Prayer. Some of the execution squad members had even hugged Alton after the baptism, causing Russ to comment, "it was like being down by the river."

The passage below starts later in the evening, as Russ is walking back to the death house after a frantic search for a tape recorder (Alton wanted to record some hymns prior to his death). During Russ's absence, corrections officers had shaved Alton's head and ankle, showered him, and given him his execution clothes.

Outside the prison, on Spring Street, a demonstration was being held. I had seen the people gathering as I entered the prison this evening, and I could hear them now. There wasn't as big a crowd as had been present when the first few executions were held after Virginia reinstated capital punishment, but there were enough to have the reporters and cameras out in force. Candles burned in defiance of the death penalty as opponents sang quiet songs. Placards with the rallying cry, "Fry the bastard!" bounced in the hands of shouting penalty proponents. And in the cells of Cell Block A above me, inmates echoed their own rage, screaming, banging on cell doors, and throwing personal property off the tiers.

I stopped in the basement lounge to collect Marie and Minister William Bell, who had grown up with Alton in Mecklenburg County. While Alton was being prepped, we had to be out of the death house. Security or something. Didn't want us changing the channel on the guard's television when they weren't watching or moving their chairs around for spite. Bell was seated in an old wooden school chair. Marie was standing near the drink machine, arms crossed, and a cigarette between her teeth.

"Got the recorder," I said.

"It work?" she asked.

"Hope so."

"With all that, you should have checked it first."

"It'll work," I said.

We pushed through the heavy door and went outside to the back hallway. It was dark, and the August air was just beginning to let go of some of its oppressive heat, although I was sweating heavily. I looked up at the sky, but the scattered clouds over Richmond reflected the city lights, obscuring the moon and stars. Just a few yards from the lounge door was the death house door. Marie knocked, we waited, and a guard let us into the hallway. Straight ahead, behind a closed door, was Virginia's death chamber. Soon it would be full of witnesses and the curious DOC officials. To the left was the door to the cells. Again, we had to wait while the guard messed with his cluster of keys. Marie grumbled around her cigarette. Bell was silent. Maybe he was praying.

The guard found the key, opened the door, and we walked in to the cell area. My fingers were tight against the recorder. The television, which was mounted on a concrete column near the guard's table, and which usually rambled in an incessant, mindless entertainment, was shut off. Harper, Mullins [two guards], and Alton stood before the first cell. Mullins was unlocking the door to let Alton in. There were always two guards on duty down here, and I asked Ray [the warden] that these two be here now, during the final hours. Others on the death squad were into playing mind games with the condemned, doing their macho thing. Mullins and Harper didn't see the need to get into that.

"Bless you!" Alton said, looking over his shoulder at me. "Praise Jesus you got the recorder!"

"Praise Jesus, I hope it'll work," I said.

Alton was in his new clothes, a pair of jeans, the right leg cut off to the knee, and a Velcro-enclosed shirt. Metal buttons or zippers would play havoc with the electrical current, so Velcro was the fastener of choice. On his feet were yellow flip-flops. He was shaved bald, the lumpy pate standing out in the dim, pinkish fluorescent lights.

Alton went into the cell. He sat on the cot, then bounded up again, sticking something through the bars to Mullins. It was the Afro pick. "We won't be needing this no more. Thanks."

Mullins stuck the pick into the pocket of his uniform shirt. He and Harper went back to the guard's table and sat. Mullins fumbled with the log, in which he was supposed to write everything anybody did, and when. He lit a cigarette and shook out the match.

"Let's get this thing hooked up," I said. "Test it out. Alton, you didn't forget those songs, now, did you?"

"No, didn't forget a thing," he said.

There was an outlet in the wall next to Alton's cell. I plugged the recorder in and carried it back. Marie dragged our chairs over, and we all sat. Alton closed his eyes and said, "Praise the Lord."

"Praise the Lord," I repeated.

"Now clap with me," Alton said. "Pat your legs for me, get with me. I'm gonna sing for you."

On our plastic chairs, we began slapping our legs with the palms of our hands. Pat, pat, pat.

Alton said, "This song I'm about to sing, I'd like to stress that the Lord placed it on my heart in a very low and lonely period of my life. He made me realize that I wasn't alone. The name of the song is called 'What You Gonna Do at the End of the Road?' "

"And this applies to any situation you face in life, no matter what it is." His words had picked up the beat of our patting. His voice was serene and steady. "If you feel you're in a situation you don't know what to do, I say the Lord Jesus is always there to help."

Pat, pat, pat. Over my shoulder, I could see Harper holding up his hand, five fingers showing. Five minutes to go.

Alton began to sing.

"What you gonna do at the end of the road? Ooo-ooh.

Who you gonna turn to where there's no one there but you? Ooo-ooh.

Put your trust in Jesus and He will see you through. Ooo-ooh.

If you make one step, He'll make two.

What you gonna do at the end of the road? Ooo-ooh.

Reach out and grab onto the unchanging hand."

In spite of the God talk which usually left me cold and suspicious, the current here was strong. My hands went with it, beating to the pulse of Alton's simple song, moving in unison with Marie and Bell's hands. Pat, pat, pat.

The song ended, and Alton praised God. Then he said, "One day I asked for a songbook. A preacher brought me one. There were songs in there I knew, but I wanted to learn some new ones. I came across one called, 'Ye Must Be Born Again.' It really caught my attention, 'cause this was me. I hadn't been saved. So I found the song, and it stopped me. But I didn't know the tune. I need a tune for to carry the song with."

With my foot, I pushed the recorder a little closer to the cell. At the guard's desk, Harper raised his hand again subtly. Three fingers.

"So," Alton said. "God placed in my heart the TV show 'The Beverly Hillbillies,' with Jed and Jethro and Ellie Mae and all that bunch."

I burst out laughing. Marie and Bell did, too. Alton smiled broadly, and told us how as he asked God for a tune, he heard banjo music coming from outside his cell. He looked up to see the opening credit of "The Beverly Hillbillies" on a pod television, and the words fit the tune perfectly. "The music caught my attention," he said. "And the Lord helped me put those things, the words and 'The Beverly Hillbillies' and everything, together. You'll see what I mean when I start singing. Here goes."

He took a deep breath, hesitated, lost the beat, and grinned. We laughed again, and Alton beamed. Then, to the bouncy tune of 'The Beverly Hillbillies' theme song, Alton sang,

"A ruler once came to Jesus by night,
To ask Him the way of salvation and light,
The Master made answer in words true and plain,
Ye must be born again.
Ye must be born again, ye must be born again.
I verily, verily say unto thee, Ye must be born again."

He sang three more verses, then began a fourth. We watched him silently.

And then the plug was pulled on the tape recorder. I looked over to see Mullins holding the cord. "It's time," he said.

Marie stood. She reached through the bars and gave Alton a hug good-bye.

"I'll see you on the other side," Alton said.

Marie left the cell area. As she went out, the death squad came in, dressed in their official black uniforms, name tags missing for this occasion. Bell and I pushed our chairs out of the way. Warden Ray Muncy stepped to the cell and read the court order. Alton stood silently, listening.

Harper then cuffed Alton's hands, and Mullins unlocked the door. Alton stepped into the aisle, and immediately the squad engulfed him, moving around him so tightly he could barely be seen.

"Give him some room," Ray said.

The men backed off a little.

Mullins said to me, "We'll take it from here, Reverend Ford."

With Johnson leading the way, we walked into the tiny hallway and then into the execution chamber. Bell and I followed the guards, Ray Muncy followed us. Alton slipped once in his yellow flip flops; Harper steadied him.

The chamber was packed with bodies. The DOC officials didn't want to move for us, they wanted us to work for it, as if we had to earn the right to get Alton to the chair. Going single file, we squeezed through. I could see DOC director Ed Murray on the phone, hand pressed over one ear, relating to the governor's office what was happening, step-by-step. He paused and shouted, "Would everyone please be quiet?" but no one was.

We made it through the crowd. The old oak chair was not more than ten feet in front of us. Two metal-hooded lights, which looked like something used in Nazi interrogations, hung from the ceiling, directly over the chair. Spotlights, lest we miss anything. To my right, witnesses sat in their enclosed box. Behind me, the officials were finally quieting, wanting to see and hear it all. To my left was a concrete pillar on which were the activation switch and light signal.

The guards were quick now, moving in unison, moving Alton into the chair with precision. Harper and Mullins strapped the legs; other guards took care of

Virginia death row inmate Alton Waye. Members of the execution team participated in Waye's death-house baptism, including taking communion, praying, and singing. Photograph courtesy of *Richmond Times-Dispatch*.

the chest strap, the arm straps, the electrode on the right leg. The back of the chair was cranked forward, pushing Alton into the straps more tightly. Alton was quiet and cooperative. He didn't fight. This was not a jailhouse conversion like I had seen in Michael Smith, who had sweated and babbled and screamed Scriptures and prayers to Jesus and God as he had been led to his death.

Before the leather hood and mask were put into place, Alton said, "I don't hate anyone involved." Then, his gaze found me and he said, "Reverend Ford, God bless you, I love you."

My jaws tightened. For the first time, I was seeing a man who was not swallowed by the chair. It had no grip on him in spite of the straps. Alton had become more than the chair.

"God bless you," I answered.

Johnson then pulled the leather helmet down tightly onto Alton's head. The leather mask was tied across Alton's face. Warden Muncy leaned to me and said softly, "You did a good job, Russ. He's prepared."

You have no idea. It wasn't me.

Ray faced the pillar and put the key into the activator switch. I turned away from Alton. I watched the faces of the witnesses, of the officials as Ray turned the key and the light above the switch went green.

There was the harsh hum of electricity, the rapt attention of witnesses.

Strange movement to my right caught my eye. William Bell was against the wall, pinned like a frantic and terrified butterfly, his hands batting the cinder block. His eyes flicked back and forth uncontrollably. I went over and put a hand on his shoulder. I knew what he was experiencing. I had seen what he was seeing. Since my first execution in 1985, I didn't watch them anymore.

Two minutes later, the current was cut off. A female guard pushed her stopwatch and the five-minute countdown began. Time needed to be given to let the body cool enough that it could be checked for a pulse. The silence in the room was as thick as the pungent smell of basted ham. And then Johnson opened Alton's shirt with a metal stick. The doctor gingerly placed the stethoscope on Alton's chest, making sure he didn't touch the body directly.

He said to the crowd, "He has expired."

I helped Bell out with the throng as quietly and discreetly as possible.

Russ would later describe the experience of singing spirituals in the death house as similar to the story contained in Acts 16, when the singing of Paul and Silas brought the prison walls tumbling down. And Russ walked away from the execution with his spirits raised. "We knew that not everybody could have that kind of experience," Russ explained to a local reporter. "We knew how the other [death house inmates] died hard, really disconnected, lost, somewhat floundering in the end. Alton was the first that walked in the light."[13]

Willie Leroy Jones (executed September 11, 1992)

Willie Leroy "Woo" Jones would be the fifteenth inmate with whom Marie would stand a death watch. A native of Richmond, Virginia, Willie served five years in the United States Army. Willie was convicted of robbing and murdering an elderly husband and wife. Willie would be one of the six inmates who escaped from death row in 1984, making his way to Vermont before turning himself in to the police.

Willie spent the last hours of his life in the death house with Marie and Russ, awaiting word of a possible stay or clemency from the governor. The wait would prove fruitless. A newspaper reporter later recounted Marie's final hours with Willie.

The phone calls finally came around suppertime. The court said no, and so did the governor. Jones took Deans's hand, she said, and told her, "Well, we didn't expect anything else, did we?" Deans had eaten nothing all day but a bagel with cream cheese; she didn't think anything else would sit on her stomach. But when Jones's last meal came, he said he ordered it for her.

"He ordered steak, baked potato, and salad, and he said, 'I want you to eat. I'm going to sit here and watch you eat,' " Deans said. Stunned, Deans tried to honor his wishes. "The potato was huge. I said, 'I can't eat that.' So I broke it like you break bread, and we all ate," she said. "It was like a communion."[14]

When Willie entered the death chamber, he quickly bent down and kissed the arm of the electric chair. Although Willie was known on death row for his sense of humor, kissing the chair was not a flippant act. "He kissed the chair to show that it didn't have any power over him," explained Russ. "He wanted to show that he was still alive, that he wasn't dead before the execution. No dead man walking. The execution team was stunned."

After Willie was strapped into the chair, Ford read a final statement in which Willie drew upon the teachings of Chinese Taoist philosopher Lao Tsu.

An ancient wise man, some six hundred years before the birth of our Lord, shared words of wisdom to be considered on occasions such as this. He advised when we gather to perform such public acts, we should always ask, "where is the great executioner? Is the great executioner here? To kill without the great executioner is like cutting wood without the master carpenter. You are most likely to cut off your own hand." The great executioner is God, our creator, the giver and receiver of life. All other taking of life is wrong. How can we heal if we become that which wounded us?

With that, Willie became the sixteenth person executed in Virginia during the "modern" death penalty era.

After the execution, a newspaper reporter noticed Marie and Russ leaving the prison with their arms around each other.

There were tears in Deans's eyes, but there was something else, too. A light that hadn't been there before. Even as Jones left his cell for the last time, she said: "He was so alive. He was glowing. I just sat there and looked at him in just utter amazement. I said to him, 'Man, they're gonna have to do some real serious killing down here because you are so alive.' "

At the very end, she said, their roles were reversed, and it was Jones who comforted Deans. He had found an inner peace, she said, and he thanked her for helping him do it. "I don't think I could stand that being for nothing," Deans said. "I want to find that spark of energy. I think I can learn that from him, how to find that peace."[15]

Even years later, Marie's eyes widened and her voice grew husky as she talked about taking a baked-potato "communion" with Willie.

Approximately twenty minutes after Willie Leroy Jones's electrocution, Willie's body was transported in a prison van to a local morgue pursuant to state law. The blue body bag containing Willie's remains was wheeled into a walk-in refrigerator, where it was stored with eleven other bodies. The next morning Willie's body, bearing the distinctive burn marks of the electric chair, was sliced apart and his blood screened for illegal drugs. The cause of death was found to be electrocution. Virginia capital defense attorney Jerry Zerkin was hardly shocked by the coroner's findings. "They fry them from the inside out . . . what's the big secret?"[16]

Final Absurdities

In Marie's eyes, the regulations and protocols surrounding the execution of a condemned man helped mask the simple fact that a human being was being murdered. "There is a ritual, you see, and the American people need ritual," Marie said. "If you deal with something straight up, you don't need a ritual. In the death house, ritual is the engine that drives the death machine and it encompasses the most absurd things."

November 1977 photograph of Michael Marnell Smith
walking into court while carrying his Bible. Smith was
denied the right to hold his Bible during his execution
because prison officials were afraid it might catch on fire.
Photograph courtesy of *Richmond Times-Dispatch*.

For Virginia death row inmate Michael Marnell Smith, the absurdity surrounded
the Bible that had been his constant companion on death row. Michael came from
a religious family, who lived and worked on a secluded dairy farm. "[It was] sort of
a closed society," explained Marie. "They did not play with or become friends with
anyone outside of the church. They just went to school, went to church, and worked
. . . dates were basically going to church."[17] When Michael confessed to police the
rape and murder of single mother Audrey Jean Weiler, he began to weep and asked
his interrogators to fall to their knees and pray with him. Michael's father, Marion
"Okie" Smith, was a preacher who wore a "robe of humility" made of sackcloth and
fasted during his son's trial. Despite the fact that his son repeatedly admitted to his

crimes, his father believed Michael was innocent and would one day be a saint in heaven. There Michael would pass judgment on his executioners.

Michael's religious fervor carried over to death row. "Michael had 'jail house religion,' and he quoted scripture all the time," explained Russ. "Sometimes an inmate will 'pull his time' by suing the state, other inmates pull their time by bucking the system. Michael pulled his time by religion. He was like a jail house preacher, and he had a very fundamentalist take on the Bible."

Michael fasted in the days before his death, and he requested permission to hold the Bible during his electrocution. The Virginia attorney general's office refused on the grounds that the Bible might erupt into flames. "It was OK to burn Michael," recalled his attorney, Lloyd Snook, "but not the Bible." In the end, prison officials permitted Michael to hold his Bible as he walked into the death chamber before placing it on the floor before the electric chair.[18] Michael was reciting scripture as he was bound to the chair, and his voice became a scream when the execution mask was placed over his face. Michael called out, "Father, I am here"[19] and then was executed.

As Michael died, a ten-year-old child stood outside of the Virginia State Penitentiary holding a sign that read "You should die. An eye for an eye, but don't waste taxpayers money, kill them right away."[20] Cries of "the party's over" and "burn, baby, burn" filled the air.[21] Death penalty abolitionists sang the spiritual "Down by the Riverside," but were drowned out by supporters who shouted "that's where she died"—a reference to the location of the murder of the young mother killed by Michael. A motorcycle with two riders waving the Confederate flag added to the surreal scene.[22]

For Gregory Warren Beaver, the absurdity involved his wedding ring. As Greg prepared to leave his cell in the death house in the Greensville Correctional Center for the short walk to the death chamber, he removed his wedding ring, handed it to Russ Ford, and asked that the ring be given to his wife. Watching from the death chamber was Ronald J. Angelone, the head of the Virginia Department of Corrections. Angelone immediately ordered that the ring be returned to Greg, who was thereafter executed while wearing the ring.

"I saw [Beaver] slip the wedding ring to Russ Ford and I had somebody go in and tell Russ Ford it should have been done earlier, before they got to the death chamber," explained Angelone. "We just don't do things late at night, that's all policy. We do not run a boy's camp. We run prisons, and we're trying to make the system safer." Marie, however, had another explanation. " 'It was just petty, petty, petty . . . they just keep coming up with one more turn of the screw.' "[23]

For Richard Whitley, the absurdity involved a hot fudge sundae. On July 6, 1987, Marie and attorney Tim Kaine stood death watch with Richard. We don't know much about Richard's background, except that Marie once commented in passing that Richard "had been hit by a fucking train when he was twelve years old" and "had enormous brain damage." Richard requested steak, French fries, a salad with French dressing, and a hot fudge sundae for his final meal. "There is a chef at the state penitentiary, he generally wears work clothes but when he serves the last meal in the death house, he wears a suit, a chef's hat, and pulls on white gloves. Even if he's

Virginia death row inmate Gregory Beaver. His last-minute request to remove his wedding ring prior to his execution was denied by a Virginia prison official, who later explained to reporters "we don't run a boy's camp here." Personal collection of Marie Deans.

serving French fries," explained Marie. "I have to tell the guys not to ask for French fries because every piece of food has to be inspected in front of the execution squad. They go through the French fries in case there is a razor blade or the like. So finally when they get their food, it's cold." Richard must not have followed Marie's advice about the fries.

After eating his dinner, Richard asked if he could save his dessert. At 9:30 p.m., less than two hours before his execution, Richard asked for the sundae—and was told that he couldn't have it. "They said, 'You can't eat anything after 9 p.m. That's the rule,'" recalls Kaine, who stayed with Richard throughout that day. "We argued and argued, but they said, 'Forget it.' He couldn't have the sundae. I think they were worried he might throw up or defecate or something during the execution. And it really struck me: Here they're going to kill this guy and the last thing he wanted to do in his life was to eat this hot fudge sundae and they wouldn't give it to him because they were worried about how it might look. So there it sat, his last dessert, on an officer's desk about five feet from his cell, and he couldn't have it, and that was that."[24]

Richard's choice of a final beverage left a haunting impression with Marie. "Now Richard wanted iced tea and he wanted tea for everybody, so they brought a jug of iced tea. I was sitting near the bars close to Richard, and they put the jug down and it says on the side 'cider vinegar' and without thinking I said, Oh, my God. 'And our Lord thirst and they gave him vinegar.'"[25] The absurdity, however, quickly faded as Richard faced the death chamber.

Before I left Richard, when the execution squad said, "Marie, you have to go now," Richard had hung onto me. As long as I was there, he was okay, but as soon

Virginia death row inmate Richard Whitley, who was denied the dessert (a hot fudge sundae) in his final meal because serving any food to a prisoner after 9:00 p.m. violated prison rules. Photograph courtesy of *Richmond Times-Dispatch*.

as I began to leave, he started shaking and he said, "I can't make it without you" and I said, "Yes, you can make it." Then I said, "Where is God, Richard?" and he raised his hand and he pulled his hand in a downward movement between the two of us. And I said, "Yes, I can feel Him, I know that God is with us, here, and when I go out there Richard, I am going into Babylon but you are staying with God." I just knew he would be alright, I just knew it. You know you can feel it.[26]

Outside the vortex of evil, in the streets surrounding the Virginia State Penitentiary, stood a small crowd of supporters and opponents of the death penalty. "As the opponents held hands in silent prayer, some proponents sat in lawn chairs or on a brick wall and jeered them. Others shouted, 'Fry him!' Shortly before 11 p.m., several in the crowd clapped hands and sang, 'Na-na-na-na, hey, hey, hey, kiss him goodbye.'"[27]

After Richard's death, Marie received a package containing his tennis shoes. The pristine white shoes were the only material item Richard could give Marie to express his gratitude for her friendship. When Marie removed the shoes from the box, her first reaction was that Richard had sent her a brand-new pair of sneakers. Then she looked at the soles of the shoes and saw the patches that Richard had used to cover the holes in the worn-out shoes.[28] And she wept.

For Charles Sylvester Stamper, the absurdity was the fact that he was carried to the electric chair. Charles had been partially paralyzed when he was attacked by Buffalo DeLong, and his injuries left him unable to walk. Marie wrote:

Charles's medication had been withheld so the autopsy wouldn't show drugs, and his arms and legs were drawing up in spasms. An hour before he was to be taken into the chamber, Charles called his mother. By the time she hung up, muscle spasms had caused his arm and hand to mold around the phone, and he couldn't let go. It took me ten minutes of massaging his hand through the bars to get the phone out of his hand and another fifteen minutes to get his arm down. Charles was unceremoniously carried by the back of his pants from his wheelchair to the electric chair.

Charles had requested to use his walker and leg braces so he could walk unassisted to the chair, but his request was denied.

For Earl Clanton, the absurdity involved his final request for a contact visit with his seven-year-old daughter before his execution. Joe Giarratano recalls:

At first the authorities here decided that he couldn't see her under those circumstances. Then they said he could. Then they said, "You can see her, but she'll have to submit to an internal search first." Now what man is going to want his seven-year-old daughter searched internally before visiting him? What would her final visit to her daddy make her think of for the rest of her life?[29]

Earl went to the electric chair without a last visit with his daughter. He, however, was allowed to visit with actor Jay North in the death house. Known primarily for his role as television's "Dennis the Menace," North had announced that he was making a documentary on the 1984 escape from death row, and he wanted to talk to Earl about his role in the escape. The documentary was never produced. It was a terrible death watch for Marie. Earl was not prepared for his death, and his final words to Marie were "help me get through this."

And for Lem Tuggle, Joseph O'Dell, and Ronald Lee Hoke, absurdity turned to uncaring cruelty when the Virginia Department of Corrections decided to house them in the new death house at the Greensville Correctional Center on the day that executions were scheduled for other inmates. Given the small size of the death house, the inmates in the other cells were able to watch as the condemned men were walked into the death chamber. "It comes across as if someone had thought of a new form of torture," Marie angrily remarked, "a kind of psychological torture . . . it makes no sense." As for the inmates who witnessed the executions, Marie said: "I've seen shock, and I've been in shock, and it's what they look like."

When a death row chaplain demanded answers, the Virginia Department of Corrections had a familiar answer ready—institutional security would be compromised if inmates were moved out of the death house during an execution. "We aren't going to jeopardize that because an inmate may feel traumatized that he's about to be executed. That's why there are three cells in the death house."[30] Chaplain Jim Griffin was not satisfied with the explanation. "It just seems unsavory to me," he commented. "There needs to be a little humanity in the whole thing. It just doesn't seem like humans would treat humans like this."[31]

For all the men of the row, the last absurdity was the lack of dignity after death. Under Virginia law, inmates must be autopsied after they are killed by the state to determine the cause of death. The rationale for the practice is simple: to refute any claims by family members that the inmate was abused or tortured. The autopsy is not about the dead inmate. It is about preventing lawsuits. Only after the prisoners' bodies have been gutted, photographed, dissected, and sewed back together are family members allowed to collect the remains of their loved ones.

For the rest of her life, Marie would be haunted by her visits to the South Carolina and Virginia death houses. Even in her dreams, she could not escape the specter of the gallows.

> After I began visiting death row, I added nightmares about executions to my nightmares about Penny's murder. After my trip to Louisiana [an Amnesty International trip taken in 1982], those nightmares began to merge into an even stranger montage of ritualized murder. In the nightmares I was given tests, and my performance determined whether the murders would go on. I failed every test and was forced to watch, helplessly, as men and women I knew were taken into death chambers one at a time and murdered."

Other nightmares involved Marie's own execution.

> It was horrible. I had finally gotten to bed about four o'clock, and was sleeping real good, and this six-man death squad appeared, carrying some kind of electrodes. "Give us the keys," one of them demanded, "and we won't execute you." I realized that I was clutching this big ring of keys with both hands. "Give us the keys, give us the keys," they began saying together, over and over, but I wouldn't let them go, I just couldn't let go. Then they took off all the insignias from their uniforms, just like they do in there, and somehow hooked the electrodes to the bed. One of them then hit the light switch, and I woke up with a shock I'll never forget and a migraine that feels like I'll never get rid of, . . . those keys must represent the lives of the men on death row.[32]

It was obvious to Marie's friends and family that her visits to the death house were exacting a terrible price. "I have execution flashbacks," Marie admitted. "I can be driving down the street and suddenly see an execution happening in front of me."[33] And in the days after executions, Marie would be driven to bed by terrible migraines and bouts of depression.

Marie resisted calls for her to back away from standing death watch. For Marie, the choice was simple: she could not, and would not, let the men of the row die alone. And she argued that being in the death house gave her a different perspective on life and the human condition. "I can't say I regret being involved in this. I appreciate every shower I have, every meal I eat, every decision I'm allowed to make for myself. Without having known condemned men, I wouldn't understand human nature."[34]

9

Marie and Joe

At heart, Marie was an abolitionist.
Her belief was simple: human beings
should not be killing each other, period.
—Joe Giarratano, April 2012

Of all the relationships between Marie and the men of death row, none is more remarkable than the enduring bond between Marie and Joe Giarratano. As discussed in Chapter 4, Marie first met Joe during a fact-finding mission to Virginia's death row on behalf of Amnesty International USA. Joe had written over thirty different death penalty and civil rights organizations, begging them to convince a former police officer on death row named Frank Coppola to resume his appeals. The head of the Southern Coalition on Jails and Prisons, Reverend Joseph Ingle, responded to Joe's plea and travelled to Virginia to meet with Coppola. Ingle's efforts were unsuccessful, and Coppola was executed on August 8, 1982. Virginia's first execution in twenty years was a gruesome affair; as electricity coursed through Coppola's body, his head and leg burst into flames, filling the death chamber with putrid smoke.[1]

Shortly after Marie opened the Virginia Coalitions on Jails and Prisons, Charlottesville attorney Lloyd Snook asked Marie to again meet with Joe. What began as a series of visits to convince Joe to pursue his appeals turned into a mutual partnership in which convict and activist struggled together to improve conditions on death row and save the lives of the condemned men—including Joe's own life. This joint crusade sparked a decades-long friendship, with Marie becoming a surrogate mother, friend, teacher, and champion for Joe.

Under any circumstances, the transformation of a death row inmate from drug addict to prison reformer would be astonishing. When one learns of Joe's life before prison, his story is almost unbelievable. Born in New York to a single mother, Joe grew up in Jacksonville, Florida, in a home filled with drugs, violence, sexual abuse, and neglect. In the passage below, Marie provides a horrifying summary of Joe's childhood.

Joe Giarratano's childhood was a nightmare come true. The very hands that should have held him in a safe, nurturing embrace instead kept him at a distance, battered him, ridiculed him, and plied his young body to satisfy the pathetic lust of a broken man. Joe's was a childhood of extreme physical and psychological abuse by his mother and her friends, and sexual abuse by his stepfather. His "home" was infested with drugs and alcohol and served as a haven and party house for drug-dealers. At best he was ignored; at worst he was tortured there.

Joe was a chubby little boy and has remained overweight all his life. As far back as Joe can remember, his mother's pet name for him was "Pig." She also referred to him as a "stupid fat-ass" and constantly told him he couldn't do anything right. When Joe was three or four years old, his mother would leave him alone for days at a time in their New York apartment. Drug dealers and other felons were frequent visitors in their home and a frequent source of "amusement" for his mother and her "friends" was to beat Giarratano with broom handles, baseball bats, and other weapons. His life was threatened by both his mother and her visitors. He was burned. He was shocked with a cattle prod. He was handcuffed to a fence at night. He also was threatened with death by his mother and her friends, and, on one occasion, a friend of his mother's attempted to run over him with a car. His mother blamed Joe for everything that was wrong, from there not being enough money to his not taking on the full responsibility of being the "man" of the house when he was fifteen years old and his stepfather died.

Joe's stepfather had begun fondling him when he was around nine and had gone on to rape him a number of times. Joe had come home one day and walked in on his stepfather and young sister Nikki having intercourse, and his stepfather forced Joe and Nikki to have intercourse while he watched. Joe told me it was after the first rape that he had begun taking drugs, which he got from a box that his mother kept in the house. It was also after the first rape that he had begun running away from home and trying to commit suicide. When running away failed to provide the escape he so desperately needed, and when authorities consistently returned him to a life of physical, psychological, and sexual abuse; Joe, at the age of eleven years old, turned to drugs, the escape that was most readily available in his home. If he, as a child, could not escape the abuse, drugs at least could dull the pain. By his early teen years, Joe Giarratano had become severely addicted to drugs and alcohol.

At the age of fourteen, Joe was charged with possession of marijuana. Just two months later, he was caught again with marijuana. Less than a month later he was caught sniffing paint thinner. Two months later, his probation was revoked for school truancy and he was committed to Dozier School, a Division of Youth Services. Unfortunately, he was returned to his mother's home a few months later.

Shortly after Joe's stepfather died in 1973, Joe made a very serious suicide attempt by overdosing on drugs and severely slashing his right wrist, and he *was committed. Because his mother reported that Joe's only drug problem was that he "OD[s] when he wants attention," his primary physician was not aware of the extent of Joe's addictions. He was aware, and he duly noted that Joe's mother projected guilt onto Joe and was so hostile to her son. The doctor ordered that her visits be severely restricted and closely supervised. The hospital staff attempted to find foster placement for Joe outside of his mother's guardianship, but those attempts failed, and once again Joe returned to the environment from which he was trying so desperately to escape.*

Records from this hospitalization show Joe to be a seriously depressed child. While hospitalized he was involved in individual and group therapy and was maintained on Librium and Thorazine. Under the discharge plan, Joe was to meet monthly with a counseling team and to remain on Librium. A child of fifteen needs a parent or guardian to fill prescriptions for Librium and see that he gets to his monthly counseling meetings. His mother did neither. Had there been any real intervention or even the minimal intervention of monthly counseling and maintenance on Librium from age fifteen, Joe might have learned to cope with the brutality of his life in a healthy way and might have overcome his drug and alcohol addiction. Instead, Joe was forced to deal with the effects of long-term physical and sexual abuse alone, while still being victimized by his mother and her friends as his addictions to drugs and alcohol intensified.

Four months after his discharge from University Hospital, Joe was charged with carrying a concealed weapon and returned to the Dozier School [a juvenile detention facility]. He escaped a little over a year later with three other boys. They were caught in Georgia with a stolen car and a weapon, and Joe and one other boy were sent to adult prison. By accident, in prison, Joe met his biological father. Joe's record in prison was good, and in November of 1976 he was paroled once again to the supervision of his mother.

By the time Joe reached the age of eighteen, his daily drug consumption alarmed his friends. One recalled that Joe "was on the verge of killing himself. He was living on that ragged edge in danger at any time of taking too much of an overdose," adding that Joe's binges often resulted in blackouts. A second friend spoke of addictions to beer, alcohol, prescription drugs, and PCP.

In the fall of 1978, Joe moved from Jacksonville, Florida, to Norfolk, Virginia, to work as a waterman on scallop boats. He spent weeks on the trawlers, working alongside a rough group of men who shared Joe's taste for alcohol and drugs. Through these men, Joe met Barbara "Toni" Kline, a small woman with dishwater blond hair, hooded eyes, and a smoker's rasp. Barbara was a single mother who worked in a nearby 7–Eleven to support her teenage daughter, Michelle. The two women lived in an old town house, which had been chopped up into smaller apartments, on Le Claire Street in Norfolk, where rooms were rented to a revolving cast of drug-addled tenants. Joe met Barbara the morning after a particularly wild party at her apartment, waking up on her couch and introducing himself. Joe had a sexual relationship with Barbara that was tense at times. During the next six months, Joe lived in a variety of places, including an abandoned car, Barbara's apartment, and in another apartment in the same run-down building.

In the early morning hours of February 6, 1979, Joe walked up to deputy sheriff Charles E. Wells, who was quietly eating breakfast in the cafeteria of the Jacksonville Greyhound bus terminal, and asked if they could talk. Later at Joe's trial, Deputy Wells would recall that Joe appeared "normal" and was wearing "dirty and sweaty" clothes. The deputy made no mention of seeing bloodstains on Joe's garments. Joe told Deputy Wells that he had killed two people and wanted to turn himself in. After the deputy advised Joe of his Miranda rights, and determined that Joe did not have a weapon, he asked Joe why he committed the murders. Joe simply responded that an argument had taken place over a thousand-dollar debt. Joe was then taken to the Jacksonville police station for questioning.

At approximately 4:00 a.m., Joe again waived his Miranda rights, including his right to have an attorney present, and over the next hour gave a series of more detailed confessions to two other Jacksonville deputies. In his second confession, he stated:

> I have been living in Norfolk, VA, for the last seven months. About three months ago I let Barbara Kline borrow $1000. On Monday, 5 February [19]79, at approximately 7:00 p.m., I went to Barbara's house . . . to ask her for the money. Barbara and I began to argue and I picked up a kitchen knife and stabbed her three or four times. Michelle Kline, Barbara's daughter, was there and began screaming so I had to strangle her to shut her up. I went outside of the house and threw the knife somewhere in the yard. I then caught a cab and went to the bus station and caught a bus to Jacksonville.

Prior to his second confession, a police officer asked Joe why he killed the two women. Joe recalls that he told the officer that he didn't know why. "I had no explanation to give him but, after he insisted that I must have had a reason, I gave a statement . . . but I have no actual memory of what I told him at that time . . . [and] I have never had any actual memory of my committing the murders. Not that night or now."

Joe gave two more confessions on the morning of February 6. In his third confession, he made no mention of Michelle ever being present at the apartment, while in the fourth confession he only discussed strangling Michelle Kline and did not reference a fight with, or murder of, Barbara. Deputy Wells would testify at Joe's trial that, during their conversation at the bus station, Joe confessed to raping Michelle, but that fact was not included in his original written report, and the testimony was elicited through a leading question. After Joe completed his fourth confession, he was examined by a doctor, given a tranquilizer, and allowed to rest.

At some point in the interview process, a Jacksonville public defender named Robert Link briefly met with Joe—a meeting Joe did not remember until he found the attorney's business card in his legal papers several years later. When interviewed by a private investigator Marie hired, Link recalled that he had warned Joe he would end up in the electric chair if he did not stop talking to the police. Joe ignored Link's pleas, telling the public defender that he had to cooperate with his captors.

By the time Joe confessed to Jacksonville law enforcement officers, Barbara and Michelle's landlord had discovered their bodies. The subsequent investigation would reveal that Barbara had been stabbed three times—once in the stomach and twice in the neck—and left in a pool of her own blood in her bathroom. Bloody footprints led away from her body. Michelle was found in one of the apartment's bedrooms, partially naked and her face covered with a blanket. She had been strangled and raped. The investigating officers carefully videotaped the crime scene, but the video would later disappear from their files after Joe's original trial. So would the biological evidence collected from the two victims.

Joe gave a fifth confession—again, without a lawyer present—on February 8, 1979, at the Jacksonville city jail. This time two Virginia detectives—Ralph J. Mears and Richard D. Whitt—conducted the interview. According to an affidavit later executed by Joe, the detectives started the interview by telling Joe they did not believe his earlier confessions.

> I told them that I had killed Barbara and Michelle, and apparently I gave them the same statement that I had given to the Jacksonville officer. They told me that it could not have happened like that. After further questioning about the statement I gave to the Jacksonville police, the Norfolk detective told me that he believed me when I said that I had murdered Barbara and Michelle, but that he needed to know the actual truth about what had happened. He then informed me that Barbara had been murdered after Michelle, and that Michelle had been raped; and that my statement to the Jacksonville officer could not have been right. I remember telling the detective then that I really couldn't remember what had happened because I was high, but that I had to have murdered them because I was the only one in the apartment. I told the officer that I would tell him what happened, but that I really could not remember.
>
> Eventually after going back and forth for several minutes the detective began asking me, "could it have happened like this, is this what happened?" And I would say "yes." The detective would then ask me to put it into my own words, and I would comply. After I would do that the other detective would write down what I had stated. He would repeat it back to me after he was finished, and ask me if that was correct. When the statement was finished they asked if I would sign and initial each page, and I agreed.

In the face of the information fed to Joe about the crime, his confession dramatically changed during the two-hour interrogation. Unlike in his four prior confessions, Joe now stated that it was Michelle, not Barbara, who was at the apartment when Joe arrived, and that he raped and then strangled Michelle after she refused to have sex. Joe also stated that he briefly left the apartment, before returning after he realized that the apartment's lights were on. When Barbara arrived at the apartment, Joe stated that he surprised her and then stabbed her two or three times with a kitchen knife with a seven-inch blade. Joe testified that he put the Kline's two dogs in the bedroom with Michelle's body, exited the apartment, locked the door, and tossed the knife (which was never found by the police) into the apartment's yard and the keys in a nearby dumpster. Then, he took a cab to a nearby Trailways bus station. When asked during the interview why he killed Barbara, he stated, "I stayed there because I knew Barbara would know I was the one that killed Michelle, and I wanted to keep her from talking."

At some point during the interrogation, the Norfolk detectives showed Joe a man's driver's license. After informing Joe that the license had been discovered at the crime scene, the detectives asked Joe if he recalled whether or not that individual had been in the apartment on the night of the murders. Joe recognized the picture on the license and told the detectives that he had seen the man around the apartments, although he did not know his name. Marie would later claim that the Norfolk police had gone as far as to prepare an arrest warrant for another man in the case, a claim the police denied. The driver's license would prove to be an elusive clue during Joe's appeals, a critical piece of evidence that the prosecution never mentioned at trial and later refused to turn over to Joe's appellate lawyers. To this day, all efforts by Joe's various teams of lawyers to obtain the license have failed.

Before discussing Joe's trial, it is important to highlight one crucial fact—to this day, Joe has no memories of the murders themselves or even waking up at the murder scene. Joe has a distinct memory of waking up in Barbara's apartment several months earlier after a hard night of partying, and Marie believed that it was this memory that Joe "conflated" with the murders. There is some evidence to support Marie's suspicions, including a witness that placed Joe in Florida at the time of the murders. And Marie hypothesized that someone in Florida may have told Joe about the murders, causing him to conclude that he committed the crimes. While subsequent teams of lawyers knew of Joe's complete lack of memory, a tactical decision was made not to challenge the portion of the confession in which Joe claimed to be at the murder scene.

The criminal justice system moved into high gear in the case of the *Commonwealth of Virginia v. Joseph Michael Giarratano*. While capital murder cases often take months, if not years, of investigation prior to trial, with flurries of motions, psychological examinations, and the careful collection of evidence, Joe's case moved with shocking speed toward resolution—aided, in part, by Joe's desire to be convicted and executed. Joe was quickly extradited to Virginia. Upon arriving at the jail, Joe noticed for the first time that he had two spots of blood on one of his boots—a fact he immediately reported to the jailor. Seeing the spots convinced Joe "that I was evil, that I had to be punished for what I did. I couldn't sleep, I couldn't keep any food down, I knew I was sick, and all I wanted to do was die." Seeking death, Joe unsuccessfully tried to hang himself in his jail cell.

After the suicide attempt, Joe was transported to Central State Hospital in Petersburg, Virginia, where doctors evaluated Joe's competency to stand trial and his mental state at the time of the offenses. During his nine-day stay at Central State, Joe reverted back to his original confession, claiming that he murdered Barbara first and then Michelle but that he did not rape either woman. And he added that he kicked in the door of the apartment before the murders, a fact not supported by the evidence. Hostile and suicidal, Joe tried to again kill himself by slashing his right wrist. And he did not help his cause by telling his doctors—falsely—that he had been admitted into a Florida mental hospital and had been in prison for trying to kill a police officer. Despite having placed Joe on a high dosage of Thorazine, the doctors at Central State Hospital determined that Joe was competent to assist in his own defense at trial and that he was sane at the time of the offenses. Joe's trial attorney never challenged the report about Joe's competency, nor was a psychiatrist or psychologist retained to be a defense expert.

Within two weeks of his confessions, Joe was indicted on capital murder charges by a Norfolk grand jury, and local attorney Albert D. Alberi was appointed to represent him. A graduate of the University of Virginia School of Law, Alberi had worked for five years in the Norfolk Commonwealth Attorney's office before opening a small law firm. Alberi would be hired by the Virginia Beach Commonwealth Attorney's Office after Joe's trial and would become a polarizing figure in the legal community. Alberi's "shenanigans" in and outside of the courtroom—including making a noose out of string during the rape trial of a black defendant, writing a threatening letter to a defense witness who testified in a death penalty trial, and failing to forward exculpatory evidence to defense attorneys in a murder trial of a juvenile defendant—led to public reprimands from several trial court judges and vocal criticism from defense attorneys. "The picture that emerges," observed the *Richmond Times-Dispatch*, "is of a man revered by his friends and colleagues, but feared and distrusted by many of the defense attorneys, police officers and defense witnesses who have opposed Alberi during his nearly twenty years as a prosecutor." One of those defense attorneys who witnessed Alberi fashion a noose in open court was more blunt, referring to Alberi as an "avenging angel" who "has no faith in the law . . . [he] feels he has to help it. He's got to give it that extra nudge to make sure it comes out right."[2]

In the 1990s, Alberi would see his repeated nominations to the judicial bench come under sustained attacks. The local bar association rated him as "unqualified" when Alberi was first nominated, although his third—and final—nomination to be a Virginia district court judge proved successful. Given Alberi's prosecutorial zeal, one wonders how much passion and energy he brought to defending a suspected killer like Joe.

Lawrence C. Lawless, a local prosecutor who would also become a state court judge, led the prosecution against Joe. Known for his biting wit, Lawless thought little of Joe—whom he later characterized as a "loser" whose weight, acne scars, and false stories of childhood abuse would not have endeared him to a jury. "Joe was not a lovable boy . . . there was very little about him that was likable that I could think of," recalled Lawless. As for the public support for Joe and his appeals, Lawless remarked that Joe had cultivated a charming air and "may have gotten himself the equivalent of a master's degree in human relationships" in an effort to avoid the electric chair. "He may find that being a celebrity is probably a very, very attractive prospect to him," opined Lawless.[3] The former prosecutor, however, was unmoved

Former Commonwealth Attorney Lawrence Lawless, who prosecuted Joe Giarratano. Lawless later volunteered to pull the electric chair switch at Giarratano's execution. Photograph courtesy of *Richmond Times-Dispatch*.

by Joe's claims of innocence. "Even a madman would not have made the confessions he did if he had not done it. He just knew too much about how it was done."[4] For Lawless, Joe's appeals were simply a means of killing time while sitting on death row. And he was so confident of Joe's guilt, Lawless volunteered to play a more active role in Joe's execution. "If they needed a volunteer to push the button I'd do it off-duty, on the weekend. I'd pay my own expenses to Richmond."[5]

When the possibility of a plea agreement was raised, in which a life sentence would be offered in exchange for a guilty plea, Joe refused and requested that he have a bench trial (a trial in which the judge serves as a fact finder) rather than a jury trial. The trial was held four months after the murders, with Norfolk Circuit Court Judge Thomas Randolph McNamara presiding. A graduate of the Virginia Military Institute and the Washington and Lee School of Law, Judge McNamara was fairly new to the trial court bench. A long-time partner at the Norfolk law firm of Williams, Cocke & Tunstall, McNamara had balanced his legal practice with service in the Virginia General Assembly before becoming a judge.

The trial itself lasted four hours. Six witnesses were called by local prosecutor Lawrence Lawless. They included Deputy Chief Medical Examiner Faruk Presswalla, who testified that Barbara Kline had died of stab wounds inflicted by a "small bladed knife" and that Michelle Kline had been raped and strangled; latent print examiner Leon C. Melcher, who testified that he recovered twenty-one finger prints from the apartment, one of which was Joe's; Peter Mohrmann, the manager of the 7–Eleven at which Barbara worked and the person who identified the bodies; Ralph J. Mears, the veteran homicide investigator to whom Joe provided his fifth confession; serologist June Browne, who testified that a pubic hair found on Michelle Kline's body was consistent with Joe's in terms of "race, color, and microscopic characteristics," but she couldn't testify that it was Joe's; and Central State psychiatrist Miller M. Ryans, who opined that Joe was not insane at the time of the murders but that drugs of the type used by Joe on February 4, 1979, could "loosen" a person's impulse control.

What was not introduced at trial was a written report, which had been provided to the prosecutor, suggesting that Barbara's stab wounds were inflicted by a right-handed person. This report would have undercut the prosecution's theory of the case, since Joe is left-handed and has a weak right hand due to a neurological defect. It is unclear from the record whether a copy of the report was given to defense counsel.

The defense called a mere two witnesses to the stand. Joe had asserted an insanity defense, and it is the responsibility of the defendant's attorney to offer the testimony and reports of expert witnesses to support such a defense. Joe's attorney, however, provided no such witnesses. Instead, he called two fact witnesses to the stand: Jacksonville Deputy Sheriffs Charles Wells and William J. Mooyham. Deputy Wells simply testified to his encounter with Joe at the Jacksonville bus station, while Deputy Mooyham discussed his interrogation of Joe at the Jacksonville jail. It is unclear why the defense called either witness, except to demonstrate the inconsistencies in Joe's confessions.

Joe was not an active participant in the bench trial. A contemporary newspaper account stated: "Clad in blue jeans and a velvet shirt, his feet chained and his hair tied tightly in a ponytail, Girratano [sic] sat motionless through the four-hour trial."[6] There was a very good reason why Joe was motionless: he was stoned. "I was drugged to the gills with Thorazine. To the point that I was drooling," Joe explained. "At one point the judge wanted to know where I was getting drugs. Both my lawyer and the prosecutor jumped up and said that I was under psychiatric care, that I was highly suicidal, and I had to be sedated." Neither the judge, the prosecutor, nor Joe's own lawyer seemed concerned that trying an incompetent defendant violated his constitutional rights to due process.[7]

Defense attorney Alberi's closing argument was brief, focusing on the defense claims that Joe could not be found guilty of capital murder because his admission of drug use and his inconsistent statements to the police demonstrated that he was too drug-addled to form the requisite premeditated intent. Judge McNamara quickly rejected the argument and pronounced from the bench that Joe was guilty of rape, murder, and capital murder. With that, the trial of the *Commonwealth of Virginia v. Joseph Michael Giarratano* was swiftly resolved.

The penalty hearings held in August were equally speedy. Under Virginia law, a defendant who is convicted of capital murder is eligible for the death penalty if the prosecutor can demonstrate either that the crime was "vile" or that the defendant poses a future risk of dangerousness to society (which includes corrections officers and fellow inmates). If the prosecution proves either factor, then the burden shifts to the defense to offer mitigation evidence, namely, evidence that the defendant's life should be spared.

The evidence and testimony offered by the prosecution at the August 7th penalty hearing went a long way in sealing Joe's fate. The first document introduced by the prosecution was a pre-sentence report prepared by a state probation officer. The report relied heavily on statements given by Joe's mother, Carol Parise, who told the probation officer that Joe was a difficult child who was depressed because he was obese. Carol claimed that, as he grew older, Joe stole money from her and was violent. As for her husband and the rest of her children, Carol described them as the "all-American family" and provided letters, later determined to be fake, from friends who praised Carol as a virtuous and loving mother. Based on interviews with Joe, the probation report further characterized him as a habitual drug addict who boasted of his criminal activities and saw the death penalty as a way of escaping a life sentence.

The prosecution also relied on the testimony of Dr. Ryans, the Central State psychiatrist who challenged Joe's assertion of insanity. Dr. Ryans testified that Joe was a "ticking time bomb" whose mental state and drug addiction made him a continuing threat to society. The defendant's own defense expert, Dr. Robert Showalter, was called by the defense to offer "mitigation evidence," namely, evidence that Joe's life should be spared. His testimony did not help Joe. Dr. Showalter opined that Joe's abusive childhood and the resulting anger toward his mother resulted in severe mental distress and a "schizoid personality disorder" at the time of the murders. Dr. Showalter added that the murder of Barbara and Michelle Kline was "symbolic" because Joe was really trying to murder his mother and his sister, both of whom Joe considered to be as sexually immoral as the Klines. During cross examination, Dr. Showalter conceded that he agreed with Dr. Ryans's assessment that Joe was a "ticking time bomb" who would likely suffer from mental illness his entire life.

The last witness at the penalty hearing was Joe's mother. She spent less than ten minutes on the stand, testifying that Dr. Showalter's testimony was "very true" and that she wished the doctor "could have helped him [Joe] when he was little." She concluded by asking the court to "have mercy" on Joe. It was not a performance by a mother desperate to save her son from the electric chair.

A second, much shorter penalty hearing was scheduled for August 13th at the request of defense counsel, who wanted to recall State Medical Examiner Presswalla. While Dr. Presswalla was unable to attend that hearing, a letter was read into evidence. In it, the doctor stated that, in his expert opinion, Michelle Kline died "some hours before" Barbara. It is unclear why Joe's attorney considered this evidence helpful to his client since it supported the most damaging of Joe's five confessions.

Immediately after the August 13th penalty hearing, Joe sat down in his jail cell and wrote a letter to Judge McNamara requesting that he be given the death penalty "to end my pain." The trial court judge accommodated Joe's wishes, sentencing him to death on August 17, 1979. The whirlwind of legal proceedings came to an abrupt end, and, within six months of his original confession, Joe walked onto Virginia's death row. He had just turned twenty-four years old. For his services in defending Joe, the Commonwealth of Virginia awarded Albert Alberi $1,400—approximately eight dollars a day for representing a man facing death at the hands of the state. Against his client's wishes, Alberi subsequently filed an unsuccessful appeal with the Virginia Supreme Court. Alberi wrote a mere ten-page brief in support of the appeal. For that, he was awarded another $300.

When later defending the quality of legal representation given to Joe, Alberi would complain that Joe would not answer questions about the case. "He [Joe] was difficult for me to fathom because in questioning him he would give very flat answers to my questions. If I'd ask him why he did something, he'd give an answer which in my estimation was not very well developed or amplified." Given Joe's belief that he deserved to die, combined with his mental state, one can sympathize with Alberi's lament that his client did not fully participate in his own defense.

Alberi was dubious of the claims that critical evidence had been withheld during the trial, and later remarked, "at no time in sixteen years [since the trial] did anything get printed [in the newspaper] where I said 'Whoops, I didn't know about that.'"[8] This statement is a bit harder to swallow. Given the new evidence discovered in the decade since Joe's original trial, evidence documented in a slew of newspaper articles and court filings, one could argue that Alberi had not been keeping up on the local news, or that his true feelings about his client and the trial were surfacing.

Summing up the process, Marie wrote:

> Joe refused to defend himself. In his mind, he was guilty and deserved to die. He tried to take his own life several times before trial. Failing that, he orchestrated his defense to assure his death. So compelling was Joe's prosecution of himself that no one involved in his case at trial—police officers, defense counsel, prosecutor, Central State Hospital staff, defense psychiatrist, or judge— entertained the possibility that he might not be guilty. No one stepped back and asked, "Could his confessions be unreliable? Could they be the product of his imagination rather than his recollection? Could his profound sense of guilt be driven by a deluded process that made him think he had committed two murders when he had not rather than a realization that what he knew he did was horrible?

At the time of Joe's conviction, Virginia's death row was located at the Mecklenburg Correctional Center near Boydton, Virginia, a small town near the North Carolina border. Built in 1977, the Department of Corrections boasted that Mecklenburg was a modern, technological wonder from which no prisoner could escape. "Yet there was a wide gulf between the prison's 'fail-safe' public face and reality," wrote authors Joe Jackson and William F. Burke Jr. "Mecklenburg was not a peaceable kingdom. The guards and inmates knew it, but prison officials placed so much faith in their [modern prison] design that they suffered from a *Titanic*-like syndrome, simply re-

Virginia death row inmate Frank Coppola at a court hearing. Coppola was a former police officer who was the first inmate executed after Virginia resumed executions in 1982. Coppola served as a mentor and friend to Giarratano. Photograph courtesy of UPI.

fusing to believe that disaster could occur."[9] Moreover, Mecklenburg was a prison boiling over with brutality, despair, and corruption. Filled with Virginia's most violent inmates and watched over by poorly paid correctional officers willing to bring contraband and drugs into the prison for the right price, Mecklenburg was akin "to Chernobyl on the eve of its meltdown."[10]

Death row was located in its own building at Mecklenburg and was separated from the violence and chaos of the prison's general population. At the time of Joe's arrival, he was one of only five inmates housed in what would become a rapidly growing death row. His fellow inmates included Frank Coppola, Morris Mason, Michael Marnell Smith, James Clark, and Alton Waye. All but Giarratano and Clark would subsequently die in Virginia's electric chair.

Of these original five inmates, Joe became closest with Coppola, whom he considered to be an older brother. Coppola was an unusual death row inmate, a man who had attended seminary and worked as a police officer before he was convicted of killing the wife of a wealthy used car dealer during a violent robbery. Joe would spend time with Coppola's wife and children when they came on visitation day, once even giving a kiss to Coppola from his young son, who wasn't allowed to make contact with his father. It was Coppola who browbeat Joe into pursuing his appeals, only to anger the younger man when Coppola himself—who was suffering from kidney disease and worried about his children being bullied at school after someone had left a tiny electric chair on his son's desk—dropped his appeals. Before his execution, Coppola announced, "it is my honest intention to rescue any semblance of dignity I have left."[11]

The impact of Coppola's death still resonates with Joe today, and he is unable to discuss his friend's death without becoming emotional. "I still feel the helplessness I experienced that day while locked in my cell, watching my friend be chained," Joe stated in an interview, "the helplessness I felt when Frank stopped in front of my cell, so that we could shake hands and say goodbye through my slot, as the guards said 'Let's go Frank,' not able to look either of us in the face."[12]

Marie re-entered Joe's life in March of 1983. By this time, Joe had tried to kill himself again, was involuntarily medicated with a daily dose of nine hundred milligrams of Thorazine, and was considering dropping his second post-conviction appeal (state habeas corpus). Lloyd Snook described Joe's physical and mental condition in the spring of 1983:

> When I first met Joe, he shuffled into the room and sat down at the table across from me. Although the temperature was over ninety degrees, he was shivering. From the very beginning Joe was a basket case. He was nervous, paranoid, sometimes actively delusional, and often angry at me for talking him into continuing his appeals. It was obvious to me that the psychiatric diagnoses were largely accurate—that Joe was under great stress, that he was on the verge of psychosis, that he was suicidal—but that he was genuinely remorseful for the crimes that he thought that he had committed, and that he believed he did not deserve to live because of those crimes.

The recent execution of Frank Coppola was still haunting Joe, and he wanted to follow the same path as his mentor and friend and volunteer to be killed. As Marie writes below, Joe would not be the first death row inmate she tried to convince to "pick up" his appeals. Working with such inmates was exhausting and terrifying, because one of the only things that stood between the condemned men and the electric chair was Marie's power of persuasion.

> I'd worked with numerous men who had dropped their appeals. All had eventually picked them up, but it's an Alice in Wonderland situation. The state becomes the man's advocate, arguing for and protecting his right to choose to be executed. The prosecutors and prison officials become possessive of the man and see themselves as protecting him from the torture his defense team is putting him through. The defense team begins to take on the full moral and legal responsibility for stopping his execution. Defense teams newly confronted with what were called "volunteers" for execution were always looking for some magic bullet—a reason to give their clients to pick up their appeals. I knew there were none. Working with these men was a long process of peeling back the layers of onion of their rationalizations until you finally reach the core of their reasons for dropping their appeals, then dealing directly with those reasons.
>
> [On March 24, 1983, Marie drove from Richmond, VA, to Boydton, VA, to visit Joe on death row and try to change his mind]. After a four-hour visit, Joe agreed to sign his habeas [petition, a type of appeal], but he told me he could not

promise me that he would be able to continue his appeals. His physical discomfort—clenching his jaws, fighting back tears, etc.—combined with his pat answers when I questioned him about his family led me to believe there was a great deal of trauma in Joe's life that he was unable to divulge.

I put Joe on my special attention list and visited him as often as I could. Over the next few months, Lloyd and I both spent hundreds of hours with Joe and retained the services of two psychologists to work with Joe as well. Joe was short, but stocky, and I was surprised to find he had a limp handshake. The handshake made me pay attention to his physical being, and I noticed that he dragged his right foot slightly. He was polite and ingratiating at each visit. He talked about the men on the row, the assistance and support they needed, their cases, the conditions on the row, anything but his own case. It was clear through these visits that his agenda was to keep me at a distance.

[In May of 1983, Joe stopped writing to Marie and ignored her telephone calls and visitation requests]. On July 13, 1983, six months after I'd gotten involved in his case, Joe filed a request to withdraw his current appeal, stating, among other things, that he fully understood that his actions "will result in my demise by means of electrocution." Lloyd promptly wrote the court requesting an examination of Joe's competency to withdraw his appeals. At the same time, the attorney general's office, confident that Joe would be found competent, petitioned for a thorough examination to be carried out at the state penitentiary in Richmond.

Joe made it clear to Lloyd that he would no longer see me, but Lloyd made a trip to Mecklenburg with the express purpose of getting Joe to allow me to visit. The best he could get was that Joe agreed to call me one time. The call started with Joe being his usual ingratiating self and thanking me for my efforts. He told me there was nothing I could do to change his mind and the other men on the row needed my time, so he certainly didn't want to waste it. I listened, then I asked him why he was afraid of me.

"I'm not afraid of you!"

"You're not? Then prove it. I will come visit you, and you will not refuse my visit."

I hung up, banking on two things: Joe's politeness and his response to any challenge. And I was right. Joe could not resist the challenge to prove that he wasn't afraid of my convincing him to pick up his appeals, nor could he refuse to come out for a visit after someone, especially a "lady," had driven more than two hours to see him.

[Marie returned to death row on August 12, 1983]. During that visit, which lasted several hours, Joe looked as if he hadn't slept in days, and he was very hyper. His agitation when I mentioned his family was more pronounced. Joe was intent on convincing me that he was not committing suicide by dropping his appeals. A Roman Catholic, he had asked Bishop Walter Sullivan, Bishop of the Diocese of Richmond, if the Church would consider his dropping his appeals to be suicide. According to Joe, the Bishop had told him it would not. I told him I

didn't care about the religious technicalities; he and I both knew he was committing suicide. He argued well, dragging out theology, but Lutherans go through the
same religious training as Catholics, so Joe soon got frustrated and switched to
talking about conditions on the row.

On August 23, 1983, Joe was transferred to the Virginia State Penitentiary
in Richmond and put in the death house to assess his competency to waive his
appeals. The death house rattled everyone who went in it, prisoner and free-
world person alike. The look of it fitted its purpose. It was in the basement of
the state pen. To get to it, you went through the administrative offices, two sets
of automatic steel doors, another set of doors out to the yard, then down a set of
steps and through a solid steel door the guard inside had to unlock. You entered a
kind of foyer with the death chamber straight ahead of you and the holding cells
behind yet another steel door to your left. The walls were painted, maybe twenty
years ago, an institutional white that had slowly peeled off to the dingy gray
concrete beneath. Water from rusting pipes constantly seeped down the walls and
square pillars used to support the cellblocks above. The water stains and mold
growing from them provided the only color in the place. There were metal pans
around the floor to catch the worst of the water flows. Water dripping into the
pans was the Chinese torture I'd heard about, but like the men and the guards,
I—or my mind for its own preservation—learned to ignore it.

What light there was came from old humming fluorescent fixtures and, on
clear days, the two squat windows that faced the concrete wall of the outside
staircase. In the past, before there was general agreement among corrections officials that death row should be separated from the death house, this had served
as both, so two rows of cells faced each other. The bars had been painted so many
times they were twice as thick as the steel they were made of. The air was dank
and musty and roaches and mice ran freely throughout. There were holes in the
ceilings of each cell about the circumference of a nickel. Every man who'd been
there told me about mice falling out of the holes while they tried to sleep at night.
Once one had run up the leg of the chair I was sitting on. Whoever was there
faced a guard who watched his every move twenty-four hours a day.

The day after Joe was moved to the death house, I showed up for what would
be my almost daily visits [Marie estimated that she and Lloyd Snook spent
hundreds of hours with Joe in the death house in the subsequent two months as
Joe was gripped with auditory and visual hallucinations]. Legal visits were held
in the "cool off room." You entered it by going down the length of the cells and
through the guards' bathroom. On the opposite wall were two barred windows.
If you got close enough to them, you were eye level with the small lawn and wall
in front of the prison. Pipes and electrical conduits ran up and down, floor to
ceiling, and crisscrossed the top of the room. To your right was another door to
the death chamber. The electric chair was about five feet from that door. The
condenser that controlled the electric chair was beside the door. On the other side
of the room was the table used to straighten the bodies of those who had just been
executed. That was where the men and their legal visitors sat. Seeing the scars

*and bits of what we assumed to be human flesh stuck to the table ratcheted up
your sense of urgency.*

Marie's visits with Joe were complicated by the fact that he stopped taking Thorazine, a high-powered psychotropic drug used to treat the mentally ill. In Joe's case, it had been passed around death row like candy in order to control the inmates. The drugs often turned the men into bleary-eyed zombies, and corrections officers used the phrase the "Thorazine shuffle" to refer to the inmates' uncertain gait. Looking back at the early days of Joe's detoxification, Marie bluntly stated that Joe was "batshit—perching in unnatural positions for hours, hearing voices."[13] Nevertheless, Marie persisted.

*We started going through those outer layers of the onion. I didn't argue with him.
I simply discounted every rationalization he gave. He started with the usual—no
reason to live, he only would be executed later, so why sit on death row waiting
for the inevitable. "How do you know what's inevitable?" I asked. Each time I
asked him a question, Joe's jaws would start clenching.*

*"Well, even if I won my case, I'd be in prison for the rest of my life. I can't do
life in prison. Why would anyone put themselves through that?"*

*"Look," I told him, "You've already demonstrated you have no respect for life,
you don't need to demonstrate that again, and if you can't do prison time, you
should have thought of that before you killed Barbara and Michelle." He stared at
me. I stared back.*

*During my visits a lot of time was spent in our staring matches. The cool off
room was around the corner from the guard's station, and our sudden silence
made the guards uneasy. Each time it would happen, a guard would soon show
up to check us out. Their presence would often serve as a way to break the staring
and let us go on. Joe would shake his head or roll his eyes and try again.*

*After a number of these visits, I said: "I'm going to keep coming here whether
you talk to me or not, so you can keep trying to feed me this crap, you can talk to
me, or you can be quiet. My preference is that you talk to me, and I don't know
what you think you have to lose by doing so."*

*After another few minutes of silence, Joe said: "You make me want to trust
you, but I can't let you get next to me for the same reason I can't let God get next
to me." Joe's jaws began to clench even as he was talking. "There's a struggle going
on in me. On one level—one side is trying to defeat the other side. One level says
keep talking, keep talking, keep talking. The other side says stop talking to her,
cut her off, cut her off, cut her off. I know what's wrong with me. I have to beat it
now. If I go over the edge, it doesn't matter. I die. If I win, if I beat it, I can live. I
can't live if I can't beat it. But there's a limit. I had to set a time limit. I couldn't
let it go on. If I don't win in time, I go to the chair."*

Part of Joe did want to live. "Then let me help you beat it," I told him.

"Why?" he asked me.

"Because I do respect life, and despite your demonstration, there is something

in you that does as well. You need to honor that. Until you do, you haven't earned the right to die, and as for letting God get next to you, do you fear his grace?"

Finally, Joe began to talk, and as he did, he began rocking back and forth in his chair, and he seemed to be watching or listening to something well outside the cool off room. He told me about "the voice" that he remembered from the time he was about three. The voice would tell him to do things, but it also told him it loved him and would take care of him. He liked the voice until it told him to kill his mother. Then he would do anything to get rid of the voice, bombard himself with drugs and alcohol, slit his wrists, anything he could think of to make the voice go away. He called the voice his imaginary friend. "Most imaginary friends come around because you're lonely, right? Mine came out of hate and fear. I was afraid to be alone. I would wake up and call my mother in the middle of the night, but she wasn't there. I'm still afraid of the dark. I cover myself up when I sleep. I guess so the boogeyman can't get me." Now the voice was laughing at him and yelling things like "whore" and "fool" at him.

Joe was convinced that he was evil and a danger to anyone around him. "Don't you understand," he asked me. "If I can brutally murder a woman and a girl, both of them friends who'd done nothing to me, and not even remember it . . . I mean, think of that. I don't even remember murdering two people. What kind of monster can kill two people and forget it? If I can do that, and I have, only God—or Satan—knows what I'm capable of doing."

Sometimes he would try to scare me away, pointing out how far the guard was, how he could get to me and "break you in half" before the guard could get to the door. Once I threw a cup half full of coffee at him. He was shocked. "Are you crazy? You don't go around throwing things at murderers. They might kill you!"

"You didn't," I told him. "That's my point."

Along with my two-hour visits to Joe and the long phone calls from him almost every night, I was still getting attorneys for men on death row, monitoring their cases, doing big hunks of investigation into their social history, counseling them over the phone, assisting in capital trials, administering the Coalition, and raising funds. I also had my own son to take care of. The physical and emotional toll of feeling responsible for what would happen to Joe was wearing me down. By the end of September, I'd have gone for amphetamines if I'd had the money and knew of sources. I'd been skinny all my life, but I was losing so much weight my clothes were hanging on me. I couldn't afford new clothes and didn't have the time to buy them if I could. Instead, I bought something called "Weight On" and doubled the recommended daily dosage.

About once a week, I'd tell Joe not to call that night. I knew the telephone calls were in large part to keep away the "voice," and I hated to deny him that sense of security, but after six days of the schedule I was attempting to keep, I had to try to get a decent night's sleep. Sleep was elusive though. The minute I slowed down I began to question my arrogance. Who was I to drag this man through this torture? Who was I to decide what should happen to him, to decide that he hadn't earned the right to die? We had learned something of Joe's background, and it was ugly. Maybe some of us couldn't survive. Maybe it was too late for Joe to learn the unconditional love and sense of self-worth the nuns had taught me. Maybe, maybe, maybe. Lloyd seemed so much surer. He had moved away from thinking of Joe as his client and worrying about his case. The lawyer was still there, but more than anything it was Lloyd, the Christian, who was responding to Joe. I drew strength from Lloyd's sureness.

The theological discussions continued with Joe always throwing Bishop Sullivan back at anything we said. One day a priest showed up. Father Jim Griffin turned out to be the Bishop's right hand man, and before he could sit down, Joe said: "I've stopped my appeals. Bishop Sullivan says I'm not committing suicide." He jerked his head toward me. "She says I am."

This was all new to Father Jim, who'd come over to the state pen to visit some of the Catholics there and had been told there was another in the death house. He asked for a little more information. "It means," I said, "that he wants the state to kill him."

"It means," Joe said, "that I accept my punishment."

Father Jim thought about this for a minute then said: "If I understand this correctly, I think the Bishop is wrong, if he actually said that to you."

All Joe could say was: "Well, you're just a priest." He clearly was shaken by Father Jim's pronouncement, and as the months wore on and Father Jim continued to visit, Joe kept going back to the suicide question. No matter what he threw at Father Jim, the answer was the same. "Joe, what you're trying to do is commit suicide."

It was the best help we had had from the clergy. In writing to Father Jim for additional help, Lloyd put Joe's spiritual crisis well: "When confronted with what seems to be a rational argument from Joe, clergymen have typically backed off, preferring to offer compassion rather than contesting what he says. Marie and I are the only two people who have disagreed with him—the only ones he simply couldn't jettison. I sent Joe a prayer from the Episcopalian prayer book, the essence of which is 'deliver us from the presumption of coming to you for solace and not strength; for pardon and not renewal.' That is precisely what Joe has been doing—coming to the Church for pardon and solace. Unfortunately, the clergy have offered pardon and solace only. We have been trying also to give him strength and renewal."

During one marathon visit, which included first a psychologist we had hired and then Father Jim, Joe's voice was growing loud enough and persistent enough to take up most of his attention. He told me on the phone that night that he couldn't make the voice shut up so he could answer the psychologist and that the room was "acting funny."

"What was the room doing?"

"It wasn't part of the building. It was moving. It was alive and more perfect. The walls were really bright, everything looked so sharp. It wasn't like we were in a building. It was just that room. I was hallucinating. That's what was going on when you got mad and slammed your hand on the table."

"I just wanted you to pay attention, but did it stop the hallucination?"

"It did," he said, "but the whole thing panicked me. I didn't know what to do. I wanted to run. Look what he did to the psychologist and the priest. He does that to everyone he's ever seen, and you and Lloyd want to argue with me. He had to put Lloyd in his place."

"Who has to put these people in their place? Who talked to all of them? Why is it important to put these people in their place?"

"I don't know. I like them."

"You trying to put me in check?"

"NO!"

"I think you are."

And then Joe's voice changed, became very harsh, brittle and hateful. "DON'T YOU TALK TO ME LIKE THAT!" He screamed at the guard to come get the phone.

I felt like I'd been kicked in the stomach and head. I was sitting on the sofa and pulled my knees up to my chin and wrapped my arms around them. Joe would be killed, and it was my fault. I'd screwed up, pushed too hard, said the wrong thing. I could see him strapped into the chair, the mask pulled over his face, the electricity coursing through his body. I could see him taken, stiff and gargoyle like, to the cool off room, the sand bags attached to his legs and arms, his bones being broken to straighten his body. I could see bits of his skin adhering to the table. I would see them the next time I had a legal visit with the man who would come after him. I cursed myself for my failure. I should have been more gentle. I shouldn't have let him think I was sure of myself. Why had I said this, why had I not said that?

An hour and a half later he called back to apologize for hanging up. I'd been given a reprieve. I uncurled my body, took a deep breath, and asked why he had hung up. He said he got angry with me, but should have said something before just hanging up like that. When I told Joe what he had said he argued at first that he would never say anything like that to me. Then he got scared.

During the next month, Joe continued to get worse. Lloyd and I began to recognize the signs when he would start hallucinating. As the time for a decision on his competency came closer, he grew more panicky.

One day he told me if I asked him to pick up his appeals, he would. "I'm not going to ask you that, Joe. It won't work. Later, when you've screwed up your courage and think you can act as if you are competent, you'll just drop them again. So, that's not going to happen. It's now, Joe. Now that you have to fight it, and now that you have to beat it."

"He is telling me you can't help me."

"Do you believe that?"

"I think if you decide you can't help me, you'll leave. You said you had no intention of holding my hand while I went to the electric chair, and you know *what I have to do to stay out of it, so I know as long as you keep coming around, you can help me."*

A few days later, Joe got angry with Lloyd and was yelling at me over the phone about it. After trying to reason with him for a while, I reminded him that I was working with Lloyd against the state in this battle over Joe's competency. "You drew that line, Joe."

He was quiet for a moment and then said: "You know what, Marie? I take too much out on you. I've got an idea. You got a magic marker, a piece of cardboard, and a piece of string? Take the magic marker and write on the piece of cardboard 'temporarily out of order' and tie it around your neck with the string."

At the end of October [of 1983] the examinations were complete, and Joe was moved back to Mecklenburg. The night before, he called me. He was worried about how he would hold up. "You make me feel safe," he told me. "You come visit me, let me call whenever I want to. I know there is someone I can grab on to." I told him he could call whenever allowed and that I would write and be thinking about him, that Lloyd and I would come visit him.

"But Joe, I'm still not holding your hand. If it comes to a competency hearing, I'm going to fight you. Remember I'll be there for one reason, to keep you out of that damned electric chair."

"I'm sure you won't let me forget it, and I like that because I need you."

"How, for what?"

"I just know I need you. I trust you, and even I know that I don't stand a chance without trusting someone."

"Wait a minute. A chance at what?"

"Of having the energy and will to fight."

"Fight for what?"

"For life, isn't that what you want me to fight for?"

"Yes."

"I promise. I will do my best."

Joe's promise helped me deal with the sense of relief I felt when he was taken back to Mecklenburg on October 31, 1983. I desperately needed sleep and some time alone in the evenings. The weekend after he went back, I slept for twenty-four hours. On Sunday, Robert and I went to Strawberry Street, our favorite area of Richmond. We bought a big cup of good coffee for me, a coke for Robert, and a dozen chocolate chip cookies from the bakery, and we ate them all on a park bench. We talked about anything and everything but Joe. Then we poked around a music store, and I bought each of us a record. Being outside with Robert on a gorgeous fall day doing ordinary things was exhilarating. I hadn't even noticed before that the leaves on the trees were turning their brilliant colors. They were so beautiful I thought they might burn my eyes. They didn't, but they did remind me of the ordinary miracles in life I shouldn't forget.

Joe had a headache when he left Richmond, which turned out to be an abscess in one of his teeth. He tried for several days to get the guards to take him to the dentist. On November 4, 1983, he refused to go back into his cell after breakfast break until he could see a dentist. His standoff lasted a couple of hours before the "goon" squad was called in. He was gassed, taken down, and dragged out of the pod and down the stairs to isolation.

Another of Lloyd's clients called to let him know what had happened. We were concerned that this might push Joe into demanding an immediate execution date, and it was important that one or both of us get in to see him. After much threatening between Lloyd and the warden, I was allowed to see Joe two days later. He was in pretty bad shape. He had not had a shower, and the water in his isolation cell had been cut off. His skin was red and raw, his eyes were blood red and watering, and he had bruises and puncture marks on his body. Yet the prison officials were insisting that Joe had not been gassed and that the only force used against him was to overcome his resistance. Mecklenburg was under court order on a conditions suit and was mandated to film all incidents, so we knew there would be a tape of this one.

Joe was amazed by our determination in getting to see him and taking on the prison about the gassing. I told him I wasn't interested in some general conditions complaint. This would be specifically about their gassing him, which meant he would have to stick around a while to give us time to get through this. "Yes, Ma'am," he said, looking very much like one of my sons after they'd been chastised.

The federal judge presiding over the conditions suit ordered a viewing of the tape with me, Lloyd, and representatives from the ACLU and attorney general's office, which was still denying that Joe had been gassed. Before the tape was shown, the attorney general gave us an introduction. He said we would see that Joe had been given more than ample time to go into his cell, that the guards had tried to reason with him, but that when they said they would have to come in, Joe had picked up a weapon (a mop), and that they had used only the minimum amount of force necessary to disarm him. We would see that during the entire length of the incident no gas had been used.

Hours into the tape, we saw a hand come up with a canister and watched as the camera slowly followed the precise stream of mace leaving the canister and going straight into Joe's eyes. Apparently, the attorney general's office had taken the word of prison officials, who were too arrogant to think their word might be challenged and so had not foreseen the tape being shown. The attorney general looked at the tape in total disbelief. "Gotcha," I thought and started laughing. The prison officials had been caught red-handed.

But it only got worse as we then watched CS gas released into the pod, and the guards, protected from head to foot, went in and pummeled Joe to the ground, dragged him out of the pod, and bumped his body down a set of concrete steps. I stopped laughing and began to get angry.

The next scene made me gag. The camera followed the guards and Joe into the isolation cell. Joe was dropped onto the floor and the guards began repeatedly kicking him. Their boots seemed to be flying into every part of his body. One guard jumped on Joe's chest as he tried to pull himself into a ball for some protec-

Death row inmates Lem Tuggle and Giarratano. Note the anti–death penalty sticker on the beam behind them. Tuggle was one of the six inmates who escaped from the Mecklenburg Correctional Center, making it as far as Vermont before being captured. Photograph courtesy of *Richmond Times-Dispatch*.

tion. There was no way the attorney general's office or the prison officials could make this look like "a reasonable use of minimal force." The guards were out of control. Finally, a senior guard came into the picture and stopped the mayhem. I couldn't imagine how every bone in Joe's body hadn't been broken at least once.

Naturally, we won that round. After all the hassle we had endured from the Virginia Department of Corrections, Joe was delighted, not for himself but for us and for the men on the row. "Wow," he told me, "these guys are in good hands."

It wasn't the response we hoped for, but after thinking about it a while, and remembering Joe's many references to being useless in prison—"all we do is take up space. You can't do anything in here that has any meaning"—I asked Joe to help us out with the problems on the row. "We can't do battle with the DOC alone, you know. We need guys on the row who can get the straight facts to us and guide us. We need men who won't be vague or embellish. We need men who are trusted by the other men, and we need men who can let us know when lawyers drop cases or courts deny appeals." The row was divided into two pods at the time, and I asked Joe to be his pod's monitor for the Coalition.

"Good try," he said, "but I've got this other thing going on." I told him whatever happened with his appeals, he would have time to set the model, and he said he'd think about it.

The reports from the evaluation came in. The prison doctor believed Joe was suffering from paranoid schizophrenia, as did one of our experts. This was the second time Joe had been diagnosed with schizophrenia, but psychiatric reports going back into his childhood noted schizoid personality disorder characterized by decompensation into psychosis in times of stress. The state, of course, found him to be competent to drop his appeals, citing as one example, his "bright-normal" IQ. Lloyd and I felt we would stand a decent chance at a competency hearing, but we knew that, in Virginia, not much works in the legal arena, and we didn't want to rely on a hearing. We kept working to get Joe to pick up his appeals.

Late in November, at the prison hearing to determine punishment for not going into his cell when ordered, Lloyd and I were allowed to represent Joe. Instead of the expected weeks or months of isolation, Joe was given what amounted to a slap on the wrist. We got to visit him for a few minutes in the hall after the hearing. "I didn't expect all this," Joe told us. "I mean, it's not like you're getting paid for any of this. In fact, it must be costing you a lot." Lloyd and I just looked at him. It wasn't a staring match this time. Joe got tears in his eyes. He was cuffed, but I reached over and held his fingers.

That night Joe got a call to me to tell me he was going to pick up his appeals. He reminded me of my telling him that I would fight with Lloyd. "Kind of like that team better than the state's," he told me. "Think I'll join it. I'll start by being your pod monitor. No, I'll start by thanking you, and telling you that I won't do this again."

"Have you beaten the demon, Joe?"

"I don't know. It could come back, but like I said, I'm on a good team. It's one I believe in. I really trust you guys. That's a strange feeling, scary, but good."

"You want to live, Joe?"

"Yeah, I do. I don't know exactly why or what for, but I do. That's kind of scary but good, too." Then he chuckled. *"Hey, you taking notes now?"*

"No, why?"

"Just thought you could use them if I zoo out on you again."

"Not to worry. I've got plenty of notes. Thank you, Joe."

He laughed again. "Right. My carrying on was just what you always wanted to deal with. You are one strange and damned stubborn lady. Well, send me a letter telling me what all you want me to do as our pod monitor, and Marie, I love you guys."

"We love you, too, Joe."

I put the phone down and went into Robert's room and told him about the conversation. "All right, Mom!" Robert jumped off his bed and gave me a big hug while I hung on laughing and crying.

I called Lloyd, and we talked about feeling the weight of the world shift off our shoulders.

I didn't have trouble sleeping that night, but as I was falling asleep, I thought about my nuns again. Maybe it is never too late.

It is true that Joe had undergone a remarkable transformation in the year that he had spent with Marie. And the changes would continue, as Joe began a rigorous process of self-education under Marie's tutelage. But it would be six long years before Marie could take a breath and conclude that it was not "too late" for Joe Giarratano and his date with the electric chair. The fight was just beginning.

10

The Fight to Save Joe Giarratano

Americans [do not] give a hoot about killing people. They
really don't give a hoot about killing them fairly, either.
As long as there is the appearance of fairness in the death
penalty, they will accept executions as a necessary evil.
—Marie Deans, November 1986

Marie may have won the battle to save Joe's soul, but the fight to save his life was only
beginning. And Joe himself was still coming to grips with his abusive childhood as
well as his apparent role in a double homicide. Marie wrote that Joe seemed "much
more relaxed and generally in good spirits" after he decided to resume his appeals,
but the other men on the row told Marie that Joe was hyperactive and often "cried
out in his sleep." "In answer to my inquiries," Marie wrote, "Joe told me he was having nightmares, but he couldn't remember what they were about."

Marie's work with Joe and the other men of the row was disrupted in May of
1984, when six inmates made a brazen escape from death row. The escape had been
planned for several months by a group of ten death row inmates, including Joe. In
the aftermath of the prison escape, Marie's efforts to help the men of the row were
undercut by a humiliated and shaken Department of Corrections intent on exacting
retribution on the inmates.

The "mastermind" of the escape was a death row inmate named Willie Lloyd
Turner, who had killed a jewelry store owner during a robbery. In recognition of his
long tenure in prison, he was nicknamed the "dean of death row." Willie was a char-
ismatic individual who designed and patented a special type of hair cutting shears
while on the row. He dazzled his fellow inmates with his skills at making and hiding
homemade knives and functional cell door keys, as well as his ability to manipulate
the corrections officers and prison staff. He even romanced a prison psychologist,
who later wrote an over-the-top account of their love affair.[1] Joe explained:

> What made Willie T. good at making weapons was that he was patient, and he
> paid attention to detail. He was extremely creative. He took all the raw material
> and fashioned the weapons used during the escape. He also hid all the weapons

and hid them so well that the staff could not find them after multiple searches. Trust me when I say this, it is not easy to conceal a lawnmower blade in any prison, much less [death row], and he hid at least three.

Joe described Willie as an intelligent, self-educated "country boy" who suffered from bouts of paranoia regarding imaginary plots against him. "Marie liked Willie," recalled Joe, "but she also thought that he was the ultimate con artist. He tried his games on her a couple times, and she let him have it." After that, Willie wised up and did not try to scam Marie. "Willie had nothing but the utmost respect, and he was smart enough to know that he needed Marie," said Joe. "He wasn't going to do anything to alienate her in any way, shape, or form."

After his execution, Willie's reputation only grew when corrections officers found a gun and a bag of bullets inside the former inmate's typewriter—a discovery prompted by a note Willie had left. The Department of Corrections was embarrassed and tried to blame Willie's lawyer, but the allegations did not stick. Given Willie's larger-than-life reputation, it is not surprising that several death row inmates claimed to have seen Willie's ghost walking through the row and peering into their cells in the days after his execution.[2]

While Joe and Willie served as the brains of the escape operation, Linwood Briley and his young brother, James "J. B." Briley served as the muscle. Over a six month period, the two brothers, along with their younger brother, Anthony Briley, and an unrelated accomplice, went on a crime spree of robbery, rape, and murder that left nine people dead—including two elderly women and a five-year-old boy. The murders were particularly gruesome, as the brothers wielded baseball bats, a cinder block, knives, scissors, a metal pipe, and an assortment of handguns to brutally assault and kill their victims.

Once on death row, Linwood and J. B. Briley used their reputations as well as threats of violence to intimidate many of the inmates. The brothers had a hand in the sale of contraband that flowed through death row, and each brother had their own "punk," an inmate that the brothers protected from violence in exchange for sexual favors.[3] The fact that the brothers had punks only enhanced the envy and respect of others on the row. The brothers were volatile and unpredictable, and Joe and Willie were concerned about joining forces with them.

In books and articles written after the escape, the Briley brothers were credited as the main force behind the escape. Joe adamantly disagrees. "If there was a mastermind behind the escape it was Willie, not the Briley brothers. They could not think themselves out of a wet paper bag." Neither brother would show remorse at their future executions; when J. B. entered the death chamber, he walked toward the small room that housed the witnesses, peered into the window, and said "Boo, are you happy now?"

The basic plan was to use homemade knives (shanks) to take the guards hostage, steal their uniforms, and then call for a prison van so the "guards" could remove a "bomb" (the death row television wrapped in a blanket). The inmates memorized the radio codes the corrections officers used, and were confident that they could communicate from the pod control room to central command warning of the bomb and request a van without raising suspicion. When the van arrived, the prisoners would drive out of the prison in order to dispose of the bomb.[4] The original date for the escape was April 15, 1984.

Over the next two months, they refined the plan. From the beginning, Joe was charged with operating the death row control room. This assignment would allow Joe to open and close cell doors and answer the phones. Other inmates would capture the guards, secure them in cells, and prepare the fake bomb.

As the escape date approached, an inmate told Marie and attorney Lloyd Snook about the pending breakout and the detailed escape plan. The inmate had grown increasingly worried about the unchecked violence that the Briley brothers might unleash during the escape, especially since the Briley brothers had sworn to kill Morris Mason and Michael Marnell Smith for being snitches. Marie and Snook did not know, at first, what they could do to stop it. They decided that Snook should not contact prison officials at the Mecklenburg Correctional Center. "They thought that I was a commie [because of my death penalty work] and if I called them up they would just blow me off,"[5] explained Snook. Instead, he called the staff of Virginia attorney general Gerald Baliles and reported the exact details of the escape.

> I told them that the breakout was planned for the night of April 20, and that it would take place by one of the inmates sneaking into the bathroom as the group came back from recreation, that the guard would then be called out of the control box by a request from one side of the pod to hand something over to another inmate on the other side of the pod, that when the door was thus opened, the inmate in the bathroom would bolt out of the bathroom, into the control room, and open all the doors, but that I did not know exactly how they planned to get out of the building or out of the institution.

Death row was immediately placed under a month-long lockdown, prisoners were interrogated, and the inmates' cells were subjected to multiple searches (or "shakedowns") by guards using X-ray machines and dogs. Astonishingly, none of the homemade weapons were found, and no additional inmates talked. The corrections officers searching for the weapons were no match for Willie and his skills at hiding contraband. He sprinkled hot pepper sauce at the door of his cell to deter the bloodhounds brought into the cellblock.

Marie and Snook also urged the attorney general's office to move several of the key members of the conspiracy to other prison facilities. Without the leadership of these inmates, they were convinced that the plan would collapse. "The AG's office kept fighting us on it," recalled Snook. "I wanted to say to them, 'You idiots, I'm trying to help you out. Come on work with me here people.' But they wouldn't do it."

Throughout the lockdown, the inmates continued to plot the mass escape, but Joe was having second thoughts. Locked in his tiny cell, Joe spent his free time reading Plato's *Crito*, a Socratic dialogue in which Socrates declines his followers' offer to help their teacher and friend escape what they believe to be an unjust death sen-

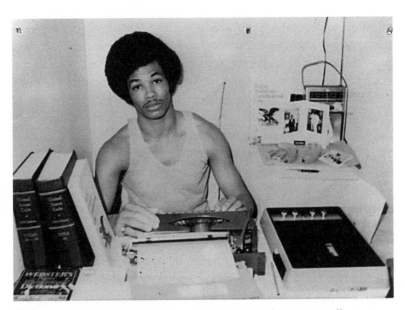

Virginia death row inmate Willie Lloyd Turner in his prison cell.
Nicknamed the "dean of death row," Turner was a skilled weapons
maker and master manipulator who was one of the main planners
behind the death row escape. Personal collection of Marie Deans.

tence. The refusal by Socrates to meet the injustice of his execution with the injustice
of an escape resonated with Joe, and he found himself questioning the wisdom of
fleeing from death row while he still had the opportunity to fight his conviction in
the court system. Additionally, Joe began to fear that the escape attempt would result
in bloodshed.

The death row lockdown ended by the middle of May, and the escape was re-
scheduled for the evening of May 31. The escape followed the precise plan conveyed
to the attorney general's office. The inmates managed to trick an officer into leaving
the control room, and another inmate burst out of the bathroom and took him hostage. Having captured the control room, the inmates telephoned officers and guards
through the building and, one-by-one, lured them to death row on the pretense that
an inmate was injured. As the staff entered the row, they were immediately captured,
stripped of their uniforms, and tied up. Two nurses were also seized and placed in
cells. When it became apparent that several inmates wanted to rape the women, Joe,
now in the control room, refused to open the cell doors and saved the women from
a sexual assault.

As the inmates prepared to leave death row with their fake bomb, they were
shocked when Joe and Willie announced that they were not leaving. The two men
had overheard one of the escaping inmates argue that the guards should be killed,
which confirmed their fears of bloodshed. Although temporarily shaken by the news
that Joe and Willie would not be leaving, the six inmates quickly departed the building and drove away in a prison van.

After giving the inmates thirty minutes to make their escape, the hostages were released and Joe allowed the senior correctional officer to contact his disbelieving superiors about the escape. As the warning went out across the state, and citizens armed themselves at the prospect of six mad dogs roaming the countryside, the inmates split up—some heading north to Philadelphia and the Canadian borders, others blundering around and never getting farther than North Carolina. All would be captured within the month.

It would be several weeks before Marie was allowed to see Joe. Death row went into lockdown, and the prisoners who helped in the escape were thrown into isolation cells. Prison officials tapped the inmates' telephone calls and tried to block prisoners from seeing their lawyers. They argued that the lawyers threatened institutional security, implying the lawyers were involved in the escape. "We remained on a state of constant lockdown," Joe explained. "Many of the guards became even more abusive. It was not uncommon to have to beg for toilet paper, and we could never be sure what we were eating when our food trays were shoved at us. Showers were rare . . . [and] recreation was non-existent."⁶ When Marie was finally permitted to return to death row, she found a group of men suffering from the month-long ordeal.

> After the escape some really bad things happened on the row, and the men left on the row—the seventeen who were still there—[the staff] just tortured them. Including things like making them all pack up and go downstairs in this conference room and stand all day long [in the summer heat]. There were windows onto the recreation area and they covered them with blankets. They made them stand there and hold all their gear. They held guns on them. They did that for hours and hours, and some of the [inmates] started passing out. Peeing on themselves—stuff like that. They all believed that they were going to be killed. They were wrecks. They moved [the inmates] around. They kept them apart. They kept them totally disoriented. No stimulation whatsoever. Total lockdown. That's another [time] where I fought with all I had to get in there. Everybody was spooked and spooky [when Marie finally saw them]. And dying to tell me what had happened. They had just gone to hell and back six times over. And they were the ones that didn't escape or hurt anybody.

As death row recovered from the prison escape, and Marie regained consistent access to the inmates, she continued to work with Joe. Through their conversations in person and over the telephone, a very different person was emerging from the dissipating fog of drugs and mental illness. Marie started to question her assumptions, not only about Joe, but about his case as well.

> It was only after Joe's mental health began to improve that we began to realize that [the earlier portrait of Joe as being violent, abusive, depressed, and a chronic abuser of drugs and alcohol] was grossly distorted. Qualities of character emerged during this time—empathy, compassion, charity, generosity, gentleness of sprit, and a searching intellect—which were wholly inconsistent with the person Joe had seemed to be up until that time. He began to show insight into

his life. For the first time he talked about how he had been made to feel in his mother's home—and in the process revealed the previously unknown and much more egregious acts of victimization he suffered. At first he only answered specific questions about his family. After a number of visits, he began to tell me about particular events in some detail. Although he tried, he was unable to place these events in any sequences. Nonetheless, a pattern of childhood and adolescent neglect, extreme abuse, and constant exposure to unhealthy influences emerged. Finally, in the late summer of 1984, Joe indicated to me that he believed I knew what his stepfather had done, [but] it took several more visits during the fall of 1984 for Joe to be able to tell me any details. Before those visits, the sexual abuse had been a subject so fraught with pain and shame that Joe simply was unable to discuss it.

As Joe's attorneys and I learned the truth about [Joe's] life history, and his frailties and vulnerabilities, and about his strengths, we began as well to wonder about the reliability of his confessions. The crime to which he confessed seemed fundamentally inconsistent with the kind of person Joe actually was. No one who cared about him and knew him well prior to the crime could believe that he was capable of committing it. Further, we learned more and more about gaps in Joe's memory. As we followed out these instincts, we realized that no one had ever done this before in Joe's case. No one had ever started at sum zero, cast aside the reflexive presumption that the confessions were true, and taken a critical look at them, at the congruence between the confessions and the physical crime scene evidence, and at the evidence of his guilt independent of the confessions.

Joe's recovery was not without its setbacks, some self-inflicted. Spooked by the rapid executions of Linwood Briley, J. B. Briley, Michael Marnell Smith, and Morris Mason following the failed escape, Joe took part in a second escape attempt in November 1985. Joe, Willie Lloyd Turner, Eddie Fitzgerald, and Lem Tuggle tried to seize the pod control room with a fake .32-caliber gun (fashioned from a flip-flop shoe, a soda can, soap, and black shoe polish) and a pipe bomb made of matches, both items courtesy of Willie. The bomb failed to destroy the control room's safety glass, and retribution was meted out swiftly.[7] Joe spent forty-five days in isolation. Marie was furious over the second escape attempt, and she let Joe know it. The fake gun was so authentic that the Department of Corrections displayed it at their training academy as a warning to new recruits.

Marie continued to review Joe's trial records and in a December 31, 1987, letter to his legal team, she expressed her growing suspicions about Joe's factual innocence. "I am about to throw a curve ball here. It always has seemed to me that there is a possibility that Joe did not kill Michelle and Toni," Marie wrote. "My reasons were basically a strange nagging about the case, Joe's continued inability to remember, along with his trying to reason the event out and fill in the gaps when we pushed him to remember." Marie added that her unease was also sparked by the inadequate cross-examination of the police and expert witnesses at Joe's trial. Until this point, however, Marie had neither the time nor the resources to mount a new investigation of the crime. That would change after a conversation with a German art gallery owner named Charlotte Zander, who had seen a BBC documentary that featured Marie and Joe.

Charlotte Zander, a gallerist in Munich, watched the documentary and was struck by Joe Giarratano. After a few weeks of not being able to forget the documentary, she contacted British ITV and was finally given my phone number. She told me Joe could be her own son's twin and asked if there was anything she could do to help him. I told her we needed funds to do an investigation into Joe's background to try to get a new sentencing hearing for him.

Within two weeks a $1,500 check came from Charlotte. I called a colleague in Florida who got a former police investigator involved. In less than a month, he called me and asked if I was sure my client was guilty. "Well," I responded. "He says he's guilty. He confessed a number of times."

The investigator had reviewed the records I'd sent him, talked with the arresting police officers in Jacksonville and looked at what reports on the confession, arrest, and crime existed there. He was convinced that we needed to conduct an investigation into the murders. "You need someone in Norfolk who knows how to do a forensic investigation," he told me, "and you need to keep an open mind about this crime. Your client just might not have done it."

The possibility of Joe being innocent had not crossed our minds. We knew the confessions were screwy and that the evidence didn't make sense, but we were searching for a psychological explanation for Joe's memory problems, believing if we could solve those problems, the crime would be clear to us. We had thought our job was for Lloyd to deal with the legal issues while I dealt with the issues of mitigation.

Lloyd was still carrying five capital cases on a pro bono basis while trying to keep his practice going and take care of his family. We had no expectations of additional donations coming from Charlotte, and neither the Coalition nor Lloyd had the money or people to conduct such an investigation. We agreed that Joe needed a defense team with more resources, and Lloyd reluctantly decided he would give up Joe's case if we could find such a team.

I reported all this to Charlotte, who volunteered to pay for an investigation in Norfolk. I hired an investigator who was a retired Norfolk Police Department homicide detective who had never worked for the defense side of a criminal case. He was skeptical of the case, telling me he was neutral, not a part of the defense team, and promising only to come back to me with the truth, just what I wanted. After several months and hundreds of hours, the investigator had become very wary of Joe's conviction and fairly certain that another man, whom he named, in the area, either alone or with an accomplice, had committed the murders. He also believed new investigators, who might be able to dig deeper, should be brought into the case.

Joe's case kept getting more complicated and demanding in every way. I had been talking with Jack Boger, head of the NAACP's Legal Defense Fund's Capital

Punishment section, about the case on about a weekly basis. Jack was leaving the LDF to become a professor at the University of North Carolina's School of Law, and Dick Burr was going to take over his position. Jack got Dick to take Joe's case. Dick would bring years of experience and the resources of the LDF to Joe's case.

In the meantime, Charlotte continued to send money for the investigation, and we hired another team of investigators, this one from California. They were experienced in interviewing people from all walks of life and continued to find evidence of Joe's innocence and the probable guilt of the man the original investigators believed was a suspect.

Through talks with the forensic scientists originally involved in working the crime and other forensic scientists who reviewed the record, the evidence of Joe's innocence continued to mount. This was not a crime where evidence had blown away or been trodden on in some field. Michelle had been raped and murdered and Barbara murdered in their own small apartment. There was plenty of evidence. It simply didn't match Joe. The stab wounds that killed Barbara were typical of a right-handed person, but Joe is left-handed and has a neurological deficit on his right side. The state claimed bloody footprints at the scene were made by Joe's boots, but its own lab tests showed otherwise. The prosecutor and police misled the court about why they didn't find the murder weapon, and the state never bothered to identify thirteen hairs found on or around the victims and numerous fingerprints found at the scene. Semen in Michelle's body also was tested but not shown to have come from Joe. In addition, we found five different confessions Joe had given, all of which contradicted one another and all of which were inconsistent with the evidence, and we learned that the original autopsy report had been changed to conform to the one confession put into evidence. On top of all that, we learned that the original videotape of the crime scene had "disappeared" from the court once we began raising questions about the case, and that a driver's license belonging to an unidentified man, but not Joe, had been found at the scene and never put into the record.

In Virginia, evidence of innocence found twenty-one days after sentencing cannot be considered by any court in Virginia, including federal courts. We would present all this evidence for the record, but we knew the likelihood of the court finding some legal error that would get Joe a new trial or even a new sentencing hearing was all but nil.

As Marie collected mitigation evidence she hoped could be used in Joe's appeal, she made repeated efforts to contact Joe's sister, Nikki Giarratano. Marie would subsequently learn that Nikki worked at a bar in Jacksonville, Florida, and during a short telephone call Nikki told Marie that she could confirm Joe's story of abuse at the hands of his stepfather. Nikki promised to provide more details, but subsequently told Marie that she could not because it would upset Joe's mother. In a tense phone call with Joe's mother, Carol, Marie was told that she could not talk to any of Joe's siblings. In short, Carol flatly refused to help her son with his mitigation defense. The maternal betrayal continued.

Joe assisted Marie in collecting and analyzing mitigation evidence for his appeals, but he was actively working to maintain order on death row (the men knew that Marie would not work on their cases if Joe reported that they were misbehaving) and helping over thirty different death row inmates draft and file lawsuits and appeals. One of these inmates was Earl Washington, a mentally-handicapped inmate facing a rapidly-approaching execution date. Convinced of Earl's innocence, Joe notified a federal district court judge of Earl's plausible claims of innocence and worked with Marie to find Earl a lawyer—setting into motion Earl's eventual exoneration, which will be discussed in the next chapter.

During the mid-to-late 1980s, Joe himself drafted and filed two different federal lawsuits: *Giarratano v. Bass*, which alleged constitutional violations regarding inmates' rights to confidential visits with their attorneys and confidential access to their legal mail, and *Giarratano v. Murray*, which argued that the state was required to provide indigent inmates with attorneys during subsequent legal appeals. Lower federal courts found in Joe's favor in both actions, although the Supreme Court would ultimately rule against Joe and his constitutional arguments in *Giarratano v. Murray*.

Despite Joe's rise from the ashes of his earlier life, he was not immune to the daily tensions of life on the row. "Seven years ago I began the process of waiting for my man-made appointment with death," Joe wrote in 1986. "Since being condemned to death, my days have been spent dealing with the guilt of having been convicted of taking the lives of two human beings, confronting the very real possibility of my own violent death, and coping with the anger, resentment, frustration, helplessness, and

Giarratano, working away as a "jailhouse lawyer" in his death row cell. Personal collection of Marie Deans.

grief of having five friends taken from my side to be ritualistically exterminated."[8] The struggle to "maintain my sanity," Joe added, was undermined by the very nature of death row.

It is almost impossible to maintain a sense of humanity in a system that ignores the fact that you are a living, breathing human being—a system where you are recognized only as a number, a compilation of legal issues open for debate, a twenty-to-fifty page legal brief before tribunals that will determine your fate without ever knowing you, as something nonhuman—a piece of tainted meat to be disposed of.[9]

The struggle for sanity was complicated by the terror and grief of watching his friends be taken away to be executed. In the passage below, Joe describes saying goodbye to fellow inmate Michael Marnell Smith.

On the night of 31 July 1986, four guards came to my unit, with handcuffs and waist-chain, to escort me to the telephone. It was a call that I had been dreading, because I would be saying my final goodbye to another friend. Within three hours after that call, Mike Smith, a man whom I had shared a life bond with for seven years, would be coldly strapped into an electric killing machine. Then 2,700 volts of raw current would fry the life out of his body.

Even now I feel the anger I felt at his death, and the pain of having a friend coldly taken from me to be ritualistically put to death. As I walked down the hallway, several guards commented on the wrongness of killing my friend, and stated that Mike was a good man. Fighting back the tears was hard because of the helplessness I experienced at not being able to save him. Memories of the times Mike and I had spent together flooded through me. I wanted to understand why Mike was being taken from me, but it was impossible. Each day I have to interact with the same guards who came to the unit and took him from me. These guards were the same guards who were telling me, "Joe, Mike is a good man. They shouldn't kill him." Each time I heard a guard say that, I could feel the anger churning within me. What they were saying made no sense to me. I wanted to scream, "NO!" I wanted to tear down the prison walls and make them stop. I hated them.

As I lifted the phone to my ear and heard my friend's voice, I didn't know what to say. Other than quick hellos, our conversation consisted of a few scattered questions tied together with long silences. I could feel the tears leaking from my eyes as the hopelessness overwhelmed me. I wanted to tell Mike to fight the guards until the last second—to take some of them down with him—but all I could say was, "I love you, my friend. I'm sorry I can't stop this." Mike's reply still rings in my ear: "I'll be fine, Joe. You know that I'm going home. Please don't do anything that you might regret later. You have to forgive them."

Walking back to my cell, I could barely move—it felt as if every muscle in my body were cramped. I could hear the guards asking me questions, but I knew *that if I responded, my hatred would spew out at them. I felt the helplessness and hopelessness in the pit of my stomach—I wanted to pull my friend back. It wasn't until later that I noticed the blood on my wrists where the cuffs bit into my flesh. I tried to pull Mike back, but I couldn't.*[10]

Michael Marnell Smith's execution highlights the dual roles that Marie and Joe often played in executions. After Smith ended his phone call with Joe, it was Marie who comforted Smith during his final hours in the death house.

Yet there was light as well as darkness for Joe. He was reading voraciously, fighting to save his fellow inmates, and growing spiritually. "I can honestly say that for the last five to six years I have known more freedom and inner peace than I ever knew before," Joe told an Amnesty International reporter. "That is something that the State of Virginia cannot snuff out. I want to live and share my experience with others, but I am at peace now, and that cannot be taken from me."[11]

As Joe's appeals were being exhausted, Marie decided that the last, best hope for Joe was a push for clemency from Virginia governor Douglas Wilder combined with a public relations campaign. Marie poured hundreds of hours into the campaign to save Joe, motivated in part by the fear that she herself could not survive his execution. "I think for each of us who do this work there is one person who is like a wall for us—and we don't know how we would ever get over that wall. I have a friend who represented [death row convict] Velma Barfield in North Carolina. She was his wall. When she was killed, it took him a year to come back. For me, Joe is that person. Even the guards come to us and say they don't know how they are going to kill Joe."[12]

Drawing attention to Joe's cause, a political action committee called "GRACE" (Giarratano Review Action Committee) was formed in the fall of 1989. Its members included former US Attorneys General Benjamin R. Civiletti and Ramsey Clark, former presidential candidates John Anderson and George McGovern, actors Mike Farrell, Robert Foxworth, Jack Lemmon, and Roy Scheider, director Oliver Stone, musicians Joan Baez and Peter Yarrow, peace activists Colman McCarthy and Joseph Ingle, and conservative newspaper columnist James J. Kilpatrick. The committee sponsored rallies, wrote op-ed pieces for national newspapers, and mailed letters of protest to Virginia politicians. At a news conference at the state capitol in Richmond, Mike Farrell handed a petition with the signatures of fifteen thousand supporters to Walter MacFarlane, legal aide to Governor Wilder. "We come today to ask for fairness for Joe Giarratano," Farrell announced at the news conference. "I think the American people are hungry for a politician who will stand on principle."[13] Despite the outpouring of support, it was uncertain how Governor Wilder, a politician with an eye on a presidential run, would respond.

In the early morning hours of February 7, 1991, Joe was roused from his sleep, placed in an unmarked prison van, and transported to the death house in preparation for his February 22 execution. The sudden departure was a shock to Joe, who wept when he learned that he would not be able to say goodbye to the other men on the row. Joe arrived at a prison that was slipping into history. The main portion of the prison had been emptied of prisoners in preparation for the demolition of the aging facility. As Joe walked down the stone steps to the basement of A building, location of the electric chair, he became the last prisoner ever to be housed at the crumbling and empty Virginia State Penitentiary.

Once at the death house, time seemed to speed up for Joe. "It's like my life stopped, and a new life begun," Joe told a reporter shortly after his arrival. "I'm just real focused. There doesn't seem to be enough hours in the day to get everything done I want to get done so every day is full. Every minute is full."[14] Yet, behind the bravado, he was afraid.

As the execution date drew closer, Joe's supporters increased the political pressure on Governor Wilder. Joe's attorneys met with MacFarlane to press for a pardon, rallies in support of Joe were held in Richmond, and the governor's office was buried in 5,475 telephone calls and letters in support of Joe's clemency petition. In newspapers across the state, op-ed pieces ran with such titles as "Death Row Inmate Merits Reprieve,"[15] "Giarratano Should Not Die under the Shadow of Our Doubt,"[16] "Why Kill Joe Giarratano Now,"[17] and "Joe Giarratano Should Have a New Trial."[18]

On February 19, 1991, Governor Wilder announced that he was granting Joe a conditional pardon. The pardon itself presented three different scenarios to Joe: (1) refuse the conditional pardon and be executed, (2) accept the pardon, cease to challenge his conviction, and be eligible for parole in 2004, or (3) give up his double jeopardy rights, ask the Virginia attorney general for a new trial—which would be "in her sole discretion and at her option"—and face the possibility of another capital conviction. No such pardon had ever been offered by a Virginia governor, or any governor for that matter. "I [am not] aware of any instance in which any governor in the United States or any United States president has ever extended his clemency powers in a manner that has either granted or allowed a new trial for any person convicted of a crime," stated Wilder in the conditional pardon.

While Joe told reporters that "I let out one hell of a cheer when I heard the news,"[19] in reality, Joe was initially angry about the conditional pardon and ready to reject it. In the late night hours of February 19, Joe, his lawyers, death penalty activist and actor Mike Farrell, and Marie huddled around a table in the small cooling room and discussed the pardon. The conversation grew heated at times, with the lawyers arguing that Joe would be a fool not to accept the pardon and Joe responding that the issue was about quality, not quantity, of life. Joe and his attorney talked for five hours, with a solemn and silent Marie simply listening.

Shortly before the meeting ended at 2:00 a.m., Marie clutched Joe's hand. With tears flowing down her cheeks, she said, "Please do this for me." Joe was shocked by the request. When he first decided to resume his appeals back in 1983, he told Marie that he was continuing to fight for her, and a furious Marie had screamed, "No, go to the fucking chair. If you aren't going to do it for yourself, then don't do it." Eight years later, Marie was asking Joe to save himself from the electric chair, if not for himself then for her. Joe didn't know what to say, so he mumbled that he would think about her request.

Shortly after Joe was escorted back to his cell, the door opened, and Captain Anthony Parker, the head of the execution team, pulled a chair into the cell and sat down. Joe had interacted before with Parker and liked him, although they had bumped heads when Joe first came to the death house and was ordered to take off his clothes and surrender all personal items—including a cross that Joe wore around his neck. Joe refused, and it took a call to the warden's office before Parker backed down. Now Parker, a professed Christian, sat with Joe and asked him to accept the pardon. It was a surreal scene, with the inmate and the executioner sitting in the bowels of an empty prison and debating life and death. Parker told Joe that God himself had intervened because He wanted Joe to live and help people. At the end of the conversation, Parker asked Joe to join him in prayer and the two men bowed their heads and asked for divine guidance and support as the hour of Joe's scheduled execution drew near.

Joe did not sleep that night. At 5:00 a.m. he called Marie, who was still awake, and told her that he would accept the governor's pardon. After she stopped weeping, a joyful Marie called Joe "a bastard" for putting her through such hell and apologized for asking him to take the clemency offer. She ended the call by telling Joe that she would never stop working to secure his freedom.

Within the hour, Marie and the attorneys returned to the death house. The jubilant lawyers promised Joe that they would not stop fighting until Joe was a free man, to which Marie fired back, "you damn well better." The promise was a hollow one, however, as the lawyers moved onto other jobs and other cases. Marie, however, would be haunted for the rest of her life by the fact that Joe remained behind bars because she had begged him to accept the clemency offer. "We couldn't talk about my time in the death house," Joe explained. "It was like a silent agreement that we weren't going to talk about it. I think she felt guilty, but I also think she was relieved."[20]

Speaking with reporters about the conditional pardon hours later, Joe gave no public indication that he and his defense team had considered rejecting the pardon. "I wish I could give the guy [the governor] a hug. He's stopped an injustice from happening and cleared the way for justice to take place."[21] In the same press conference, Joe repeated his hope that Virginia attorney general Mary Sue Terry would follow the governor's wishes and grant him a new trial. "I don't see any justification for Mary Sue Terry not to petition for a new trial," stated Joe. "I believe that Governor Wilder clearly expects a new trial will take place."[22]

Privately, Joe did not believe that Terry would grant him a new trial. A former prosecutor, Terry was known as a competent attorney who carefully worked up her cases. "I'd cringe when I see Mary Sue in court," a local prosecutor recalled. "She'd beat you to death with motions. She'd pick on every bit of evidence. I knew when Mary Sue was on the other side, I had my work cut out for me. . . . It was like walking into a buzz saw."[23]

After eight years in the Virginia General Assembly, where her conservative voting record was at odds with her Democratic Party affiliation, Terry ran a successful campaign to become the state's first female attorney general. She won the election despite her opponent's campaign efforts to raise suspicions about Terry's commitment to family values (stemming from her status as an unmarried woman). At one

Joe Giarratano at the press conference after accepting Governor Wilder's conditional pardon. Photograph courtesy of *Richmond Times-Dispatch*.

fundraiser, a local politician had claimed that Terry's opponent "knows more about criminal law in his little finger than his opponent knows in all five of her ringless fingers."[24]

As attorney general, it was no secret that Terry had her eye on the governor's office. And it was no secret that a reputation of being soft on crime would hurt Terry's chances of achieving her future political goals. A year after Joe's conditional pardon, Terry tried to tamp down a similar groundswell of support for death row inmate Edward Fitzgerald by having her assistants hold a private briefing for reporters on the gory details of Fitzgerald's crimes. "It's as if they're holding a pep rally for an execution," complained a local member of the ACLU. "The enthusiasm with which the attorney general's office defends the death penalty—and in this case promotes it—is appalling."[25]

As Marie and Joe waited for the attorney general to make her announcement, others voiced their opinions about the conditional pardon. While Joe's supporters were relieved and thrilled, others were furious that Joe had escaped the electric chair. "It's the most unjust thing I've ever seen in my life,"[26] said Earl Jones, uncle of Barbara Kline. "The Bible says an eye for an eye . . . we haven't had the eye yet. We won't be satisfied until we get that eye."[27] Accusing Virginia of being "too damn chicken to pull the switch on him," Jones volunteered to do the deed himself. "I thought our family could have a minute's peace" with the execution, Jones added. "But we can't have that, knowing he's laughing at us."[28] Ralph J. Mears, the former Norfolk detective who conducted Joe's fifth and final confession, echoed a similar sentiment. Convinced of Joe's guilt, Mears denounced the pardon. "To me it's a bunch of crap . . . he should have fried a long time ago, no question about it."[29]

The joy Joe and his supporters felt was short-lived. Several hours after Joe accepted the conditional pardon, Attorney General Terry issued a written press release stating that she would not grant Joe's request for a new trial. "I am intimately familiar with the facts of the case, and I am convinced that Mr. Giarratano committed the crimes of which he stands," she announced. "He is not entitled to a new trial, and I shall initiate no further legal proceedings." In a subsequent interview, Terry told reporters that she had spent a year examining Joe's case and had concluded that Joe's claims of innocence were unbelievable. "A child was raped and killed, and a mother was left bleeding to death on the floor. . . . It wasn't until nine years after this tragedy that Joe Giarratano raised any questions whether he committed the murder at all."[30] As for Joe, Terry simply stated "I think that Joe Giarratano tonight is a lucky person."[31] While Terry claimed that her decision was based solely on her belief of Joe's guilt, others wondered if Terry's plans to run for governor also played a role in her decision. Marie herself had predicted, prior to Joe's pardon, that Terry did not want to grant Joe a new trial because she feared he would be acquitted. In researching this book, I wrote Terry and asked to interview her regarding Joe. I received no response.

Dejected followers pledged to fight the attorney general's decision, but there was no legal basis to challenge Terry. Joe was transferred to the Augusta Correctional Center, where Marie and death penalty activist Colman McCarthy helped him establish a highly successful peace studies program. Marie sat on the program's board of directors, and she sponsored several workshops for the prisoners. "[Marie tried] to have prisoners reconcile with the victims of their crimes when it was possible," Joe explained. "We actually tried to set up meetings in some cases. She would come in and give seminars about basically just telling the guys to grow up. Being Marie. Pounding on heads and getting guys to change and focus on self-reformation."

The prisoners quickly grew to admire and respect Marie.

> They loved her. Some of them saw her as a mother figure—a big sister. Some of 'em just saw her as one of the guys. She could sit down and cuss just like they could. She'd come into the visiting room and sit down—there was no smoking in the visiting room even when we had our seminars and they'd all get together and go sneak off into a corner and go smoke a cigarette.
>
> She was trying to teach them that they could make a difference in the world generally. Marie was this grand idealist and she thought—she was trying to create an army for change I guess that is the best way to put it. She was encouraging guys to take on these new roles—cut loose from the system. Don't ask the system to do anything for you. Don't depend on the system for anything. Do this yourselves.

In early 1995, the Virginia Department of Corrections ordered that the peace studies program be terminated because of claimed financial irregularities in the program.

While the charge did not stick—the peace studies program had just passed an audit by the IRS—the program was doomed, victim of the correctional policies of the new head of the Virginia Department of Corrections, who believed that prisoners were being coddled and conditions of confinement must be made more Spartan. Despite its undeniable record of success, the program was ended. But the attack on Joe was just beginning.

In July, Joe was transferred abruptly to the Buckingham Correctional Center. There he met with a prison official, who Joe claims tried to recruit him as a snitch.

> He said, "Listen, Giarratano, you're well liked in the prison. Prisoners trust you—they know you. You move in circles that a lot of people can't move in. You know everybody. We want you to come work for us." He wanted me to wear a wire. I said, "No, that's not going to happen." I took his business card, tore it up, and threw it at him. I said, "Don't call me no more."

Joe believes that prison officials put out the word that he was a snitch in order to punish him for not accepting their offer. If that was the plan, it worked brilliantly; shortly after the meeting, Joe was attacked in the prison yard by an inmate who yelled, "die, you snitch" before stabbing him with a knife. The wound was not life-threatening, but the message had been delivered.

Claiming they were concerned for Joe's safety, on September 4, 1996, plainclothes prison officials arrived at Joe's cell at 2:00 a.m., placed him in a car, drove him to the Richmond airport, loaded him into a private plane once used by Governor Wilder, and spirited him out of Virginia. Joe's final destination was a maximum security prison in Utah. Neither Joe nor his attorneys had received advance notice of the transfer.

At the Salt Lake City airport, Joe was met with a squad of heavily armed guards. "I was supposed to be this mad dog," Joe recounted in a bemused voice. "I got off the plane and one guy said, 'You don't look so tough.' I said, 'Well, this is a surprise to me too, buddy.'" Once at the prison, Joe was placed in a death row cell that the guards claimed was the former home of the late Gary Gilmore.

> When I got there, they said they were there to break me. They put me in a cell with no windows—solid steel door—closed it. It's black [inside the cell]. You hear the mice. They came in once a day and threw a meal bag on the floor. You could hear the mice go for it. I just sat in there and laughed and didn't pay them no mind.
>
> Mike Farrell and Marie got the local ACLU to come into the prison and demand to see me. They brought me out [but first] covered my eyes up so I wouldn't mess my eyes. Tried to give me a bath [before meeting with the ACLU] and I said, "Nope I'm going out just like this." It wasn't long after that I went on the hunger strike. I wound up getting tubed up—they hooked me up to the [feeding] tubes.

Joe's supporters were outraged by the secret operation, and the public outcry forced the Virginia Department of Corrections to meet with reporters. At the press conference, Department spokesman David Botkins announced that Joe himself was to blame for the stabbing and the subsequent transfer to Utah: "Joe Giarratano by his own doing made himself a high-profile inmate." Botkins did not define what he meant by the phrase "by his own doing," but Joe had already anticipated his transfer and explained its true motivation in a handwritten letter to his supporters: "Contrary to the assertions of Virginia DOC officials, my involuntary transfer was effectuated as a retaliation against me because of my political and nonviolent activities; and my longstanding political and legal efforts on behalf of myself and my fellow prisoners."[32]

When challenged as to the costs of transporting Joe on a private plane, Botkins cited Joe's alleged dangerousness as the reason. "You don't take a convicted felon of the magnitude and notoriety of Joe Giarratano on a commercial flight."[33] No mention was made of Joe's efforts to create a peace studies program. And the Department of Corrections refused to release information on the cost of the jet ride.

Attorney Jerry Zerkin was furious at the contrived reasoning behind his client's transfer and blasted the Department of Corrections in an interview. "It was absolutely not his idea, he did not want to go," Zerkin said. "He's a lightning rod for attention. He's a symbol. What better thing than to pack him off to Utah." Marie also rejected the claim that the transfer was motivated by safety concerns. "The first thing they [the Virginia Department of Corrections] could do to make prisoners safe is not label them snitches, particularly when they're not snitches."[34]

Joe's hunger strike lasted sixty days and resulted in the burly inmate losing over sixty pounds. A frantic Marie travelled to Utah during the hunger strike, saw Joe, and raised hell with the prison officials, who were beginning to realize that Virginia prison officials had duped them into taking a prisoner who could not be broken. "She was angry," recounted Joe. "She was ready to blow the place up. And it was shortly after that [Marie's visit] that they decided I would be leaving."

After six months, Utah prison officials transferred Joe to the violent Statesville Correctional Center in Joliet, IL. Alarmed by the open gang violence of the prison, Joe underwent a second hunger strike in order to protest prison conditions and to get placed in the relative safety of isolation.[35] Illinois prison officials were as flummoxed by Joe's passive resistance as their Utah counterparts were, and in September of 1996 Joe's efforts were rewarded with a transfer back to Virginia. His exile was over, but Joe was far from safe.

Any celebration about Joe's return to Virginia was short lived. Joe was sent to the Red Onion State Prison, referred to by a local reporter as a "modern-day Alcatraz atop a Wise County mountain ridge."[36] The relatively new facility had already earned a reputation of violence and brutality on the part of prisoners and guards. In a newspaper exposé written by Joe regarding prison conditions at Red Onion, he labeled the new prison as "another expensive house of pain and dehumanization."[37] He wrote that prisoners were subjected to electric shocks for talking back to guards and that "excessive force was the rule" in dealing with inmates.[38]

Fitting the prison's reputation, Joe's initial encounter with the prison staff was equally warm. Tossed in an isolation cell upon his arrival, a gun-toting corrections officer gave Joe a chilling greeting: "Don't care who you are or where you come from. You're at Red Onion now. You will do what you are told, when you are told, how you are told, for how long you are told. Or you will be shot, shocked, taken down, injured or even killed. Do you understand, boy?"[39] Now a veteran of seventeen years in the Virginia prison system, Joe understood all too well. But Joe was not cowed, and he continued to help inmates with grievances during his time at Red Onion. He even filed a lawsuit against the Virginia Department of Corrections regarding their treatment protocols for inmates with Hepatitis C.

In 2006, Joe was transferred to the slightly less violent Wallens Ridge State Prison, located on a mountaintop near Fancy Gap, Virginia. That is where I first met Joe, when Marie asked me to check on him after a young prison inmate assaulted Joe and broke his wrists. It was my first visit with an inmate in a maximum security prison, and I had resolved to not be conned by a con. Within an hour into the visit, however, I realized what a bright and unique individual Joe was.

As I formed a friendship with Joe, Marie—now in ill health—was working with attorneys to mount a second appeal for clemency. This time the petition would be served on Governor Tim Kaine, a former attorney who had previously represented death row inmates Lem Tuggle and Richard Whitley and had sat in the death house with Marie. It was Kaine who fought so bitterly with prison officials when they would not let Richard Whitley eat the dessert from his last meal. Additionally, Kaine served as an expert witness in Joe's lawsuit that involved access to court appointed attorneys and testified in court as to the complexity of habeas appeals. Because of Kaine's relationship with Marie, and their joint work together, Marie thought that Kaine was her "ace in the hole" when it came to the new clemency petition.

The rough-and-tumble world of politics, where individuals mortgage their personal beliefs for electoral advantage, could not be ignored. While Kaine, a Democrat and a devout Catholic, stated during an earlier political campaign "I just don't believe the death penalty is right, because we human beings make mistakes,"[40] Kaine unveiled a more nuanced position when he ran for governor. Facing withering criticism of his past death penalty work from a conservative opponent who delighted in telling voters that Kaine was a liberal lawyer and that one of his clients, Lem Tuggle, had escaped from death row (thereby suggesting that Kaine himself was partially to blame), Kaine changed his position. While he still expressed his moral and religious opposition to the death penalty, Kaine pivoted—repeatedly telling the electorate that his religious faith would not interfere with his duties as chief executive. "As a Christian missionary in Honduras, I learned that life is sacred. That's why I oppose the death penalty," Kaine explained in a campaign ad.[41] "I'll carry out a death sentence because that's the law."[42] He later added, "I'm not going to change my religion just to get elected. I'll sign death warrants."[43]

Some political observers viewed the distinction as disingenuous at best and craven at worst. Kaine's political dance continued as he reassured voters that he would not spare convicted killers who sought clemency. At yet another political debate,

Kaine told the assembled audience that, if elected, he would only use his powers of executive clemency in death penalty cases in "exceedingly rare circumstances where someone can show their innocence."[44] These were ominous signs from Marie's "ace in the hole," and she recognized them. "My fear is that he [Kaine] might give fewer clemencies because he feels he has to prove himself," Marie wrote in an e-mail. "However, I support him because he is a good person, because he cares about all the people, not just the rich, and he has good fiscal sense and good leadership qualities." And, Marie added for emphasis, she thought that Kaine's opponent "is the worst kind of old Southern rural redneck slime bag."

Kaine won the governor's race and served as Virginia's chief executive from 2006 to 2010. In 2009, he also became head of the Democratic National Committee. He was clearly a political star on the rise. Marie and a team of lawyers submitted a clemency petition to the governor's office in September of 2009. When he learned that the petition had been sent to Kaine, Joe wrote Marie. "It is done. It would not have happened without you. It would really be the highlight of my life to be able to stand at your side outside of prison and raise your arm in victory . . . and thank you. I want that opportunity. I could get hit by a truck or die of a heart attack after that, and I'd be content."[45]

On November 16, 2009, Marie sat at her antiquated word processor and wrote the following letter to the governor:

> I write in support of the petition for Joe Giarratano. I realize you have a lot on your plate, but I pray you will make clemency for Joe Giarratano a priority before leaving office. He won't have another chance.
>
> You know I did my best to get a new trial for Joe. It was what he wanted and still wants—the chance to prove his innocence. But Mary Sue Terry squelched that chance. Then our hopes for exoneration through DNA testing were dashed when we learned the only testable evidence from Joe's case had been destroyed or lost.
>
> Tim, remember when you and I were in the death house with Richard the night of his execution [and] he wanted to share his last meal with us. The guards brought a gallon of iced tea in a vinegar jar. It stunned me, and I blurted out "Our Lord thirst, and we gave him vinegar." I've never forgotten that night, and the memory of that vinegar jug is as strong as the sight of it that night. I'm grateful that Governor Wilder spared Joe's life. But I also know that we cannot simply say "too bad the evidence was destroyed" and continue to deny to Joe whatever justice remains available to him, [we] cannot continue to give him vinegar. That justice is in your hands alone. As I said, I truly do not believe his chance will come again. Shalom.

We do not know if Kaine received Marie's letter. After having his staff conduct an independent investigation, which included talking to former Governor Wilder, Kaine concluded that Joe's claims of actual innocence were not supported by the evidence.

"I did not reach a level of comfort that he was not a participant in that crime," Kaine explained to me. "And that's why I did not issue clemency in that case."[46]

Marie was devastated by Kaine's decision, and in an October 23, 2010, letter she poured out her feelings to Joe:

> You ask if I'm okay. Not really, but I'm trying, Joe. Part of the trying is probably the kicking myself for feeling convinced that you were coming out and therefore making the fall harder . . . I, too, had allowed myself to believe you would be released. I'd started making plans, emailing lots of people asking them to pledge donations to you . . . I'd made a list of things you'd need to do and how I could help—like getting identification, a coat, clothes, and even asking if anyone knew how we could get you a computer. I even made a run to the grocery store to get ingredients for spaghetti Bolognese, a fresh salad and a crusty loaf of Italian bread. I can't believe I allowed myself to fall into that.
>
> It is clear that the man I once knew [Kaine], the man I spent so much time with at MCC [death row] and in the death house, is gone, and that his soul has been scoured out by politics. . . . Tim Kaine is a stranger. Should I ever confront him, and he speaks to me, he'll get a piece of my mind. Other than that, I've got nothing for him.
>
> Is hope an illusion, Joe, or is false hope an illusion? You know I have a streak of blithering optimism in me. Right now I have no value for either hope or that optimism, yet I'm ready to do battle for you again, and again, and again if necessary. Remember, Joe, the struggles continue. I've come to the conclusion that for some that is what life is. Maybe we don't have the sugar to make lemonade, but we keep squeezing the lemons. It's better than just leaving them to rot.

In an e-mail to a friend, Marie confessed that she was hurting and wanted to hide. "[My mother] always said when I was sick or hurting I was like a hound dog. Hound dogs go off when they are sick or hurting, dig a hole and get in it until they heal or feel better. My mother used to say I [would] find a space for myself and go into it. I wanted to find a space for myself this time and mourn."[47]

When Joe learned of the clemency decision, he was more worried about Marie than himself. "If I have any regrets about Kaine's moral/political cowardice, it's that I've been denied the opportunity to be out there for you where I could have been of some real help to you," Joe wrote Marie.[48] And he reassured Marie that it wasn't her fault. "We didn't fail Deans," he wrote, "Kaine did."[49] Joe was also deeply affected by the decision, confessing that he had allowed himself to be optimistic about the clemency petition. "I reckon I let myself have a bit too much hope with Kaine and didn't anticipate my still being here," he said. "That sounds a bit nutty, but right now I just feel a bit frozen in space. Really not sure what to do with myself."[50] Allowing himself to hope was a mistake that Joe could not let himself repeat. "Hope is just too damned costly," he wrote, "and dangerous for me."[51]

At fifty-four years old, Joe took an honest look at his future in the Virginia prison system. "I am really getting too old for this kind of nonsense," he admitted to Marie. "And all I can see in front of me is more the same. I'm too old and not in the best of shape to be fending off young knuckleheads [who are] one half my age."[52] Joe was tired of the "constant struggle to find meaning/purpose in this madness and to grow and develop in this constantly dehumanizing environment."[53] The prison system was not designed for the person that Joe had become. "The fact that I am truly reformed . . . actually works against me in this system," Joe said. "The reality is that the penal system is not designed or equipped to deal with truly reformed individuals. Our system is designed and operated in a manner to control and manage unregenerate, degenerate, immoral, amoral, dysfunctional offenders."[54] Now thirty years into his prison sentence, all Joe wanted to do was "head to seg[regation], let my beard and hair grow, take a vow of silence, put a "bite me" sign on the window of the cell, and check out. I'm not staying on the roller coaster. I'm done."[55]

But the roller coaster ride continued. In the fall of 2014, Joe was abruptly transferred back to Red Onion. The official explanation was a weapons charge, but Joe believed that he was set up by a prison administrator who was angry at a blog that Joe was writing about his life at Wallens Ridge. In protest, Joe went on another hunger strike. Although hunger strikes had been an effective tool to fight prison abuses in the past, Joe's aging body could not handle the pressure of another hunger strike and he collapsed in his cell only a few days into the strike. Finding Joe on the cell floor, corrections officers forced Joe to dress himself before he was transported to a prison hospital in Richmond, Virginia. Emergency surgery resulted in the amputation of Joe's right leg, but doctors were able to save his damaged left leg. In the weeks following his surgery, Joe suffered through infections and pneumonia, but he survived.

Ironically, Joe finally received a lower offender classification after the amputation. This classification determined which facilities could house Joe. Marie and his lawyers had fought for decades to have Joe's offender classification reduced, but grudges die slowly at the Virginia Department of Corrections, and their efforts were rebuffed repeatedly. With this lower classification, Joe could finally be housed in a facility appropriate for Joe's age, parole eligibility, and non-violent prison record.

Joe is presently incarcerated at the Deerfield Correctional Center in Capron, Virginia, which has a sizable population of geriatric prisoners. Over thirty years in prison have taken a toll on Joe's health, but he is gamely learning to use his new artificial leg. In the spring of 2015, Joe was turned down for parole for the tenth time in ten years. Ever the fighter, Joe has submitted another parole application.

Throughout Joe's travails over the last five years, he has been an enthusiastic supporter of this book. Joe has talked to me over the telephone, visited with me at Wallens Ridge State Prison, the Department of Corrections facility at the Medical College of Virginia, and at the Powhatan and Deerfield Correctional Centers, and answered an endless stream of e-mails. Trudging through memories of death row and the death house is not pleasant for Joe, but he has done it for Marie.

11

The Death of the Coalition

I'll keep going now until one of us drops dead, me or the
death penalty. . . . I just hope the death penalty goes first.
— Marie Deans, November 1991

In the early 1990s, Marie's energies were primarily focused on saving the lives of
two Virginia death row inmates: Roger Keith Coleman and Earl Washington Jr.
The men were convicted in separate and unrelated cases for the rape and murder of
nineteen-year-old women, and the lawyers handling their appeals were convinced
of their clients' factual innocence. Both Roger and Earl would find themselves facing execution dates without lawyers, and they would desperately turn to Marie to
help stay their executions. Over the course of a decade, Marie would experience the
heights of joy and the depths of the blackest grief as she worked to exonerate the two
men.

Roger Keith Coleman was born in 1958 at an army base in Georgia and raised in
Grundy, Virginia, a small coal-mining town in the southwestern corner of the state.
Essentially abandoned by his parents at the age of seven, Roger was adopted and
raised by his paternal grandparents. While many men who land on death row share
the common experiences of suffering abuse and deprivation in their childhoods,
there is no evidence of such factors in Roger's youth. Other than making some "dirty
phone calls" when he was in eighth grade, Roger's adolescence was unremarkable.
He was an above-average student in high school, and, despite his slight stature, Roger
played on the basketball and football teams. He also ran track and spent his free time
hunting, fishing, and reading science fiction novels. He had no interest in working
in the local coal mines after graduation, planning instead on a career in the Army.[1]

Any hopes of enlisting in the military ended in the spring of 1977, when Roger
was charged with the attempted rape of a local school teacher named Brenda Rife.
She testified at trial that Roger stopped at her home and asked for a drink of water.
Once inside, he produced a gun and ordered her to tie up her young daughter before forcing Brenda into a bedroom. Roger's subsequent efforts to rape Brenda were
thwarted when she escaped, grabbed her daughter, and screamed for help. A trial
and conviction quickly followed, and Roger subsequently served almost two years
in prison.

After his release in March of 1979, Roger returned to Grundy, started working in the coal mines, and began dating fifteen-year-old Patricia Thompson. Biographer John C. Tucker writes that the young teenager was "entranced by the older boy, especially by his reputation as a tough ex-convict who at the same time seemed thoughtful, articulate, and intelligent."[2] Not surprisingly, Patricia's parents were initially wary of Roger, but he was eventually embraced by the large Thompson clan. They would marry two years later and live with Roger's grandmother in a small trailer home.

Earl Washington Jr. was born on May 3, 1960, in rural Fauquier County, Virginia. Earl was raised in extreme poverty by hard-working, hard-drinking parents who struggled to provide food, shelter, and clothing for their five children. Their economic situation was so grim that one of Earl's siblings died of malnutrition at three months old, and the children sometimes did not have clothes or shoes to wear to school. The Washington family "lived like dogs," according to a local school bus driver. Earl's younger sister Linda was "sure" that their mother, Marie Mudd Washington, drank heavily during her pregnancies, and she recalled that their mother put beer in her children's baby bottles at night. As an adult, Earl would also develop a taste for alcohol.

Harsh discipline and violence were hallmarks of Earl's youth, as recounted by biographer Margaret Edds:

> Once, Washington said, he had a kitten that made the mistake of climbing onto the table and eating out of his father's dinner plate. "He'd told us kids, 'Don't you ever let no cat get on there, or I've got a surprise for him.'" The "surprise" was swift and permanent. When Earl Sr. saw the kitten, he picked it up, opened the door to the heating stove and threw the cat into the fire.[3]

The children were routinely beaten by their parents for infractions both serious and minor, such as spending too much time in front of the television or for "looking at them funny."

The violence continued into Earl's teen years. When he was sixteen years old, Earl was shot by an uncle who wanted Earl to do his chores faster. The uncle told the police that it was meant as a joke. The bullet punctured Earl's kidney and liver, and he had to have an appendectomy. Later diagnosed as mentally handicapped (his IQ score at age 10 was 62), Earl repeated multiple grades in elementary school. "Teacher after teacher described Earl Jr. as a lovable child who tried hard to please but was stymied by frequent absences and difficulty in comprehension."[4] Earl left school after tenth grade and started working as a farmhand.

While Roger and Earl had different childhoods, the crimes of which they were accused, and how they were tried, were eerily similar. On March 10, 1981, the small town of Grundy was shocked by the vicious murder of nineteen-year-old Wanda McCoy, the sister of Roger Coleman's wife, Patricia. Wanda had been stabbed, raped, sodomized, and nearly decapitated by a deep knife wound to her throat. While her family and neighbors described Wanda as a shy young woman, newspaper reporters were not satisfied with a shrinking violet as a victim and instead referred to her as "a victim out of American folklore: a member of the hillbilly clan that had battled the Hatfields in the nineteenth century."[5]

Roger was immediately a prime suspect in the murders. Not only was he a convicted felon, but Roger also had been caught publicly masturbating in a local library a month before the murder. In the initial weeks after Wanda's death, Roger remained a free man as police investigated the murder. He even served as a pallbearer at her funeral. A month later, however, Roger would be indicted by a grand jury for Wanda's death.

Like most defendants charged with capital murder in Virginia in the 1980s, Roger was assigned two court-appointed lawyers with limited experience representing criminal defendants.[6] Kathleen A. Behan, who represented Roger on his final set of appeals, was blunt in her assessment of Roger's trial attorneys; when asked to characterize their level of experience defending a murder case, she simply replied: "None. Zero. Zilch." And she was correct. Behan further alleged that the attorneys did not zealously defend Roger. "They never went to the crime scene in this case, [and] they never interviewed most of the witnesses until the day of trial."[7]

Roger rejected a plea deal (a guilty plea in exchange for two life sentences) and his three-day trial started on March 15, 1982. Many of the citizens in Grundy had already concluded that Roger was guilty, but that did not stop them from lining up outside the courthouse to get a seat in the courtroom. A sign that read "Time to Bring Back the Hanging Tree" was posted at a gas station a short distance from the courthouse. The gas station was owned by Preston Rife, a man with a special interest in the trial—he was the husband of Brenda Ratliff Rife, the woman that Roger attempted to rape.

No witness could place Roger at the crime scene, and the evidence against Roger was largely circumstantial and based on physical evidence. At the time, science had not sufficiently advanced to let investigators perform DNA testing on the two pubic hairs and seminal fluid left by the attacker or a drop of blood found on Roger's jeans. Testing, however, did establish that the pubic hairs were "consistent" with Roger's hair, that the individual who left the seminal fluid shared Roger's blood type, and that the blood on his jeans matched Wanda's blood type.

As with many criminal cases, a cellmate of Roger's provided damning testimony—testifying that Roger confessed that he and a second man had raped Wanda after the unidentified man stabbed her. Like many cases involving "jail house snitches," the former cellmate received a reduction in his sentence after testifying against Roger. While prosecutors claimed that the informant received a lesser sentence because he helped stop a jailbreak, Roger's lawyers maintained he was rewarded for his testimony. Years later, the mother-in-law of the informant claimed that he had lied under oath.

Not content with the damning testimony of one former cellmate, prosecutors also sought to introduce the testimony of Thurman Taylor, a convicted murderer who was housed at the same jail for two months. Taylor was called as a witness to testify to incriminating statements Coleman allegedly muttered in his sleep. Given the inherent unreliability of the evidence, the presiding judge ruled that the testimony was inadmissible.[8]

Roger's defense team tried to undercut the prosecution's case by claiming that Roger had neither a motive to kill Wanda nor the opportunity to do so given his movements on the night of the murder. The only unusual aspect of the capital murder trial was that Roger took the stand in his own defense, vehemently denying any involvement in Wanda's murder. The jury clearly was not convinced by Roger's testimony. They deliberated for only three hours before returning a verdict of guilt on the charges of rape and murder.

The sentencing hearing was held the next day. In order to show proof of future dangerousness, the prosecution called Brenda Ratliff Rife to the stand. Brenda was the school teacher whom Roger was convicted of attempting to rape, and she told the jury of her grim encounter with a gun-waving Roger. For a jury deciding if Roger posed a risk of future danger to society, Brenda's testimony was compelling.

Roger's defense attorney introduced testimony of only two character witnesses, both ministers, who had visited Roger in jail and witnessed his "sincere" religious beliefs. The first minister called to testify was the jail's chaplain, and Roger started loudly weeping when the chaplain took the stand. He later explained that he did not think that "the Lord would be drug into this."[9]

When Roger took the stand for a second time, he told the jury that it did not matter if he lived or died.

> Really, I feel there is nothing the jury can do to me . . . Last night when the verdict of guilty came back, I lost the only things that ever meant anything to me: my freedom, my life, and my wife, whom I love very much. At this point, the death penalty or life. It doesn't matter. It's up to the Lord now, anyway. . . . There is nothing more you can do to me. It all happened last night.[10]

The testimony completed, the attorneys rose to give their closing statements. The prosecution made a simple plea to the jury: "purge our community of Roger Keith Coleman . . . and sentence him to death."[11] Again, the jury did not take long to deliberate. Before the verdict was read, the drama mounted as the judge ordered the courtroom cleared and each spectator searched before they could return. Threats had been made against Roger, and the possibility of violence in the courtroom was real. Finally, the verdict was announced. Roger Coleman would die. By the end of April 1982, Roger Coleman arrived at death row.

Approximately two weeks after the trial and conviction of Roger Coleman, a nineteen-year-old woman was raped and murdered at the Village Square apartment complex in Culpeper, Virginia. Her name was Rebecca Lynn Williams, and she was a mother of three young children—two of whom were in the first-floor apartment at the time of the attack. Rebecca's slaying was even more brutal than the murder of Wanda McCoy. Rebecca's body was riddled with thirty-eight stab wounds. Remarkably, Rebecca was still alive when rescuers found her on the front steps of her apartment, nude, bloodied, and crying for help. The dying woman repeatedly identified her sole attacker as a "black man."

The crime remained unsolved until May of 1983, when police arrested and interrogated Earl for the assault of an elderly neighbor named Hazel Weeks. An alcohol-fueled evening and a subsequent fight with a family member sent a drunk Earl on a mission to find a weapon, and he recalled that Ms. Weeks kept a handgun on top of her refrigerator. When Ms. Weeks confronted Earl in her home, he beat her with a chair. There is conflicting evidence as to whether Earl also ordered her to take off her robe, but no sexual assault occurred. When Earl returned home, he accidently shot one of his brothers in the foot and then hid in a nearby grove of trees until he was found by the police.

Once in custody, Earl confessed to the attack on Ms. Weeks. He did not stop there. He also—when asked by the police—confessed to four different unsolved crimes. His confessions to three of the crimes—two rapes and a robbery—were so patently false that Earl was never prosecuted for the crimes. One of the police interrogators, however, thought that Earl had not fully confessed to all his crimes, and he decided to ask Earl about the Rebecca Williams murder. When directly asked, "did you kill that girl in Culpeper?" Earl shook his head "yes" and started crying. When Earl stopped crying, the interrogator asked the first of what would be a long stream of leading questions, that is, questions designed to feed information to Earl and suggest the answer to him. "I'm talking about the girl that was found stabbed, lying naked outside of the apartment in Culpeper," said the officer. Earl responded in the affirmative.[12]

What followed were multiple interrogations (Earl's appellate lawyers scornfully called them "rehearsal" sessions) where different teams of investigators essentially corrected Earl's testimony in order to get a credible confession. Earl initially described his victim as black, short, and alone; but the victim in question was white, five feet eight inches, and with a toddler and a baby in the apartment. He told the officers that he had stabbed the woman two or three times, when, in actuality, Rebecca had been stabbed thirty-eight times. (The original team of interrogators had told Earl that the victim had been stabbed.) Earl stated that he kicked in the door of the apartment, but there was no evidence of a forced entry. Earl said that the victim was unconscious when he left, but Rebecca Williams was conscious and able to provide a description of her attacker.

When taken to the apartment complex where the crime occurred, Earl was asked to show the police where the murder occurred. At first, Earl said that he did not recognize the complex. He then directed the police to the wrong end of the complex. After police pointed to the correct apartment and asked Earl if that was the crime scene, he changed his answer. It was only then that the police typed up the eight-page confession and had Earl sign it.[13] An expert witness would later comment that Earl's multiple confessions were "archetypes of what can happen to people with mental retardation during intense questioning."[14]

When Earl was asked about the confession years later, he said "At first, they started asking me about this crime. Then they got to telling me how it happened and all this and that. I was just agreeing with what they were saying. That's the way they wrote it down, I guess."[15] As for the police officers, all that Earl could say was that "they talked nice."[16] He added, without a trace of irony, "I'm a pretty easy guy to get along with."[17]

Earl's trial took place in January of 1984 in the Circuit Court of Culpeper County. As with Roger's case, Earl's lawyer had little experience defending criminal cases. The only evidence presented by the prosecution was Earl's confession and a shirt that was found six weeks after the crime in a dresser at the victim's apartment. When shown the shirt by investigators, Earl agreeably identified it as his; Earl's sister, who washed his clothes, later testified that she did not recognize it.

While police had found seminal fluid and blood (Type A) on a blanket at the crime scene, an expert witness retained by the prosecution concluded that Earl was not the source of the fluids (he was Type O). The prosecution had no reason to bring up this exculpatory piece of evidence; the defense had every reason to present the evidence to the jury but, astonishingly, did not. Nor did defense counsel attack the interrogation techniques used to generate Earl's confession.

Like Roger, Earl took the unusual step of testifying in his own defense. Earl denied killing Rebecca Williams. While Earl admitted signing his confession, he testified both that the confession was false and that he could not remember the contents of the written confession. Finally, Earl stated that the police were lying when they said that he had implicated himself in the murders. In short, Earl's testimony was a disaster.

During his closing statement, Earl's attorney did not discuss any of the evidence presented by the prosecution. He did not review any of the testimony provided by Earl himself. Instead, he reminded the jury that the prosecution had the burden of proving Earl's guilt beyond a reasonable doubt and that the jury had the right to decide if Earl's confession was credible. The jury only deliberated fifty minutes before returning a verdict of guilt.

The sentencing phase of Earl's trial was worse. The prosecution must convince the jury that a murder is vile in order to make the defendant eligible for the death penalty. In order to prove that Earl's crime was "vile," the prosecution put Rebecca Williams's mother on the stand. Her testimony was devastating, as she talked about how Rebecca's murder had traumatized her grandchildren:

> They have a telephone that is just used for talking to their mama in heaven and this is the way they talk about their problems. They sit down on the phone and they take turns talking to mama in heaven, to let her know how things are going, especially if they're very, very upset or something has upset them. . . . It's not an easy thing to work with children that are emotionally disturbed like this. They're beautiful children.[18]

Under existing law at the time, testimony at sentencing hearings could not include the impact of a murder on family members. No objections to the testimony, however, were made by Earl's attorney, and the jury heard the story of phone calls to heaven.

Defense counsel did not call a single witness to testify why Earl Washington should not be condemned to death. His closing comments were brief, as he simply told the jury that "this is Earl Washington's day in court and you must do him justice."[19] This time, the jury deliberated ninety minutes before sentencing Earl to die for the rape and murder of Rebecca Williams. A stunned and frightened Earl Washington Jr. arrived on death row on May 9, 1984—approximately two years after Roger Coleman first walked onto the row.

Both men would have a guardian angel and protector in Marie. She met Roger in the winter of 1983, eight weeks after she opened the Virginia Coalition on Jails and Prisons. Marie's first impressions of Roger were not positive. Coleman biographer John Tucker wrote of their first meeting:

> In their initial encounter he did little but whine, reciting a litany of complaints about conditions on death row and all he had lost as a result of a conviction that he insisted was unjust—his wife, his family, his job and so on. Marie responded in typical fashion. "Okay," she said, "you're right. Conditions are miserable and you've lost all those things. So, what are you going to do now? Sit here and complain, or do something for yourself?" For a while, Coleman mostly continued to complain.[20]

An irritated Marie finally grew tired of Roger's whining. "Look Roger," she said, "if you're really innocent, I'd think you would want to get out of here rather than be executed." Marie recalled that Roger "just sat there for a few minutes, and then got this little grin on his face and said 'Okay, I want to work with you.'"[21]

Marie's fight to save Roger, however, had just begun. In the months that followed, Roger was one of seven death row inmates who dropped their appeals. Marie swung into action, spending hours on the telephone beseeching attorneys to take the cases and hours in the visiting room at death row begging the inmates to pursue their appeals. The irony that Marie was working to find lawyers for inmates who did not want them was not lost on Marie. While having an inmate who might be factually innocent certainly caught Marie's attention, she worked just as hard to find lawyers for inmates who clearly committed their crimes. Her goal was the same for all the men: keep them out of the electric chair.

It was not until the end of the year that Marie returned for a second visit with Roger, who acted bored as Marie explained how she was searching for a competent attorney to represent him and re-file his appeal. As she talked, Roger's demeanor suddenly changed. "Suddenly, she realized he was crying," wrote Tucker. "He was desperately ashamed of crying in front of her and, worst yet, his fellow inmates. Marie reached her hand between the gray steel bars of Coleman's cell and touched him on the arm. He did not pull away, as she had half expected. Instead, he moved closer to her. Before she left he had agreed to resume his appeals."[22]

Tucker refers to Marie and Roger as "friends," which is inaccurate. While liking an inmate was never a prerequisite for Marie to help an inmate, she neither trusted nor particularly liked Roger. And Marie did not think that Roger was being truth-

Virginia death row inmate Roger Coleman, who maintained his innocence to the very end. Marie's involvement in his case would result in the closing of the Virginia Coalition on Jails and Prisons. Photograph courtesy of *Richmond Times-Dispatch.*

ful with her. "Roger was guarded and had built a wall of defenses around the beast within," Russ Ford recalled. "We knew he was not being genuine or dealing from any real depth. If an opening appeared we would move in, but he would be quick to recover."

Roger's fellow inmates shared Marie's distaste. "The men on death row were luke-warm toward Roger," Russ stated. "He was a 'gamer' and they didn't like him." Roger was aggressive toward some of the men and stole from them. Joe Giarratano found Roger to be arrogant. "He thought that he was more intelligent than anyone on the row, and more intelligent than almost anyone else," Joe stated. "He kept to himself on the row, and he wasn't sociable unless it suited him to be so. Roger was tolerated [by the men of the row]."

Soon after arriving on death row, Roger became involved in a Scared Straight program in which he and other inmates mailed letters to high school students and warned them away from the evils of drugs and alcohol. Roger had started the pro-gram, called "The Choice is Yours," with the Briley brothers, but he quietly removed their names from mailing materials after the brothers escaped from death row.

"It [the program] keeps me in touch with the outside world; it gives me a good feeling and it shows I'm not powerless to help," Coleman explained in a newspaper interview. "I wanted to do something to help others. When I first went to jail in 1977 . . . I saw that everyone around me was young and they could have made a different choice. The project's all about making up your own mind and living responsibly."[23] The program was originally only a letter-writing campaign. A videotape of Roger giving his presentation was later recorded and circulated to Virginia high schools. "If just one kid is kept from prison by this film, it will have been worth it," Roger stated. "It's as simple as that."[24] Eventually small groups of teenagers from nearby churches and schools travelled to the Mecklenburg Correctional Center to hear Roger speak about the realities of prison life. "Meeting with Roger had a tremendous impact on our kids who are still talking about the visit," a school principal gushed after his at-risk students met with Roger. "It wasn't just a prison visit. These boys had thought prison was an OK place with TV and basketball. They had no idea how lonely and how violent prison life can be."[25] No one appeared to question the wisdom of taking minors to death row to talk with a convicted rapist and murderer.

Talking to a reporter, Roger pointed to the program as evidence for his puzzling claim that death row was "one of the best things that's ever happened to me—because if I hadn't come here, I'm certain I never would have grown up." Describing himself as immature, selfish, and friendless prior to his conviction for capital murder, Roger pointed to the isolation and depravations of death row as freeing him from the shackles of past mistakes. "I had to come to prison to learn what freedom is. I've been more free in prison than I've ever been before in my life. . . . If they execute me, the joke's on them. The things that I've gained they can't take."[26]

Those who knew Roger were skeptical of both his actions and words, arguing that Roger was a transparent manipulator engaged in a crass publicity campaign. "I think the message on the tape is skewed," said former Coleman prosecutor Michael McGlothlin. "It doesn't deal with the morality of the issue. He has not repented for anything that he's done wrong. He's telling children, 'Don't violate the law or this is where you'll end up,' but the reason he shouldn't have killed Wanda McCoy is not because it puts him on death row. The reason he shouldn't have killed her was because she was a human being."[27]

When it came to Earl Washington, Marie was protective and motherly toward the shy young man. Years later she wrote:

> My visits to Earl while he was in the death house are especially poignant to me today. . . . Earl's brave front reminded me of the little-boy bravado of my eleven-year-old son. But my son could understand better what was happening than could Earl. Earl knew only that he was in a frightening and threatening place. Earl's face would light up when he'd see me, because my presence made him feel safe. Earl told people that I would not let anything happen to him. I, of course, was all too aware of how helpless Earl and I both were before the power of the State.[28]

And Marie's feelings were reciprocated. "He [Earl] would say to people, 'She loves me and she takes care of me,' " recalled Marie. He accepted her as a mother figure.

Earl was a popular inmate on death row, and he was protected by prisoners like Joe Giarratano against the violence and scams that were part of everyday life. "I do remember one incident when Roger [Coleman] and [Alton] Waye were teaching Earl to play poker," Joe said. "They convinced Earl that he was good. They set him up

[and] then began cheating him." Joe got into the game, won all the money that Earl lost, and gave it back to him. The other inmates "got the message" from Earl's burly protector, and they left him alone.

Earl's adjustment to death row was not easy. Joe clearly recalls when the terrified and lost young farmhand arrived at Mecklenburg.

> One of the most notable things about Earl during those first few months was that I had to basically lead him around the unit by the arm. He was just plain frightened of everyone and every sound around him . . . Whenever someone new arrived on the row I would, at the first opportunity, seek to learn all the basic information that I could: name, prison ID number, county where convicted, any attorney's name and address, medical needs, family contacts . . . and get that information to Ms. Deans. I would also try to explain some of the ins and outs of the strange world the person just entered.
>
> Getting basic information from Earl was difficult. It was obvious to me that Earl was slow, and more, he was scared out of his wits. He would not speak or when he did he would only mumble. More often than not he would just nod his head yes or no to questions I would ask, and it was difficult to ascertain whether or not he was even understanding my questions. He clearly did not realize or comprehend where he was.
>
> For the first few days, Earl would not leave his cell at all, not even to pick up his meal trays, shower, or participate in recreation. During my periods of out of cell time, I would spend a good period of that time at Earl's cell door talking to him through the tray slot in the door, though the conversation tended to be quite one-sided. Slowly Earl began to come out of his shell a bit, and began to come out on his own. He seemed to be the most comfortable around me and would come out in the unit if he saw me out there. We made sure that he had hygiene items, some cigarettes to smoke, made sure he got his meals, and I loaned him my radio to listen to. Slowly Earl began to feel more comfortable around the other men [but] he rarely talked much at all. When some of the other men would try to engage him in conversation, he would usually just hang his head and listen, or he'd find me and ask if he could go listen to the radio.

From the start, Marie suspected that both Roger Coleman and Earl Washington suffered from significant cognitive problems. During one of our meals at a cheap Chinese restaurant that Marie preferred, she explained how Roger's "peculiarities" surfaced.

> I was doing the mitigation interviews [with Roger], and I was also just talking to him. Actually, it was more listening. Roger talked more than I do. So I would mostly listen to him. I found peculiarities that I was pretty sure he wasn't making them up. These are the kind of symptoms that many, many mitigation people would not recognize. So I just seriously doubt that he was making them up. Like hearing what he termed 'Greek" out of one of his ears.

We're talking [on the telephone and] I said something about my ear getting tired but I don't like to switch because I can't—it doesn't come in as well. He said, "Oh, you have that too?" I said "Yeah, you don't switch ears?" "No," he said. "What do you hear?" He said, "I don't know what it is—Greek-like. I don't know what it is." So I went along with it. "But it's not English," I said. "No, it's not English." "Not just a funny accent?" "No, I don't know what it is," he said. "I say Greek because that's the most outrageously outlandish kind of language I can think . . . if I've got the phone in the wrong ear, I find myself wandering off. The other half of my brain has gone and done something else."

But he was hearing something different. He did these check outs where he'd just go to his cell and nobody would see him for five days or ten days. I learned that he always had excuses for these disappearances. Then he finally told me that he didn't know what was happening—that he'd feel different and he'd go to his cell. Next thing he knew it was five days later.

Marie believed that the punishment meted out by prison officials after the 1984 prison break worsened Roger's mental problems. In the weeks after the recapture of the inmates, Marie fought to see the men on the row. When she was finally let back into Mecklenburg, Roger was one of the first inmates that she demanded to see. "It took me fifteen to twenty minutes to get him to realize that he was not hallucinating and that I was really there," said Marie. "I wasn't allowed to touch him, so I was kicking him under the table—where they [the guards] couldn't see—and talking to him. He really thought he was hallucinating [when he saw me]. I was really worried about him."

In Marie's opinion, Roger never fully recovered from the escape attempt and the resulting retaliation. "After the escape, [and] seeing how bad off he was, [my feeling was that] he was kooky, not even really hanging on, just gone away. I brought him back a little, but not completely." Marie added that Roger suffered from more than trauma related to the escape. "I thought there was something dreadfully wrong with him," Marie explained. "I was convinced that there was something neurologically wrong. And that's why I wanted [him] examined."

As for Earl Washington, Marie suspected after their initial meeting that he was mentally handicapped. During their first interview, Marie asked Earl for his parents' address and telephone number. He couldn't answer her questions. When Marie tried a different tack and asked if his parents "lived on a particular road," Earl responded "No. They live in a house." Marie concluded, "Joe was right. Earl needed a lot of help."[29] Subsequent testing showed that Earl had an IQ of 69, which meant he had the comprehension of an average ten-year-old child.

Both Marie and Russ also saw how easy it was to manipulate the mentally handicapped Earl. "We could have convinced Earl that he shot JFK in Dallas," said Russ. The fact that Earl could be so easily coerced into admitting anything immediately alarmed Marie, and soon she questioned Earl's confession and his guilt. Russ shared Marie's belief that Earl was innocent. "If they had tried to kill him, it would have been my last execution," explained Russ. "I would have fought the death squad."

Marie's first priority was to find lawyers for Roger and Earl. Roger's direct appeal was denied by the Virginia Supreme Court on September 9, 1983, while Earl's appeal was denied on November 30, 1984. After the United States Supreme Court declined to grant Earl's request to review his appeals, Earl's execution was set for September 5, 1985. Marie anticipated that Roger would soon receive his execution date as well. To avoid the electric chair, both Earl and Roger would have to find lawyers to file complicated appeals for post-conviction relief—lawyers who would work for free.

Three months after Roger's direct appeal was denied, Marie convinced the Washington-based law firm of Arnold & Porter to represent him. When it came time to find Earl an appellate lawyer, however, Marie was not so lucky. Shortly after the denial of his direct appeal, Earl received a letter from his attorney. He could not read it, so he asked Joe Giarratano to tell him its contents. The message was simple: "Your appeal has been denied. I am no longer your attorney. And the state will be setting a date of execution."

"I sat him down and tried my best to explain what was going on," Joe recalled. "He understood and he was scared. He kept telling me that 'Ms. Deans won't let them. She'll get me a lawyer.' What Earl did not understand was that Marie was having great difficulty finding volunteer lawyers willing to take a capital case appeal."

Then a second letter arrived for Earl. He went again to Joe's cell. This letter was from the Virginia attorney general, asking when Earl would be filing his next round of appeals. "I wrote to the attorney general and the trial court on Earl's behalf," Joe said. "I explained that Earl could not read or write, suffered [from] mental retardation, and that it was not possible for him to draft complicated legal pleadings or otherwise represent himself. I asked the court to appoint a lawyer to help Earl. Those pleas fell on deaf ears."

While Joe could write letters and draft legal documents from his prison cell, he did not have the resources to place mass phone calls to potential attorneys. That job fell to Marie. "I began frantically searching for a lawyer [for Earl]," Marie wrote. "I called over 160 lawyers in Virginia and around the country. They all refused. Some had legitimate reasons, but most simply did not want to expend the time, energy, and money, nor did they want to deal with the opprobrium incurred in defending a human being we have determined unfit to live." As attorney after attorney rebuffed Marie, she sent Earl's case file to Joe. If all else failed, Joe would have to draft Earl's appeals.

Marie's efforts became more frenzied when Earl, still without a lawyer, was moved to the death house in the middle of August 1985. "In the flurry of activity that ensued, and before I or anyone could file a petition for Earl, they came for him," Joe wrote. "I tried my best to prepare Earl for what to expect and to assure him that Marie Deans and I were on top of things. I tried hard not to let him see just how worried I really was, but Earl could tell. All he would say was, 'I don't want to go, Joe. Why can't I stay here with you and Baydar?' All I could muster in response was to tell him not to worry, he'd get to visit with Marie." In his cell, Joe watched as an elite group of black-uniformed guards called the "Prison Emergency Response Team" ("PERT") pulled a shaking Earl from his cell and walked him out of the pod.

Days passed slowly in the death house for the frightened Earl, as he listened to the guards repeatedly test the electric chair. Marie continued to call attorneys. Joe Giarratano tried a different tack. In July, Joe drafted and filed a civil rights complaint in federal court. In essence, Joe asserted that death row inmates' constitutional rights were being violated because Virginia did not provide legal counsel to assist them in exhausting all appeals prior to execution. In a letter sent to the judge assigned to hear the case, Joe used Earl Washington's case to highlight why the failure to provide attorneys to the inmates was unjust: "I feel an enormous sense of responsibility with Mr. Washington's life at stake. It appears to me that if Mr. Washington is executed, that fundamental principles of Due Process and Equal Protection would . . . be thrown out the window."[30]

Joe's lawsuit was like a signal flare fired desperately into the night sky. He hoped that a large law firm would take notice of the lawsuit, agree to represent him, turn the suit into a class action, add Earl Washington as one of the plaintiffs in the lawsuit, and then seek a stay of execution for Earl while the civil action worked its way through the court system. And Joe hoped that the firm would represent Earl on his remaining criminal appeals.

The signal flare worked. The law firm of Paul Weiss was intrigued by the lawsuit, and they sent a young attorney named Marty Geer to death row to meet with Joe. When Marie and Geer arrived in the small death row visiting room, however, Joe was not in the mood to talk about his lawsuit. Instead, he confronted Geer and said, "Earl Washington has an IQ of 69, an execution date three weeks away, and no lawyer. What the hell are you going to do about it?"[31] Moved by Joe's passion, Geer called her office and asked if they should take Earl as a client. Not willing to commit, a senior partner instructed Geer to meet Earl.

The next day, Geer returned with Marie to the same visitation room. Waiting for the two women was Earl Washington. Like Marie, it did not take Geer long to determine that Earl was significantly disabled; his new attorneys would soon discover that Earl "was unable to name the colors of the flag, describe what a thermometer does, or recite the alphabet."[32] The idea that he could draft and file his own criminal appeals was inconceivable.

Attorneys at Paul Weiss agreed to take Earl's case. They would file an appeal on Earl's behalf, thus stopping the execution clock. The appeal, called a writ of habeas corpus, had to be carefully written or Earl's chances in court would be compromised. A team of lawyers, led by Eric Freedman and Marty Geer, worked around the clock to fashion an appropriate appeal. Earl's state habeas corpus petition was filed on August 27, 1985. A stay was entered in his case, and Earl was returned to death row after fourteen days in the death house.

Despite the obvious problems in Earl's case, not everyone was happy to learn about Earl's new team of lawyers. The chief prosecutor in Earl's case announced that the new round of appeals did not promote the ends of justice. "The man had a three-day trial," said John C. Bennett. "The matter has been reviewed by the Virginia and US supreme courts. At some point, the matter has to become final."[33]

For the moment, Earl was safe. He was also badly shaken by his visit to the death house. "Earl went back into his shell and, for a few months, really didn't communicate much," recalled Joe. "He spent a lot of time sleeping, chain smoking, eating all he could get his hands on, and just sat like a fixture in front of the pod TV when he did come out of his cell . . . whenever the PERT team came to escort one of us somewhere . . . Earl would become visibly agitated. He would often ask if the person was going to be okay."

Over time, Earl did slowly adjust to the ebb and flow of life at Mecklenburg, but it was never easy for him. "I can state with a certainty of having lived those years with Earl that, even if there was much he did not understand, he felt every hard and painful moment," Joe asserted. "One could not help but sense it, know it, see it in his face, in his body language, [and] in his uncontrollable shaking."

Looking back on Earl's close brush with the electric chair, some might argue that Virginia would never have executed a mentally handicapped inmate with viable legal appeals remaining but no lawyer. A member of the Virginia attorney general's office, however, said otherwise in open court. During a hearing before Judge Robert Merhige, a sympathetic federal judge who supported Marie's work, an assistant attorney general testified that Earl's execution would have gone forward if Marie had not secured a lawyer or if Earl had not filed an appeal himself.

At the moment, one crisis was averted. Roger and Earl had attorneys who could use their talents and experience to fight to save the two men. While the lawyers would draw on Marie's skills in collecting mitigation evidence for the appeals, and would depend on Marie to be a conduit between their law offices and the two men, Marie would no longer have to worry about Roger and Earl facing the electric chair without legal counsel. This did not mean, however, that there were not other men on the row without lawyers. Marie's work was not finished, and the terror of other men being executed without exhausting their appeals continued.

Roger's and Earl's appeals were both grounded on the fundamental argument that they were factually innocent. At this stage in the appeals process, however, state and federal procedural law held that the lawyers could not simply argue their clients were innocent. Those claims should have been raised during the inmates' direct appeals. Rather, the attorneys had to argue that the men's trial attorneys were incompetent—and thus denied the men their constitutional right to counsel—because the attorneys did not present evidence of the men's innocence. In other words, listing all the different pieces of evidence showing Roger's and Earl's innocence was how their appellate lawyers could make the case that the trial court lawyers did a mediocre job representing the two men. This was more difficult than it seems. Not only did the appellate lawyers have to present evidence of incompetence, but they had to also demonstrate that the outcome of the trials would have been different but for the trial court lawyers' incompetence.

As trial court transcripts were examined, witnesses were re-interviewed, and appeals were drafted, it became apparent that the evidence of actual innocence was much stronger in Earl's case. Not only did Earl's trial lawyers fail to challenge critical pieces of forensic evidence introduced by the prosecution, but the attorney did not challenge the admissibility of a confession that Earl's appellate lawyers viewed as the result of police manipulating the brain-damaged Earl.

Kathleen A. Behan was the Arnold & Porter attorney who worked on Roger's case during the final stages of his appeals. Described by a reporter for the *Washington Post* as "tall, slim, and deeply earnest . . . with an abiding hostility toward the death penalty,"[34] Behan was a graduate of Columbia Law School who worked for the American Civil Liberties Union after graduation. She joined Arnold & Porter in the summer of 1990 and was almost immediately assigned to the Coleman case. Working by her side was James McCloskey, who was the head of Centurion Ministries—an organization dedicated to investigating wrongful convictions and securing the exoneration of innocent men. They were a formidable team, motivated by their unshakeable conviction that investigators had ignored other leads and "shoehorned" Roger into a conviction.[35] Again and again they would return to the small town of Grundy, re-examining the forensic evidence and looking for new witnesses who could support Roger's claims of innocence.

Behan and McCloskey's hopes were sent soaring when they were contacted by a woman named Teresa Horn, a Grundy resident who claimed that a local man assaulted her in the spring of 1987. During the attack, Horn stated that the man told her to be quiet or he "was going to do me like he did that girl on Slate Creek." Horn added that her friends later explained to her that the "girl on Slate Creek" was Wanda McCoy. Upon investigating the man, Behan and McCloskey found that he lived less than fifty yards from the McCoy house. Horn executed an affidavit containing her allegations, and several months later she repeated them to a news reporter. The day after her television interview, Horn was found dead. A medical examiner later ruled that Horn died from a drug overdose, but rumors spread through Grundy that she had been murdered. Frightened by the incident, Grundy residents stopped talking to Behan and McCloskey.[36]

It would take approximately eight years for Roger and Earl's appeals to work their way through the state and federal courts. The volunteer attorneys working on behalf of Roger and Earl spent hundreds of hours collecting new evidence, drafting briefs, and appearing in court. The odds that any judge would find in favor of a death row inmate who had filed a petition of habeas corpus were not good. In the case of Roger, the odds became worse after his attorneys missed a critical filing deadline with the Virginia Supreme Court. Because of this procedural error, all subsequent appeals filed in the federal courts were dismissed without considering the merits of Roger's claims.

As Roger and Earl exhausted their appeals, it became more and more apparent to their attorneys that the only way to save their clients' lives was to ask Virginia governor Douglas Wilder to grant clemency based on their clients' claims of factual innocence. Such a tactic worked in Joe Giarratano's case, but it was a long shot at best. In the last year Governor Wilder had intervened and spared the lives of death row inmates Joe Giarratano and Herbert R. Bassette Jr., decisions that had cost the governor precious political capital. Time was running out.

On May 1, 1992, Roger was transferred to the new death house at the Greensville Correctional Center in Jarratt, Virginia. At Greensville, Roger spent fifteen days shivering in a frigid cell. Russ Ford believed that prison administrators were deliberately keeping the cell cold to cause Roger discomfort, and he was furious. "That's when my anger toward the Department of Corrections turned to hate," Russ later explained.

Shortly after Roger arrived at the death house, *Time* magazine ran a picture of Roger on its cover with the caption "This Man Might Be Innocent. This Man is Due to Die." One of the guards was so impressed that he brought a copy of *Time* into the death house and asked Roger to autograph it. Roger's attorneys had worked hard to get Roger's story in national press, and they hoped that the publicity would increase the pressure on Governor Wilder to grant clemency. Their efforts at drumming up support paid off, and Governor Wilder's office received over six thousand letters and telephone calls—including a call from Mother Teresa—urging the governor to grant clemency.

The publicity campaign triggered a backlash from a furious Brenda Ratliff, the Grundy school teacher who Roger attempted to rape. At an emotional news conference, Brenda recounted Roger's attack and accused the media of reopening old wounds by trumpeting Roger's claims of innocence. "I have been a victim of Roger Keith Coleman for fifteen years," she told the assembled reporters. "And I am angry now. I am angry at the media . . . It's getting to where I can't deal with it."[37]

In a later interview, Pat Hatfield, the librarian who witnessed Roger masturbating in the public library, also criticized the media's portrayal of the Grundy community. "All these reporters and all these people have come out here and tried to stereotype us as illiterate and uneducated, and people who have not tried to give him a fair trial," she stated. "We've all suffered . . . because we have to look on national TV and see the whole legal system of the county discredited."[38] Hatfield's ire was also directed at Coleman's lawyers, who issued a press release in which they named the "real" killer. "They were trying to build this case for Roger's innocence, and they didn't care who they threw to the dogs," she said. "It didn't matter whose life was destroyed as long as they could save Roger."[39]

As Roger awaited the governor's decision, he spoke with newspaper reporters, appeared on *Good Morning America*, *Larry King Live*, *Nightline*, *Today*, and *The Phil Donahue Show*, and filled his free time by rereading the science fiction stories of Robert Heinlein, whose books featured the character of time-travelling space explorer Lazarus Long. He also negotiated with prison officials for extra visits with his girlfriend, Sharon Paul. A former University of Virginia student, Sharon had read the following personal ad that the now-divorced Roger had run in a student newspaper in late 1983:

Thirteen steps from eternity. Death Row prisoner seeks sincere people to correspond with and for possible visits. White, 24 years old, 5'9" tall, 155 pounds, brown hair and green eyes. Photos appreciated but not necessary. Sincerity is what counts.[40]

Sharon responded. "I was captured by the vulnerability," she explained. " 'Here's me, and all I want is someone to write to me' . . . It was letting the world see his loneliness. I guess I admired that honesty and openness from the very start."[41]

Letters and phone calls were exchanged. In one of his early letters, Roger wrote Sharon, told her that he did not kill Wanda McCoy, and told Sharon to ask any questions that she had about the murder. Roger sent Sharon small gifts and homemade cassette tapes of romantic music. Visits followed. Years passed, the friendship deepened, and they fell in love. Sharon became utterly convinced not only that Roger was innocent but that he would be exonerated if the world discovered Roger's true character. "I wish that the people who have the power to do something for Roger could know the Roger Coleman that I know," she lamented to a reporter. "That he is a warm, caring, generous person, and he has taught me what it is to love."[42] Now their fantasies of a life together were shattered, and a devastated Sharon prepared to say goodbye to Roger.

Two days before Roger's execution date, Governor Wilder announced that he would not grant clemency. A sliver of hope remained. After a flurry of telephone calls with the governor's office, Roger's lawyers learned that Governor Wilder might be willing to revisit the clemency petition if Roger would take a polygraph test. Roger's legal team was divided on whether Roger should accept the governor's offer, with Marie and Russ arguing that the physically and emotionally exhausted inmate could not possibly pass the test. Siding with his lawyers, Roger decided to take the test.

At 6:00 a.m. on the morning of his execution, a caravan of police cars transported Roger to Richmond for the polygraph. As the polygraph examiner started attaching the electrodes to Roger, the condemned man began "shaking and sobbing uncontrollably."[43] The test was delayed until Roger recovered, but Marie and Russ's fears were later confirmed. Roger failed the test. Any chance at clemency was gone.

Roger spent the last afternoon of his life visiting with Sharon and Marie. Unlike prior executions, Marie would not stand death watch. "Roger had always said that he knew I would be with him if they killed him," Marie said. "He had this recurring dream that he would be in the electric chair, and I would be by his foot. They would pull him away, and I would have his toe. I wouldn't let go."

At the end, however, Roger asked Marie to forgo the death watch and watch over Sharon. "I was stunned but not totally surprised," Marie said. "He loved that girl with everything he had. He knew that Sharon and I had come to care very much for each other. He really believed I was the only one that could take care of her. It turned out that he was probably right." Marie and Sharon would spend the night in Marie's apartment, with Marie comforting Sharon as she wavered between grief and denial over Roger's execution.

It was Russ Ford who stood death watch with Roger, along with Behan and McCloskey. During those final hours, the game show "Wheel of Fortune" blared from the television outside of Roger's cell. McCloskey later bitterly recalled watching a contestant solve one of the word puzzles—the answer was "miscarriage of justice."[44] Together they joined Roger for his final meal.

He [Roger] has seen a television ad in which a condemned man orders a Tomb-stone Pizza for his last meal, and partly because he thinks it would be a good joke to do what the ad suggests and partly because he really does love pizza, he has ordered it for his meal, along with Sprite and fudge-stick cookies. The meal, however, was delivered to the death house in mid-afternoon and has sat on the guards' desk ever since. The pizza is cold, with the cheese hard and yellow, and the Sprite is warm. The guards have not bothered to refrigerate it, or to heat the pizza before serving it.[45]

Roger was not put off by the stale food, devouring half the pepperoni pizza and the cookies.

In Washington, DC, another meal was being impacted by Roger's looming death. Dining with President George H. W. Bush at a black-tie dinner in honor of Canadian Prime Minister Brian Mulroney, Chief Justice William H. Rehnquist and Associate Justice Anthony Kennedy repeatedly excused themselves to deal with multiple tele-phone calls regarding a last minute stay of execution filed by Roger's lawyers. The stay was ultimately denied, and the justices were able to return to the dinner.[46]

After his final dinner, the other familiar rituals followed. Head and eyebrows shaved. Final shower. Conducting gel applied to his bald scalp. New clothes. Because of alleged fears about suicide, the death squad confiscated Roger's glasses and dental plate. When Roger's legal team returned to the cell, McCloskey silently thought that Roger resembled a miniature Buddha with his shaved head.[47]

As the final hours before the execution drained away, the conversation among the small group ebbed and flowed. Behan later commented, "the last two hours I spent with Roger were the hardest two hours of my life."[48] Roger remained preternaturally calm as the execution time drew near and, at one point, mused out loud as to the positive aspects of being a condemned man. "If I hadn't been wrongfully convicted, I would be a nobody from Grundy for my entire life . . . and here I am, I've met Sharon, she means the world to me, I'm famous, my face is on Time magazine. I'm a somebody."[49]

At 11:26 p.m. on May 20, 1992, Roger Coleman walked into the death chamber and was strapped into the electric chair. After he was secured, Russ Ford gave him a kiss on the head and walked away. His final words to Roger were simple: "Go with the flow."[50] Roger's glasses and dental plate were returned so Roger could see his final statement and read it without a lisp. "An innocent man is going to be murdered tonight," Roger told the assembled crowd of prison officials, guards, and witnesses. "When my innocence is proven I hope Americans will recognize the injustice of the death penalty as all other civilized nations have."

Roger's final words were directed to Sharon. "My last words are for the woman I love. Love is eternal. My love for you will last forever. I love you, Sharon."[51] Roger ap-peared "calm and composed" in the eyes of a witness, and he spoke in a "clear [and] crisp" voice. With that, the switch was thrown, and 1,750 volts of electricity raced through Roger's body. A second charge followed. Smoke rose from his right leg. And he was gone.[52] Outside the prison, Wanda McCoy's husband announced to the assembled reporters, "Roger was his own executioner by the act of his own hands. He's not going to be able to hurt anyone again."[53]

A memorial service was held four days later in the mountains surrounding Grundy. It was a warm and windless Saturday afternoon, and a small group of family and friends—including Kathleen Behan, Marie Deans, and Russ Ford—gathered to say goodbye to Roger. A small table had been brought to the site to bear pictures of Roger and several vases of flowers.

As the sounds of a bagpipe recording of "Amazing Grace" filled the air, Sharon Paul walked the short distance from the gathered mourners to a rocky overlook, which was one of Roger's favorite spots. "She opened the container, and, taking out a handful of ashes, kissed her hand and tossed the ashes into the wind. She stopped a minute, and then, gathering herself, repeated the gesture until the box was empty."[54] "I cried and carried on," remembered Marie. "Afterward we [family and friends] all sat around and talked about Roger. How we knew him and what we thought of him."

Although Marie did not know it at the time, the frantic efforts by Roger's attorneys to save his life would result in the death of the Virginia Coalition on Jails and Prisons. Press releases drafted by his lawyers in the months before Roger's death buttressed his claims of innocence by naming another man as the real killer. Marie was aghast. Not only had the attorneys accused another man of the murder, but the press releases listed Marie as one of the parties issuing the releases. "I said, 'Don't put my name on anything that says [the other suspect's name],'" Marie said, "and they put my name on it anyway."

Not only did Marie believe that there was no evidence to support the defense team's claims that they had identified the real killer,[55] but Marie did not want another man to take Roger's place in the electric chair. "I'm not in the business of exchanging people on death row. I just want to get them out." Marie's worst fears were confirmed when the newly accused man filed a five million dollar libel suit against Roger's lawyers and Marie.

After receiving a copy of the complaint, a panicked Marie called David Kendall. Now a prominent Washington lawyer, Kendall and Marie had first met when he worked for the NAACP Legal Defense Fund. Kendall immediately agreed to represent Marie, who was frightened that a judgment in the lawsuit would wipe out a small college fund that she had saved for Robert. Marie was ultimately dismissed from the libel suit and did not have to pay damages. When I asked Kendall why he did not charge Marie for his legal services, his answer was simple: "I thought that Marie Deans walked on water."[56]

Arnold & Porter, the law firm that represented Roger during his final appeals, settled the libel suit for a "considerable" sum of money and issued a bland press release: "We complied with our professional responsibility and stand by our representation of Roger Coleman."[57] Marie herself did not blame the lawyers for the libel suit, pointing to their inexperience in a capital murder case. She did, however, feel used by the "spin" the lawyers employed to deflect the blame from Roger.[58]

Despite the fact that Marie was not found liable, the damage was done. "After Roger was killed, I spent several weeks doing almost nothing but writing grants, but, once we were sued, foundations that had agreed to give us grants all said they would have to hold them until the suit was resolved," wrote Marie in an e-mail to a friend. "Our major donors did the same thing."

As Marie desperately tried to raise money to save the Coalition, she counted on one last source of money to come through, namely, funds Marie maintained that an Arnold & Porter lawyer had promised Roger they would pay her for the hundreds of hours she worked on Roger's case.[59] When Marie learned that the law firm had decided not to pay her the funds, she was devastated and furious. "I never got a penny. I would have felt better about that if they just hadn't made any promises. But, they promised me and they promised their own client [Roger] as he's going in the fucking electric chair that they're gonna do this [pay Marie for her work on the case] and they didn't."

Marie and the Coalition limped along for a year. Marie cut her staff down to two unpaid volunteers (one of whom was her son, Robert), and Marie herself stopped drawing a salary. Reducing her staff meant that Marie took on more job duties, which left little time to look for new grants. "I'm the fundraiser and chief cook and the bottle washer," Marie explained to a reporter. "We just have too much work for me to concentrate on fundraising."[60] From his prison cell, Joe Giarratano launched a fundraising campaign, but it did little to increase the trickle of donations coming into the Coalition.

The Virginia Coalition on Jails and Prisons permanently closed its doors on August 31, 1993. The demise of the Coalition was lamented in newspapers around the state, with reporters referring to Marie was "the last best friend of Virginia's death row"[61] and "one of the most influential advocates of death row inmates in the state."[62] Marie vowed that she would work full-time to raise money and re-open the Coalition, but she was a realist and knew that the chances of finding funding were remote at best. "I had no clue where my next meal was coming from," Marie recalled years later. "You didn't even know if you had fought the good fight at that point. None of it was working out."[63] When I asked Marie if she bore any animus toward Roger for the closing of the Coalition, she quickly replied that she did not. And Marie added that Roger would have been "miserable" if he knew how his case helped close the Coalition.

While Marie mourned the death of the Coalition, one more battle loomed before her: Earl Washington had a date with the executioner. By the fall of 1993, Earl's appeals were all but exhausted. The only remaining option was to petition Governor Wilder for clemency. In October, a DNA test on seminal fluid left at the crime scene was finally conducted, but the results were contested by the attorney general's office. In short, the report stated that the genetic material could not have been from Earl Washington *alone*. The logical conclusion was that Earl was not the rapist. Now the attorney general's office argued for the first time that Earl could have been one of two rapists who attacked and killed Rebecca Williams, and their combined genetic material explained the test results.

Marie and Earl's lawyers were furious at the state's new theory of the case. "It is clear from the tests and the report that Earl is excluded from guilt," Marie told a newspaper reporter. "We know there were not two perpetrators. There was one."[64] Despite the attorney general's office's response, Marie shared the news with Earl. "I told him, 'You are leaving Mecklenburg. You will never need to be afraid of the electric chair again,'" she told Earl. "He was giggling like a child. . . . He gave me a big hug. He kept looking at me and grinning and touching my hand. I told him that now the whole world will know he did not kill or rape Rebecca."[65] In hindsight, Marie's decision to share the news with Earl was a mistake.

There was little that Earl's supporters could do regarding the attorney general's refusal to acknowledge the significance of the DNA test. So Marie concentrated on raising public support for Earl's clemency petition. Time, however, was running out. Governor Wilder's term of office ended on January 15, 1994. Wilder's successor was a conservative Republican named George Allen, and Earl's attorneys had little hope that he would look favorably on the clemency petition. As Governor Wilder pondered the petition, he ordered another DNA test to be run on the seminal stains found at the crime scene. On the afternoon of Governor Wilder's final day in office, attorney Barry Weinstein, one of Earl's lawyers, received a call from Wilder's office. A staffer announced that the governor would grant Earl a conditional pardon and reduce his sentence to life with the possibility of parole. The pardon would also allow for a new trial if Virginia ever repealed its twenty-one-day rule. The staffer added that Earl had two hours to decide whether or not to accept the offer.

The next five hours were a blur for Weinstein and Marie. They jumped into Weinstein's car and started the two-hour drive from Richmond to the Mecklenburg Correctional Center. Talking intensely about the conditional pardon, Marie and Weinstein were startled when the car suddenly rolled to a stop. It was out of gas. Jumping out of the stalled car, Weinstein and Marie started waving at passing cars to stop. Finally, an old Buick pulled over and its occupants helped push Weinstein's car to a gas station. Precious time had been lost, and they did not arrive at Mecklenburg until 7:00 p.m.—two full hours after the expiration of the clemency offer.

For the next hour, Marie and Weinstein met with Earl and discussed the advantages and disadvantages of accepting the governor's proposal. When Earl announced that he would accept the clemency offer, Marie started to cry. "I'll be alright," Earl said as he took Marie's hand. The comforted had become the comforter. "He signs it, and I was just devastated," Marie said. "There was a huge part of me saying, 'Don't sign. Don't sign. Keep fighting. Maybe we can win.' But this other part of me was going, 'Yeah, but they'll kill him.'"[66]

When Robert Hall, another one of Earl's attorneys, called the governor's office to announce that Earl had accepted the offer, a staffer informed Hall that the clemency offer had expired. Hall was furious. "You advise the governor that once we determine what [inaugural] ball he's attending tonight, we'll have a press conference outside, and I have reason to believe that it will be well attended by the press," Hall fired back. Approximately a half hour later, the governor's office called to say that Governor Wilder would shortly be announcing to the press that he had granted Earl Washington clemency.

As phone calls were going back and forth, Weinstein and Marie returned to Richmond. It was a somber car ride home. Marie would later say: "I felt like a puppet on a political string, hopeless [and] devastated."[67] The Coalition was gone. Marie was unemployed. She was exhausted and suffering from post-traumatic stress disorder. And Earl, like Joe Giarratano, would spend the rest of his life in prison for a crime he did not commit. The prospect of Earl being transferred out of the relatively safe confines of death row and into the more dangerous environment of a prison's general population frightened Marie. "I was afraid for him," she said. "I didn't think that Earl was prepared to live in prison without getting hurt."[68]

Over the next six years, Earl disappeared into the Virginia correctional system. He would be incarcerated at six different prisons during that time period. Marie's fears about Earl's safety proved to be unfounded, and Earl was a model inmate who seldom received infractions.

With the closing of the Coalition, Marie slowly disengaged from the men of Virginia's death row. Marie continued to stand death watch with the men she befriended prior to the shutting of the Coalition's doors, but her visits to death row stopped. Another connection to death row was severed in 1994, when Russ Ford stepped down as the death row prison chaplain. Other organizations providing specially trained attorneys to death row inmates sprang up in Virginia, and the specter of condemned men being marched to the death house without legal counsel faded away.

In 1997, Marie moved from her small apartment in Richmond to a townhouse in Charlottesville. Robert was now a student at the University of Virginia, and Marie wanted to be close to her youngest son. The townhouse was the first house that Marie ever owned, and she was only able to purchase it because of a government housing program. Having no money to hire a contractor, Marie painstakingly remodeled the townhouse, doing the painting, wallpapering, and building bookshelves and cabinets all herself. Slowly she turned the house into a cozy home. Marie supported herself by taking court-appointed mitigation work in death penalty cases, but, over the next ten years, Marie took fewer cases. Her health was declining, and Marie no longer had the stomach for the grim work.

Yet Marie remained committed to freeing Earl Washington. In the years after Earl's pardon, his attorneys repeatedly tried to obtain a copy of the DNA test ordered by Governor Wilder, but the state crime lab refused to release them. The attorneys eventually stopped asking. Earl's family stopped writing and visiting him, and Earl went a stretch of three years without a single visitor. Some members of Earl's former legal team, however, diligently worked to stay in touch, and Barry Weinstein tried to lift Earl's sagging spirits with regular telephone calls, letters, and deposits to Earl's prison commissary account.

The final step in Earl's exoneration began in the spring of 1999. A filmmaker named Ofra Bikel was producing a documentary on inmates who remained in prison despite exoneration by DNA evidence. Bikel was interested in Earl's case, and one day she walked into the Virginia state crime laboratory and requested a copy of the January 1994 DNA report ordered by Governor Wilder. Bikel was surprised when it was handed to her without a murmur of protest. While the report ordered by Earl's attorneys in the fall of 1993 stated that Earl was not the sole source of the semen stains at the crime scene, this later report went further: Earl was "eliminated" as a source of the biological material. Earl was innocent, and nobody but Bikel knew.

Bikel's findings were presented on a January 2000 episode of the television show *Nightline*. Despite the DNA report's conclusion that Earl was not the source of the DNA, then-Governor James Gilmore remained unconvinced. Months passed. Earl's lawyers continued to lobby the governor's office for Earl's release.

In June of 2000, Governor Gilmore ordered a third DNA test on the remaining materials. More delays ensued as the test, which should have taken two weeks to conduct, was not finished for three months. Finally, the governor's office announced that the test results were complete. The governor, however, would not release the results until they were analyzed by his own experts and an investigation was completed by the Virginia State Police. In newspaper articles across the state, the governor's reluctance to release the test results was criticized roundly as politics at its worst. "Why is Earl Washington still in prison, and why won't [Governor] Gilmore say what the most recent DNA test results showed?" asked the editorial page of the *Virginia-Pilot*. "The lack of straight answers is suspicious, reinforcing the appearance that Washington, who is forty, has been left to rot even longer in prison for crimes he did not commit."

Finally, on October 2, 2000, Governor Gilmore announced that Earl Washington had been granted a full pardon for the murder and rape of Rebecca Williams and that the new DNA evidence linked another convict to the crime. In the press release, the governor stated:

> In my judgment, a jury afforded the benefit of the DNA evidence and analysis available to me today would have reached a different conclusion regarding the guilt of Earl Washington. . . . Upon careful deliberation and review of all of the evidence, as well as the circumstances of this matter, I have decided it is just and appropriate to intervene in the judicial process by granting Earl Washington an absolute pardon for the capital murder and rape of Rebecca Williams.[69]

Marie was overjoyed at Earl's pardon, but she was angry at the language used by the governor. "Gilmore never said, 'The man is innocent,' or 'Geez, we're sorry.' Nothing."[70] And in her own press release, Marie fired off a stinging indictment of Virginia's criminal justice system. Marie wrote:

> Today all of Virginia knows what we always knew. Earl Washington is innocent. We have kept a man-child on our death row for almost ten years and came within days of killing him because the State has placed finality over truth, because our laws and rules address procedure and technicalities over justice, and because we simply refuse to recognize that our system is far from perfect. . . . It is time for us to change the rules and laws and attitudes that allow for stories like Earl's to happen.

When asked about Governor Gilmore's decision, Earl was characteristically succinct. "I feel good," Earl said. "I've been telling everybody I didn't do it." And then Earl added, "I guess I'm freed."[71] But he was wrong. There was another turn of the screw.

In 1983, Earl was convicted of the robbery and assault of Hazel Weeks, the elderly woman whose gun Earl had sought to steal and use in a fight. Earl received two consecutive sentences of fifteen years for the crime. At the time of Earl's conviction, Virginia still granted parole to prisoners. Nobody had thought to have a parole board review these convictions and determine if Earl had earned "good time credits" toward parole, however, because Earl was on death row for a separate crime. Now Governor Gilmore announced that Earl would not be freed until a parole board reviewed his case and determined if he was eligible for parole. By passing the buck to the parole board, Gilmore had washed his hands of Earl Washington.

Earl's attorneys were incredulous that the governor would not order Earl's immediate release from prison. "It's an act of political cowardice and bureaucratic buck passing that compounds the original injustice," said Eric Freedman, the attorney who had drafted Earl's original state habeas petition. "No one doubts that Mr. Washington would have been released six or seven years ago on the noncapital charge, which is the governor's excuse for continuing to hold him."[72] Another one of Earl's attorneys blasted the governor's decision as "gutless."[73]

The anger Earl's lawyers felt came to a head when the parole board determined that Earl should not be released until February of 2001. The parole board had the authority to immediately release Earl, but in December of 2000 the board announced that they were denying Earl early release based on the "serious nature of his offense" (namely, the robbery and assault of Hazel Weeks). Earl would remain in prison until his mandatory parole date on February 12, 2001. "It's a moral, political, and legal outrage and, from these people, utterly not surprising," commented Jerry Zerkin, another one of Earl's lawyers. "Earl will survive the additional time because he is a bigger man than they are."[74]

The disappointment and outrage expressed by Earl's legal team stemmed from more than the fact that Earl would spend two more needless months in prison; they all shared the concern that the Department of Corrections might use trumped-up disciplinary charges to overturn Earl's mandatory parole date and extend his prison stay. "I was very, very concerned that they were going to find some way to keep him in prison," said Marie. "I felt it very strongly."[75] Their fears proved unfounded. Fortune finally favored Earl, and his last months in prison were without incident.

On February 12, 2001, Earl Washington was released from the Greensville Correctional Center and transported to Virginia Beach, where he was met by a jubilant Marie Deans and attorney Barry Weinstein. "He just let out that big grin when I walked in [the room]," Marie said. "It was all worth it with that grin of his."[76] Marie thought it was "cute" when the excited Earl showed her his new wallet with dollars inside. Despite the frigid temperatures, the Department of Corrections had not prepared Earl for the winter weather. "He was dressed in a short-sleeved cotton shirt and work pants," wrote biographer Edds. "He had a $25 check from the Department of Corrections in his pocket, but he had no hat, no coat, and no gloves."[77] A jacket and a heavier polo shirt were quickly found for him.

Faced with the prospect of a press conference, Earl turned to Marie for support. Like she had for the last seventeen years, Marie knew exactly what to say to calm his fears.

Taking in the scene, Marie put her head close to his and spoke softly. "You know how I am about press conferences," she said. "They make me really nervous. You can't make me go in there by myself." Drawing in a deep breath, Earl took her hand, and together they faced the crowd.[78]

As Earl faced the crush of reporters and camera crews, he would continue to hold Marie's hand. As he once told a fellow inmate, Earl knew that Marie wouldn't let anything happen to him.

Earl Washington presently lives in Virginia Beach with his wife. He works for Support Services of Virginia, an organization that provides jobs and support to mentally handicapped adults. Earl's modest salary is supplemented by a $1.9 million settlement with the Commonwealth of Virginia. The settlement was the result of a civil lawsuit filed by Earl's lawyers, alleging that investigators coerced Earl into falsely confessing to the rape and murder of Rebecca Williams. The moneys received by Earl have been placed in a trust administered by his attorneys.

Based on the DNA evidence in Earl's case, a convicted rapist named Kenneth Maurice Tinsley pled guilty in April 2007 to the rape of Rebecca Williams. Although Tinsley did not admit to her murder, the signed plea agreement acknowledged that sufficient evidence existed to convict him of the slaying. In exchange for his plea, he received two life sentences for the crime. "I'm sorry for everything I did," the wheelchair-bound Tinsley stated at his sentencing hearing.[79] The plea agreement had no practical impact on Tinsley, who was in poor health and already serving two life sentences for rape.[80] Despite his heart problems, Tinsley is alive today and is housed at the Sussex II State Prison in Waverly, Virginia.

Tinsley's conviction prompted Virginia governor Tim Kaine to issue a revised pardon, which formally proclaimed Earl's innocence. "It is now evident that Mr. Washington was, and is, innocent of the crimes against Mrs. Williams," Kaine stated. "I have decided it is just and appropriate to grant this revised absolute pardon that reflects Mr. Washington's innocence."[81] When asked by the reporters how he felt about the new pardon, Earl simply said, "It makes me feel good that the governor did that."[82] Marie allowed herself, briefly, to feel a sense of accomplishment over the exoneration of Earl Washington. "I won something worth fighting for when Earl walk[ed] free."[83] But the victory also felt hollow to Marie. "I still don't feel Earl [was] a success," she later explained. "He spent all those years in prison. Finally, he just got a little bit of what he deserved."[84]

Earl was now free. While Marie continued to fight to free Joe Giarratano, her career as a death penalty activist was essentially over. One ghost, however, returned to her life: Roger Coleman. In the years after his execution, Roger's supporters main-

An elated Marie meets Earl Washington Jr. after his release from prison. Photograph courtesy of *Richmond Times-Dispatch*.

tained that Virginia had executed the wrong man. Books and articles were written. Interviews were given. And, as technology advanced, Jim McCloskey repeatedly demanded that the biological evidence in Roger's case be subject to DNA testing. His supporters raised the funds necessary for a DNA test. They demanded that Virginia release the evidence for testing, and finally Virginia agreed.

In January 2006, Governor Mark Warner announced that a posthumous DNA test proved that Roger Coleman was, in fact, guilty. The results left Coleman's supporters dumbfounded. James McCloskey, the Director of Centurion Ministries, had led the effort to prove Roger's innocence. Upon hearing the news, he stated that he "felt betrayed by the man whose last words included the statement, 'An innocent man is going to be murdered tonight.' "[85] "This particular truth feels like a kick in the stomach,"[86] confessed McCloskey.

When asked about his decision to permit DNA testing, Senator Mark Warner reflected on his time as governor during this historical time in Virginia. "It [posthumous DNA testing] was a difficult decision to make. At that time, I thought Coleman might be innocent. We also experienced a difficult legal custody battle over the DNA sample from the case. I also wondered, could the DNA be tainted as it had been so long since his case was open? There was a lot going through my mind." Warner added, "As a governor, I presided over executions and considered it to be the most serious and solemn responsibility of the job. That obligation also entails a special duty to seek out the truth, no matter where it takes you. . . . As the governor, you are not a second judge in these sorts of criminal cases—it is not your job to second guess facts. In the case of Roger Coleman, it was the right thing to do."[87]

Unlike Jim McCloskey, Sharon Paul—Roger's girlfriend and his staunchest supporter—did not feel betrayed by the test results. "I have to believe something," she said. "What I believe is, if Roger committed the crime, he had no memory of it, and that's why he was able to be such a strong advocate for his own innocence right until the end." Curiously, Paul expressed surprise that Roger duped his legal team. "I just can't believe they were so wrong. I mean, these are people who do this for a living; they're not naive, they don't get duped," she explained. "And that Roger, this little person from southwest Virginia, could have fooled them for so long—that's the most difficult part for me to believe." According to her friends, the only person who did not accept the test results was attorney Kathleen Behan.[88]

Marie and Russ Ford were not surprised by the findings. "Maybe Roger had fought so hard to live that he came to believe his own lie," Russ said. "Roger presented himself as a victim of faulty police work and ambitious prosecutors. He died an imposter." Dying an imposter had widespread consequences. Roger's deception disillusioned the anti-death penalty community and undercut the believability of future claims of innocence asserted by death row inmates. "Never believe a killer," wrote one Virginia columnist, who concluded that Roger's supporters "didn't really care" about him. "What they wanted was a martyr. He was the best they could find." The columnist's parting advice for death penalty activists was "Your [anti-death penalty] arguments might be more persuasive if they weren't always accompanied by phony campaigns that try to turn sociopaths into heroes."[89] "Stop the presses: It turns out that rapists and killers are also liars," wrote Michael Paranzino, head of the pro-death penalty organization Throw Away the Key. "Roger Keith Coleman, like every killer on death row, professes his innocence until the very moment he took his last breath. The only problem was, prominent liberals fell for Coleman's lies hook, line, and sinker."[90]

As the flurry of publicity over Roger's guilt faded, Marie focused on one last dream: to write a book about her experiences with the men on the row. Marie was working part-time for a non-profit organization, and she finally had the time to sit, reflect on her decades-long battle against the death penalty, and write about her unique experiences. Making her dream a reality, however, would prove far more difficult than she imagined.

12

The Final Years Alone

What I've wanted all my life is to get out of the
storm, [to] stop struggling to reach land.
　　　—Marie Deans, undated

The last decade of Marie's life was filled with sadness, illness, and unfulfilled goals. With the exception of working on Joe Giarratano's clemency petition, her death penalty work was essentially finished, and the name "Marie Deans" meant little to the newest generation of attorneys, activists, and abolitionists. Isolated in her small Charlottesville townhouse, doing transcription and editing work in order to pay her bills, Marie felt like the world had forgotten her.

Our window into Marie's daily existence comes primarily from her letters to Joe, who lovingly saved them. The letters give us insights into Marie's daily travails as well as the diverse and dynamic intellectual relationship between Marie and Joe. In the letters, they discuss a dizzying array of topics: Zen Buddhism, mankind's assault on the earth and its resources, globalization, new research on migraines, presidential elections, the strategic military skills of Robert E. Lee and Stonewall Jackson (Marie believed that her distant relative General Jackson was a great strategist but "a nut and stone cold killer"), professional hockey, *The Federalist Papers*, the merits of homemade versus store-bought pimento cheese, the theory of consilience, and the various books that Marie was simultaneously reading (*Confessions of an Economic Hitman, The Sixth Lamentation, Ex Libris, How the Scots Invented the Modern World, The Killer Angels, One Market Under God, The Outermost House, A Year by the Sea,* and *The Lacuna*).

While opportunities existed for Marie to work as a mitigation specialist, she was conflicted about continuing death penalty work. On one hand, Marie was upset that attorneys were not calling her with offers of mitigation assignments. "I don't care about getting credit for whatever I've done over the years, but I do get angry that people assume I don't need the work," she wrote to Joe. "I suppose they think that I can live off my reputation."[1] And she was fearful that her poor health would cause judges to think twice about appointing her to serve as a mitigation specialist on individual federal and state cases. "Very few people know how bad my back/arthritis is, and I don't want them to," she wrote. "It would just give them another excuse not to give me paying work."[2] As she wryly noted in an earlier letter to Joe, "The world is not crying out to give jobs to sixty-two-year-old women with bum backs, and I will have to do some serious scrambling to keep food on the table . . . as always since I left Charleston, there is NO ONE I can fall back on."[3]

On the other hand, Marie no longer had the stomach for the stress associated with death penalty work. "As you know, I would give a lot to get away from capital cases," she wrote to Joe. "Maybe it is that I would give a lot to get away from lawyers, from the backbiting that has never stopped in the work, and the general wear and tear and insecurity."[4] In a subsequent letter to Joe, Marie touched upon a familiar theme, namely, being used by lawyers and not being properly compensated for her work. "I also think I'm getting less and less tolerant of people pushing me. I don't feel sorry for myself, but I do feel used, and feeling used makes me very cranky these days."[5]

Marie was incensed because she believed that death penalty work had turned into a profitable enterprise for attorneys, a trend she believed signaled the end of the abolition movement.

> Once again, we seem to see lawyers tucking themselves into any issue or situation that pays well, and, again in my opinion, managing to destroy movements and perpetuate the very things those movements were trying to dismantle. What was so disheartening to me hearing this was the rock that fell into my stomach, because I truly felt like I'd just heard the death knell of any hope of abolishing the death penalty. Maybe one day it will fall in on itself, but it seems very clear to me that it won't be stopped by any abolition movement in this country. That movement has been usurped and turned into a new lawyers association, in large part because they have managed to drain all resources away from the actual movement.
>
> This kind of thing infuriates Robert for another reason. He feels people like me and other old movement people broke our physical and psychic health and basically starved ourselves in order to build a movement that was then taken over by the money grubbing pros. He calls us the slaves that built the abolition plantation. I can't argue with him. I can only feel sicker in heart and soul for having been part of that and hope to God that the work of the Virginia Coalition and other work I have done can stand in some way on its own as having done some good for a small group of people, because I do not feel that any of my efforts toward abolition were worth anything.[6]

Disheartened by what she saw, Marie wanted to be that old hound dog and hide. "I have the deepest longing to just go away and tell everyone to leave me the hell alone, that I'd like a little time before I die to do a few things that I simply want to do, and do them in some semblance of peace."[7]

What Marie desired was financial security and time to write. In 2002, she wrote Joe and excitedly told him that she had begun her memoir. Marie had pursued a career as a short story author in the 1970s, but she found the process of writing a memoir to be very different. "When I wrote and published regularly, I was very disciplined, writing every day for several hours," she said. "Now, writing when I have time not dedicated to work or family, it feels like the damn thing is having to drip out of me at the rate of one drop a week. Pretty frustrating."

Marie was also daunted by the subject matter of her new project. Before Marie had written short works of fiction. Now she was focusing her unblinking gaze on her own life. "I've not written about myself before," she confessed, "and it's very foreign territory for me, so the flow ain't exactly comfy."[8] Marie, however, did see a benefit to writing about herself. "Talking to a counselor would open a can of worms I don't want to mess with. Doing the book, talking about all of that is enough, [is] probably more than enough. I just keep hoping the book will be some kind of catharsis for me."[9]

In the fall of 2003, Marie applied for a writing fellowship with the Virginia Foundation for the Humanities. She hoped that a fellowship would give her the financial freedom to spend six months writing without worrying about finding work to pay her bills. When Marie received a rejection letter from the Foundation in the spring of 2004, after spending months "praying to the fellowship gods," she was crushed.

I was turned down for a fellowship with the VA Foundation for the Humanities. . . . I was truly stupid to count on it. But I did, and because I did, I keep spending the bulk of my time doing pro bono and volunteer work, which meant I was truly squeaking by and draining my little savings account. Now I have just enough money (maybe) to survive until I get paid for this federal case, and nothing coming in after that. My first reaction to being turned down . . . was to think, well, [maybe] this book isn't supposed to be written, because I've been able to do basically zilch on it over the past eight months. But then I trudged out to the yard to do whatever heavy lifting I could (need to work off some of the feelings from that letter, you know, and really want that yard to look decent), and though the truth is if I stopped doing all pro bono cases and volunteer work and concentrated on two things only—getting and working paying cases and working on the book, although it would take me much longer to get it done, I could get it done—well, if I don't die first.

The hardest part of all this is the kind of writer I am. Even when I was publishing short stories and articles and doing volunteer work, I had to block the writing time. I have never been able to make my mind go from writing to other things and back to writing in short periods of time, like a ping-pong ball. I need long periods of time just to sit and muse. It probably looks unproductive to other people, but that is my most productive writing time. I did so long for that six-month period of time when I would have had enough financial support to cover me for that period and have that nice long block of time to write (musing included). On a usual schedule, even giving up volunteer and pro bono work, it will no doubt take me several years to get this book done, and who knows if it will be published. So, it is looking like my dream of getting back to writing as a lifestyle was just that—a dream.

Truth is I'm pretty depressed. Robert called as soon as I sent out the email about the turndown, and I started crying so hard, I just had to hang up on him. I'm really tired, Joe. Tired of struggling for every case, tired of struggling against the system, tired of struggling for every dime. Having a little pot of something that looked like gold to me sitting at the end of this long tunnel I've lived was all the reward I need to keep moving toward it. But I just don't feel like I have the energy to live like this the rest of my life.[10]

As she always did, Marie pressed on and continued to work on the book. Her frustrations, however, mounted as her progress slowed. "I feel like I'm caught up in some undercurrent that is keeping me from reaching any shore," she wrote to Joe. "There are all these possibilities, but I keep getting sucked under trying to feed myself and keep my house."[11] In another letter Marie lamented the limited time to write. "I have to put the writing aside again," she stated. "That not only makes me cranky, it even makes me a little bitter, like are the gods ever going to cut me a break?"[12]

The lack of money was not the only reason why Marie could not move forward on the book. Marie began circulating copies of what she referred to as either "three short chapters or one long chapter with three parts" to friends to review and critique. When the chapters returned to Marie, she found that her well-meaning friends were giving her contradictory advice about the content and structure of the book. Her friends even debated choices about grammar, word choice, and verb tense. Marie was paralyzed by the conflicting voices, as she obsessively rewrote and rewrote existing chapters.

Marie also looked for literary agents who could promote her book proposal to publishers. She sent proposals directly to publishers. She spoke to friends who were published authors, asking them to help her find agents and publishers. Her friends spoke to publishers and agents. She had no success. When a friend suggested that Marie forgo a large publishing house and approach an academic press, pointing out that prestige was better than profits, Marie was aghast. "Here we go again," she wrote to Joe. "I can't afford to [be paid] in prestige."[13]

I met Marie in approximately 2005, when I was working on a death penalty book.[14] My co-author was Laura Trevvett Anderson, who had served as a spiritual advisor for a death row inmate named Chris Thomas, the young man that Marie asked Buffalo DeLong to protect on death row. What made Chris's story so unique is that Laura was first his high school teacher and then became his spiritual adviser after his conviction. Laura stood death watch with Chris at the Greensville Correctional Center, and she witnessed his execution. Now Laura and I had joined forces to tell Chris's story.

Marie worked on Chris's case as his mitigation specialist, and Laura and I met with Marie to interview her about Chris. Like many, I was instantly struck by Marie's dedication to the cause, and we became friends. After the book was published, I told Marie that I would help her with her memoir. But, by the time we started meeting to work on her project, Marie's health was failing. A severe break of her ankle limited her mobility. Breathing difficulties and lung cancer would soon follow.

Marie Deans, Todd C. Peppers, and Helen Prejean, CSJ, at a death penalty panel at Roanoke College. This would be Marie's last public appearance. Photograph courtesy of Michele Peppers.

During our conversations around her kitchen table, I would see glimpses of her old passions and energy as she recalled her time with the men of the row. Marie was a master storyteller, and the hours would race by as she told tales of prison administrators both competent and incompetent, guards both vicious and kind, and inmates both damned and redeemed. Marie seemed younger during these talks, with her face flush with emotion, her voice rising, her eyes flashing, and her cigarette waving in the air.

More often, however, her predominate emotion was sadness. Marie felt abandoned by her colleagues, forgotten by history, and ignored by her two sons, whose infrequent visits and telephone calls left Marie feeling isolated and depressed. In a 2004 letter to Joe, Marie wrote: "My place is pretty trashy in certain ways—ways I can't afford to do better with or ways I don't have [what] it takes physically to take care of. My children know that as well, and they don't do anything about it. I know they both have wives who have their own wants, but—here I go whining again—it does hurt that they don't have even a weekend a year to help out in the yard or around the house."[15]

There were still glimpses of Marie's keen powers of observation and her deep reservoirs of compassion and humor. On August 4, 2004, Marie wrote Joe about a new resident who was living in her small back courtyard. "A tiny little frog moved into the yard about a week ago," she wrote. "I have a dogwood, which the water treatment sits under. Beside the water treatment is a piece of pottery in the shape of a fish . . . at night the little frog lives in the fish pottery. During the day he mainly stays on a rock in the water treatment, sometimes jumping around the plants, getting bugs, I assume. He's about three [inches]."

It wasn't long before Marie had a "standoff" with her new friend.

> I went to take the trash out . . . and he was on the walkway. He just sat there, so I figured I could walk around him, but he had a hissy fit when I got close to him. He started jumping around and screeching like a crazy frog. He seemed terrified. So, I backed off and put the bag down and came up again trying to shoo him back into the water (actually leaning over and going "shoo, shoo"). Didn't work. He just started all the jumping and screeching again. He was so discombobulated, he looked like he was going to hurt himself. So I just came back inside.
>
> I waited for several hours, but he didn't move, I had to get the garbage out . . . so I tried again, and he just started quivering when I got near him. I finally got the hose out and sprayed him (gently) from a distance. That made him move just enough [to] get under the Salvia by the walk. He seemed to feel safe there, so I got the garbage can to the street. I hope the lesson he learned was to stay off the walk. I worry about him getting stepped on. Maybe I should put a sign on the gate saying "Do Not Walk on Frog."

Marie's adventures with her little frog continued for the next six weeks. On August 14, Marie wrote Joe and announced that the frog was staying away from the sidewalk and instead taking long swims in her small fountain. The friendship was not destined to last. On September 22, 2004, Marie wrote that the frog was dead—but that a new amphibian had entered her life.

> My resident frog died . . . it looked like something got him. I saw him in bad shape on the walkway and tried to get him into the water, but that scared him so much that all I could do for him was to keep a very gentle spray of water on him. It didn't revive him enough, but I hope it made his death more comfortable. Last week, a new frog appeared. This one is about half the size of the first one. He's also pluckier in that he doesn't jump into the water when I come outside unless I walk more than halfway between the door and him. I just hope nothing gets him. The storms did scare him. He stayed in the water, mostly under the rocks for the entire three-day period.

Only Marie with her oversized heart would stand death watch with a frog and try to make his last minutes on earth as peaceful as possible.

Marie drew strength from her relationship with Joe, and often she scolded herself for complaining while Joe sat in prison. "I'm glad you're running on stubborn," Marie wrote to Joe. "You need something to run on. And tell you the truth, Joe, you help me keep running on whatever stubborn I've got left. When my stubborn runs out, I think of your situation and how you keep going, and I figure out I'd look pretty damned silly knowing that and not keeping going."[16] Joe, in response, urged Marie to keep writing.

As Marie's health declined, her fears about keeping a roof over her head grew. "There are days/times . . . when I feel like I cannot deal with the pain from my spine another minute, when I think I'm going to lose my house and end up on the streets because I can't get work, or paid for the work I do, and I ask myself if this is worth it."[17] Marie came to depend on a small circle of friends to run errands for her, to help with small purchases, and to keep her company. My wife and I spent several "day after" holidays with Marie, coming to her house on the day after Thanksgiving or Christmas with a huge spread of leftovers and some modest presents.

By 2010, Marie could barely move around her two-story home, and her needs increased. Some members of her circle, including myself, felt overwhelmed by her economic, medical, and emotional needs. Marie's sharp intellect had been blunted by depression and anxiety as well as the growing cocktail of drugs prescribed for her pain. In such times, the darkest places of our psyches are exposed, and it was no different with Marie. Conversations in the last year of her life were challenging, as Marie became alternately forgetful, frightened, angry, childlike, and confused. From prison, Joe felt helpless. In his letters to Marie, he lamented the fact that he could not be there to care for her.

In the last weeks of her life, Marie was housed in a two-person room in the basement of a Charlottesville rehabilitation clinic. It was a large, shabby facility filled with chemical smells and damaged people. Her guardian angel in those final weeks was Denise Lunsford, an attorney who had worked with Marie at the Virginia Mitigation Project before becoming a local prosecutor. Like Marie, Denise was a tall woman with a no-nonsense demeanor and a quick wit. Denise visited Marie daily, bringing her food and making sure that she was getting proper care. A steady stream of friends came to see Marie in those final weeks, and we all walked away knowing that she was dying. Several days before her death, Marie was moved to a local hospice. She died on April 15, 2011, in Denise's arms. She was only seventy years old and, in our opinion, was another victim of the death penalty.

Decades before her death, Marie wrote about the deaths of her father-in-law and her grandfather. In her unpublished essay, she compared the two men and their experiences during their final weeks of life.

My father-in-law died alone in a Lysol-swabbed, pale green cell [hospital room] in the early morning hours. His body was found by a new nurse coming on duty. She read his name from a plastic band around his still wrist. We had visited him in shifts, day after day, night after night, for two years. But we were not with him in those last gray hours.

The visits had been awkward. We stood around his bed or sat on plastic chairs trying to be cheerful, embarrassed by long silences we would have felt no need to fill had we been at home. We were shunted aside for his every physical need, told to wait outside while strangers emptied the bag of urine that hung at the side of his bed, or exposed his buttocks for shots, or dressed wounds of operations meant to satisfy us more than heal him. Toward the end he begged them to leave him alone. "I am a man," he implored. They called him "difficult" and put guardrails around his bed.

I took one young nurse aside. "Don't you see? He is embarrassed." "There are things that must be done, care he must be given." She was irritated by my interference. "Care, yes, but you must not—diminish him." My hand was on her arm "Look." She brushed my hand away. "He hardly knows what's going on."

But even pain and humiliation are real. His death was no more than a period of time to make arrangements for getting his body out of the hospital and into the ground.

It was a very efficient process. The hospital released his body to us, and a funeral director took it away. That night the same funeral director led us to a velvet-draped, thickly carpeted room. It was also green, though a deeper shade. "He looks quite good, thin, of course, but very natural." The body looked much as I would expect the figures in Madame Tussauds museum to look.

There were no memories for us in that room. We sat stiffly in damask-covered chairs, acutely aware of our own discomfort. Visitors signed in, paused at the casket, then came over to us. The room commanded quiet, and so they leaned toward us as if they had some secret to impart. At first we would sit forward, eager to hear. "He looks good, as if he'd never been sick." "He looks so peaceful." "What a blessing that he is out of his pain." We sat back.

The next day we followed his body to a church he had attended once or twice. A man in a dark blue suit talked about resurrection and never mentioned my father-in-law's name. There were no children there, but then there was nothing of value for children to learn there.

We filed out of the church and into a long line of cars that held up traffic and annoyed shoppers and women heading home to fix supper. We took him to a cemetery on the edge of the subdivisions—the year before he had signed a perpetual care contract—and put his body in a precise hole in a sterile expanse of lawn neatly punctuated with envelope-sized bronze plaques. "In fifteen years," I thought, "they will cover this place with the same plastic grass our chairs are sitting on." And then, foolishly, "they will suffocate."

That was eleven years ago. We have been back only once, to bury my mother-in-law beside her husband. Why go back? That place, like his lonely death and impersonal funeral, has nothing at all to do with his life.

There was a time when dying was not sanitized and death not formalized.

My grandfather died almost thirty years ago. I was still a child, and his death was the first that had come close to me. Granddaddy was sick for a long time too, and he spent some of that time in a hospital, but when it became evident that they could not bring health back to him, we brought him home.

He spent his last months in his own bed with the smell of his newly plowed fields coming in the window on strong breezes that filled the curtains he had watched Grandmama make years before. He heard his family moving about the house he had built for his new bride. He ate the food he had grown and his wife had cooked for him. He took part in the nightly family devotions. He spent his last days sinking into death with the hands of his family on his body.

He died with his daughter-in-law beside him. He had loved her dearly, de-lighting in her bustling cheerfulness since he had first laid eyes on her, when she stood beside his son's wheelchair acting as if it were the most everyday occurrence for a Yankee city girl to leave her family and come to live on a remote southern farm with a paraplegic.

We came together in that room, wife, children, grandchildren, sister, brothers, nieces, and nephews. Soon the cousins and friends came. They filled the kitchen with food and the house with flowers and greenery from their yards. They added their memories to ours. We cried together, and we laughed together. I remember trying to hear them all, hungry for more of his life.

Late that night I was put to bed in a room adjoining Granddaddy's. The door was left open. I could see my grandfather's casket and hear the murmur of my family's voices as I fell asleep.

The next afternoon we took Granddaddy to the church he had helped build. We passed his fields and the fields of his sister and brothers, cousins and friends. It was a weekday, but no one was in the fields. People walked along the road toward the church. They turned and watched us pass. The men took off their hats and pressed them to their hearts. Others waited in their cars to fall in behind the funeral cortege. No one, black or white, would work that day. A man among them had died.

Though my grandfather had suffered as had my father-in-law years later, no one called his death a blessing. Instead the minister talked of the blessings of Granddaddy's life. He talked about his habits, his mischievous sense of humor, his work in the church, of what he had given to all of us, of what he meant to each of us. We were a family, not put asunder by suffering, but part of a community brought together in remembrance.

We stood around in the churchyard meeting old friends and hugging distant cousins who had come for the day. Then we took Granddaddy to the community cemetery. Now and then we passed a car with an out of state license the patrolmen had pulled over. One of the drivers, an old man, stood at erect attention beside his car. He must have died years ago, but for me, he still lives there beside my cousins' fields honoring a man's life and death.

That old cemetery is a lush, beautiful place of huge oaks, moss and ferns, grasses and wild flowers. Over the oldest grave, a carved stone reads in part: "John McFaddien. Born 1708, arrived America 1730 . . . He overcame obstacles that we might enjoy freedom and opportunity. We shall not permit his memory to die."

There is no vanity in those words. There must be thousands of stories like this in America. But this one is for us. Its message is neither grand nor sentimental. It tells us simply that there is continuity in life, that we are part of a place, part of a people and, therefore, none of our lives are meaningless. We are connected, connected to John McFaddien and all his progeny before and after us, connected to life and death. We have made and kept rituals within our family and community to reinforce this message. One of these rituals, I think the most important, always ends here, so we know at the end of our lives we will come to this place that quietly and familiarly reclaims its own.

Watching my grandfather being lowered into this ground, I began to know that death is but part of the ever-changing mystery of life. Today I have vivid memories of him. I don't often think of his dying and death, but when I do, I know they were an appropriate part of his life, a part that informed of the intrinsic value of the individual life.

It is my father-in-law's death that haunts me. When he was too ill to be a productive part of our daily lives, we put him under the care of paid strangers. When he died we walked through a perfunctory ritual that seemed to be telling us an anonymous life of utility was over.

I have one small photograph of my grandfather. I do not need it for memory. We have a large cardboard box of photographs of my father-in-law. I search that box again and again trying to find the life we so carelessly put away.

When we pull death apart from life, when we deny the special, individual worth of any human's life in death, we deny the continuity of life. Without continuity, memory is blocked, the value of a life is diminished, and so, in turn, are we all.

Marie did not have the death that she wanted. She did not die at home, surrounded by her familiar books and family members. Marie, however, did return to that "place that quietly and familiarly reclaims its own." After a memorial service in Charlottesville, Marie's body was returned to her beloved South Carolina. She was buried in the family cemetery in Clarendon County, the same county in which she was born seventy years before. Marie now lies amongst generations of McFaddens. We hope that she has made it through the storm and found peace.

Afterword

After Marie Deans's memorial service in Charlottesville, Virginia, Todd Peppers shared with me the work Marie had been doing on her memoir. I encouraged him to pick up the threads Marie left and complete the tapestry of her life. This book is an admirable job of telling Marie's story, and I am grateful he and Maggie Anderson completed the task.

In 1982, the Southern Coalition on Jails and Prisons (SCJP), an organization working to abolish the death penalty and promote prison reform, decided to make Virginia a ninth project state. As Director of the SCJP, I hired Marie Deans to begin the Virginia Coalition on Jails and Prisons (VCJP). After being with Frank Coppola in the death house in Richmond, Virginia, in a desperate and futile attempt to stop his electrocution, I had witnessed the anti–death penalty effort in the state and learned about conditions on death row and the absence of lawyers for the condemned. It was a discouraging experience. So my colleagues and I sent Marie to deal with the appalling situation regarding the death penalty in Virginia. It was as bleak as any I had observed in any Southern state in which I had worked (and I had worked in all of them, visiting death rows and the prisoners on the row).

Todd has written a fine description of the ten years of hell when Marie ran the VCJP. What I would like to discuss is the spiritual dimension of her life. Through my friendship with her, I discovered it was the spiritual element that made Marie Deans the force of nature she became in Virginia. It was the spiritual impetus that took her into the death house thirty-four times to be with the condemned as they experienced their final hours before their ritual slaughter and to beg, plead, and demand lawyers for them.

James McBride Dabbs, like Marie a South Carolinian, wrote a book entitled *Haunted by God*. Marie, like Dabbs, was one of those white Southerners haunted by God and compelled to move beyond whiteness to address civil rights. For us in the South, fighting the death penalty was that challenge despite the Supreme Court pronouncing it constitutionally acceptable in 1976. We all knew that the Supreme Court justices had changed since the 1972 decision outlawing the death penalty, but the reality on the ground was still the same: only the poor faced the death penalty, a disproportionate number of them were black, and the race of the victim was almost always white.

Given that social reality, how does one respond when haunted by God? And what does haunted by God mean? It does not connote that the experience is eerie, paranormal, or hallucinatory. Nor does it mean one is obliged to be a churchgoer or act as a member of the dominant culture. Rather, it is a calling, a summons, and through the murder of Penny Deans, Marie discerned a call. It led to her founding Murder Victims' Families for Reconciliation and through that effort to the fight to abolish the death penalty.

I met Marie at one of the conferences against the death penalty we organized in the South. Later, I supported her when she ministered to J. C. Shaw, the first man executed in South Carolina under its new death penalty law. We shared a fondness for bourbon and Dietrich Bonhoeffer.

Marie defined herself as a Christian in keeping with Bonhoeffer's definition of the term: "A person for others." Bonhoeffer was her spiritual North Star. She oriented her Christian faith to Bonhoeffer as her Polaris in the dark Virginia nights in the death house. Otherwise, one might deduce Marie was a lunatic for her visits to the thirty-four condemned men facing extermination. Who would possibly want to take that action once much less thirty-four times?

Dietrich Bonhoeffer wrote *The Cost of Discipleship*. As a German Lutheran, he scorned the "cheap grace" the German church bestowed through its acceptance of the Third Reich. Rather, Bonhoeffer proclaimed that a Christian was summoned to follow Jesus of Nazareth, even unto the cross, if that should be the cost of discipleship. Although Bonhoeffer's criticism was directed at the church and the Third Reich in Germany, it is equally applicable today in the United States regarding the American church and its relationship to the government. That cozy dynamic was completely clear to Marie. She was haunted by Jesus of Nazareth who asked her to challenge the American sacrifice of human life on the altar of state killing. Hence she moved to Richmond, Virginia, the former capital of the Confederacy, to work on behalf of the men of Virginia's death row.

Marie, a Lutheran, also worked on the Lutheran church to change its position so it would oppose the death penalty. But she was a Bonhoeffer Lutheran, a person with a vision called to challenge the state even if its actions implementing the death penalty were wildly popular. If the Lutheran denomination would prove slow to respond, Marie moved ahead to fulfill her summons to discipleship, to be "with the least of these, my brothers and sisters" (Matthew 25:45).

Bonhoeffer paid the ultimate price for his opposition to the Third Reich with his execution on April 9, 1945. Marie, too, suffered a costly price for her discipleship. A part of her was devoured by the beast of state killing each time she was with a man about to be exterminated. The experience had a corrosive effect. This is why Marie so strongly opposed people calling her a "saint" or an "angel" for her work. State-mandated ritual killing of human beings has no good quality in it. Everyone is corrupted, pained, deeply damaged by the process and the consummation of killing. The person in that environment is confined within the official madness, and that was the cost of discipleship for Marie. One does not go into that killing zone pure, and one does not emerge a hero. Rather, all are traumatized by the violence, the pain, the killing. The soul is damaged—sometimes irrevocably so.

The experience of waiting with the condemned for official extermination is painful, exhausting and produces mind-numbing trauma. Or to be precise, the mind encases the body in numbness in order to function and to protect. If one can imagine being in a glass tunnel and looking outside through the glass, it is akin to the feelings generated within the belly of the beast as it kills prisoners. People are moving, speaking to one another, and reaching out to touch. But being encapsulated in the glass-like tunnel, those outside are not heard, not felt, not experienced as being real. The outside world is sealed away, and it is as if one is engaged in a pantomime of communication. Thus, when one can, one seeks solitude, quiet, a time to heal, if possible, as soon as the ordeal is complete.

The world gazes upon this behavior with uncomprehending vision. The work with the condemned on the verge of extinction defies understanding so categories are chosen: angel, saint, or fool. Any objective delineation is chosen to keep the reality of it at bay. After all, what if one was to realize the summons to discipleship was directed not to the angel or fool but to one's self?

Marie was certainly a fool. Indeed, this volume terms her "a courageous fool," as she once referred to herself. But as I shared with her, she was a fool in the sense Reinhold Niebuhr described a fool when teaching at Union Theological Seminary some years before I arrived there. Niebuhr and the Swiss theologian Karl Barth were theological rivals in the 1950s and 1960s. In class, a student asked Niebuhr what he thought about Dr. Barth's description of the Apostle Paul's epistle in which a Christian was described as "a fool for Christ." Niebuhr eyed the student, paused, and responded: "I suppose it's all right to be a fool for Christ. Just be sure you're not a damn fool." Marie was certainly a fool. Whether Marie was a fool for Christ or a damn fool, this volume will enable the reader to decide. Her behavior with the condemned confounded the world. But her God-haunted soul, which profoundly felt the call of discipleship from Jesus, responded to the grace of that urging.

When Marie and I sat outside Morris Mason's cell on death watch on the eve of his destruction on June 25, 1985, the man with the mental acuity of a child reached out to us. Sensing our sadness, he assured us: "I'm gonna be strong. I'm gonna be brave. I'm gonna make you proud." This came from a man who thought he would return from his execution to play basketball with his death row brothers. A man who, even as he heard the clanging of the chains as the death squad approached to "extract" him from his cell, sought to reassure us, his surrogate parents.

In recalling that story, I testify that Marie Deans made me, the men on the Row, and those who knew her and worked with her, stronger, braver, and proud—proud to have been in the struggle with her and, hopefully, in some modest way, to have been stronger and braver for our friendship.

Such is the cost of discipleship to which Dietrich Bonhoeffer bore witness and what Marie strove to become: "A person for others." May we all be such a person.

—Joseph B. Ingle
August 15, 2015

Joseph Ingle is a United Church of Christ minister who works with the condemned on the Tennessee death row. He has written *Last Rights: 13 Fatal Encounters with the State's Justice* (1990), *The Inferno: A Southern Morality Tale* (2012), and *Slouching Toward Tyranny: Mass Incarceration, Death Sentences and Racism* (2015). One of the founders of the Southern Coalition on Jails and Prisons, Ingle has been nominated twice for the Nobel Peace Prize.

Timeline of Major Events

June 8, 1940	Marie McFadden (Deans) born in South Carolina
August 26, 1956	Joseph Michael Giarratano born in Bronx, New York
August 18, 1958	Marie marries William Tremper
Fall 1959	Marie moves back to Charleston and divorces Tremper
1960	Joel Tremper is born (Marie's first son) (a/k/a Joel "Mac" McFadden)
1961	Marie marries Peter Anderson (not his real name)
1967	Marie divorces Anderson
1968	Marie marries Robert Deans
Spring 1972	Mac moves in with grandparents
August 20, 1972	Penny Deans is murdered
January 1973	Robert Deans is born (Marie's second son)
1976	Marie founds Victims' Families for Alternatives to the Death Penalty, renamed Murder Victims' Families for Reconciliation in 1986
1979	Marie founds a Charleston chapter of Amnesty International
April 1981	Marie tours South Carolina death row—first time in maximum security prison
1981	Marie meets South Carolina death row inmate J. C. Shaw
1982	Marie and Rose Styron investigate conditions in death rows across the South
1982	Marie injured in Amtrak train wreck
August 1982	Marie makes initial visit to Virginia's death row
Fall 1982	Marie meets Virginia death row inmate Joseph Giarratano
1982	Frank Coppola is executed
January 1983	Marie moves to Virginia and opens Virginia Coalition on Jails and Prisons
1983	Marie's mother Hettie dies. Marie divorces Robert Deans
1983	Marie meets Virginia death row inmate Roger Keith Coleman
1984	Marie meets Virginia death row inmate Earl Washington Jr.
May 1984	Prison escape from Virginia death row
1985	Marie's father Joel dies
January 11, 1985	J. C. Shaw is executed
June 25, 1985	Morris Odell Mason is executed
August 27, 1985	Earl Washington Jr.'s execution is stayed

November 1985	Second Virginia death row prison escape attempt fails
January 10, 1986	Terry Roach is executed
July 31, 1986	Michael Smith is executed
November 1986	British ITV airs a documentary about Marie's work
1987	Charlotte Zander contacts Marie and provides funding for investigation into Joe's case
Fall 1989	Joe founds "Giarratano Review Action Committee"
April 27, 1990	Raymond Woomer is executed
July 19, 1990	Ricky Boggs is executed
February 7, 1991	Joe moved to Virginia State Penitentiary to await February 22 execution date
February 19, 1991	Joe receives conditional pardon from Virginia governor Douglas Wilder
August 22, 1991	Derick Lynn Peterson is executed
May 20, 1992	Roger Coleman is executed
August 31, 1993	Virginia Coalition on Jails and Prisons closed its doors
July 17, 1996	Joe Savino is executed
September 4, 1996	Joe is transported to a prison in Utah
1997	Marie moves from Richmond, Virginia to Charlottesville, Virginia
March 1997	Joe is transported to a prison in Illinois
October 2, 2000	Earl Washington, Jr. is granted full pardon by Virginia governor James Gilmore
February 12, 2001	Earl is released from prison
2005	Posthumous DNA evidence proves Roger Coleman murdered Wanda McCoy
2006	Joe is transferred to Wallens Ridge Prison in Virginia
2010	Virginia governor Tim Kaine denies Joe's petition for clemency
April 15, 2011	Marie dies from lung cancer
Fall 2014	Joe is transferred back to Red Onion Prison
Spring 2015	Joe is denied parole for the tenth time in ten years
Today	Joe resides at Deerfield Correctional Center in Capron, Virginia

The Men of the Row

The following is a list of men of the South Carolina and Virginia death rows (and their dates of execution) with whom Marie Deans stood death watch.

Linwood Earl Briley (October 12, 1984)
Joseph Carl "J. C." Shaw (January 11, 1985)*
James Dyral "J. B." Briley (April 18, 1985)
Morris Odell Mason (June 25, 1985)
James Terry Roach (January 10, 1986)*
Michael Marnell Smith (July 31, 1986)
Richard Lee Whitley (July 6, 1987)
Earl "Goldie" Clanton Jr. (April 14, 1988)
Alton Waye (August 30, 1989)
Ronald Raymond "Rusty" Woomer (April 27, 1990)*
Richard T. "Ricky" Boggs (July 19, 1990)
Wilbert Lee Evans (October 17, 1990)
Buddy Earl Justus (December 13, 1990)
Albert Jay Clozza (July 24, 1991)
Derick Lynn "Baydar" Peterson (August 22, 1991)
Roger Keith Coleman (May 20, 1992)**
Edward B. "Fitz" Fitzgerald Jr. (July 23, 1992)
Willie Leroy "Woo" Jones (September 15, 1992)
Timothy Dale Bunch (December 10, 1992)
Charles Sylvester Stamper (January 19, 1993)
Syvasky L. Poyner (March 18, 1993)
David Mark Pruett (December 16, 1993)**
Johnny Watkins Jr. (March 3, 1994)
Willie Lloyd "T" Turner (May 25, 1995)
Dennis Wayne Stockton (September 27, 1995)**
Herman Charles Barnes (November 13, 1995)
Richard Townes Jr. (January 23, 1996)
Gregory Warren Beaver (December 3, 1996)
Larry Allen "Taz" Stout (December 10, 1996)
Lem Davis Tuggle Jr. (December 12, 1996)
Ronald Lee "Ronnie" Hoke Sr. (December 16, 1996)
Mario Benjamin Murphy (September 17, 1997)
George Adrian Quisenberry Jr. (March 9, 1999)**

Executed in South Carolina
**Visited in the death house, but not on night of execution*

The Runaway

"The Runaway" is an unpublished story Marie wrote in the 1970s. Because of the undeniable fact that it is based on Marie's relationship with her mother, we have decided to include it. Of course, some of the details in the story are fictitious. Nevertheless, we believe that it provides a window into the anger and pain that Marie felt toward Hettie.

■

My mother had a high, clear voice. It wasn't whiny, shrill or raspy, but I hated it. Now and then when I say something out loud, I hear my mother saying those very words in that very tone, and I hush. Her voice was like a finger poking in your shoulder, tamping a small, defined hole deeper and deeper until you could think of nothing but that place and that persistent rhythm.

Maybe it was because she had no use for what she called small talk. If things were going well, if neither my father nor I had done anything to upset her, our house was quiet. But if one of us did something she did not like, she could talk for hours. She remembered everything. She would pull out our past misdeeds and lay them out like an accountant's ledger, turning the pages, adding page by page to the debit side, subtracting page by page from the credit. Her voice gave them shape and weight. When I was a child, I saw the consequences of any wrong action as the solid words of my mother's voice.

My father and I would do almost anything to keep her voice quiet, but we were never able to know what it was she wanted of us. She was our conscience, and we spent half our time trying to appease that conscience and the other half trying to escape it. For me it meant indecision in anything, from which color stockings to wear to which man to marry, and the foolish escape of marrying the one I knew full well was the wrong one. For my father it meant letting go of his natural simplicity and uncomplicated desires, and the foolish escape of an occasional binge.

A night would come when he would not come home. He would be gone one, two, sometimes three nights, and then he would simply show up, looking just as he had when he left. She never asked where he had been, what he had been doing. She started right in at the beginning. Poke, poke, poke, adding up, piling on. He never answered. We went on fixing supper, eating, cleaning the kitchen, putting out the trash, locking up. And over everything her voice was going on and on and on.

Finally she would dismiss me. I would go to my room and close the door, and her voice would become a murmur brushing against my door like moths brushing against my window screen. Late into the night the murmur would cease, and we would all sleep in our separate rooms with our separate nightmares.

Slowly my father's binges began to come closer together so that those quiet spaces were pushed further apart. Then things began to happen that made her voice grow harsher, louder, more persistent than ever. My father began to come home drunk. He began to let the bills go. Creditors were calling, and his business began to lose money.

Now at night the murmur rose and pushed against my door. I learned to sleep before it stopped. But one night the murmur grew so loud it broke into separate words. My door could no longer keep it out.

"You. You were the one who was so sensitive. You were the one who felt everything. You were the one in pain. Oh god, how sick I am of your pain. But it was a lie. Don't you know that by now? Don't you know even that?"

Her voice came stronger, then weaker, then stronger again. He was walking, trying to escape her, and she was following him from one end of the house to the other.

"There's nothing left inside of you that can feel. There's nothing inside of you but plumbing to run the whiskey through."

I knew he would have his hands deep in his pockets, his head down and pushed to one side, the left side. His body would show shame, but his eyes would be staring out beyond her words, beyond the house, trying to see the way he got in, trying to find the way out.

"You are nothing. Nothing to me. I don't care anymore. I don't. I don't. And you are nothing to your child. Nothing to yourself."

I wanted to scream at her, to tell her it wasn't true. It was not true that my father was nothing to me. She had no right to say that to him.

"No, that's not true, is it? You are something. You are a lie. You are a sham. You are a coward. You are all those things you once said you despised."

She said more, but I don't remember the words now. Even this much only came back to me later. What I heard next was his voice, no words, just the low, quiet drawl of his voice, and then the door to his room slammed.

I knew when Mother and I got up in the morning, my father would be gone. He was always gone the morning after a fight. He would leave no trace of himself, no dishes in the sink, no cigarette butts in the ashtrays, no damp towel in the bathroom. He would have cleaned himself out of the house as if, in taking away all signs of himself, he had escaped.

Then she opened my door, pushing it hard enough for it to hit and bounce away from the wall. "Get up and pack your suitcase. We're leaving here. Now."

It did not occur to me to ask why or to do anything other than what she said. We were packed, dressed, and on the road within an hour. My father never came out of his room. We were going to my grandfather's, two states and nine hours away. Once we were in the car, I began to wonder if my father would remember to call the school, and what he would say when Angie showed up Friday night to go with me to the Junior Sock Hop. I hoped he wouldn't be there. I hoped he would go out and get drunk as the lord. Back then I envied him that escape. I pictured him with his male friends in a noisy bar telling stories and slapping each other on the back and laughing.

I liked thinking of him like that, and I fell asleep. Mother woke me outside of an all-night restaurant just across the Florida border. We ate pecan pie and yawned and drank cups of coffee. She told me I'd have to wake up to help keep her awake. Going to her dad's always put her in a better frame of mind, and I was feeling pretty good too. My grandfather's house was as quiet as ours had been, but it was a warm, friendly kind of quiet. It was best when I was there without Mother, but even with her, it was better than our house.

After all that coffee, I was more concerned about having to go to the bathroom than I was about falling asleep. There was plenty of hard traffic, interstate trucks and tourists. Mother was warming up the way the Yankee tourists warmed up the farther they got into Florida. She wouldn't have liked the comparison. She hated tourists. She started telling me about the Scrub and Barney Dillard, her favorite Florida character. I had heard the stories often on trips to Granddaddy's, but I never tired of Barney. He represented Florida and the Scrub before the revenuers came.

She no longer talked in the dreary monotone she used at home. Her voice was like the older girls at school when they talked about their dates. She told me about Barney's twenty or so children and how he had lost his arm to a gator saving one of those children. She told me about Scarface Al Capone and his gang stopping at her aunt's hotel and how her cousin had let him know she knew who they were by pointing out a back entrance "just in case." I never could understand how she could be so silent and hold so much anger at home, yet become such a wonderful storyteller just by crossing a state line. When the oncoming lights shined into the car, I would see her face, animated, almost pretty. It was like having two mothers. This one I loved. Over the years it was this one who made me try to understand the other one.

She was telling about the Seminoles when we turned off Highway 17 and left the traffic. The sky was just beginning to tinge gray. I hated this desolate road, but she loved it. She had gone with a kind of wild fellow from Mt. Dora, and they had raced this road in her dad's '32 Ford. She picked up speed and fell quiet, acting out instead of talking. She lit a cigarette and sped up a little more. She was doing eighty. I sat back, holding on to the door handle and feeling like one of the "chicken kids" in that old Ford.

My dad told me once that it was his motorcycle and black leather jacket that had first attracted my mother. There was a picture of him taken back then that I looked at a lot. He was handsome and daring-looking. I could imagine this Florida mother wanting to ride behind him on that motorcycle. They got married and rode for almost a year before the guy riding next to them was thrown off his motorcycle when it hit a pothole. They found him way back off the road. My dad said they couldn't move him because his back was broken. The man's name was Cale, and he lived sixteen years after that.

When I was around eight my dad starting taking me with him on Sunday afternoons when he went to visit Cale in the nursing home. My mother never went and only mentioned his name once that I can remember; that was the day my dad and I came home from Cale's funeral. She said now that Cale was dead maybe my dad could stop being afraid of him.

We'd gone for miles and hadn't passed a car, a house or anything. She didn't need cars or people. She just needed the road. She lit another cigarette, and when I looked up, I saw something glint back at us. At first I couldn't figure out what it was, maybe a piece of glass or a beer can, but it would have to be two beer cans. As we came closer, I could just make out a form.

"Slow down."

She jerked her foot away from the gas pedal. The car slumped a little. "What is it?"

"Up there. I think there's a deer at the edge of the road."

"For Pete's sake. You scared me half to death." She shoved her foot hard against the pedal and the car sprang forward.

"You'll hit him."

"They're afraid of lights. He'll go back into the woods."

But he didn't. He started moving slowly, almost reluctantly out into the road. He kept staring at us. The lights blinded him, and I don't think he saw beyond them to the car until we were almost beside him. Then he leaped.

He was beautiful, delicate and graceful, poised in the air before us. Right now I can close my eyes and see him there, an exquisite, frightened and doomed creature.

He came down on the right fender, crashing and bouncing back into the air. His slender legs looked like a puppet's whose strings had gotten tangled, but he was real and pulsing blood. He fell away from the car and onto the side of the road.

Then he was gone, and I slammed against the door and saw the shoulder of the road rise, in slowed-down-time and hold quivering, before it came down again. The car slapped against the pavement, tried to move into and dip under it, and then began to skid. Road, trees, then road again moved across the windshield. It was like a ride I shouldn't have gotten on at the fair. I wanted to get the operator to stop. Then somehow it did stop. The car slid into the edge of the woods, pushing into the vines and undergrowth.

I don't know how long we sat staring into the trees. I remember the sounds of the crash coming back to me like a movie track out of sync with the picture. I remember feeling numb and cold and seeing Mother holding her head.

"Did you hit it? Your head?"

"I don't know. It hurts. Are you all right?"

"I'm just cold."

She nodded, and reached down and put her hand over the ignition key. She sat like that for a minute before she turned the key. The motor didn't catch. She jerked her hand off, then on again. This time it caught. She backed the car onto the road, ground the gears and pulled away.

"What are you doing? What about the deer?"

"He's dead."

"No. You don't know that. You can't just leave him there."

"Are you crazy?" She was shrieking. "That god-damned stupid deer could have killed us. He almost did kill us."

"It wasn't his fault. He was scared. He was blinded. He couldn't even see us. We could see him, but he couldn't see us. He couldn't."

She wouldn't answer me. She wouldn't even look at me.

"Please go back. Please. I can't stand him lying there all broken up. He hurts. You know he must hurt. Please." I knew my crying would make her madder, but I couldn't stop.

She couldn't stop either. Now I know that she was afraid. I know that she could no more stand to look on that deer than I could stand to imagine his pain and the way he must have died.

We were almost to Mt. Dora when I had to make her stop. I stood on the side of the road and vomited into the weeds. I threw up pie and coffee and more coffee, until I was just gagging and heaving and still crying. When I finally came back to the car, she was smoking and looking out her window. She threw the cigarette out and pulled off as soon as I closed the door.

She didn't say another word until we pulled up in Granddaddy's yard. She handed me a half-eaten pack of lifesavers with a hair and pieces of tobacco stuck to it. "You can smell the vomit. Don't say anything about the accident."

We slept off and on during the first day, getting up late in the evening to eat supper and talk about cousins and friends and Granddaddy's oranges and lemons and the little boy in Honduras that Grandmother's church circle had adopted. Listening to them it was as if my mother had had no other life but the one here in this house where she had been born. Our life and my father simply did not exist. I felt I was not part of her. She was someone I vaguely remembered from my last visit. Our reason for being there, the trip, the deer—none of it was mentioned.

I dreamed about the deer though and woke up cold and wet with my grandmother hovering over me. "Here child, here." An incantation to bring me out of the nightmare world.

The next morning Grandmother and I made orange peel preserves while Mother and Granddaddy sat on the porch. We could hear Mother's voice and the squeak, squeak of Granddaddy's rocking chair.

After the third day there, I began to notice my grandparents' daughter becoming my mother. She would grow quiet in the middle of a conversation and look over at the telephone. I started watching the phone, too, and both of us would sit up straight, waiting when it rang. Usually my father would have called by now.

Two mornings later we left. Mother was edgy, tired of talking. She sat in the car with her hands on the steering wheel, one foot on the accelerator and one on the brake while Grandmother and Granddaddy shoved a cake, a boxed lunch and admonitions to be careful into the car. We backed out of the drive, and she raised her hand at them, not even looking in their direction. I watched them until the grove cut them off from sight.

The sun was hot, traffic was heavy, and we could see the ruined groves and read the signs advertising new subdivisions, new sights, new thrills. Mother's Florida had already begun to harden into plastic. Once she snorted at a worksight [sic] where men and bulldozers were crawling all over what had obviously been a large grove. "We should have driven back last night." She lit a cigarette, almost biting off the end.

I had not really thought about the deer until we got to the Mt. Dora road. Mother hesitated, but then eager to push this new Florida behind her, she turned onto the old highway.

Once we left Mt. Dora there was no traffic. With no stories to listen to and no dark-covered fear of speed, I began to look for some signs of the deer. Maybe even now there was something we could do. This time Mother might stop. She was angry at the destroyers. She would see the deer, not as a threat, but as part of the old, primitive Florida pushed out of its habitat and sent into the world of cars and people by bulldozers making the way for shoddy trailers and attractions.

But then half way between Mt. Dora and Sanford, we saw another part of the old land. Ahead and high above us a buzzard glided slowly over the road and into the treetops. We both saw him and knew what he was. Nothing else moves with such patient, certain grace. We did not try to see him when we came to the trees he had gone into. We knew there would be nothing left of his grace. He would be hunched and hideous, his efficiently skinned head turning slowly as we passed. I slumped down in the seat and closed my eyes.

At Sanford we turned back onto the main highway. When we passed Jacksonville and crossed the line into Georgia, Mother opened the box Grandmother had put between us. At Darien we stopped for gas and Cokes to wash down the sandwiches we had eaten. We walked around drinking our Cokes while the man filled the gas tank and cleaned the windshield. Once Mother stopped in front of the phone booth for a minute.

We came into Charleston just after five-thirty. Traffic thinned out when we reached the Ashley River Bridge and thickened again in the city. Mother was drumming on the steering wheel and riding both pedals again.

We pulled up in front of the house, tooted the horn, and began gathering up magazines, food, and empty cigarette packages, but my father did not come out. Mother hit the horn again, two quick taps, then slid out of the car. We both dawdled a little waiting on him to come help us, waiting on him to come out and greet us as if we had left on a planned and routine trip. The first floor was dark, and only the hall light was on upstairs. Something splatted down to the ground beside me, and I looked up at a row of birds on the telephone wire running in front of the house.

"Well, maybe he's late getting home. Let's get the suitcases." She opened the trunk and groaned. "I forgot the oranges. We'll have to leave them for now."

"He'll get them later."

She pursed her lips then nodded.

We lugged the suitcases up the walk and saw the newspapers. Two for each day we'd been gone. It must have rained, half of them were soggy and yellowed. It looked like we had been gone for weeks instead of days. She turned the lock and pushed the front door in over a scattered pile of mail.

We stood in the hall with the suitcases and food and magazines and mail around our feet looking into and around the hall like we had never been there before. Then Mother reached past me and turned on the light. She put her hand on my shoulder and told me to wait.

I watched her go slowly up the stairs, heard her cross the hall and waited outside his room. Then I heard the whine his door always made, and I waited again.

I remember gathering up the mail and newspapers and pushing the front door closed. Then Mother standing at the head of the stairs looking down, not at me, not really at anything, just looking down. I had never seen her look like this before, as if she wasn't sure where she was or even maybe who she was. She looked too young and too afraid to be anyone's mother. But when I put my hand on the newel post, she focused on me and pushed her hand out.

"No, don't come up here."

It is very strange that something as total and devastating as a suicide can completely change a person's life without changing the person. Nothing at all seemed to change within my mother. She grew a little harder, a little quieter, a little more efficient.

She did not bend under the weight of getting my father's body out of the house and into the ground. She did not break down when she watched me cling, sobbing, to my grandmother. She did not turn away when her father explained the financial mess we were in. She simply did what she had to do and went on doing it for years.

So how to explain this afternoon? She had, a little reluctantly, taken my two girls to the park. She is not a doting grandmother, but my sitter had come down with the flu, and my boss was in a dither. I was pasting up the front page of the paper when my older daughter called. As scared as she was, she was able to tell me exactly where they were, and I got there within minutes.

I found my mother crouched on the ground, holding herself, pushing off the hands of the small crowd that had gathered around her. She didn't recognize me at first, and then she reached out and grabbed my face and then my shoulders and then my hands. "We have to go back. We have to go back." It was almost as if some crazy old woman had stopped me on the street. I had to keep telling myself that this person was my mother.

Later when I had gotten her home, when the doctor had given her a shot, when we had watched her slowly give way and fall asleep, I questioned my daughters.

"Nothing. She was fine. She was the same as always. But then she just started crying—just a little crying. We couldn't even hear her. She was just standing at the fence crying. Then she was crying more and more. She didn't pay any attention to us. She didn't even act like we were there. We tried to get her hands off the fence, and she fell down. She wouldn't get up."

"What fence? Why wouldn't she let go of the fence?"

"She said the deer knew."

The deer? And then the trip and the accident and my father's death came back. On the highway I had an automatic braking reaction to any animal that came into my vision. Other than that, had I even thought about the deer?

The deer. After all these years Mother had simply gone into a petting zoo with a handful of just-bought seeds, but instead of eating her seeds, the deer had skittered and backed away from her.

I fed and settled my girls down and then went into the bedroom. I sat down on the bed beside Mother and smoothed her spiked hair and straightened the covers around her. I hadn't really noticed how grey her hair had become. There was too much skin on the hand I held and more folds of skin under her eyebrows and chin. My mother was old. Her husband was gone. Her mother and father were gone, and they had taken Mother's Florida with them. She had no one to run from, no place to run to.

I had been mistaken about my mother. She had courted pain all her life, not because she was indifferent to it, but because she knew and despised herself as a coward. She had been so afraid of those things she could not control—pain, ugliness, attachment, love—that she, too, had leaped into the light of fear and been broken by the hard reality of her own destructiveness.

Those things she had screamed at my father the night we left were the things she had felt about herself. I had held her responsible for my father's suicide because I had been so sure she had felt no responsibility.

I could almost feel her hands grabbing at me again. "We have to go back. We have to go back." How many times had she gone back and relived their life together up to and including that evening when she had gone alone up those stairs and stood alone outside that door knowing what she would find?

I pulled the rocking chair out of the corner and brought it up beside the bed. I rocked slowly back and forth, remembering my mother in Florida and at home, my father, Cale, my grandparents and the deer. I had thought my father and I morally superior to my mother because we had visited Cale and we had removed ourselves from her. I had forgotten those hours she spent with Cale beside the road and I had refused to see her standing alone outside by father's door.

I rocked on into the night and waited for my mother to wake up. We had all been cowards. She was right. We had to go back. This time I would go back with her.

The Gift

"The Gift" is another unpublished story Marie wrote in the 1970s. Again, it is loosely auto-biographical and provides additional insights into how Marie was impacted by the loss of her oldest son and the birth of her youngest.

■

Johnny. Always Johnny. She couldn't forget, and she couldn't live remembering. "Momma, I can't live with you anymore. I love you, but I can't. Goodbye, Momma." She no longer needed to read the letter. She only needed to close her eyes to see every scrawl and smudge.

For twelve years Johnny had been her stability, her hope, the one constant in her life that made her able to endure the bad times and enjoy the good times.

Laura pushed the covers off and lay shivering in the empty bed. She had heard Paul leave and felt the bed getting colder. They were so alone. Paul huddled into his loss, and she into hers. He was incensed by her mother taking Johnny. "The only person that woman can stand up to is someone flat on his or her back. She's been planning this for years, but she had to wait, didn't she? Wait till you were too sick to fight her, and I was burying my dad. She's indecent. And Johnny is no better." He resented Laura's inability to be angry with Johnny. "Why do you defend him?" "He's a child."

Oh, damn it. Would she ever stop crying? She got up and punched her arms into the old chenille robe. She brushed her teeth until her gums started bleeding. She watched the blood, pink with saliva, run down the drain. Into the sewers. Take. Drink. This is the blood of Laura. Oh, Christ. You can't bleed to death from the gums.

Shut up, Laura. Wash your face, Laura. Get dressed, Laura. Go to the kitchen, Laura. You forgot to take your medicine, Laura. Did you, Laura? Did you "forget" to take your medicine? She sat at the kitchen table holding a cup of hot coffee, embracing its tiny warmth.

It can't be over 60 degrees in here. It was less. She had forgotten to order more fuel oil. She picked up the phone, hung it up again. Her voice would break. She would cry. She got another sweater and tied a scarf around her head.

She looked through the paper, not really seeing any of it, then took it into the den. She started over to the wing chair beside the fireplace. No. She would not sit curled up in the chair all day, watching the clock, waiting for Paul to come home, hoping he would light a fire, sit across from her, and talk with her the way he had so long ago—two years ago.

She pulled the vacuum cleaner out of the closet and dragged it into the living room. She would do a thorough cleaning. She would suck up all the cobwebs from the corners of the ceiling, chase down the dust balls, strip away the grime. She would be full of energy. When she finished, she would shower, fix her face, and put on fresh clothes. Paul would be surprised and pleased. They would go to The Chowder House, sit in their old booth and eat oysters and hush puppies. Then they would drink pots of coffee and talk.

She cleaned the wood work and windows and felt the winter sun on her face. She stood at the front bay and watched the cars and people going by. When was the last time she and Paul had gone for a walk before supper?

She switched on the vacuum, pulled the sofa out from the wall, and stood staring at the floor behind it. "Oh, God, Johnny." Slowly she stooped down and picked up a sock. It was dirty, and the top was pulled out of shape. She rubbed it against her face and smelled his sweaty, little-boy body. "Johnny. Please, Johnny, come back. I can't stand it, Johnny. I can't. I can't."

Paul found her there. The vacuum was still running. He pulled the sock out of her hand and helped her to bed.

She woke during the night and went to the bathroom. Back in the bed, she couldn't sleep. She got up again and put on her nightgown. Still she couldn't sleep. Her heart was racing. She went back to the bathroom and took a phenobarbital. Later she took another and finally fell asleep.

Laura heard the mail slot cover fall back against the door. It was almost one-thirty. Maybe there was a letter from Johnny. Maybe the sock had been a sign.

There were bills, advertisements, a house magazine. She left them and started looking for the sock. She went through the garbage in the kitchen, the trash in the den, bedroom, and bathroom. Nothing. She pushed Johnny's door open, but each time she tried to walk into the room, everything went black, and she had to hold on to the doorframe. Her heart started racing. She couldn't get her breath. She edged along the wall to the bathroom and took two pills. "One every four hours. No more. No less." But this was different. Her heart couldn't take this. It would blow up in her chest.

In the bed she lay waiting for her heart to slow down, waiting for her breath to come normally, waiting to fall asleep, waiting for Johnny. But he was not coming back. She knew that. No one was coming back, not her father, not John, not Paul's father, not Johnny, not even Paul. In five years she had lost them all, and they would never come back.

She was gasping and feeling her fear of suffocation move up with the pain. Johnny. Johnny. Don't think, Laura. Don't think. But it was getting worse. Her whole body was shaking. She was strangling on her own heart. She tried to get up and fell off the bed. She lay there trying to gasp enough oxygen to get up. Finally she crawled to the bathroom. She pulled herself up to the sink and leaned against the cold porcelain. It seemed to take forever to get the bottle open. She spilled half the water down her front before she could steady the glass against her teeth. The pills stuck in her throat. At last she was able to swallow enough water to get them down.

Laura felt herself being dragged, dragged out of the warmth she had found, dragged out of the soft darkness, dragged back into life. "No. Leave me alone." She tried to find the dark warmth again.

"Get up. Stand up. Damn it, stand up. Walk. Come on, Laura, walk!"

She fought him, but he was stronger. He had always been stronger. What was he doing to her? Where was he taking her? Why couldn't he leave her alone?

Icy water hit her head and body. She screamed and tried to get away, but his hands were everywhere she tried to go. Exhausted, she stopped fighting and leaned into the corner of the shower. "All right. Please. Enough. Please, let me out."

Paul shut off the water and shoved a towel at her. "Dry yourself and get dressed. I'll make coffee. And don't put that god damned robe back on. It stinks."

She found clean jeans and a sweater, but she had just gotten them on when she smelled the coffee. It was like releasing the valve on a pressure hose. She drenched the toilet, the wall behind it, and herself.

"Oh, Christ." Paul stood in the bathroom door looking at her as if she were no more than her own vomit.

"Get out! Get out!" She pushed him, knocking him off balance and into the hall. "Get out!" She slammed the door and locked it. He yelled something, but she ignored him. She took the clothes off, cleaned up the mess and got back into the shower.

There were no more clean clothes. She gathered up the clothes from the bathroom floor and the bottom of her closet and took them to the washing machine. Paul was waiting in the kitchen.

"You'll get pneumonia."

She looked over at him and went on arranging the clothes in the washer.

"Don't you even know you're naked and wet? Have you completely lost your mind?"

She poured detergent into the washer and closed the lid. She felt warmed by his anger. She heard him get up and leave the kitchen. Go away then. I don't care.

He came back and handed her his robe. "Sit down. You still need coffee. It's not Sanka. I thought you should have regular."

She was afraid it would make her sick again, but it went down and tasted good. "Why did you do that? I was sleeping. I don't get to sleep much."

"What the hell are you talking about? I come home and find trash and garbage strewn all over the house, you dead to the world, and your pills—what you'd left of them—dumped on the bathroom floor. You expect me to sit around here calmly and watch you commit suicide? What in God's name do you take me for?"

"Suicide?" It was worse than the cold water. "No. No. I wasn't. I didn't. Look, I was trying to find the sock. You hid the sock from me. I went to Johnny's room, and . . ." She was crying again. She looked at him and shook her head. She wanted so badly for him to touch her. "Listen to me. You've got to let me hire someone to come in here and help you."

"A keeper?"

"That's not fair." But he still wouldn't look at her. "None of this is fair. I can't go to work and wonder day after day how I'm going to find you when I get home." He turned then. "Can't you understand what this is doing to me?"

She drank more coffee, made herself stop crying. She had to think. She knew what he was doing. He wanted someone to come into the house and find all the socks, someone who would pack up the things in Johnny's room and give them away. He wanted Johnny cleaned out of his house the way her mother had cleaned her father out of their house, the way she had let them make her clean John out of their apartment. Paul was just like the rest of them. She would have to be very careful.

"Yes, you're right. I know you're right. This isn't fair to you or me. What I need is to get back to work." She looked up and smiled at him. "I'll call Dr. Blanchard tomorrow and tell him we need to work out a new regimen, one that will give my heart time to heal, but still let me work. He and I can work something out. I'd like to be able to pick away at putting the house back in order and paint a couple of hours a day. Maybe I can take, say, half a dose of the medicine and short naps or just lie on the sofa a while every couple of hours and catch up on my reading." She got up and took his hand. "I know it's been hard on you."

For three weeks Laura lived her lie. Paul helped her stretch a canvas, and she got her paints out and started working from a sketch she had done before Johnny left. She was getting the house back in order, and she had supper going every evening when Paul came home. She did it all while her heart raced and she gasped for breath. She was hoarding her pills, taking them only when Paul was home. She saved two a day, but they weren't as strong as the first ones Dr. Blanchard had prescribed, and even so, the druggist would only give her thirty at a time. She thought she would need a hundred to be sure. If she took less, they might not work fast enough. But she could stand the waiting now, because she knew it would end.

Knowing she would not have to spend all those years without Johnny, she could go back and remember the years with him. She hardly noticed the pain in her chest. Every day she went about the routine work of the house while her mind lived in the past with Johnny. Every day she took the hidden bottle out and counted the pills.

She gave no thought to the rightness or wrongness of what she was doing. She was a problem to Paul, and God had deserted her years ago. Only once did she stop to think about it in any sense other than as her plan. She woke one morning having dreamed that Johnny was a grown man knocking on the door. Paul let him come in just long enough to show him her body rotting in a casket in the living room. Johnny's screams had waked her. She got up and wrote a letter to him, explaining, exonerating him, asking him to understand and forgive her. She believed there was no one else whose forgiveness she needed.

She had just over a week to go when she was cleaning out the closet and found the box of tampons. At first she pushed them aside, but later she put down her paint brushes and went back to the closet. How long? She checked her calendar. Two months. It was impossible. It was the medicine. It was losing Johnny. It was her heart. It could not be, not now, not when her plan was so close. The calendar fell out of her hands. She was shaking. The pain in her chest was horrible. She wanted to scream. She wanted to run. Don't think. You know it can't be true.

But I have to think. I would have to give up my plan. I couldn't go on with it. I couldn't do that. Even now I couldn't do that.

Listen to me, the doctors—four doctors—have said you are sterile. This is something else.

But I have to know. I have to know.

You do know. You've missed two periods. Johnny left three months ago. This is a trick, a false pregnancy, nothing more. It is nature playing tricks on you. It is God playing tricks on you. Nature, God, they never want to let go. They want to suck everything out of you before they let you go. They don't care about your pain. Go on with your plan.

She called Dr. Blanchard.

"All right. You get ready, and we'll have a look, but you must not be disappointed at what we find. Emotions have a great deal to do with our bodies, and you've had a lot to deal with lately." Dr. Blanchard squeezed her shoulder. She knew he thought she was pathetic, and she hated him for that. "I'll ask Mrs. Christie to come in."

Laura let Mrs. Christie's chatter numb her like canned music while she undressed and stuck her heels into the icy stirrups of the examining table.

She thought suddenly of Johnny, of autopsies, and tensed. "Relax now, Laura. Come on, take a deep breath. That's better."

It seemed to Laura that he would find all her secrets in his probing, that somehow those organs designed to conceive and nurture life would be drying up and hardening in the face of her plan.

Dr. Blanchard pulled off the gloves and patted her knee. "Okay. I'll give you a few minutes to dress, and then we'll talk."

Mrs. Christie handed her a paper towel. "You just open the door when you're ready."

After she had used the paper tower, Laura looked for some sign of dampness. It told her nothing. She wadded it in the paper sheet and shoved the whole mess into the trashcan. She fumbled with her clothes, first buttoning her blouse wrong then getting it caught in the skirt zipper. She opened the door a crack and sat down beside the big, paper-laden desk. She wished she had brought something to read, but knew it wouldn't have helped. Twice she got up and paced the room. She jumped when Dr. Blanchard finally pushed the door in.

It wasn't a trick. She was three month pregnant. Dr. Blanchard called it a miracle. "There's just no other way to explain it, is there?"

Laura went home, took the pills out and watched them fall into the toilet and disintegrate. She burned the letter she had written Johnny. She took out the instructions Dr. Blanchard had given her, and re-reading them, began crying as she had not done in weeks.

A miracle. You and your damned miracles. Are you there? Did you do this? Why?

Why couldn't you leave me alone? One child for another. Is it so damned simple for you? Are we nothing more to you than pieces to be moved around your game board, knocked off, replaced? We feel, damn you. We hurt. Oh, God, how we hurt.

It was not an easy pregnancy. Laura had to fight, to put all her energy into saving a pregnancy she hadn't wanted and didn't understand, yet, in fighting, she could feel her heart slowing down, growing stronger. She no longer had to gasp for breath. Maybe it was only nature doing what was necessary to get a new creature into the world. Whatever was causing her health to return, she could feel herself responding, becoming this child's mother and nurturer. She began to make bargains with God. I'm not sure. You can't expect that, not yet, but let this baby be born well and whole, and I'll leave the door open.

And he was. The doctor laid him in her arms while he cut the umbilical cord. She felt the weight of him against her empty belly and saw his puckered face and gray-red skin. He was life itself in her arms, life that she had brought into this world. She had never felt so whole, well and alive. She heard her son crying, throwing his newfound voice into the world, and she felt he and she were part of eternity. They had touched the beginning and the end.

For a year Laura kept Scott beside her. Awake or asleep, they were constantly together. She not only loved having him near her, she was too anxious to let him be without her. She didn't trust anyone else with him, not even Paul.

Laura was sitting on the grass, enjoying the hot sun and watching Scott toddle around the yard He loved showing her his treasures—"Momma, Momma," and he would point to a flowering weed. "Flower," she would tell him. "Okay," he would answer. He would go to the gate and peek through the slats until a car or large dog came down the street, then he would waddle back to her in his funny, propelled walk-run. "Ooh, big!" She would hold him and play with him until he felt secure enough to go search for more treasures.

He spotted a small, yellow butterfly and tried to catch it. The butterfly fluttered around his head, and Scott squealed and clapped his hands. "Momma, Momma!" "Butterfly, Scott."

He became oblivious to everything else. He waddled, turned, reached, fell, pushed himself up and started following his special treasure again. Laura laughed and urged him on. "There he is, behind you."

Then he went down face first. Laura waited a moment, but he didn't get up. By the time she reached him, he had caught his breath and was screaming. She picked him up and saw blood all over his face. He began clawing at her.

She held him tightly against her and ran to her neighbor's house. Standing on the front stoop waiting for Mrs. Kirkland to find her keys, Laura spoke quietly, soothingly to Scott, but her mind was shrieking, Not Scott . . . Not Scott . . . Not Scott . . .

Every time Laura thought about the needle moving into the flesh just above Scott's eye and saw the pain and fear register in his face, her stomach convulsed and her mouth filled with bile.

It was over a week before the extreme swelling went down, another two weeks before his natural color came back. A quarter of an inch and he would have lost his eye. Yet she had been right there. He hadn't been out of her sight for a moment.

She began to hover over him. Her body pitched toward him at every stumble or falter. She was afraid to leave him for any reason. Even when she left Paul to watch Scott, she was nervous until she could get back to him.

Scott was playing on the floor with his blocks when Laura came back into the den after taking a quick shower. She smiled at Scott's teetering tower and then saw Paul asleep on the sofa. Scott was perfectly all right, but Laura could see flashes of all that could have happened, and she was furious.

"Paul!"

He jerked awake and came off the sofa in one movement. "Oh, I thought . . . I must have fallen asleep."

"Do you know what could have happened while you were supposed to be watching Scott? He could have gone into the kitchen and—and swallowed something poisonous. He could have wandered out into the yard, into the street. He could have pulled something over on himself. Can't you be trusted with him even for a few minutes a day?"

"Me? Listen, Laura, Scott wasn't with me when he got hurt. He was with you."

She saw herself slap him, felt the bone beneath her hand, heard the smack, felt the sting of her palm, then saw his hand fly up to his face and watched the red whelps develop around his fingers like a color portrait of her guilt. He stared at her. His hand came away from his face and moved toward her. She braced herself, closed her eyes and then felt his arms around her. "Oh, Laura, Laura. I'm so sorry."

She had forgotten what it was like to lean on Paul. She remembered something from Mauriac about a man who always looked for the limits of love and so always found them at once. She had not carried out her plan, but she suddenly knew that she had never given it up. She had held it in reserve, waiting for the day when she would lose Scott, sure that he was her last lifeline, sure then, that she would lose him.

She relaxed against Paul, smelled the tobacco and aftershave mixed with the faint odor of his sweat, felt his beard scratch her forehead. Scott had been a gift of life, and Paul was part of that gift. But it had been a gift she had not truly understood, a gift she had not accepted with grace. For the first time, she was deeply grateful for that gift.

That night they moved the crib out of their bedroom into the nursery. They were both worried that Scott might be afraid or feel neglected, but he was only excited. "Momma, Momma, Scott's room."

Paul helped Laura get Scott ready for bed, then he kissed him good night and left them alone.

Laura rocked Scott and read him a story about water babies. She had to read it three times before he calmed down. She held him until his eyelids began to droop with sleep. Still she couldn't leave him. She stood beside the crib, her hand curled over his fist, watching his eyelids quiver, seeing the scar. "There'll be just a tiny, white line above the crease of his eye, hardly noticeable. These things happen to everyone,

Laura. I doubt you'd find a person in this world without some similar scar." Gently she drew her finger over the scar. She did not feel the lurching in her stomach, nor taste bile.

Scott was so beautiful, peaceful and trusting. Looking at him, feeling the wonder of him, she knew that Johnny would come back, not tomorrow, maybe not for years, but he would come back. The gift of Scott made all things possible.

Words she had not thought of in many years formed in her mind. She tucked the blanket around Scott, brushed the hair away from his eyebrows and saw him smile in his sleep. "Now I lay you down to sleep. I pray the Lord your soul to keep." She was trembling when she reached for the switch to turn off the lamp, but the expected darkness was only a gentler light. Paul had plugged in a nightlight beside the doorway. She could still see Scott in the soft glow. "Good night my son. Until tomorrow."

Notes

Introduction
1. George Plimpton, "The Story Behind a Nonfiction Novel," *New York Times*, January 16, 1966.
2. Kevin Helliker, "Capote Classic 'In Cold Blood' Tainted by Long-Lost Files," *Wall Street Journal*, February 8, 2013.
3. Gore Vidal, *Palimpsest* (Random House, 1995).

Chapter 1
1. Michael Hardy, "Hope on Death Row is Kept Alive," *Richmond Times-Dispatch*, date unknown.
2. Marie M. Deans, "Let's Forget Revenge and Stop This Violence," *Virginia Pilot and Ledger Star*, July 17, 1983.
3. Hardy, "Hope on Death Row."
4. Deans, "Let's Forget Revenge."
5. Marie Deans, "Living in Babylon," in *A Punishment in Search of a Crime: Americans Speak Out Against the Death Penalty*, ed. Ian Gray and Moria Stanley (New York: Avon Books, 1989), 73.
6. Ibid., 74.

Chapter 2
1. Marie Deans, "How Society Handles the Abused Child Who Becomes a Criminal Adult," *Richmond Times-Dispatch*, May 23, 1984.
2. Ibid.
3. Robert Deans, interview with author.
4. Eula Garrison, "Why I Am an Abolitionist," *Washington Coalition to Abolish the Death Penalty* (2005): 3.
5. Georgia Caldwell, "The Electric Chair: Who Sits in It?," *Virginia Country*, vol. 12, no. 1.
6. Marie Deans, "Caring Nations Have Abolished Death Penalty," *Lynchburg News & Daily Advance*, September 4, 1990.
7. "Courting Death: Speaking Out on Capital Punishment," *The Plough: Publication of the Bruderhof Communities*, no. 18 (January/February 1988): 8.
8. Marie Deans to Joe Giarratano, November 10, 2004.
9. William F. Tremper, interview with author.
10. Zackary Zeid, "Marie Deans, Death Penalty Abolitionist, Dies at 70," *Richmond-Times Dispatch*, April 17, 2011.
11. Mike Farrell, interview with author.
12. Tim Kaine, interview with author.

13. Lloyd Snook, interview with author.
14. Helen Prejean, interview with author.
15. Steve Northup, interview with author.
16. Barry Weinstein, interview with author.
17. Bart Stamper, interview with author.
18. Pamela Tucker, interview with author.
19. Former death penalty activist, interview with author.
20. Joel "Mac" McFadden, interview with author.
21. Larry Cox, interview with author.
22. Deans to Giarratano, July 21, 2004.
23. Jerry Zerkin, interview with author.
24. Molly Cupp, interview with author.
25. Matt Seiden, "This Victim Lobbies for Criminals," *Baltimore Sun*, March 16, 1983.

Chapter 3

1. Lynne Langley, "Letters to Prisoners of Conscience," *Charleston News and Courtier*, June 3, 1980.
2. Larry Cox, interview with author.
3. Amnesty International, "Texas Death Row Biggest," *Texas Observer*, May 7, 1982.
4. Marie M. Deans, "Revenge on Murderers: There are Better Ways to Go," *Los Angeles Times*, June 7, 1983.
5. Stuart Banner, *The Death Penalty: An American History* (Cambridge, MA: Harvard University Press, 2002): 9.
6. Deanna Pan, "The George Stinney Case is Back: Attorneys Plan Civil Rights Suit," *Post and Courier*, August 25, 2016.
7. David Bruck to Joseph Ingle, November 10, 1983.
8. Deans, "Living in Babylon."
9. Ibid., 74.
10. Ibid., 74–75.
11. Marie Deans, unpublished essay.
12. Deans, "Living in Babylon," 75.
13. Marie Deans, unpublished essay.
14. "Killer of Teen-agers is Executed in Carolina," *New York Times*, January 12, 1985.
15. David Bruck, "Banality of Evil," in *A Punishment in Search of a Crime: Americans Speak Out Against the Death Penalty*, Ian Gray and Moria Stanley (New York: Avon Books, 1989): 81.
16. Colman McCarthy, "A Last Talk with a Condemned Man," *Washington Post*, January 13, 1986.
17. David Bruck, interview with author.
18. David Bruck to "Vance," February 5, 1986.
19. Bruck, "Banality of Evil."
20. Marie Deans to "Nick," April 3, 1986.
21. Alison Whyte, "Victims of State Torture," *Independent*, August 23, 1989.
22. John Mock, "Killer of Two Executed in S. Carolina," *Philadelphia Inquirer*, January 11, 1986.
23. Bruck, "Banality of Evil," 85.
24. Whyte, "Victims of State Torture."
25. "Solicitor Would Seek Death Sentence Again," *Charlotte Observer*, January 12, 1989.
26. Deans to "Nick," April 3, 1986.
27. Jeff Miller, "Court Halts Execution of Woomer," *The State* (Columbia, SC), June 16, 1989.
28. Margaret N. O'Shea, "Rusty Woomer Put to Death," *The State* (Columbia, SC), April 27, 1990.

Chapter 4

1. "Iowa Floods Derail Amtrak Train," *New York Times*, June 16, 1982.
2. Joseph Ingle, interview with author.
3. Marie Deans, unpublished essay.
4. Joe Giarratano, interview with author.
5. Joseph Ingle, interview with author.

Chapter 5

1. Report from the Virginia Coalition on Jails and Prisons, February 11, 1988.
2. Lloyd Snook, interview with author.
3. Lloyd Snook to Assistant Attorney General Richard Gorman, February 6, 1984.
4. Marie Deans to Attorneys for DR Prisoners, August 24, 1984.
5. Tom Sherwood, "Judge Orders Halt to Restrictions on Lawyers' Visits to Prison," *Washington Post*, October 3, 1984; Randolph Goode, "Lawyer Prison Visit Rules Voided," *Richmond News Leader*, October 1984.
6. Marie Deans to Mecklenburg Assistant Warden William Crenshaw, August 9, 1984.
7. Marie Deans to Federal Bureau of Investigation (Richmond Office), January 30, 1989.
8. January 30, 1988, FBI Report.
9. Marie Deans to Federal Bureau of Investigation (Richmond Office), January 30, 1989.
10. Edward C. Fennell and John Heilprin, "Killer Kornahrens Executed," *Post and Courier* (Charleston, SC), July 19, 1996.
11. Russ Ford, interview with author.
12. Georgia Caldwell, "The Electric Chair: Who Sits in It?," *Virginia Country*, vol. 12, no. 1.
13. Marie Deans to the men of death row, memorandum, November 11, 1983.
14. Maria Glod and Anita Kumar, "Thomas Haynesworth Exonerated in Rape Case After 27 Years in Prison," *Washington Post*, December 6, 2011.
15. Mike Allen, "Death Penalty Foes See Terry Conflict," *Richmond Times-Dispatch*, May 13, 1993.
16. Marie Deans to John L. Carroll, August 21, 1986.
17. Larry O'Dell, "Court in Virginia Examines Death Row Isolation Policy," Associated Press, October 27, 2014.
18. *Prieto v. Clarke*, 780 F.3d 245 (2015).
19. Albert Camus, "Reflections on the Guillotine: An Essay on Capital Punishment," trans. Richard Howard (1957).
20. "Victims of State Torture," *The Independent*, August 23, 1989.
21. Doug Struck, "Slaying Victim's Kin Fights to Save Other Murders," *Baltimore Sun*, April 22, 1990.
22. Joe Giarratano, interview with author.
23. "Public Execution Denied," *Washington Post*, May 24, 1990.
24. Monica Davey, "Execution Date June 29: Savino Asks Court to Film his Death," *Roanoke Times*, May 24, 1990.
25. Frank Green, "Inmate Says Officers Gave Dose of Drug," *Richmond Times-Dispatch*, June 8, 1994.
26. Frank Green, "Va. Inmate is Executed for Slaying: Joseph Savino was Third Person Put to Death in State This Year," *Richmond Times-Dispatch*, July 18, 1996.
27. Ibid.
28. Joe Giarratano, interview with author.
29. William Hoffer, "Medical Care on Death Row," *American Medical News*, March 9, 1984.
30. Frank Green, "Prison Officials Believe that DeLong Killed Himself," *Richmond Times-*

Dispatch, June 15, 1993; Mike Allen, "DeLong was Drunk, Officials Say," *Richmond Times-Dispatch*, July 28, 1993.

31. "Inmate on Death Row Killed Self," Associated Press, July 28, 1993; Frank Green, "Latest Chapter in Sad History of Prison War—State Now Fighting Death Row Drugs," *Richmond Times-Dispatch*, July 29, 1993; "This is Maximum Security: Cocaine on Death Row," *Virginian Pilot*, July 30, 1993.

32. Ibid.

33. Code of Virginia § 19.2–264.4.

34. Ibid.

35. "The Nature of the Beast," *Angolite: The Prison Newsmagazine*, vol. 12, no. 3 (May/June 1987): 14.

36. Tony Germanotta, "Woman Toils to Ban Executions," *Virginian-Pilot*, February 9, 1986.

Chapter 6

1. Lynn Waltz, "Death Walk Chaplain Russ Ford has Accompanied 19 Condemned Murders to Virginia's Electric Chair," *Virginian-Pilot*, August 28, 1994.

2. Russ Ford, interview with author.

3. Marie Deans, interview with author.

4. Erik Brady, "Bringing God to Death Row," *USA Today*, August 25, 1995.

5. Waltz, "Death Walk Chaplain."

6. Brady, "Bringing God to Death Row."

7. Ibid.

8. Russ Ford to Rev. George F. Ricketts, Inter-Office Memorandum, August 24, 1992.

9. Paul Dellinger and Laurence Hammack, "Death Row Prisoner Executed," *Roanoke Times*, October 20, 1995.

10. Clemency Petition of Richard T. Boggs.

11. Ibid.

12. Ibid., Exhibit 2, "Autobiography."

Chapter 7

1. Mike Allen, "Death Diary: Pleas, Anger Fill Days Before Execution," *Richmond Times-Dispatch*, August 25, 1991.

2. Robert Johnson, *Death Work: A Study of the Modern Execution Process* (Mason. OH: Cengage Learning, 2005): 152.

3. Johnson, *Death Work*, 153.

4. Alison Whyte, "Victims of State Torture," *The Independent*, August 23, 1989.

5. Jim Mason, "Prison Doomed, but Chair to be Spared," *Richmond Times-Dispatch*, October 12, 1990.

6. Whyte, "Victims of State Torture."

7. Margaret Edds, *An Expendable Man: The Near Execution of Earl Washington, Jr.* (New York: New York University Press, 2003): 5.

8. Germanotta, "Woman Toils to Ban Executions."

9. Deborah W. Denno, "Is Electrocution an Unconstitutional Method of Execution? The Engineering of Death Over the Century," *William and Mary Law Review*, vol. 35 (Winter 1994): 551–693; 665.

10. Frank Green, "Death Row Captive—Role in Execution Took an Emotional Toll," *Richmond Times-Dispatch*, May 24, 1998.

11. Denno, "Is Electrocution An Unconstitutional Method," 670–71.

12. Ibid.

13. Jeff Gammage, "Virginia's Old 'Pen' to Close Chapter on Human Suffering," *Philadelphia Inquirer*, November 13, 1990.

14. Nelson Schwartz and Mike Allen, "Death Penalty Opponents Angry about Latest Execution," *Richmond Times-Dispatch*, August 24, 1991.

15. Joe Jackson and William F. Burke Jr., *Dead Run: The Untold Story of Dennis Stockton and America's Only Mass Escape from Death Row* (New York: Random House, 1999): 184.

16. Molly Moore and Sandra Sugawara, "Sorrowful, Satisfied Crowds Greet Briley Execution in Va.," *Washington Post*, October 14, 1984.

17. Marie Deans, unpublished manuscript.

18. Ibid.

19. Green, "Death Row Captive."

20. Russ Ford, interview with author.

21. Ibid.

22. Alison Whyte, "Victims of State Torture," *The Independent*, August 23, 1989.

23. Joe Giarratano, correspondence with author.

24. Barry Weinstein, interview with author.

25. In *The Cost of Discipleship*, Dietrich Bonhoeffer defines cheap grace as "the preaching of forgiveness without requiring repentance, *baptism* without church discipline, *Communion* without *confession*. Cheap grace is grace without *discipleship*, grace without the cross, grace without Jesus Christ."

26. Sue Anne Pressley, "Guiding the Trip 'Through the Darkness'; Chaplain, Counselor Are Immersed in the Haunting Relationships of Death Row," *Washington Post*, September 2, 1992.

Chapter 8

1. Michael Crowley, "A Fight Against Ignorance," *Amnesty: Journal of the British Section of Amnesty International*, no. 41 (October/November 1989): 21.

2. See Joseph B. Ingle, *Last Rights: 13 Fatal Encounters with the State's Justice* (Nashville: Abingdon Press): 247–49.

3. Joe Giarratano, in *Last Rights* (250–51).

4. Russ Ford, interview with author.

5. See Sheila Isenberg, *Women Who Love Men Who Kill* (Lincoln, NE: iUniverse, 2000).

6. Joe Giarratano, in *Last Rights* (250–51).

7. "Their Last Days," *Virginian-Pilot*, September 5, 1993.

8. Evans D. Hopkins, "My Life Above Virginia's Electric Chair: The Sleepless Night Morris Mason was Executed," *Washington Post*, July 21, 1985.

9. Lynn Waltz, "Death Walk Chaplain," *Virginia Pilot*, August 28, 1994.

10. Russ Ford, unpublished manuscript.

11. Ronnie Crocker, "VA's Next Execution Puts Focus on Retarded," *Daily Press* (Newport News, VA), July 17, 1989.

12. Joe Giarratano, interview with author.

13. Waltz, "Death Walk Chaplain."

14. Greg Schneider, "Suffering with Death Row Prisoners Awaiting the Chair," *Virginian-Pilot*, September 17, 1992.

15. Schneider, "Suffering with Death Row Prisoners."

16. Mike Allen, "Autopsy is Final Chapter in Executions," *Richmond Times-Dispatch*, September 28, 1992.

17. Rex Springston, "Smith's Execution Not Worry to Family," *Richmond Times-Dispatch*, July 29, 1986.

18. "Their Last Days," *Virginian-Pilot*, September 5, 1993.

19. Dennis Montgomery, "Condemned Murderer: 'Father, I Am Here,'" Associated Press, August 1, 1986.

20. Donald P. Baker, "Va. Killer Executed as Appeals Fail," *Washington Post*, July 31, 1986.

21. Mark Smith, Joseph Williams, and Frank Douglas, "Smith Executed for '77 Death," *Richmond Times-Dispatch*, August 1, 1986.

22. Jim Mason and Bill Wasson, "Killer Asks Forgiveness, Dies in Chair," *Richmond Times-Dispatch*, August 1, 1986.

23. Frank Green, "'One More Turn of the Screw.'" *Richmond Times-Dispatch*, December 29, 1996.

24. "Their Last Days," *Virginian-Pilot*, September 5, 1993.

25. Deans, "Living in Babylon," 76.

26. Ibid.

27. Gregory Gilligan, "Whitley Is Executed for 1980 Slaying," *Richmond Times-Dispatch*, July 7, 1987.

28. Pressley, "Guiding the Trip through the Darkness."

29. Georgia Caldwell, "The Electric Chair: Who Sits in It?," *Virginia Country*, vol. 12, no. 1.

30. Frank Green, "Death House Cell Assignments Called Torture," *Richmond Times-Dispatch*, December 15, 1996.

31. Ibid.

32. Evans D. Hopkins, "Marie Deans: Keeper of the Keys," *Style Weekly*, April 23, 1985.

33. Kirk Makin, "Killing the Killers" (a four-part series), *Globe and Mail* (Canada), June 10, 1987.

34. Makin, "Killing the Killers."

Chapter 9

1. Unless otherwise noted, the quotations and information in this chapter are taken from the following sources: an unpublished, partially completed book chapter that Marie Deans wrote on Joe Giarratano; interviews with Marie and Joe; the 1990 clemency petition written by Marie and attorneys Richard Burr, Julius L. Chambers, and Richard L. Schaeffer; the attachments to the clemency petition; and the 1990 petition for writ of certiorari to the United States Supreme Court written by Richard J. Bonnie, Richard H. Burr III, Julius L. Chambers, Kay L. Ely-Pierce, and Gerald Zerkin.

2. See, generally, Jon Frank, "Tenacious Bench Judge Dies at 60," *Virginia-Pilot*, September 21, 2004; Joe Jackson and June Arney, "Controversies Trail Alberi in his Quest for Judgeship," *Virginia-Pilot*, March 3, 1996; "Alberi Judged 'Not Qualified' By Bar Association," *Virginia-Pilot*, March 5, 1996; June Arney, "Prosecutor's Error Frees Teen in Killing," *Virginia Pilot*, May 13, 1995.

3. Green, "Lawless—No Second Thoughts."

4. Jim Mason, "Evidence Clears Condemned Man, Lawyer Contends," *Richmond Times-Dispatch*, May 13, 1989.

5. Green, "Lawless—No Second Thoughts;" Mason, "Evidence Clears Condemned Man."

6. "Slayer of 2 Awaits Decision on Fate," *Richmond Times-Dispatch*, May 24, 1979.

7. *Pate v. Robinson*, 383 US 375 (1966).

8. June Arney, "Joseph M. Giarratano Blood Footprints Led Him to Doubt His Own Confession," *Virginia Pilot*, June 26, 1994.

9. Jackson and Burke, *Dead Run*, 8.

10. Ibid., 9.

11. United Press International, "Ex-Cop Set to Die in Electric Chair," August 8, 1982.

12. Joe Giarratano, "An Experience in Life," *Southern Coalition Report on Jails and Prisons*, vol. 13, no. 2 (Summer 1986).
13. Maryanne Vollers, "As His Date with the Executioner Nears, Joe Giarratano Says He's No Killer—and Some People Believe Him," *People*, vol. 33, no. 21 (May 28, 1990).

Chapter 10
1. Caroline M. Schloss, *The Life of Willie Lloyd Turner, Virginia's Dean of Death Row* (Virginia Beach, VA: Donning Co., 2000).
2. L. B. Taylor Jr., *The Big Book of Virginia Ghost Stories* (Mechanicsburg, PA: Stackpole Books, 2010): 367.
3. Jackson and Burke, *Dead Run*, 16–25. Unless otherwise noted, the information in this chapter on the escape is drawn from *Dead Run*.
4. Jackson and Burke, *Dead Run*: 94–95.
5. Lloyd Snook, interview with author.
6. Joe Giarratano, interview with author.
7. Jackson and Burke, *Dead Run*: 195; Donald P. Baker, "6 Va. Death Row Prisoners Fail in Escape Attempt," *Washington Post*, November 27, 1985.
8. Joseph Giarratano, "The Pains of Life," in *Facing the Death Penalty: Essays on a Cruel and Unusual Punishment*, ed. Michael L. Radelet (Philadelphia, PA: Temple University Press, 1989), 193.
9. Ibid.
10. Ibid., 194–95.
11. Frank Jennings, "USA—The Risk of Executing the Innocent," *NUACHT Amnesty International*, no. 62 (September/October 1989): 12.
12. Kirk Makin, "Killing the Killers" (a four-part series), *Globe and Mail* (Canada), June 10, 1987.
13. Frank Green, "15,000 Sign Petitions Asking New Trial for Giarratano," *Richmond-Times Dispatch*, November 15, 1990.
14. Kirk Saville, "Inmate Awaits Word—Giarratano Set to Die Friday," *Daily Press* (Newport News), February 17, 1991.
15. James Kilpatrick, "Death Row Inmate Merits Reprieve," *Richmond Times-Dispatch*, October 22, 1990.
16. Richard H. Morefield, "Giarratano Should Not Die under the Shadow of Our Doubt," *Roanoke Times*, November 6, 1990.
17. James Kilpatrick, "Why Kill Joe Giarratano Now," *Virginia-Pilot*, January 30, 1991.
18. "Joe Giarratano Should Have a New Trial," *Roanoke Times*, February 11, 1990.
19. Jim Mason, Tyler Whitley, and Bill Masson, "Wilder Grants Giarratano Pardon," *Richmond Times-Dispatch*, February 19, 1991.
20. Joe Giarratano, interview with author.
21. Jim Mason, "Inmate Signs Pardon, Asks Trial," *Richmond Times-Dispatch*, February 20, 1991.
22. Ibid.
23. Molly Moore, "Politics Outstrips Legal Expertise in Va. Attorney General Race," *Washington Post*, July 8, 1985.
24. Molly Moore and Tom Sherwood, "Raising the Family Factor: Virginia Candidates Use Marital Status as an Issue against Their Opponents," *Washington Post*, October 13, 1985.
25. John F. Harris, "Va. Takes PR Initiative in Execution, *Washington Post*, June 23, 1992.
26. Tony Germanotta, "It's Up to Giarratano to Decide: Life or Death," *Virginian-Pilot*, February 20, 1991.
27. Ronnie Crocker, "Wilder Spares Inmate's Life with Conditional Pardon—Decision Disgusts Victims' Family," *Daily Press* (Newport News), February 20, 1991.

28. Ibid.
29. Germanotta, "It's Up to Giarratano to Decide."
30. Warren Fiske, "I'd Like to Give the Governor a Hug," *Virginia Pilot*, February 21, 1991.
31. John F. Harris, "Terry Rules Out New Trial for Pardoned Killer," *Washington Post*, February 20, 1991.
32. Dan McCauley, "Nonviolence Studies Founder Transferred to Utah Prison," *Daily News Record* (Harrisonburg, VA), September 9, 1996.
33. Frank Green, "Inmate Flown to Utah for Safety," *Richmond Times-Dispatch*, September 6, 1996.
34. Ibid.
35. Frank Green, "Ex-Death Row Inmate is on a Hunger Strike," *Richmond Times-Dispatch*, September 6, 1996.
36. Laurence Hammack, "Critics Question Supermax Need," *Roanoke Times*, April 11, 1999.
37. Ibid.
38. Laurence Hammack, "Human Rights Attorney Seeks Prison Meeting," *Roanoke Times*, January 22, 1999.
39. Laurence Hammack, "ACLU Questions Inmate Placement at Red Onion," *Roanoke Times*, January 3, 1999.
40. Michael Sluss, "Tim Kaine: Death Penalty is a 'Moral Concern,'" *Roanoke Times*, October 6, 2001.
41. Jeff E. Shapiro, "Campaign Spot Watch," *Richmond Times-Dispatch*, June 23, 2005.
42. Ibid.
43. Chelyen Davis, "Kilgore and Kaine Battle to a Draw," *Free Lance Star* (Fredericksburg, VA), October 10, 2005.
44. Hugh Lessig, "Governor Hopefuls Spar During Forum," *Daily Press* (Newport News, VA), December 9, 2004.
45. Giarratano to Deans, September 9, 2009.
46. Tim Kaine, interview with author.
47. Deans to Firthiof, e-mail, January 20, 2010.
48. Giarratano to Deans, February 7, 2011.
49. Giarratano to Deans, December 17, 2010.
50. Giarratano to Deans, October 3, 2010.
51. Giarratano to Deans, February 7, 2011.
52. Giarratano to Deans, March 13, 2010.
53. Giarratano to Deans, March 18, 2010.
54. Giarratano to Deans, February 21, 2010.
55. Giarratano to Deans, January 19, 2011.

Chapter 11

1. John C. Tucker, *May God Have Mercy: A True Story of Crime and Punishment* (New York: WW Norton, 1997): 98. Unless otherwise noted, information in this chapter on Roger Coleman comes from *May God Have Mercy*. General information on the Coleman case was also found in *Coleman v. Commonwealth of Virginia*, 307 S.E.2d 864 (1983); Glen Frankel, "Burden of Proof. Jim McCloskey Desperately Wanted to Save Roger Coleman from the Electric Chair. Maybe a Little too Desperately," *Washington Post*, May 14, 2006; Trip Gabriel, "Freedom Fighter," *New York Times*, May 10, 1992; Margaret Edds, "Pending Execution Grips Uncertain Town," *Roanoke Times*, April 20, 1992.
2. Tucker, *May God Have Mercy*, 25.
3. Margaret Edds, *An Expendable Man: The Near-Execution of Earl Washington, Jr.* (New York: New York University Press, 2003): 21. Unless otherwise noted, all information in this

chapter on Earl Washington comes from *An Expendable Man*. General information on the Washington case was also found in "Earl Washington, Jr.: Petition for Executive Pardon," written by Robert T. Hall, Barry A. Weinstein, Eric M. Freedman, and Marie Deans; Eric M. Freedman, "Earl Washington's Ordeal," *Hofstra Law Review*, vol. 29, no. 4 (2001).

4. Edds, *Expendable Man*, 22.
5. Trip Gabriel, "Freedom Fighter," *New York Times*, May 10, 1992.
6. Information on the murder, investigation and trial is drawn from *May God Have Mercy*; Jim Mason, "11 Years Later, Murder Case Debate Lingers," *Richmond Times-Dispatch*, May 13, 1992; and Frankel, "Burden of Proof."
7. "Virginia's Controversial Roger Coleman Case," *Nightline*, May 18, 1992.
8. "Death Recommended for Roger Coleman," *Virginia Mountaineer*, March 25, 1982.
9. Ibid.
10. Tucker, *May God Have Mercy*, 88.
11. "Death Recommended for Roger Coleman," *Virginia Mountaineer*, March 25, 1982.
12. "Earl Washington, Jr.: Petition for Executive Pardon," 7.
13. Ibid., 8–9.
14. Ibid., 1.
15. Frank Green, "Confession or Confusion on Death Row," *Richmond Times-Dispatch*, June 6, 1993.
16. Margaret Edds, "Wrongly Accused and Sentenced: Freeing Washington Would Destroy Myth of Justice," *Virginian-Pilot*, April 16, 2000.
17. Green, "Confession or Confusion on Death Row."
18. Eric M. Freedman, "Earl Washington's Ordeal," *Hofstra Law Review* vol. 29, no. 4 (2001): 1096.
19. "Earl Washington, Jr.: Petition for Executive Pardon," 11.
20. Tucker, *May God Have Mercy*, 98.
21. Frankel, "Burden of Proof."
22. Tucker, *May God Have Mercy*, 99.
23. Michael Hardy, "Let Us Be a Lesson, Inmates Say," *Richmond Times-Dispatch*, July 27, 1986.
24. Ibid.
25. Michael Hardy, "Death Row Inmate Warns Teens," *Richmond Times-Dispatch*, April 27, 1987.
26. Jim Mason, "Inmate's 'Freedom' Found on Death Row," *Richmond Times-Dispatch*, May 13, 1989.
27. James McBride, "The Tragic Choice of Roger Coleman," *Washington Post*, July 16, 1987.
28. Marie Deans, "Press Statement of Marie Deans," October 26, 1993.
29. Frank Green, "Confession or Confusion on Death Row," *Richmond Times-Dispatch*, June 6, 1993.
30. Edds, *An Expendable Man*, 88.
31. Ibid., 83.
32. "Firm Takes Culpeper Slaying Case," *Richmond Times-Dispatch*, October 19, 1985.
33. Ibid.
34. Frankel, "Burden of Proof."
35. Frankel, "Burden of Proof."
36. Trip Gabriel, "Freedom Fighter," *New York Times*," May 10, 1992.
37. Paul Dellinger, "Coleman's Assault Victim: I'm Angry,'" *Roanoke Times*, May 15, 1992.
38. Paul Dellinger, "Coleman Did It, Town Says," *Roanoke Times*, May 15, 1992.
39. Frankel, "Burden of Proof."
40. Tucker, *May God Have Mercy*, 100.
41. Frankel, "Burden of Proof."
42. "Virginia's Controversial Roger Coleman Case," *Nightline*, May 18, 1992.

43. Tucker, *May God Have Mercy*, 312.
44. Tamar Lewin, "Lawyer Relives Sorrow of Execution," *New York Times*, May 25, 1992.
45. Tucker, *May God Have Mercy*, 319.
46. Peter Applebome, "Virginia Executes Inmate Despite Claim of Innocence," *New York Times*, May 21, 1992.
47. Ibid.
48. Tamar Lewin, "Lawyer Relives Sorrow of Execution."
49. Frankel, "Burden of Proof."
50. Tucker, *May God Have Mercy*, 329.
51. Ibid.
52. Peter Applebome, "Virginia Executes Inmate Despite Claim of Innocence."
53. Ibid.
54. Tucker, *May God Have Mercy*, 155.
55. Frankel, "Burden of Proof."
56. Peppers's interview with David Kendall.
57. Frankel, "Burden of Proof."
58. Ibid.
59. Ibid.
60. Deona Landes Houff, "Death Watch: Virginia's Leading Anti-Death Penalty Group Closes When It's Needed Most," *Style Weekly*, August 24, 1993.
61. Joe Jackson, "Va. Inmates on Death Row Lose Chief Ally," *Virginia Pilot*, September 4, 1993.
62. Frank Green, "Death Penalty Foes Endure Rough Season," *Richmond Times-Dispatch*, March 27, 1994.
63. Edds, *An Expendable Man*, 158.
64. Frank Green, "Guilt in Doubt in Rape, Slaying," *Richmond Times-Dispatch*, October 26, 1993.
65. Bill Miller and Steve Bates, "DNA Test Could Lead to Man's Release," *Washington Post*, October 26, 1993.
66. Edds, *An Expendable Man*, 155.
67. Ibid., 157.
68. Ibid., 159.
69. Frank Green, "DNA Clears Washington," *Richmond Times-Dispatch*, October 3, 2000.
70. Edds, *An Expendable Man*, 186.
71. Frank Green, "DNA Clears Washington."
72. Ibid.
73. Ibid.
74. Frank Green, "Early Release Denied," *Richmond Times-Dispatch*, December 23, 2000.
75. Edds, *An Expendable Man*, 186.
76. Margaret Edds, interview with Marie Deans, April 15, 2002.
77. Edds, *An Expendable Man*, 194.
78. Ibid.
79. Frank Green, "Tinsley Pleads Guilty in '82 Death," *Richmond Times-Dispatch*, April 12, 2007.
80. "Man Pleads Guilty to '82 Rape, Murder," *Daily News* (Newport News), April 12, 2007.
81. Michael Felberbaum, "Kaine Issues Pardon in '82 Rape, Murder," *Daily News* (Newport News), July 7, 2007.
82. Ibid.
83. Margaret Edds, interview with Marie Deans, April 15, 2002.
84. Margaret Edds, interview with Marie Deans, January 31, 2002.
85. Maria Glod and Michael D. Shear, "DNA Tests Confirm Guilt of Executed Man," *Washington Post*, January 13, 2006.

86. Kristen Gelineau, "DNA Test Confirms Guilt in '81 Case," *Daily Press* (Newport News), January 13, 2006.
87. Margaret Anderson interview with Senator Mark Warner.
88. Frankel, "Burden of Proof," *Washington Post*, May 14, 2006.
89. Kerry Dougherty, "Supporters of Dead Killer Can Eat Crow at DNA Result," *Virginian-Pilot*, January 14, 2006.
90. Kristen Gelineau, "DNA Test Confirms Guilt in '81 Case," *Daily Press* (Newport News), January 13, 2006.

Chapter 12
1. Deans to Giarratano, May 8, 2005.
2. Deans to Giarratano, March 8, 2004.
3. Deans to Giarratano, December 16, 2002.
4. Deans to Giarratano, October 24, 2003.
5. Deans to Giarratano, March 17, 2004.
6. Deans to Giarratano, August 26, 2004.
7. Deans to Giarratano, March 17, 2004.
8. Deans to Giarratano, September 9, 2002.
9. Deans to Giarratano, October 24, 2003.
10. Deans to Giarratano, March 20, 2004.
11. Deans to Giarratano, May 22, 2004.
12. Deans to Giarratano, March 16, 2003.
13. Deans to Giarratano, May 8, 2004.
14. Todd C. Peppers and Laura Trevvett Anderson, *Anatomy of an Execution: The Life and Death of Douglas Christopher Thomas* (Lebanon, NH: Northeastern University Press, 2009).
15. Deans to Giarratano, March 20, 2004.
16. Deans to Giarratano, April 11, 2004.
17. Deans to Giarratano, January 6, 2006.

Index

Numbers in italic refer to photographs.

Muncy, Ray, 152–54
Murder Victims' Families for Reconciliation
    (MVFR), 47–48, 78–79, 246
Murray, Edward W., 137
Murray, Patricia, 75–77

NAACP Legal Defense Fund, 225
Niebuhr, Reinhold, 247
Nightline (television show), 229
non-fiction novel, 6–7
North, Jay, 160
North Carolina, 49–50
Northup, Steve, 42, 115
Northup, Wayne, 14–15, 16–17, 19–20

O'Dell, Joseph, 160
Oklahoma, 49–50

Paranzino, Michael, 233
Parise, Carol, 171, 193
Parker, Anthony, 140–41, 197–98
Paul, Sharon, 222–23, 224, 225, 233
peace studies program, 200–201
Peppers, Todd C., 1, 2–3, 7, 237–38, *238*, 240,
    245
Peterson, Derick L. "Baydar," 89–93, *91*, *94*,
    129–30, 136–37
Plato, 188–89
Prejean, Helen, 41–42, *238*
Presswalla, Faruk, 169–70, 171

Quintana, Manuel, 101–2

Red Onion State Prison (Wise County, VA),
    202–3, 206
"Reflections on the Guillotine" (Camus), 32
Rehnquist, William H., 224
Richmond Times-Dispatch (newspaper), 31, 82,
    168
Rife, Brenda Ratliff, 207, 209, 210, 222
Rife, Preston, 209
Riley, Richard, 64
Roach, James Terry, 52, 60, 65–68, *66–67*
"Runaway, The" (Deans), 253–60
Ryans, Miller M., 169–70, 171

San Francisco Zephyr, 70–74
Savino, Joseph John, III, 98–101, *99*
Scheider, Roy, 196
schizophrenia, 22, 52, 60, 144, 184

segregation, 32
sexual abuse, 87, 88, 98, 163, 191
Shaw, Joseph Carl "J. C."
    Deans and, 20, 52–60, *60*, 63–65, 106, 246
    execution of, 63–65
    photographs of, *57*, *60–61*
Shaw, Treeby, 117–18
Showalter, Robert, 171
Sisters of Charity of Our Lady of Mercy, 24,
    28–30, *29*, 31
slavery, 25–26, 53, 85, 136–37
Smith, Henry, 130
Smith, Marion "Okie," 156–57
Smith, Michael Marnell
    Deans and, 112–13
    execution of, 156–57, 191
    Ford and, 153
    Giarratano and, 173, 195–96
    photograph of, *156*
    prison escape and, 188
    Snook and, 80
Snook, Lloyd
    on Deans, 41
    Deans and, 80–82
    Giarratano and, 162, 174, 175, 179–82, 184,
        192
    Mason and, 80, 145, 146, 147
    prison escape and, 188
    Smith and, 80, 157
South Carolina, 52–53. *See also* Broad River
    Correctional Institution (Columbia,
    SC); Central Correctional Institution
    (Columbia, SC)
South Carolina Citizens Against the Death
    Penalty, 70
South Carolina Review, The (magazine), 17
Southern Coalition on Jails and Prisons (SCJP),
    74, 76, 78, 109, 245. *See also* Virginia
    Coalition on Jails and Prisons (VCJP)
St. Angela Academy (Aiken, SC), 24, 28–30, 31
Stamper, Bart, 42
Stamper, Charles Sylvester, *94*, 102, 159–60
state habeas corpus, 103, 174–81, 219
Statesville Correctional Center (Joliet, IL), 202
Stinney, George, 53
Stone, Oliver, 196
Styron, Rose, 48–50
suicide, 129–30
Sullivan, Walter, 102, 111, 175–76, 179
Support Services of Virginia, 231